ENEMY IMAGES IN AMERICAN HISTORY

ENEMY IMAGES IN AMERICAN HISTORY

Edited by

Ragnhild Fiebig-von Hase

and

Ursula Lehmkuhl

Berghahn Books
Providence • Oxford

E
179
.E56
1997

Published in 1997 by

Berghahn Books
Editorial offices:
165 Taber Avenue, Providence, RI 02906, USA
Bush House, Merewood Avenue, Oxford, OX3 8EF, UK

Library of Congress Cataloging-in-Publication Data
Enemy images in American history / edited by Ragnhild Fiebig-von
Hase and Ursula Lehmkuhl.
       p.   cm.
   Includes bibliographical references (p.   ) and index.
   ISBN 1-57181-031-5 (alk. paper)
      1. Enemies (Persons)--United States--History--Congresses.
   2. Hate--Social aspects--United States--History--Congresses.
   3. Social conflict--United States--History--Congresses. 4. United
   States--Foreign relations--Psychological aspects--Congresses.
   5. United States--Politics and government--Psychological aspects--
   Congresses. 6. United States--Emigration and immigration--
   Government policy--Congresses. I. Fiebig-von Hase, Ragnhild.
   II. Lehmkuhl, Ursula.
   E179.E56   1996
   303.3'8--dc20   96-21144
                                                           CIP

British Library Cataloguing in Publication Data
A CIP catalogue record for this book is available from
the British Library.

Printed in the United States on acid-free paper

CONTENTS

LIST OF ILLUSTRATIONS

FIGURES

PREFACE

How do enemy images develop? How do they influence societies as well as the domestic and foreign policies of a political community or nation state? Are there national peculiarities with regard to the sources and uses of enemy images? These questions were bundled under the topic "Enemy Images in American History" and discussed by eighty historians at the Annual Conference of the Historians in the German Association of American Studies which met at the Akademie für Politische Bildung, Tutzing (Germany) in February 1994. Most of the contributions came from historians and concentrated on the historical experience of the United States, with David Kennedy presenting a most remarkable synthesis in his keynote speech. In addition, there were important and thought-provoking papers from the neighboring fields—from political science (Kurt R. Spillmann, Zurich), psychology (Kati Spillmann, Zurich), sociology (Ulrich Beck, Munich), and American studies (Berndt Ostendorf, Munich). This volume presents the revised versions of all the papers. Both well-known and younger scholars endeavored to meet the challenge of the topic, a challenge that led all participants deeply into the fields of individual and social psychology, social and political history, as well as international history.

The editors want to thank all the participants of the conference for their lively contributions which helped to make the endeavor a success. We also wish to express our gratitude to Professor Jürgen Heideking and Professor Gustav Schmidt, who provided the necessary support for planning and organizing the conference as well as the publication of this volume. Additional support came from our colleagues and the staff at the Institute of Anglo-American History, Cologne University, and the Institute of International Politics of the Ruhr-University at Bochum, especially from Sigrid Schneider and Elisabeth Lebert. Our editor Marion Berghahn and her team at Berghahn Books, above all Janine Treves and Shawn Kendrick, have proven to be extremely competent, patient, and understanding. Last, but not least, our thanks go to our hosts, the former director of the Akademie für Politische Bildung at Tutzing, Professor Manfred Hättich, his team, and especially Klaus Grosch, who supported us with most valuable suggestions and concrete arrangements in every respect, and who excelled in their hospitality during the conference. One could not ask for a more inspiring environment than this extraordinary institution on the shores of Lake Starnberg south of Munich.

The volume itself does not pretend to give a final answer to the question of enemy images in American history. There are many important subjects that could not be covered. The book is meant rather as an encouragement to further interdisciplinary studies in a field where intense cooperation among psychologists, sociologists, political scientists, anthropologists, experts in cultural studies, and historians seems to be extremely rewarding.

Ursula Lehmkuhl
Ragnhild Fiebig-von Hase

INTRODUCTION

Ragnhild Fiebig-von Hase

As enthusiasm about the end of the Cold War has ebbed, the widespread expectation of a peaceful world has given way to the more sober realization that the familiar balance of terror between the two superpowers has only been superseded by other, long subdued forms of conflict. Parallel to the appearance of "new" antagonisms, an equally breathtaking array of enemy images is emerging. They assume political and economic conflict, but are also charged with ideological assumptions along religious, cultural, ethnic, racial, and gender lines.[1] This process is closely intertwined with an intensified debate on national identity. Even in democratic societies the disappearance of the omnipotent and omnipresent "enemy" seems to create not so much a feeling of liberation and relief, but rather of uncertainty and insecurity: nothing seems worse than the loss of the "enemy."

But, although so many unanswered questions emerge concerning the future, the following contributions concentrate on the past.

1. The search for the "enemy" of the present and the future is in full swing. Lester Thurow in his *Head to Head: The Coming Economic Battle among Japan, Europe and America* (New York, 1992), and Jeffrey Garden, *A Cold Peace: The Fight for Supremacy* (New York, 1992), stress the conflicting interests between the three great economic powers, the United States, Japan, and western Europe under German leadership. Samuel P. Huntington puts forward in his article, "The Clash of Civilizations?", *Foreign Affairs* 72 (1993): 22–49, a gloomy vision of a cultural clash between the "West" and the allied Islamic and Confucian civilizations. See also:

Is it a "natural" predisposition of the human species to have enemies? Does history provide us with a clue as to whether nations need enemy images to secure internal coherence and stability? This book concentrates on enemy images, their genesis, changing patterns, and functional uses in American history, beginning in the early period of nation building and ending in the 1960s. To the editors the historical experience of the multiethnic, multicultural society of the American democracy appears to be an especially gratifying research field for analyzing the development and maintenance of enemy images and their impact on society. Do these characteristics of the American nation, combined with the democratic political system, reflect themselves in a special form of dealing with enmity within the country itself and in its relations with the rest of the world? Does it make sense to speak of an American "exceptionalism" as far as enemy images are concerned?

In order to answer such questions, the importance of enemy images for the behavior of the individual as well as of social groups and nations has to be clarified. Therefore, this volume pursues an interdisciplinary approach and starts with two chapters discussing the psychological and sociological dimension of enmity. The presentation of a wide variety of historical research findings follows.

Enemy images seem to be omnipresent in modern societies, but still the paradigm enemy image is a complex and imprecise one. The difficulties start with definition. In its widest and colloquial form, an enemy image is a culturally influenced, very negative, and stereotyped evaluation of the "other"—be it individuals, groups, nations, or ideologies. "Others" are classified as "enemies" if their appearance is coupled with some kind of extreme

---

Samuel P. Huntington, *The Clash of Civilization* (New York, 1996). Among the American conservative elite, intellectuals like James Kurth in "The Real Clash," *The National Interest* 37 (1994): 3–15, claim that the "clash" is already a reality as a "clash between the West and the post-West, within the West itself." Western civilization is said to be under attack by the "multicultural and the feminist movements." Encouraged by the American intellectual elite, ethnic groups within the United States are believed to be forming "beachheads or even colonies" of other cultures which are contesting Western hegemony. And certainly others detect their enemies within their own nation — minority groups fighting against racial and ethnic prejudices, feminists against "male chauvinism," and fundamentalists against religious tolerance. The search for new enemies appears not only in the United States, but in Germany as well, where the former FRG and the GDR were fixed on each other as enemies during the East-West conflict. The whole West appears to be in a victory crisis. See in this volume: Ulrich Beck, "The Sociological Anatomy of Enemy Images: The Military and Democracy After the End of the Cold War."

threat perception.[2] A perceived menace often provokes violent behavior. Therefore the social relevance of imagined or verbalized enmity consists in its close relationship to aggression: enemy perception can be instrumental for aggressive behavior, and both can reinforce each other.

Research on the genesis, appearance, and consequences of enemy images has to consider also the functional uses of enmity within societies and in the field of international relations. The image of an external enemy can help to legitimize the power structure of a state and enforce the loyalty of its citizens. Ulrich Beck observes in his chapter that there are different rules for handling conflict within and between modern nation-states. Therefore, he pleads for a strict differentiation between images of the *external* "enemy" and "stereotypes of the other" (heterostereotypes) that concern animosity *within* a society. The differentiation provided by Beck certainly helps to clarify the levels of analysis. However, the line between the external and the internal enemy is difficult to draw for an immigrant society such as the United States, in which citizens may still feel a double loyalty towards their old and their new home country. In American history it is easy to find examples where the perception of the so-called "hyphenated Americans" as collaborators and saboteurs influenced the national climate, the decisions of the political elite, and the outcome of political situations. In addition, "hetereostereotype" has a broad meaning that is not restricted to the characteristics of extremely negative images combined with threat perception. David M. Kennedy emphasizes in his contribution to this volume the "complicated nexus of 'alterity' and 'enmity,' internality and externality": alterity might be a necessary attribute of enmity, but it is not sufficient to create it. Therefore, the more general definition of enemy images has some advantages. Most of the contributors to this volume use the colloquial definition, but also point out quite clearly the functional uses of enmity in American history.

The Individual Dimension

It is only the individual, not human groups as such, that can hate and fear. Enemy images are the result of individual perception, passion, and reason, and every functional utilization of enmity

2. David J. Finlay, Ole R. Holsti, and Richard R. Fagen, *Enemies in Politics* (Chicago, 1967), 1–3.

has to address the individual's capacity for aggression and hatred. Therefore, an analysis of enemy images cannot neglect the individual dimension and profits from all theories explaining human behavior. Among the theories focusing on the individual perspective, three seem to be of special importance: (1) the sociobiological approach explaining the function of enmity in terms of the biological evolution of humankind; (2) psychoanalysis, focusing on the relationship between aggression as well as enmity and the early childhood experiences of an individual; and (3) the cognitive approach stressing the cognitive processes that generate enemy images.

Sociobiology

There is a long tradition of seeing human beings as aggressive animals. This assumption received new, intense impulses from Social Darwinism.[3] Sociobiologists or ethologists referring to the innate aggressive drive argue that, as a result of the long process of biological evolution, certain fundamental forms of social behavior were imprinted into our genes. Especially aggressive behavior and the assumedly instinctive tendency to perceive aliens as enemies is considered as having been essential for the survival of the individual and the group in an early evolutionary stage of humankind. Aggression is then evaluated as a behavior residual etched into specific parts of our brains. Recent versions of this theory argue, as Kurt R. and Kati Spillmann point out in their chapter, that even today extreme stress, fear, and threat perception mobilize these patterns of "archaic behavior."

Critics of the ethological approach concede that the biological predisposition of human beings is an important cause of their behavior. But they object to the ethologists' assumptions that human nature is determined by biology and that the "natural" dimension of human actions can be explained by analogies drawn from experiments on animal behavior. They warn against the "idolatry of evolution" and stress the socially destructive implications of Social Darwinism, which encouraged a reckless national and racial egotism by declaring this to be not only "natural" but

3. Peter Gay, *The Cultivation of Hatred*, vol. 3 of *The Bourgeois Experience, Victorianism to Freud*, 3 vols. (New York, 1984–1993), 39–68. For the American experience with Social Darwinism and the vogue of Spencer's theories: Richard Hofstadter, *Social Darwinism in American Thought* (Boston, 1955).

also the moral norm.[4] The Spillmanns take such objections into consideration in their analysis of the more advanced new research in the field of ethology. They warn against the "naturalistic fallacy" and introduce culture as the second important variable besides sociobiology for explaining human behavior.

Psychoanalysis

For Sigmund Freud human aggression was also ubiquitous and had an archaic character rooted in biology. But Freud's most important achievement was that he transcended the biological approach by advancing psychological explanations and stressed the importance of early childhood experiences for human behavior. For him human beings have individual characters. They have "natural" aggressive impulses like animals, but in addition they show a unique ability for sadistic conduct and destructive action not known in animal behavior. This potential has to be explained. On the other hand, aggression and enmity do not emerge for Freud as the insurmountable fate of humankind. Humans are not passive victims of nature. As individuals, they organize their life and can learn to understand and control their subconscious instincts with the help of psychoanalysis.[5]

In Freud's early libido theory, aggression was not a main topic, although he stressed the "ambiguity" and inextricable entanglement of love and hate. But then in December 1914, after the beginning of World War I, he stated that the "primitive, savage and evil impulses of mankind have not vanished in any individual, but continue their existence, although in a repressed state" and only wait for "opportunities to display their activity."[6] The "opportunities" he had in mind were extreme stress, social pressure, and fear. One possible emotional reaction to such challenges is regression into affectively loaded types of early childhood behavior. In such situations, as the Spillmanns maintain, enemy images can serve as the mental background for aggression, distrust, guilt projection, negative anticipation, identification with all evil, zero sum thinking, stereotyping, deindividualization, and the refusal of empathy.

4. Erich Fromm, *The Anatomy of Human Destructiveness* (New York, Chicago, San Francisco, 1973); German ed.: *Anatomie der menschlichen Destruktivität* (Hamburg, 1977), 30–50.

5. Fromm, *Anatomy*, German ed., 30–31, 98–107, 492–532.

6. Cf.: Gay, 532.

It was only in the 1920s when Freud emphasized the dichotomy of Eros, the life impulse, and Tanatos, the death drive, that he defined aggression as projection of the self-destructive energies of the death drive against others.[7] Enemy images can be interpreted as such projections. Psychoanalytical research has emphasized the importance of projection as the favorite medium of racism. In this context, racist theories have an alibi function for human destructiveness: the enemy appears as the convenient other, legitimizing aggressive behavior.[8]

In this context enemy images can be extremely helpful tools for the individual. The Manichaean fantasies rampant in certain circles of American cultural fundamentalism during the 1960s, a phenomenon which Berndt Ostendorf presents so ironically and masterfully in his chapter, can hardly be understood otherwise than as sadomasochistic projections. The writings of David A. Noebel, which Ostendorf describes, demonstrate the typical overestimation of the imagined adversary as monolithic and almighty. By denouncing the performers of African-American music and beat as tools of world communism, Noebel painted a grotesque picture of reality despite his pseudoscholarly quotations from all sorts of documents. In analyzing similar phenomena in American history, Richard Hofstadter spoke of the paranoid style in American politics and characterized as products of projection certain "qualities of heated exaggeration, suspiciousness, and conspirational fantasy," which he had observed emerging cyclically in situations of social conflict.[9]

The psychoanalytical interpretation of personality structure influenced the theory of the "authoritarian personality," which was developed by the so-called Frankfurter Schule in their effort to understand Nazism and the Holocaust. This theory became important in explaining the correlation between individual and societal aggression. Authoritarian personalities feel constantly surrounded by "enemies." Deep-seated, unconscious insecurity and anxiety, which can be traced back to early childhood experiences of emotional deprivation and authoritarian parent behavior, are seen as the main characteristics of an authoritarian personality. Such individuals prefer a rigid morality, and show a tendency towards projection and dichotomization in cognitive perception, an extremely

7. Fromm, *Anatomy*, German ed., 31.
8. Gay, 68–95; Gordon W. Allport, *The Nature of Prejudice* (Cambridge, MA, 1954), 381–91.
9. Richard Hofstadter, *The Paranoid Style in American Politics and Other Essays* (New York, 1965), 3–40, cf. 3.

stereotyped form of thinking in the categories of friend/enemy, and an early readiness to violent behavior. They welcome strict social hierarchies and believe in a rigidly institutionalized social order that promises safety and definiteness.[10] In foreign policy they prefer military solutions and stress ethnic conflict potential. War means to them escape out of a threatening complexity.[11] Here again, the imaginative simplicity and rigidity of Ostendorf's main characters provide good examples for such an explanation.

Cognitive Theory

A third possibility for analysis of the individual dimension of enemy images is provided by theories of cognitive psychology. "Cognition" is defined as "a collective term for the psychological processes involved in the acquisition, organization, and use of knowledge." Its main presupposition is "that any interaction between an organism and its environment changes not only its overt behavior or psychological condition but also its knowledge or information about the environment, and that this latter change may affect not only present responses but also future orientation to the environment."[12] Central to the approach is the assumption that human beings organize their perceptions, knowledge, and preferences, and that they construct a "value system" or "belief system" for their orientation. "Images"[13] or "schemas"[14] work as a set of

10. Theodore W. Adorno, Else Frenkel-Brunswick, D. J. Levinson, and R. N. Sanford, *The Authoritarian Personality* (New York, 1950).

11. Daniel Levinson, "Authoritarian Personality and Foreign Policy," in *War,* ed. Albert Lepawsky and George Goethals, 2nd ed. (New York, 1968), 133–46.

12. *The Harper Dictionary of Modern Thought,* ed. A. Bullock and O. Stallybrass (New York, 1977), 109, as cf. in: Martha L. Cottam, *Foreign Policy Decision Making: The Influence of Cognition* (Boulder and London, 1986), 6–7.

13. The "image" approach was first used in marketing psychology, but became particularly popular for evaluating decision-making processes in international relations. See especially: Kenneth E. Boulding, *The Image* (Ann Arbor, 1956); Ole R. Holsti, "The Belief System and National Images: A Case Study," *Journal of Conflict Resolution* 4 (1967): 244–52; Finlay, Holsti, and Fagen, *Enemies in Politics,* especially 1–24.

14. The "schema" approach takes up theories that Jean Piaget (*Structuralism,* English ed., London, 1971) had already developed during the 1920s. Schema theories profited from the new research field of artificial intelligence and the rapid development of computer technology. There are three important differences between image and schema theory. First, while the image approach assumes a hierarchical order of images and values within the belief system, schema theory works with the idea that the value system has a much more diffuse and chaotic structure. Second, schema theory assumes that intellectual capacity and spontaneous day-to-day experience are constantly combined in the perception of the environment,

lenses, which filter and organize all newly received information according to the prevailing set of the individual's established values, goals, and preferences. Schemas refer to cognitive structures that represent organized knowledge about a given concept, context, or type of stimulus. They consist of structured, simplified information, and vary with expertise and involvement.[15]

Empirical research demonstrates that the human mind easily integrates new information that fits into the individual's existing value system. A one-sided bias might be the result of worst case or, in contrast, wishful thinking or emotional defense mechanisms. In addition, the desire to find a scapegoat or a safety valve for aggressive impulses might lead to a distorted world-view. The more the core values are threatened, the more the distortions intensify. Since the whole process remains mainly within the sphere of the subconscious, it is rather unlikely that such false information will be corrected.[16]

Stereotypes can be viewed as schemas, and stereotyping an individual implies categorizing him or her into schemas about groups according to certain attributes or characteristics.[17] From this perspective—highlighting the *content* of schemas—enemy images can be interpreted as the result of extremely negative attitudes toward certain others, or as imprinted into the individual's value system. But, since schemas influence also the *manner* of perception, enemy images might just as well be the outcome of manipulations and distortions caused by the individual's endeavor to integrate incoming information into the existing schemas, i.e., from information processing.

---

while the image approach concentrates only on rational reasoning. Third, image theory sees the belief system as a compelling factor, while schema theory assumes that it leaves the individual a rather broad freedom of action to choose between different schemata. The individual is here supposed to be an active, not passive, participant in the construction of schemata. Schema theory postulates that information processing is influenced more by the perceiver's intuitive theories than by the stimulating information. For an overview, see Susan T. Fiske and Shelley E. Taylor, *Social Cognition*, 2d ed. (New York, 1991); Jakob Schissler and Christian Tuschhoff, "Kognitive Schemata: Zur Bedeutung neuerer soziapsychologischer Forschung für die Politikwissenschaft," *Aus Politik und Zeitgeschichte* B 52–53/88 (23.12.1988): 3–13.

15. Schissler and Tuschhoff, "Kognitive Schemata," 6.

16. Allport, *The Nature of Prejudice*, 165–77.

17. For the perception of group stereotypes as schemas, see Walter G. Stephan, "Intergroup Relations," in *Handbook of Social Psychology*, ed. Gardner Linsey and Elliot Aronson, 5 vols. (New York, 1985), 2: 251–89; David L. Hamilton and Tina K. Trolier, "Stereotypes and Stereotyping: An Overview of the Cognitive Approach," in *Prejudice, Discrimination, and Racism*, ed. John F. Dovidio and Samuel L. Gaertner (New York, 1986), 127–63.

The cognitive approach can offer a clue to understanding the seemingly inconsistent behavior of the German author Baron Dietrich Heinrich von Bülow, whom Volker Depkat portrays in his contribution to this book. Bülow had to remove the inconsistency between his utopian image of America as a happy isle of enlightened virtue and his own experiences in the United States. The result was that the friend became the enemy. It seems that the change in evaluation was relatively unproblematic for Bülow, because he could return to the elitist aristocratic ideology which was familiar to him since his childhood. In a similar case study, Hartmut Keil presents Alexander von Humboldt's and Ottilie Assing's reaction to slavery as a good example of the powerful influence of a consistent value system in shaping individual friend/enemy perception and resistance to racial prejudice.

Within the broader frame of schema theory, the "scripts" or "lessons of the past" approach concentrates on the impact of past experiences and historical analogies on perceptions and reactions. The search for antecedents helps to explain current events and seems to be one of the basic cognitive steps in political decision making. The impact of historical experience on enemy perception can be proved in many instances.[18] In this volume Michaela Hönicke refers to Franklin D. Roosevelt's tendency to interpret the German historical record by drawing a line from Frederician tradition to Bismarck's power politics and Hitler's brutalities. This image of the German enemy clearly influenced the president's wartime policy.

During the Cold War, decision making in foreign policy became one of the main research fields in which cognitive theories were applied. Enemy perception played an important role in this context. With the advent of the nuclear age and the atomic bomb, the

18. Deborah W. Larson, "The Role of the Belief System and Schemas in Foreign Policy Decision Making," *Political Psychology* 15 (1994): 20–21; Deborah W. Larson, *Origins of Containment: A Psychological Explanation* (Princeton, NJ, 1989), 54–57; Michael Shapiro and G. Matthew Bonham, "Introduction," in *Thought and Action in Foreign Policy: Proceedings of the London Conference on Cognitive Process Models for Foreign Policy, March 1973* (Basel, Stuttgart, 1977), 1–9; Ernest R. May, *Lessons of the Past: The Use and Misuse of History in American Foreign Policy* (New York, 1973); Yuen Foong Khong, *Analogies at War: Korea, Munich, Dien bien Phu, and the Vietnam Decision of 1965* (Princeton, NJ, 1992) is a good example of the usefulness of such an approach. Foong Khong focuses on how and why decision makers in foreign policy use historical analogies. He also studies whether such analogies really shape policies, or whether they only serve the purpose of legitimizing political decisions before the public.

time factor became of crucial importance for diplomatic crisis management. Quick and adequate answers by the relevant decision makers to external challenges could decide the fate of humankind. Naturally, the shrinking time limit for rational consulting procedures spurred the interest in information processing and evaluation within the human mind.[19]

Image and schema theories interpret foreign policy as the outcome of decision making by the leading statesmen and their advisers. Attention focuses on the world-view of foreign policy makers, the assessment of the adversary, and the impact of these considerations on policy outcomes. A main concern is that leading statesmen might be influenced by a distorted or misperceived enemy image and thereby reach inadequate conclusions about the intention of their adversary, with grave implications for their own actions. An important assumption is that decisions are shaped far more by the subjective beliefs of the actor than by the rational appraisal of available information and, therefore, that all sorts of distortions of reality are the rule. It becomes essential to find out whether "misperceptions" occurred, and why this happened. The most widely discussed perceptual model is Robert Jervis's explanation of distortions as reactions to "cognitive inconsistency." Dislike of a country is supposedly determined not so much by concrete events, but rather by the degree of conflict believed to exist between this country and one's own. This perceptual bias enters the decision-making process. The distortions are supposed to be gravest when antagonistic relationships are involved, as is the case in most critical situations in international relations.[20]

19. Richard C. Snyder, H.W. Bruck, and Burton Sapin, *Decision Making As an Approach to the Study of International Politics* (Princeton, NJ, 1954); Boulding, *Image;* Holsti, "Belief System"; *Psychological Models in International Politics,* ed. Lawrence S. Falkowski (Boulder, CO, 1979); Alexander L. George, *Presidential Decision Making in Foreign Policy: The Effective Use of Information and Advice* (Boulder, CO, 1980); Larson, *Origins,* and Cottam, *Foreign Policy Decision Making,* are sophisticated, newer contributions to this research field. Larson integrates cognitive-psychological analysis of decision making into a multilevel explanation model of foreign policy.

20. Robert Jervis, *Perception and Misperception in International Politics* (Princeton, NJ, 1976). A particularly interesting chapter for historians (217–82) deals with the misperception of historical evidence by decision makers. For a good discussion of the underlying problems see: Richard Hermann, "The Empirical Challenge of the Cognitive Revolution: A Strategy for Drawing Inferences about Perceptions," *International Studies Quarterly* 32 (1988): 175–203; Jerel A. Rosati, "A Cognitive Approach to the Study of Foreign Policy," in *Foreign Policy Analysis: Continuity and Change in Its Second Generation,* ed. Laura Neack et al. (Englewood Cliffs, NJ, 1995), 49–70.

In his studies of John Foster Dulles's image of the Soviet Union, Ole Holsti found that hostile images tend to be self-perpetuating.[21] Each of the conflicting parties believes in its own virtue and constructs a diabolical image of the adversary. Both adversaries cling to an image of their enemy that is diametrically opposite of what the opponent believes about himself or herself. Therefore, hostile relationships produce mirror images. This kind of black-and-white thinking leads to conflict escalation and war, as Ralph White maintained in his study on enemy perception during the two World Wars and the Vietnam War.[22] The enemy is demonized and brutalized, as David Kennedy points out in his chapter with regard to the Japanese and German enemy image during the two World Wars. Jürgen Heideking describes in his contribution how for Americans the enemy image of England served as a mirror image of the virtues claimed for their own colonial society. The constant reciprocal reinforcements of the Soviet and American enemy images during the Cold War became one of the main obstacles to disarmament.[23]

The exceptional circumstances of decision making in Washington and Moscow during the Cold War attracted much attention. As Richard K. Hermann observed: "Because of the importance of Soviet-American relations and strategic deterrence, Americans have been preoccupied with the psychology of enemy relationships."[24] Therefore, critics argue that decision-making approaches highlight only the most negative aspects of the international system by concentrating on hostile relationships, while the psychology of international cooperation is more or less neglected. This bias in research planning leads to a one-sided evaluation. Another serious flaw of the theory is that no clear norms exist for distinguishing a "valid" assessment of a situation from a distortion and for defining the intensity or the amount of the latter.[25] Further, the analyst might have a distorted perception of the observed situation and the relevant decision-making process. Then, perceived distortions are possibly only the result of the analyst's misperceptions, while the observed actors evaluated the situation adequately and reacted accordingly. Third, environmental factors

21. Finlay, Holsti, and Fagen, *Enemies in Politics*, 25–99.

22. Ralph White, *Nobody Wanted War: Misperception in Vietnam and Other Wars* (Garden City, NJ, 1966).

23. Daniel Frei, *Feindbilder und Abrüstung: Die gegenseitige Einschätzung der UdSSR und der USA* (Munich, 1985).

24. Richard Hermann, "The Empirical Challenge," 186.

25. Robert Mandel, "Psychological Approaches to International Relations," in *Political Psychology*, ed. Margaret G. Hermann (San Francisco, London, 1986): 251–58.

have to be taken into consideration. Political decision making occurs within bureaucratic organizations that normally place constraints on the individual decision maker. Fourth, the structural attributes of the individual nation-state and the international system shape and limit policy choices. Whether structural variables have a deeper impact on decision making than psychological ones will always remain an open question.[26] Therefore, although all these theories are very useful tools to enlarge our perception of the important aspects of decision making and enmity evaluation, it is necessary to keep their speculative nature in mind. Human nature on the one hand and the societal and international environment on the other are far too complex entities to permit simplistic generalizations.

Sociological Insights

Enemy images develop as social attitudes in the process of constant interaction between the individual and the social environment. In this context, the interest centers on the questions of socialization and group behavior. To what extent do ethnic, racial, gender, or age differences and the plurality of ideological, religious, and cultural values affect threat perception? How far do the economic, social, and political structures of the environment intervene as variables? Is there a relationship between the intensity of economic or social conflict and perceived enmity in a given society? Are multiethnic, multicultural societies such as the United States more easily susceptible to the emergence of enemy images?

Socialization

Sociopsychological theories assert that an individual's value system, his or her images or schemas, are developed during the process of primary socialization in early childhood. During this period of life individuals not only enlarge their cognitive capacities, but also adopt the cultural values of their primary group, the family, including the stereotypes and with them certain dispositions for friend/enemy distinction. The child develops its own identity by

26. Ole R. Holsti, "Foreign Policy Decision Makers Viewed Psychologically: Cognitive Processes Approaches," in *Thought and Action*, 10–74; Irving L. Janis, *Crucial Decisions: Leadership in Policymaking and Crisis Management* (New York and London, 1989), 13–17.

accepting the roles and attitudes of significant others. Then, in the second phase of socialization, the individual comes into closer contact with society as a whole and internalizes its predominant structure, its role attributions and institutions. During this phase the child already has stereotypes at its disposal as socially institutionalized programs that provide help in mastering daily life. A multitude of agents, such as schools, churches, political parties, the workplace, sport clubs, and other groups, now assumes greater importance. Secondary socialization is a lifelong process and accordingly the individual is confronted with a never-ending array of social impulses that affect his or her value system.[27] Together with all sorts of stereotypes, enemy images are embedded in the contents of socialization. Orthodoxy or dogmatism in education and socialization foster polarization and black-and-white thinking, as well as perception in friend/enemy categories.[28]

Schools and the mass media play an important role in the process of secondary socialization. They are essential transmitters of stereotypes and stereotyped perceptions of the external and internal "enemy."[29] Public utterances and the writings of public opinion leaders like politicians, church representatives, journalists, teachers and university professors, historians, and political scientists might influence the enemy perception of the individual as well as of groups. The phenomenon of historians serving on the "home front" during wartime is well known in all great nations during the twentieth century.[30]

27. George H. Mead, *Mind, Self, and Society from the Standpoint of a Social Behaviorist*, ed. with introduction by Charles Morris, 14th ed. (Chicago, 1967); Charles H. Cooley, *Human Nature and the Social Order*, 1st ed. (1902), 4th ed. (New York, 1964); Erik H. Erikson, *Childhood and the Society* (New York, 1950); Peter L. Berger and Thomas Luckmann, *The Social Construction of Reality: A Treatise in the Sociology of Knowledge* (New York, 1966), German translation: *Die gesellschaftliche Konstruktion der Wirklichkeit. Eine Theorie der Wissenssoziologie* (Frankfurt, 1980), 139–85.

28. Finlay, Holsti, and Fagen, *Enemies in Politics*, 17.

29. Otto Klineberg, *The Human Dimension in International Relations* (New York, 1964), German ed.: *Die menschliche Dimension in den internationalen Beziehungen* (Bern, Stuttgart, 1966), 48–50; for mass communication: Paul M. Sniderman and Philip Tetlock, "Interrelationship of Political Ideology and Public Opinion," in *Political Psychology*, ed. Margaret G. Hermann, 62–96; Gerald F. Lindemann, *The Mirror of War: American Society and the Spanish American War* (Ann Arbor, 1974), 114f. refers to the importance of grammar school teachers and schoolbooks for the spread of the Spanish enemy image before and during the Spanish-American War.

30. For the American case during World War I: Peter Novick, *That Noble Dream: The "Objectivity Question" and the American Historical Profession* (Cambridge, New York, Melbourne, 1988, reprint 1995), 111–32; Carol S. Gruber, *Mars and Minerva: World War I and the Uses of Higher Learning in America* (Baton Rouge, LA, 1975); for

Many of the following contributions refer to the importance of
the media for the dissemination of enemy images and provide
important insights into the governmental strategies of influencing
public opinion with regard to enmity. Consistency of the message
with the internalized cultural and social values as well as the
prevalent political attitudes of the addressees seem to determine
the success of these strategies. Modern governments are well
aware of these possibilities. Mark Ellis mentions in his chapter the
German government's endeavors to influence American public
opinion during World War I. These activities and the previous
endeavors of some German-Americans to set themselves culturally apart from the American mainstream had devastating results
for the entire group of Americans of German descent. The coun-
terpropaganda of the American government unleashed a heated
campaign against them. National support for the war effort was
strengthened through stigmatizing the hyphenated Americans as
potentially disloyal traitors. The emotional hysteria deliberately
created by propaganda developed into racial discrimination and
the "Red Scare" after the war. The image of the German enemy
was transformed into a more general hate campaign against African-Americans and Communists. David Kennedy insists that after
1917 the German enemy image was "manufactured" by political
and cultural elites, and disseminated by organs of mass communication, because the American government had a "need for an
enemy image" to mobilize the nation for war.

Michaela Hönicke analyzes the endeavors of Franklin D. Roosevelt's administration during World War II to focus propaganda on
a convincing image of the German enemy that would prevent the
repetition of such excesses. Opinion surveys registered a diffuse
understanding of the enemy and the causes of the war. The government had to overcome "the discrepancy between the psychological
requirements for total war and the lack of resolve to fight" and had
to educate Americans about what the country was fighting for without endangering domestic unity. Dramatizing the consequences of a
Nazi victory for their own country in a way that concentrated on the
personal consequences of such a development for every American
proved successful. The enemy image was concentrated mainly

the German experience during World War I: Klaus Schwabe, *Wisssenschaft und
Kriegsmoral. Die deutschen Hochschullehrer und die politischen Grundfragen des Ersten
Weltkrieges* (Göttingen, Zürich, Frankfurt, 1969); Wolfgang J. Mommsen ed., *Kultur
und Krieg: Die Rolle der Intellektuellen, Künstler und Schriftsteller im Ersten Weltkrieg*
(Munich, 1996).

around the ideological threat to the "American way of life" and thereby provided a mirror image of American values. Wendy L. Wall demonstrates how the war in Europe increased the endeavors to propagate a national spiritual unity and to enhance tolerance as the core value of "Americanism." She leaves no doubt that this debate on American identity was motivated by threat perception and the existence of a common enemy.

In the aftermath of World War II the Justice for Greece Committee, representing a relatively small and isolated American ethnic minority, tried to mobilize public opinion with anti-communist propaganda to promote its own nationalistic interests. The Committee was successful in its campaign against the communist "enemy," as Peter Zervakis points out in his chapter, because communism was perceived as a threat to the "American creed."

A changed political climate with a new set of enemy images and different propaganda preferences might have grave personal consequences for journalists. Jessica Gienow-Hecht refers in her chapter to the consequences of McCarthyism for the German-Jewish editors of *Die Neue Zeitung,* the paper of the U.S. military government in Germany. Although these Jewish emigrants from Nazi Germany had proved their allegiance to the United States through their work in the Psychological Warfare Division during World War II and the reeducation program in occupied Germany, they became suspect as pro-communist and were finally dismissed as editors. Their specific brand of liberalism and their German, often socialist, past had induced them to resist the crude anti-communism that was demanded as an ideological guideline by their superiors, who yielded to political pressure from above. Loyalty became synonymous with sharing the prescribed enmity of the Cold War.

Group Theory: The In-Group/Out-Group Bias

In his definition of "enemy images" in this volume, David Kennedy stresses the importance of groups. The other is perceived as embodying some deeply menacing threat to the integrity and survival of the own group. This "enemy image" might have little or nothing to do with reality. The invention of the "enemy" might just be a response to the internal requirements of a group. Hatred and enmity appear as attributes of groups and group interaction.

Group aggression is the result of aggregated individual hatred, but the specific mix of this aggression is determined by a special "group dynamic," i.e., by certain behavioral patterns of individuals belonging to and acting as members of a group.[31] Social psychology stresses the importance of the group for an individual's self-identification. Group membership creates the emotional satisfaction of social affiliation, and this induces individuals to accept group values and group stereotypes. Conflict among groups is considered to strengthen group cohesiveness and reduce tension and deviation within the group. Concerning enemy images, the most important behavioral pattern of groups is in-group/out-group discrimination. Empirical research suggests that members of a group react with a decided bias toward alien groups. This bias is sustained by a set of stereotype assumptions about the attributes of the members' own group as contrasted to those of others. Gordon W. Allport contends that there exists within a group a certain pressure for value conformity among its members that helps to sustain the group's identity. Threat perception will intensify this pressure and produce a clear differentiation between friends and enemies. Those members who do not concur will be threatened with sanctions. Such reactions might explain how group integration is being improved by stigmatizing out-groups as enemies. The possibility of functionalizing enmity for group cohesion seems to be one of the reasons which make the propagation of enemy images attractive for group leaders.[32] In this context, Kennedy calls attention to the fact that Freud spoke of the "inherent psychopathology of groups."[33]

One has to bear in mind, however, that the concept of group dynamics and the findings on in-group/out-group discrimination result from research on small, especially peer groups. These classic group theories postulate interaction or interdependency between group members or shared values as constituent characteristics of a group. Role differentiation and a feeling of solidarity among members are considered as essential for defining an aggregation of people as a group.[34] The research findings cannot per se be applied to larger or more informal groups, and especially not to whole nations with completely different structural characteristics. Secondly,

31. The classic work is Kurt Lewin, *Resolving Social Conflict* (New York, 1948); see also: *Group Dynamics: Research and Theory*, ed. D. Cartwright and Z. Zander (Evanston, IL, 1953).

32. Lewis Coser suggests in *The Functions of Social Conflict* (New York, 1956), 110, that "struggle groups may actually search for enemies with the deliberate purpose or the unwitting result of maintaining unity and internal cohesion."

33. See David M. Kennedy's contribution in this volume.

34. See for example: George Homans, *The Human Group*, 5th ed. (New York, 1956); Cooley, *Human Nature*.

the question of how exactly the group influences the values of its members remains open. The difficult balancing act between "deindividuation" within groups as subjugation under the norms of a group on the one hand, and the development, maintenance, and defense of personal identity on the other remains a lifelong challenge for every human being. Also, cultural differences in the evaluation of the individual/society relationship are immense, and these differences influence the individual's behavior within and toward groups.[35] In addition, the complex structure and the value pluralism of modern societies provide the individual with some choice in group affiliations. While the family retains a privileged but not unchallenged position in primary socialization, multiple-group membership is common in later-life phases, and the values of the chosen groups might be contradictory. As a result, the individual is confronted with value conflicts in many forms. This refers also to enemy perception: there are no clearly defined "natural" enemies in modern democratic societies. The individual's choice of enemy images will depend on personal preferences for certain ideologies, persons, or groups, and the person's status within society.

Cognition theories, when applied to group theory, use a very different concept of a group—the "minimal group paradigm." Here, groups are nothing more than aggregations of people with certain common attributes. The starting point of analysis is not individual behavior, but assumptions about the structure and dynamics of the social context. The social environment is defined as a multitude of distinguishable social groups that correspond with each other. Individuals are categorized into groups according to their race, ethnicity, age, status, religion, profession, gender, etc., and this does not involve assumptions about group structure, interaction, or cohesion. Out-group discrimination is explained as emanating from the cognitive processes that accompany the application of schemas and stereotypes to incoming information about individuals and their categorization into groups.[36] The empirical evidence on individual attitudes toward members of other groups is collected through interviews and surveys. In his research on

35. Alexander Thomas, *Grundriß der Sozialpsychologie*, 2 vols. (Göttingen et al., 1992), 2: 209–12; S. Prentice-Dunn and R. W. Rodgers, "Deindividuation and the Self-Regulation of Behavior," in *Psychology of Group Influence*, ed. Paulus B. Paulus (Hillsdale, NJ, 1989), 87–109.

36. A good summary of this type of approach is: *Theories of Group Behavior*, ed. Brian Mullen and G. B. Goethals (New York, 1986); Brian Mullen, *The Phenomenology of Being in a Group: Meta-Analytic Integrations of Social Cognition and Group Processes* (New York, 1991).

"social identity" Henri Tajfel demonstrates not only the general tendency for such categorization, but also that group members evaluate their own group positively while they show a negative bias toward alien ones. They concentrate interest and engagement on their own group, and, therefore, judgments on the capacities and opinions of the in-group show a careful differentiation. This contrasts markedly with the tendency to develop stereotypes for out-group attributes. The development of the individual's social identity seems to be closely related to group identity and differentiation among groups. The existence of other groups is necessary to develop a "we-feeling," even with regard to the minimal group situation.[37]

On the other hand, experiments show that discrimination against out-group members can be blocked by strategies of fairness that individuals develop to attain a positive social identity.[38] Lewis Coser pointed also to the disintegrative effects of intergroup and internation conflicts on groups/nations unless there exists already a strong group cohesion before the beginning of a struggle.[39] Exploiting enemy images might provide short-term integrative advantages with problematic long-term results. In addition, the functional value of enemy images for group cohesion, although certainly important, can be overestimated. A successful integrative group strategy will probably rely more on positive group aims than on negative differentiation toward others.[40] At least David Kennedy doubts that enmity is necessary to perform this function of differentiation; he claims that for Americans the "otherness" of Europe and of the neighboring Latin American states sufficed to form their national identity during the nineteenth century.[41]

The categorization of groups by the human mind explains a disposition for discrimination, but it cannot in itself explain

37. Henri Tajfel, *Human Groups and Social Categories: Studies in Social Psychology* (Cambridge, 1981); Henry Tajfel, *Differentiation between Social Groups* (London, 1978); *Social Identity and Intergroup Relations*, ed. Henri Tajfel (Cambridge, 1982).

38. See the references to such experiments in Thomas, *Grundriß der Sozialpsychologie*, 2:235.

39. Coser, *Functions*.

40. Essien U. Essien-Udom describes in his *Black Nationalism: A Search for an Identity in America* (Chicago and London, 1962), 124, 166, the case of the Nation of Islam. Founded and led by Elijah Muhammad, the Nation of Islam developed a clear enemy image, the Caucasian race and its claim to racial superiority, but endeavored also to create a new identity for black Americans by encouraging self-respect and economic respectability, as well as a sense of responsibility for their own community.

41. Kennedy, "Culture Wars," in this volume.

enmity, unless the differentiation between "we" and "they"—the others—is coupled with a feeling of extreme threat. The question remains unanswered: what causes threat perception? Enemy images do not emanate only from group dynamics.

The Construction of National and Ethnic Identities

How important is the existence of an "enemy" for the development of a national or ethnic identity? The answer to this question depends on certain assumptions about the nature of ethnicity, nationalism, the nation, and the nation-state. In modern political theory and historiography, the debate concentrates mainly on three questions: first, whether the feeling of ethnic belonging and nationalism reflects an anthropological/psychological need of human beings for group affiliation; second, whether ethnic and racial entities as well as nations are natural organisms or social constructs and whether belonging to such entities is hereditary or contractual, that is, established by descent or consent; and third, whether nationalism is a process accompanying social change, i.e., industrialization, democratization, bureaucratization, and modernization.[42]

Authors stressing a psychologically motivated need of human beings for ethnic identification and national identity maintain that both are integrative group ideologies and as such evoke the "natural" desire of human beings for affiliation with groups. Nationalism as an ideological construct creates the satisfying feeling of

---

42. For the general debate: Eric J. Hobsbawm, *Nations and Nationalism Since 1780, Programme, Myth, Reality* (Cambridge, New York, etc., 1990); Hans Kohn, *The Idea of Nationalism* (New York, 1944); Ernest Gellner, *Nations and Nationalism* (Ithaca, NY, 1983); Louis C. Snyder, *Encyclopedia of Nationalism* (Chicago, London, 1990); Anthony D. Smith, *Theories of Nationalism*, 2d ed. (New York, 1983); Hans Mommsen, "Der Nationalismus als weltgeschichtlicher Faktor. Probleme einer Theorie des Nationalismus," in Hans Mommsen, *Arbeiterbewegung und Nationale Frage. Ausgewählte Aufsätze* (Göttingen, 1979), 15–60; Heinrich August Winkler, "Einleitung: Der Nationalismus und seine Funktionen," in *Nationalismus*, ed. Heinrich August Winkler, 2d ed. (Königstein/Ts., 1985): 5–46; for Europe during the years after 1945: *Nationalismus, Nationalitäten, Supranationalität: Europa nach 1945*, ed. Heinrich August Winkler and Hartmut Kaelble (Stuttgart, 1993); good summaries of recent literature are: Dieter Langewiesche, "Nation, Nationalismus, Nationalstaat: Forschungsstand und Forschungsperspektiven," *Neue Politische Literatur* 40 (1995): 190–236; and especially for the development of nationalism during the early period of the nineteenth century: Reinhard Stauber, "Nationalismus vor dem Nationalismus? Eine Bestandsaufnahme der Forschung zu Nation und Nationalismus in der Frühen Neuzeit," *Geschichte in Wissenschaft und Unterricht* 47 (1996): 139–65.

belonging to a *Volk*, nation, or nation-state, provides the idea of a common history and future, and creates a feeling of mutual security by defending the "national interest" against competitors and enemies. Nationalism constructs "nation" as a supposedly eternal basis for a new collective identity of society through recourse to common descent, history, language, religion, culture, and customs. As such, it created emotional security for the individual in a historical period in which rapid modernization had loosened older dynastic and religious ties. Formulated at first by the intellectual elite, the important phase of modern nationalism began when its ideas were widely disseminated and when nationalistic programs found mass support. Eric Hobsbawm and Terence Ranger speak of the "invention of tradition" in the name of nationalism, as a "set of practices ... which seek to inculcate certain values and norms of behavior by repetition, which automatically implies continuity with the past."[43] National ideology constructs the "fiction of a fateful, objective and inescapable unity of *Volk*, nation, history, language and state."[44] An important aspect of this "imagined community" is inclusion and exclusion, the naming of the in-group and the out-group; at least in Europe, nationalism excelled in "enemy" invention. "Enemies" of all sorts served as scapegoats when the invention of "nation" was used to overcome the destabilizing effects of social transformation into modernity. During the high phase of modern nationalism between 1870 and 1950, ethnicity and language, supported by pseudoscientific biological theories and enmity construction, developed into the main characteristics of nation building in Europe.

Critics of this approach stress the primacy of ethnic belonging as a real feeling of social identity and reject the idea of an invented tradition with regard to ethnicity. Ethnicity is perceived as a natural model of group identity. These theories assert that nations emerge only when ethnic identity becomes the dominating force for the creation of political structures.[45] Other contributions interpret ethnicity as a sociobiological force, as a natural power. Descent is seen as crucial in shaping character. Boundaries between groups

43. Eric J. Hobsbawm, "Inventing Traditions," in *The Invention of Tradition*, ed. Eric J. Hobsbawm and Terrence Ranger (Cambridge, 1983), 1–14, cf. 1; see also: Benedict Anderson, *Imagined Communities: Reflections on the Origin and Spread of Nationalism* (London, 1983).

44. Cf.: Hagen Schulze, *Staat und Nation in der europäischen Geschichte* (Munich, 1994), 337.

45. Anthony D. Smith, *The Ethnic Origins of Nations* (Oxford, 1986, repr. 1993); John A. Armstrong, *Nations before Nationalism* (Chapel Hill, 1982).

are constructed. Ethnicity appears as exclusive otherness.[46] Nathan Glazer and Daniel Patrick Moynihan envision for the United States a future in which race and religion determine "the major groups into which the American society is evolving."[47]

But the primacy of ethnic identity is also challenged, at least for the American experience, and ethnicity emerges as a concept for the construction of a collective identity similar to nationalism. The only difference is that it concentrates on group construction within a nation-state instead of nation building within the global environment. Werner Sollors in particular maintains that ethnicity is a rather recent invention and that ethnic groups are also "typically imagined as if they were natural, real, eternal, stable, and static units." Under the specific historical conditions of the United States, ethnic groups are the result of "ethnicization" or "ethnification": new group consciousness emerges among people who previously had other bases of group identity. Ethnicity appears as "the modern and modernizing feature of a contrasting strategy ... an acquired modern sense of belonging that replaces visible, concrete communities." In the United States, the preoccupation with ethnic difference stems from an act of self-defense by ethnic minorities against the dominating majority that controls the political discourse. Ethnicity in the United States is, as Sollors insists, the modern "result of interactions" within a polyethnic culture.[48]

The response to ethnic revival has been divided even among ethnics. Some African-Americans have been particularly outspoken in their rejection of the invention of supposedly "natural" ethnic purity, criticizing it as a "modern invention of the white people,

---

46. Andrew M. Greeley, *Ethnicity in the United States: A Preliminary Reconnaissance* (New York, London, etc., 1974); Michael Novack, *The Rise of the Unmeltable Ethnics: Politics and Culture in the Seventies* (New York, 1975); Pierre L. van den Berghe, *Race and Racism: A Comparative Perspective* (New York, 1967).

47. Nathan Glazer and Daniel Patrick Moynihan, *Beyond the Melting Pot: The Negroes, Puerto Ricans, Jews, Italians, and Irish of New York* (Cambridge, MA, 1963); compare also Richard Alba, *Ethnic Identity: The Transformation of White America* (New Haven, CT, 1990), who believes that while differences between ethnic groups of European origin will fade, African-Americans and Hispanics will stand out even more and a racially defined pluralism will emerge.

48. See the excellent contributions for different American ethnic groups and Werner Sollors "Introduction," in *The Invention of Ethnicity*, ed. Werner Sollors (New York, Oxford, 1989), ix–xx, cf. xii–xix; Werner Sollors, *Beyond Ethnicity: Consent and Descent in American Culture* (New York, Oxford, 1986); Greeley, *Ethnicity*; a useful survey of American thought on assimilation and ethnicity is: Russell A. Kazal, "Revisiting Assimilation: The Rise, Fall, and Reappraisal of a Concept in American Ethnic History," *American Historical Review* 100 (1995): 437–71.

to perpetuate the color line" and justify racial discrimination.[49] Leading representatives of the intellectual establishment also consider the endeavors to construct specific ethnic identities and define the American nation as a "nation of nations" as highly explosive and socially dangerous. These critics maintain that the multicultural and multiethnic aspects of American society are deliberately inflated by the interested lobbies of ethnic minority leaders and that common national experiences and concerns are minimized and neglected. Both approaches are part of the present intense dispute over the appropriate definition of American identity and the underlying struggle for social opportunity and political power. While the perception of an external threat weakens and the feeling of a common national identity diminishes, images of the internal enemy have a high priority in all these endeavors of ethnic group construction. This is the reason why thinking in terms of ethnic group affiliation is considered "disuniting" and disruptive.[50] The main question is, how much individuality, group differentiation and multicultural values can a democratic society tolerate without falling apart?

The idea of the nation as an organic body, into which its members are born, emerged from German political philosophy during the nineteenth century. It reflects the historical situation of a country in which the national aspirations of the bourgeoisie were concentrated on cultural unity, since political unification could not be attained before 1870–71. The idea of an ethnic homogeneous German *Volk* with a common language and common culture was propagated by the intellectual elite in their endeavors to legitimate their demand for political unity. Even today, German citizenship laws are based on the idea that ethnic descent construes nationality. But the perception of German ethnic homogeneity is a myth. New research on German nationalism leaves no doubt that Germany was always a melting pot of people from different ethnic origins—although certainly not as pronounced as the United States.[51] The German ethnic group had and has the status of an overwhelming majority. But the idea of an "organic" German *Gemeinschaft* (community) based on common descent prevailed in

49. Sollors, *Invention of Ethnicity*, xvii–xix.

50. Arthur M. Schlesinger Jr., *The Disuniting of America: Reflections on a Multicultural Society* (New York, London, 1991).

51. For a convincing comparison see Dirk Hoerder, *People on the Move: Migration, Acculturation, and Ethnic Interaction in Europe and North America*, German Historical Institute, Annual Lecture Series No. 6 (Providence, RI and Oxford, 1993).

German political thought and national identity until the perversion of the concept *Volksgemeinschaft* by the Nazis discredited the whole idea. The dangers inherent in the descent concept of national identity were exposed when a brutal racism and the persecution of imagined enemies became the main component of Nazi ideology and political strategy.[52]

Contrary to this traditional German self-perception as a "descent community," American immigrant society developed a self-image as a nation created by contract and consent, as a "consent community." American nationalism centers on the political values of liberal and democratic republicanism as proclaimed by the founding fathers and fixed in the Constitution. It is quite appropriate that the American discussion of nationalism concentrated on "nation building" and its preconditions.[53] In this volume, Jürgen Heideking analyzes the process of American self-discovery as a nation during the Revolutionary period. American virtue was contrasted with English decadence and corruption. This image of the English enemy contributed to the idea of an American missionary drive and American "exceptionalism." The ideological dissociation from the mother country was extremely important for the development of the American identity, since there were no ethnic or other common attributes among the settlers that could be used for this purpose. The idea of a specific civil virtue and of a mission to fight for liberty, equality, and freedom remained the main characteristic of American national identity. Being an American means

52. For German nationalism: Otto Dann, *Nation und Nationalismus in Deutschland, 1770–1990*, 3d enlarged ed. (Munich, 1996); Harold James, *A German Identity: Seventeen Seventy to Nineteen Ninety* (New York, 1991); Hans-Ulrich Wehler, "Nationalismus und Nation in der deutschen Geschichte," in *Nationales Bewußtsein und kollektive Identität: Studien zur Entwicklung des kollektiven Bewußtseins in der Neuzeit 2*, ed. Helmut Berding (Frankfurt, 1994), 163–75; *Nation und Gesellschaft in Deutschland: Historische Essays*, ed. Manfred Hettling and Paul Nolte (Munich, 1996), especially the papers of James J. Sheehan, Dieter Langewiesche, Klaus von Beyme, Jürgen Habermas, Wolfgang J. Mommsen, and Henry Ashby Turner Jr.; for an excellent analysis of the contribution of enmity to the emerging national identity in Germany and France: Michael Jeismann, *Das Vaterland der Feinde: Studien zum nationalen Feindbegriff und Selbstverständnis in Deutschland und Frankreich 1792–1918* (Stuttgart, 1992).

53. Hans Kohn, *American Nationalism: An Interpretive Essay* (New York, 1957); Donald J. Devine, *The Political Culture of the United States* (Boston, 1972); Lloyd A. Free and Hadley Cantril, *The Political Beliefs of Americans* (New Brunswick, NJ, 1967); Seymour Martin Lipset, *The First New Nation: The United States in Historical and Comparative Perspective* (London, 1964); Gabriel A. Almond and Sidney Verba, *The Civic Culture* (Boston, 1965); *The Civic Culture Revisited*, ed. Gabriel A. Almond and Sidney Verba (Newbury Park, London, New Delhi, 1989).

believing in the "American Creed," holding American political culture in high esteem, and living the "American way of life." Differing behavior and beliefs are suspected as disloyal in moments of national crisis. Various religions—Catholicism during the 1850s and Islam nowadays—as well as ideologies like communism, fascism, or totalitarianism were stigmatized as "un-American" and served as the archenemy.[54] Racial theories became the basis for defining the enemy during the Civil War and after 1906 when the slogan of the "Yellow Peril" emerged. The contributions of Mark Ellis, Michaela Hönicke, Wendy Wall, Peter Zervakis, and Jessica Gienow-Hecht to this volume provide ample evidence of such ideological enemy construction and perception: Americans define their enemies by explaining their antagonism against others as struggles between value systems. The administration of Woodrow Wilson provided the German enemy image with an ideological overtone by interpreting World War I as the fight of "Democracy vs. Militarism." Similarly, Franklin D. Roosevelt concentrated on the ideological antagonism between Nazi totalitarianism and American democratic values. Ideology was the overriding theme of enmity during the Cold War. Antagonistic ideologies were even combined into one enemy image, as was the case with Nazism and communism together forming the construct of "Red Fascism" or totalitarianism.[55]

Structural Factors

Antagonistic human attitudes like enmity cannot be explained by sociopsychological theory only, i.e., the "soft facts" of human mental dispositions. The "hard facts" of the environment have to be taken into account.[56] Ulrich Beck reminds us that enmity might

54. A useful compilation of texts and documents on subversion is: David Brion Davis, ed., *The Fear of Conspiracy: Images of Un-American Subversion from the Revolution to the Present* (Ithaca, NY, 1971); see also the contributions in: *Conspiracy: The Fear of Subversion in American History*, ed. Richard O. Curry and Thomas M. Brown (New York, 1972).

55. Les K. Adler and Thomas G. Paterson, "Red Fascism: The Merger of Nazi Germany and Soviet Russia in the American Image of Totalitarianism, 1930s-1950s," *American Historical Review* 75 (1969–1970): 1046–64.

56. Neglect of the "hard facts" is the major objection of the structuralist school to sociopsychological explanations of enmity and aggression. For representatives of this school the sociopsychologists' refusal to discuss the structural causes of strife and enmity has an alibi function, since the construction of "misperception" enables them to neglect the underlying power structures within a society as the essential precondition of human existence and perception.

not be only an invention. The Jewish perception of the Nazis as enemies after 1933 was not only imagined. The threat was extremely real, whether it was perceived or not. Enmity is usually based on some concrete facts that permit the enemy image to appear as plausible and real. The causes of antagonism are not only embedded in the personal character traits of individuals, but also exist in the economic, cultural, and political structures of society and the international system. They constitute the framework for all human interactions and that means also for enemy perception and enemy behavior.

Social change is an important variable, since it mobilizes society and requires individuals to readjust their behavior and to face an uncertain future. As a result, a general feeling of insecurity might develop which provides an ideal hotbed for all sorts of projections. It might result in political intolerance, ethnic prejudice, religious fundamentalism, and heated nationalism with their stereotyped black-and-white thinking and witch-hunting.[57] Social strain of all varieties seems to be the main reason why people succumb so easily to hate propaganda. It is in times of social unrest, economic depression, questioned cultural identity, and war that internal enemy images are propagated to confirm old or construct new group cohesion and that external enmities are emphasized in order to create or consolidate national unity. "Community" is one of the ideological constructs frequently used in modern times to overcome periods of crisis and insecurity.[58] In the context of a cultural crisis, enmity can be helpful for the construction of a surrogate identity. Enemy images appear as by-products of the desire for new social identities, since in-group/out-group differentiation promotes the process of group construction and definition. Jürgen Heideking's analysis of the American identity crisis during the Revolutionary period and the transformation of the American settlers' old loyalty to the British crown into a specific American nationalism describes such a process. Substantial clashes of interest had created a crisis in the relationship between motherland and colony and had raised doubts about British intentions among the settlers, who began to question their own identity as subjects of the British Crown. The English enemy image proved helpful for the construction of the new national identity. Social conflict enhances enmity,

57. Ted R. Gurr, "The Revolution—Social Change Nexus: Some Old Theories and New Hypotheses," *Comparative Politics* 5 (1972–73): 359–92, is still a useful survey.
58. Gérard Raulet, "Die Modernität der Gemeinschaft," in *Gemeinschaft und Gerechtigkeit*, ed. Micha Brumlik and Hauke Brunkhorst (Frankfurt, 1993), 72–93.

since, as Georg Simmel has put it, "it is expedient to hate the adversary with whom one fights." He believed that external conflicts have an integrative effect on society, but warned also that feelings of hatred are generally much more intense in close relationships.[59] Civil strife arouses more hatred than international conflict, because all participating groups are in dire need of enemy images to justify their violent behavior against fellow citizens. The violation of old loyalties and the refusal of solidarity and empathy to neighbors, friends, or even family members needs a strong, convincing explanation to be acceptable to most individuals.[60] Jürgen Heideking's findings support this hypothesis, and the American experience of the Civil War certainly confirms such a theory. Wars and their aftermath are also times of social hardship, encouraging group conflict. In this volume, Mark Ellis describes the persecution of German-Americans as internal enemies during World War I. While the uses of hate propaganda against the enemy during wars are a by-product of the official efforts to mobilize society for war, intense internal friction after wars is to be explained as a response to the social and economic changes that occurred during wartime. At the end of wars, the community-building glue of the collective effort for victory disappears. Disillusion spreads and a reorientation becomes necessary. In the United States the nativist battle cry against the hated other increased after World War I when it was combined with anti-socialism and racism and, during the "Red Scare," directed its fervor not only against "Communists" but also against black Americans. Wendy Wall points to the difficult position of the American Jews in the United States before and during World War II. Japanese-Americans fared even worse after Pearl Harbor. Discrimination against German émigré Jews during the first period of the Cold War and the main wave of McCarthyism is the subject of Jessica Gienow-Hecht's chapter. Berndt Ostendorf describes how racism mixed with anti-communism and anti-modernism in the ideology of rightist fundamentalism during the Cold War.

The differences of class, race, ethnic origin, gender, or age, as well as the plurality of ideological, religious, and cultural values, might provide the strain that promotes threat perceptions. Form and intensity of such antagonisms as well as the accompanying enemy images will vary according to the composition of a society,

---

59. Georg Simmel, *Der Streit* (1908), repr. in *Soziologie*, 3d ed. (Berlin, 1958), cf. from English ed. *Conflict*, translated by K. H. Wolff (New York, 1955), 33.
60. Coser, *Functions*; Ted R. Gurr, *Why Men Rebel* (Princeton, NJ, 1970).

its cultural identity, and its political structure. In the case of the United States, the exceptional centrality of multiethnic immigration, as well as the race question, and, secondly, egalitarian liberal ideology seem to be most important for explaining antagonistic group thinking. Each major wave of immigrants led to xenophobic nativist reactions against the newcomers that transcended the perception of otherness, since the immigrants were seen as a danger to the community. Although the ideological contents of this enmity varied with the specific characteristics of the newcomers, taken together, they produced a mirror image of American self-perception: the aim of all nativist movements was to uphold "Americanism" and fight for Protestant Christianity as well as white, Anglo-Saxon supremacy. The fight was directed against Catholic, Irish, German, and later southeast European newcomers; against radicals, especially socialists and communists; most vehemently against Chinese and Japanese immigrants; and most recently against Hispanics. Nativism did not simply emanate from the perception of ideological or cultural differences and the fear of cultural alienation. Often ethnic and racial conflict also bore elements of class antagonism, since immigrants and black Americans constantly provided the American labor market with a source of cheap labor. The immigrating newcomers threatened the economic and social position of the lower stratum of American society in many respects. Nativism has been most successful in periods of economic depression.[61]

Personal contact and close neighborhoods make cultural difference, social status anxiety, and economic competition more visible and might therefore produce enmity. Racism and xenophobia remain abstract for people who are not confronted with the other. The visible "enemy" appears more threatening than an antagonist living far away. Hartmut Keil maintains in his chapter that racism was not an important issue among German-Americans, since most of them settled in the rural Midwest and did not come into close contact with African-Americans. His findings on the importance of physical contact are confirmed by studies on racial discrimination against blacks and Asians.[62] The civil rights movement of the 1960s

61. John Higham, *Strangers in the Land: Patterns of American Nativism, 1860–1925* (New Brunswick, NJ, 1955).

62. Cf. for example: Kenneth L. Kusmer, *A Ghetto Takes Shape: Black Cleveland, 1870–1930* (Urbana and Chicago, IL, 1976), 53–65, 174–89; Roger Daniels, *Coming to America: A History of Immigration and Ethnicity in American Life* (New York, 1992), 238–64; Roger Daniels, *Asian America: Chinese and Japanese in the United States Since 1850* (Seattle, 1988); Roger Daniels and Harry H. L. Kitano, *American Racism: Exploration of the Nature of Prejudice* (Englewood Cliffs, NJ, 1970).

was optimistic that personal contact and racial coeducation would help to overcome racial prejudices. But this hope has by now disappeared, as social psychologists doubt the positive effects of school busing and similar efforts toward racial integration. The racial dilemma did not wane; it only changed its appearance, and its causality became more complex. Racism is no longer characterized only by prejudices of white people against colored ones. Issues of race now are two-sided, and they are to be judged from the perspective of whites as well as blacks and Asians. Modern racism is the result of a complex process of interaction between the races.[63]

The second important possible structural source of social conflict and enmity is the American political system itself, particularly the persistent gap between individual expectations with regard to citizens' rights and political reality. The American political value system is defined flexibly and abstractly enough to provide room for a certain amount of value pluralism and social change. But this vagueness of the ideological framework creates inconsistencies that are a constant source of social strain. The promise of liberty as well as freedom can never be fulfilled for all individuals alike, and this creates discontent and enmity among the underprivileged groups toward the more successful and respected majority. Samuel P. Huntington argues that liberty and equality contradict each other to a certain degree and that therefore the "promise of disharmony" is built into the American political system. Protest movements claim equal opportunity and access to political power. Thus, the "liberal creed" itself appears responsible for "creedal passion periods." Although, compared to Europe, class conflict was and is less obvious and dominant in the United States, "the United States has had more sociopolitical conflict and violence than many European countries."[64]

Huntington refers only to the "passion-periods" of left-wing radicalism with its insistence on equal rights, but does not consider the passionate fundamentalism of the conservative right. The latter's "Americanism" and their will to fight the assumed "enemy" is no less guided by assumptions about the real meaning of the

---

63. *Prejudice, Politics, and the American Dilemma*, ed. Paul M. Sniderman, Philip E. Tetlock, and Edward G. Carmines (Stanford, CA, 1993); Berndt Ostendorf, "Probleme mit der Differenz: Historische Ursachen und gesellschaftliche Konsequenzen der Selbstethnisierung in den USA," in *Die bedrängte Toleranz*, ed. Wilhelm Heitmeyer and Rainer Dollase (Frankfurt, 1996), 155–78.

64. Samuel P. Huntington, *American Politics, the Promise of Disharmony* (Cambridge, MA, 1981).

Constitution and its transformation into political institutions. As Hofstadter has put it for the McCarthy era, "the modern right wing ... feels dispossessed: America has been largely taken away from them and their kind, though they are determined to try to repossess it and to prevent the final destructive act of subversion." In Hofstadter's eyes, the American right feared the destruction of capitalism, the increasing power of the federal government, and communism, and believed in the existence of a vast and sinister conspiracy. Cosmopolitans and intellectuals, socialists and communists appeared as enemies.[65] Enemy images serve as a weapon in the internal fight for the definition of the national ideological and cultural identity, for economic opportunity as well as political influence and power.

For the American experience, geographical remoteness from Europe, the center of great power conflict until World War I, has been a third important structural factor for constructing enmity. Enemy images have to be plausible for the majority of people to serve their purpose. Since Americans did not lack in self-esteem, only a mighty nation could be considered as a real threat. Mexico did not qualify, and the relationship towards England remained ambivalent, but not outrightly antagonistic. David Kennedy maintains in his contribution that the struggle with England and its aftermath resembled more a family feud, while Jürgen Heideking obviously takes Anglo-American antagonism more seriously. Edward P. Crapol points to the potential for economic conflict between the two nations and American resentment of British naval mastery on the Atlantic during the nineteenth century. But the British acquiescence in the Monroe Doctrine in 1895 and the rise of the United States to first rank as an industrial power placated American enmity towards Britain and made a "fragile rapprochement" possible.[66] While Kennedy claims in his chapter that the German enemy image evolved during World War I, Ragnhild Fiebig-von Hase maintains that the American enemy image of Germany had already begun to develop with the proclamation of

65. Hofstadter, "Paranoid Style," 23–29; compare: Seymour M. Lipset, *The Politics of Unreason: Right-Wing Extremism in America 1790–1970* (London, 1971).

66. Edward P. Crapol, *America for Americans: Economic Nationalism and Anglophobia in the Late Nineteenth Century* (Westport, CT, 1973); Edward P. Crapol, "From Anglophobia to Fragile Rapprochement: Anglo-American Relations in the Early Twentieth Century," in *Confrontation and Cooperation: Germany and the United States in the Era of World War I, 1900–1924,* ed. Hans-Jürgen Schröder (Providence, RI and Oxford, 1993), 13–31.

Weltpolitik by Kaiser Wilhelm II and the building of the German battle fleet in the years after 1896. Combined with the German economic expansion in Latin America, the decision to build such a huge fleet encouraged speculation and suspicion. The image of the German enemy and a possible naval clash with the *Kaiserreich* became the basis of American security policy in 1900. Isolation was gone: the Atlantic Ocean no longer provided a sufficient security barrier for the Western Hemisphere against European expansionist ambitions. Americans did not fear an outright German invasion of their country, but perceived German ambitions as a threat to the cherished Monroe Doctrine and feared a further elimination of the advantages of an isolated geographic location.[67]

The American image of the Japanese enemy emerged after the Japanese-Russian War of 1904–05, and was fueled by American racial antagonism against Japanese immigrants and clashing expansionist aims in East Asia. The administration of Theodore Roosevelt realized the strategic implications of this new enmity: the United States had become vulnerable on both coastlines—on the Pacific as well as the Atlantic. From then until 1945, subsequent administrations from Theodore Roosevelt to Franklin D. Roosevelt perceived American vulnerability on two maritime frontiers as a serious security dilemma. American foreign policy and naval armament plans were adjusted to acknowledge this fact.[68] Already well before 1914, technological advancement in communications and armaments had considerably diminished the geostrategical advantages that the United States had enjoyed, and several "war scares" give an impression of the rise of anti-German and anti-Japanese feelings.

The new enmities reflected the rise of the United States to world power status and the spread of American interests around the world. America's future world leadership became obvious during World War I, but the trend was already clearly visible before 1914 and was only further enhanced by the war. European,

---

67. Ragnhild Fiebig-von Hase, *Lateinamerika als Konfliktherd der deutsch-amerikanischen Beziehungen, 1890–1903* (Göttingen, 1986); Ragnhild Fiebig-von Hase, "The United States and Germany in the World Arena," in *Confrontation and Cooperation*, 33–68.

68. William R. Braisted, *The United States Navy in the Pacific*, 2 vols. (Austin, TX, 1958 and 1971); for the American two-ocean security dilemma since 1906: Ute Mehnert, *Deutschland, Amerika und die "Gelbe Gefahr": Zur Karriere eines Schlagworts in der Großen Politik, 1905–1917* (Stuttgart, 1995); Ute Mehnert, "German Weltpolitik and the American Two-Front Dilemma: The 'Japanese Peril' in German-American Relations, 1904–1917," *Journal of American History* 82 (1996): 1452–1477.

and especially German, politicians, intellectuals, business management, and workers perceived American competition as *the* future threat to the existing European global hegemony and adjusted their policies as far as possible according to the perceived "American danger." Many individuals and interest groups interpreted European-American competition as "enmity."[69]

The Political Functionalization of Enemy Images

Finally, enemy images are used in the fight for political power and material advantage on the national as well as the international level. This is why the uses and misuses of enemy images deserve to be analyzed with utmost scrutiny. Whom do enemy images serve? When, how, and under what circumstances? How far do they reflect the reality of the political power structure within a state? What kind of individual and social costs do they produce? How far does the perception of external enemies and its manipulative use influence a political system and serve to justify a specific resource allocation? How much does this affect discussions about wealth distribution?

The Enforcement of Loyalty: Ulrich Beck's "Militarily Bisected Modernity"

In his chapter, Ulrich Beck points to the qualitative difference between "heterostereotypes" and "enemy images" in their relation to the power monopoly of the state. In modern democracies, enemy images are closely associated with the state and the military. In his theory of the "militarily bisected modernity," Beck stresses the functional value of enmity in legitimizing a given power structure and preserving the existing social status quo. All of the achievements of modernity have a double face for the citizens, since universal military conscription bisects their newly gained freedom and enlarges the power of the state. Enemy images supply the ruling elite with the necessary consensus on defense that justifies these restrictions of personal freedom: "Military consensus delimits democratic consensus and vice versa." Enemy images also provide the chance to reduce a complex and often unmanageable given reality into a stringent bipolar friend/enemy alternative.

---

69. Fiebig-von Hase, "United States."

They justify aggressive behavior against foreign nations that would never be tolerated within the state itself. A double standard of values is deliberately created—one for the citizens, one for the enemy.[70] All citizens can be forced to take sides, to identify themselves with a certain enemy perception, or face the alternative of being stigmatized as saboteurs and traitors of the fatherland. Doubts and ambivalence are no longer tolerated. Enemy images are therefore the most powerful instrument for enforcing internal consensus and disciplining a society. The repressive potential accompanying the functionalization of enemy images exposes their "contramodern character." In modern Western democracies, Beck maintains, social integration was accomplished until 1989 less by positive achievements than through enemy images—the stigmatizing of communism as the external archenemy and the exaggeration of the Soviet military threat.[71] The research contributions in this volume provide much material to substantiate such a theory.

The International Dimension

There are different explanations for aggression and enmity in the international system. All of them are closely related to a set of assumptions about the nature of people, society, and the global environment. Beck discusses four theoretical approaches: first, the liberal theory of "peaceful capitalism" with its belief that in the modern world anachronistic preindustrial elites are responsible for international aggression, that capitalism concentrates on conquering markets not people, and that therefore, a capitalistic world will be competitive but "nonbelligerent"; second, the neo-Marxist approach of "military capitalism" that explains enmity and war in the international field as the logical outcome of capitalistic reproduction and class conflict within nation-states; third, "political nationalism" (Max Weber) with its political construct of a *Staatsnation* stressing "ethnic identity, political community, the readiness to use force, and the state monopoly on the use of force" as its

70. The idea that there exist in modern societies "two codes of morals, two sets of mores, one for the comrades inside and the other for strangers outside" and that concerning outsiders it was "meritorious to kill, plunder, practice blood revenge, and to steal women and slaves" can already be found in the work of William Graham Sumner. Among other factors, Sumner named religion as being responsible for this double standard. Cf. in: Gay, *Cultivation*, 91f.

71. For the historical aspects see also Anthony Giddens, *The Nation-State and Violence*, vol. 2 of: *A Contemporary Critique of Historical Materialism* (Cambridge, 1985, reprint 1992).

characteristics. In a world of nation-states, the anarchic character of the international system makes military force the essential tool in the fight for national survival. Lastly, Beck discusses Talcott Parsons's "civic nation" concept, as a contrast to Weber's *Staatsnation,* with its "societal community," "citizenship," "solidarity," and "mutual loyalty among its members" as core values. International cooperation through the creation of common institutions for conflict solution appears as the logical behavior of such states in the global environment. States will seek their enemies according to their ideological self-definition: communism vs. capitalism, authoritarian nation-states vs. civic nations. A *Staatsnation* will search for enemy images that refer to interstate conflict in its efforts to enhance national unity; a "civic nation" will use enemy images that stress the superiority of its moral values and contrast them with the "evil" ideology of the foe.

Beck also combines the internal aspect with a global view in his concept of the "militarily bisected modernity": after the collapse of the Soviet Union and the end of the Cold War, the trend is towards renationalization and revitalization of the anarchic structure of the international system. The usefulness of enemy images as a source of legitimation for the state survived the Cold War. The search for new enemies reflects the necessity of external enmity for stabilizing power structures that lost their justification when the old enemy images collapsed. But, at the same time, the process of individuation is heightened by growing social mobility and increasing economic globalization and by the establishment of international communication networks. In Beck's "global risk society," individuals loose their clear social identity, the concept of the other is generalized, and enemy images are arbitrary and variable. Arguing against doubts that human beings can stand that much disintegration, Beck puts forward the facts that identity is not based only on national enemy images, and that global orientations like ecological morality can also provide order. The source of integration is now the targeting of false ways of production, false nutrition, and false lifestyles and their devastating effects on the global community. To strengthen this new possibility of a social identity, supranational networks and institutions have to be created and supported.

Unfortunately, it is already clear enough that the ecological movement does not abstain from black-and-white painting and also uses enemy images to mobilize support for its concerns. Multinational corporations and the atomic industry are main targets.

In the postmodern debate on cultural identity, another theoretical model emerges. It visualizes states and regions as cultural
entities struggling for survival in an anarchic global environment in which the Western concept of civilization can no longer
claim superiority. In Samuel P. Huntington's prophecy of future
culture wars, enmity is defined culturally. In the search for a lost
national identity, other cultures serve as the convenient other,
the "enemy." The Islamic and Confucian cultures are the preferred targets.[72] The idea reflects conservative skepticism of the
postmodern discourse on cultural and ethnic difference. While
postmodern thought considers the idea of the other "progressive," since it respects the other as such under all circumstances,
the pronounced concern for ethnic and national otherness leads
to reactions that construe anew a deterministic and stereotyped
friend/foe thinking in world affairs: Western culture vs. the rest.[73]
After the loss of the Cold War enemy, the "culture war" concept
promises an easy escape from confusing uncertainty for those
who have difficulties in adjusting to the new pluralism in global
power distribution.

Power Politics and the "Cult of the Offensive"

Concepts of foreign policy and military strategy determine the
functional usefulness of enemy images. The political concept of
"deterrence" and the military "cult of the offensive" especially
appear to further aggressive behavior within the international
system and to promote the propagation of enemy images for its
justification. Both concepts rest on a Hobbesian perception of humankind and society and on Social Darwinist assumptions about
the nature of the global system. If the anarchic nature of the
international system forces the nation-states into a permanent
competition for power, war becomes the ultimate expression of
this fight. Diplomacy is the normal medium of this power struggle, war the calculated exception. Enmity among states appears
as endemic and "natural," as a structural component of the system. States are not surrounded by friends, but "encircled" by

72. Huntington, *Clash of Civilizations*.

73. Preferably Islam is the subject of such theories, as Huntington's contributions
demonstrate. But the Western perception of "Islam" is a stereotype for which
Islamic fundamentalists as well as Western "experts" share responsibility. It neg-
lects the diversity of existing Muslim societies. Aziz Al-Azmeh, *Islamisierung des
Islam: Imaginäre Welten einer politischen Theorie* (Frankfurt, 1996).

actual or at least potential enemies, and have to stay constantly on the alert by building alliances and concentrating on military preparedness. For the realist school, national security is the central issue of politics.[74]

The trend to "organized peacelessness" increases when the "cult of the offensive" is added, and the political and military elites believe in the advantages of "first strike" military capability. The belief in an easy victory through early military preparation further enhances the danger of preemptive war. The history of the European "concert of powers" before 1914 provides an object lesson on how the concept of deterrence developed into a diplomacy of extreme brinkmanship characterized by the constant exaggeration of enmity, an irrational evaluation of information, and worst-case thinking.[75] The policy of nuclear deterrence in the bipolar system during the years from 1945 to 1989 serves as another example. The political and military deterrence strategies of the Soviet Union and the United States during the Cold War created the arms race and threatened the survival of humankind.[76]

Deterrence is a psychostrategy, since the credibility of the "deterring threat" is the central issue. The adversary must be convinced that the threatened measures will be realized if he does not comply with the verbalized demands of the "deterrer." Otherwise he will expose the maneuver as a "bluff." The deterrer will seek the approval of his own citizens for his political brinkmanship, because wide popular support will increase the plausibility of his arguments and therefore his chances to convince the adversary. The "coercive potency of publicity" is part of the bargaining power. But at first, public opinion has to be persuaded that the risks involved are justified by considerations of national security. At the same time there is the provocative effect of a public threat. The position of the adversary might harden under the pressure of

74. Hans J. Morgenthau, *Politics Among Nations*, 6th rev. ed. (New York, 1985).

75. Stephen Van Evera, "The Cult of the Offensive and the Origins of the First World War," in *Military Strategy and the Origins of the First World War: An International Security Reader*, ed. Stephen E. Miller (Princeton, NJ, 1985), 58–107; Glenn H. Snyder, *From Deterrence and Defense Toward a Theory of National Security* (Princeton, NJ, 1961); Dieter Senghaas, *Rüstung und Militarismus* (Frankfurt, 1972), 28–93.

76. Robert Jervis, *The Illogic of American Nuclear Strategy* (Ithaca, NY, 1984); Jervis maintains that deterrence theory became the "most influential school of thought in the American study of international relations" between the late 1950s and the end of the 1970s. Robert Jervis, "Deterrence Theory Revisited," *World Politics* 31 (1978–1979): 289–324; Alexander George and Richard Smoke, *Deterrence in American Foreign Policy: Theory and Practice* (New York, 1974).

public opinion, and this will result in conflict escalation.[77] It is quite clear that in this context the propagation of enemy images has not only an immensely important functional value for streamlining public opinion at home, but also for conveying the "message" to the enemy.[78]

Enmity becomes normalcy and peaceful cooperation the exception in this concept, as the first is considered to be the result of rational "realism," the second of irrational "idealism." This is only the logical consequence of the underlying general ideas about human nature, the national interest of states, and the global system. Different ideological assumptions will immediately lead to contrasting assessments of enmity and the function of enemy images.

"Militarism," "Militarization," and the "Military-Industrial Complex"

Theories of the "martial spirit," "militarism," and the "militarization" of society provide such a contrasting view. Militarism is commonly defined as the prevalence of military values within society, as the "dominance of the military over civilian authority."[79] Militarization concerns the process through which society is increasingly organized around the preparation for war. Successful militarization seems to depend on the promulgation of enemy images. Patrick M. Regan believes that increased militarization leads to an increase in violent behavior by the state, and, at the same time, an increasingly violent foreign policy leads to greater societal militarization. Thereby a vicious circle is created that represents a "self-amplifying feedback relationship": "The more militarized a society, the greater is the extent to which the perception of a threat will be maintained in the mass media." If the external danger lessens, "an increase in the manipulation of the perception of a threat" by the ruling elite will occur. Since the powerful "security elite" controls public information to a large extent, its capabilities of creating an

77. Glenn H. Snyder, *Conflict Among Nations: Bargaining Decision Making and System Structure in International Crises* (Princeton, NJ, 1977), 251–54. Snyder uses game models to explain international relations and analyzes the strategy and tactics of crisis bargaining.

78. Snyder, *Deterrence;* Senghaas, *Rüstung*, 42–43.

79. Volker R. Berghahn, *Militarism: The History of an International Debate, 1861–1979* (Cambridge, 1981); *Militarismus*, ed. Volker R. Berghahn (Cologne, 1975); Ekkehart Krippendorff, *Staat und Krieg: Die historische Logik politischer Unvernunft* (Frankfurt, 1985); *The Militarization of the Western World*, ed. John Gillis (New Brunswick, NJ, 1989).

"armament culture" are great.[80] These theories insist that the causes of war do not emanate primarily from the nature of the international system but rather from the power structures of the modern nation-state. The "martial spirit" with all its modern brutalities is not considered inherent in human nature but rather is seen as a product of socialization. Hero cults and enemy images are the instruments with which the ruling elite conditions people to endure war and accept deprivations of freedom during peacetime. A certain emotionally loaded atmosphere of hatred is necessary to achieve the desired result. At the same time, modern war has no use for individual hatred; the latter becomes even dysfunctional for the complex technical requirements of modern warfare. The disciplining of the citizens as soldiers has become one of the most essential prerequisites of victory.

The contrast between the German and the American experience demonstrates that the intensity of militarism differs. During the Cold War, the degree of militarization in the United States seemed to be considerable, while West Germany's record appeared less pronounced in this respect. In contrast to this finding, the German Kaiserreich was a "garrison state" before 1914, despite the beginnings of democratization. Germany possessed the largest army of the world and ranked second as a naval power after Great Britain. Militarization was for Imperial Germany one, but certainly not the only, possible answer to the specific geostrategic, political, and economic challenges imposed on the country by its history and the European environment. In contrast, the American Army was small before 1917, and American defense policy concentrated on naval power. Certainly the reason was not that Americans were born with less potential for aggression in their character, but military virtue was less popular in the United States at that time. In contrast to Germany, military conscription was not considered a positive influence in the process of socialization but rather rejected as an impediment to personal freedom. Fierce opposition to standing armies was a popular credo. David Kennedy points out the reasons: Americans could afford to neglect enmity towards other nations during the nineteenth century, because geography provided them with sufficient security. Enemy images had no functional value as long as it was impossible to present a plausible threat to the public. Standing armies were ideologically

---

80. Patrick M. Regan, *Organizing Societies for War: The Process and Consequences of Societal Militarization* (Westport, CT, 1994), passim, quotations, 23, 100, 116.

suspicious and of little practical value. All this changed during the twentieth century. While Americans concentrated on internal wars during most of the nineteenth century, involvement in international conflicts characterized the American historical record during the twentieth. New comparative research on the military professionalization of American and German naval officers before 1914 moderates this thesis. In pointing to the similarities in the world-view of the naval establishment in both countries, and stressing the importance of the German enemy image for the development of the American Navy before 1914, Dirk Bönker argues that American "exceptionalism" in militarization should, as far as the Navy is concerned, be reduced to a question of degree rather than principle.[81]

Comparisons of societal attitudes towards peace movements can be used as another indicator for the degree of militarization. Here, the differences between the American and the German historical experience before 1914 are immense. While in the United States the peace movement was highly respected as an influential political force and sponsored by the economic, cultural, and social elites, German peace advocates were a comparatively small group without any access to political power and were stigmatized as antinational traitors by the government, the churches, and a large majority of Germans.[82]

The question of whether the ascendancy of the United States to the rank of the world's most powerful military nation is accompanied by a lasting militarization of the American value system has to remain open. In his recent book Michael S. Sherry reminds us once more that the intense preoccupation with war since the 1930s, as he sees it, left deep scars on American society. Although he realizes that the spell of military euphoria was broken when the Cold War ended, he argues that only a consistent modification in political thinking and rhetoric as well as institutional reorientation will change militaristic attitudes.[83]

---

81. Dirk Bönker, "Maritime Aufrüstung zwischen Partei- und Weltpolitik: Schlachtflottenbau in Deutschland und den USA um die Jahrhundertwende," in *Zwei Wege in die Moderne: Aspekte der deutsch-amerikanischen Beziehungen, 1900–1918,* ed. Ragnhild Fiebig-von Hase and Jürgen Heideking (Trier, 1997, forthcoming).

82. With an excellent summary of the literature on the peace movement of both nations before 1918: Christof Mauch, "Pazifismus und politische Kultur. Die organisierte Friedensbewegung in den USA und Deutschland in vergleichender Perspektive, 1900–1917," in *Zwei Wege in die Moderne.*

83. Michael S. Sherry, *In the Shadow of War: The United States Since the 1930's* (New Haven, CT and London, 1995).

Closely related to the theories on militarism are assumptions about the dominance of the military-industrial complex in modern industrial societies. The debate about the military-industrial complex developed as a reaction to the internal implications of the American-Soviet arms race during the Cold War. The immense influence and power of the armament industry and its close interrelationship with the military and intelligence bureaucracy as well as with the political and scientific elite is stressed. Several studies confirm the large impact of the armament industry on the economic life of the new "Gunbelt."[84] "Pentagon capitalism" threatens to destroy the autonomy of the free enterprise economy. It induces "parasitic" growth and hinders the economic development of the nation as a whole.[85] In this concept, enemy images are considered instrumental in sustaining popular consent to constantly increasing armament costs. The military-industrial complex appears as the main culprit for international enmity—another enemy image is thereby created.[86]

Theories on militarism, militarization, and the military-industrial complex have an emancipatory and progressive touch. Their proponents hope to strengthen the democratic structures of society by exposing the deformational effects of militarization. Their strength is that they stress the importance of threat perception and point to the profiteers of militarization. Their weakness is that they provide no analytical tools to distinguish between threats that are real and those that are only imagined—between necessary defensive security preparations and aggressive militarism. Such criteria seem to be indispensable for an assessment of enmity in the international context.

84. Roger W. Lotchin, *Fortress California, 1910–1961: From Warfare to Welfare* (New York, 1992); *The Rise of the Gunbelt: The Military Remapping of Industrial America*, ed. Ann Markusen, Scott Campbell, Peter Hall, and Sabina Deitrick (New York, 1991).

85. Seymour Melman, *Pentagon Capitalism* (New York, 1970); Seymour Melman, "Pentagon Bourgeoisie," in *Beyond Conflict and Containment: Critical Studies of Military and Foreign Policy* (New Brunswick, NJ, 1972), 184–97.

86. *War, Business, and American Society: Historical Perspectives on the Military-Industrial Complex*, ed. Benjamin F. Cooling (Port Washington, NY, 1977); Paul A. C. Koistinen, *The Military-Industrial Complex: A Historical Perspective* (New York, 1980); Senghaas, *Rüstung; The War Economy of the United States: Readings on Military Industry and Economy*, ed. Seymour Melman (New York, 1971); *Testing the Theory of the Military-Industrial Complex*, ed. Stephen Rosen (Lexington, MA, 1973); *Science, Technology, and the Military*, ed. Everett Mendelsohn, Merritt R. Smith, and Peter Weingart, 2 vols. (Boston, 1988); Jacob Van der Meulen, *The Politics of Aircraft: Building an American Military Industry* (Lawrence, KA, 1991); Patrick M. Regan's book on societal militarization is an interesting attempt to combine the approaches of militarism and the military-industrial complex in the broadest sense.

Conclusion

The preceding survey of possible analytical approaches to the intricate problem of enemy images as well as the results of new empirical research on the American experience presented in this volume provide only an ambivalent answer to the question of American "exceptionalism" in enemy perception and construction. Many intervening variables complicate the picture. There is much evidence that the specific composition of the immigrant society played an outstanding role. A liberal political ideology that stressed individualism and tolerance mitigated at least partly ethnic discrimination, racial hatred, and religious intolerance. Among the exceptional factors shaping American enemy images, the ascendancy of the nation to world leadership was certainly the most important one. By birth, Americans certainly did not have a more peaceful or aggressive character than the rest of humanity, but in response to the peculiar circumstances of the country's cultural, economic, and political development, its social composition, and its role within the international community, Americans developed their own patterns of enemy perception.

PART I

SOCIOLOGICAL AND PSYCHOLOGICAL ASPECTS

Chapter One

SOME SOCIOBIOLOGICAL AND PSYCHOLOGICAL ASPECTS OF "IMAGES OF THE ENEMY"

Kurt R. Spillmann and Kati Spillmann

Relevance of the Topic

The fabric of human history is shot through with the thread of images of the enemy and their consequences in conflicts of all types. Wars and violent conflicts continue to be waged with atrocious results. There have always been violent conflicts among enemy groups. The historical records of all nations are filled with them, and the majority of early literary documents—such as, for example, *The Iliad*—deal with such themes. Concepts of the enemy are factors usually effective in the background, and important in the mobilization and escalation of conflicts, even if very different proximate causes of conflict stand in the foreground.

The history of the United States is no exception in this regard. Concepts of the enemy played an important role from the founding of the Massachusetts Bay Company (1629) onwards in defining an identity which was their own, at first as New Englanders and later as Americans. Through changing times and circumstances, the visible enemies could be the Anglican bishops under William Laud, the Indians, the French, the Confederates, the blacks, immigrating southern Europeans and Slavs, fascists and National Socialists, the Japanese, Communists, or the Soviet "Evil Empire."

The worldwide relevance and the unbroken virulence of the subject "images of the enemy" is being demonstrated today by the violence in the former Yugoslavia, in various states of the former Soviet Union, in Angola, in Rwanda, and South Africa. In the approximately fifty other wars currently recorded by the Arbeitsgemeinschaft für Kriegsursachenforschung (Research Unit on the Causes of War, AKUF) at the University of Hamburg, concepts of the enemy, or the archaic patterns of behavior connected with them, also continue to play a significant role.

Why Do Humans Wage War Against Humans?

The question of why humans still behave toward other humans in a manner in no way compatible with our modern ethical criteria pursues us just as persistently as it did Thucydides at the time of the Peloponnesian War. And yet more than 190 states have today committed themselves, by signing the United Nations Charter, to uphold worldwide behavioral rules in the service of peace and the safeguarding of human rights. But theory and practice are poles apart, as are the postulates and the reality of law and peace. This wide gap is found at all levels—at the global, regional, international, and domestic levels—continuing down to the level of day-to-day social interactions. Why have we not succeeded in creating peace on the basis of justice? Why are humans enemies, why do they stay enemies, and why do they become enemies, both as individuals and in groups?

Reflections on these questions and speculations on human nature and the probable sources of injustice and violence fill whole libraries. Thoughts oscillate in endless variations between negative assessments of human makeup and intentions, as formulated, for example, by Thomas Hobbes, who believed humans could be made peaceful only through a "Leviathan," or strict submission to the absolute power of a state, and *positive* evaluations of free, and by their very nature good, humans, as depicted by Rousseau. These speculations all remain at the level of conjecture and postulate on the way humans should be and behave, how the just state should be organized and governed, and how people and institutions should act. A solid theory of human behavior or a comprehensive model that may be tested scientifically has been lacking, if one does not consider Sigmund Freud's body of theory, intended to be natural-scientific, as such.

From Helplessness to Sociobiology

The lack of a consistent, natural-scientific theory of the motivation of human behavior was until just recently comparable to the state of affairs in the fields of natural history and natural philosophy prior to Darwin: numerous researchers collected, sifted, and described endless amounts of observations and facts, constructed classification systems, and offered theologically anchored explanations of the existing diversity of life forms. But only with the publication of Charles Darwin's epoch-making work *On the Origin of the Species by Means of Natural Selection* (London, 1859) did a comprehensive theory become available which explained the most important mechanisms behind the variety of life forms in a verifiable fashion. With this, scientific investigation of evolution was underway.

As the most important consequence, Darwin, through homology evidence, ended humanity's status as the "crown of creation" and returned the species to the total interrelation of all living beings. Homo sapiens was now seen, as were all life forms, as the product of an evolution of many million years' duration. This was humankind's second dethroning (Copernicus had already pushed humans from the center of creation and transformed the earth into a normal celestial body somewhere in the universe).

Darwin's explanatory model is based mainly upon the three principles of competition, variation, and heredity, that is:

1. In all organisms, more progeny are born than can reproduce (= competition).
2. Individuals differ in their ability to survive and reproduce (= variation).
3. At least a part of this variation is inherited, in the sense that progeny show more similarity to their parents than to any individual in the population chosen at random (= heredity).[1]

With this explanatory approach, Darwin was able to plausibly substantiate that the diversity of life forms is based on a principle—the principle of evolution—having recognizable laws, as a countermovement, so to speak, to the Second Law of Thermodynamics.

1. According to Paul Schmid-Hempel, in "Lebenslaufstrategien, Fortpflanzungsunterschiede und biologische Optimierung," in *Fortpflanzung, Natur und Kultur im Wechselspiel, Versuch eines Dialogs zwischen Biologen und Sozialwissenschaftlern,* ed. Eckart Voland (Frankfurt, 1992), 75f.

It was not until much later, however, that *patterns of behavior* were also recognized and studied as evolved control systems serving to increase chances of survival and reproduction. The behavior of animals and humans was more difficult to bring into agreement with Darwin's basic laws of evolution; in particular, the phenomenon of cooperation led to problems in understanding.

The British biologist William D. Hamilton asked himself why it was that Darwin's postulated competition does not show up indiscriminately through all life forms, while in most life forms various forms of cooperation and altruism can be observed. How, for example, can we explain the observation that animals show readiness to sacrifice themselves? Marmots, for instance, whistle a warning of the approach of birds of prey, thus drawing attention to themselves and putting themselves in danger.

These and other basic questions about the biological roots of social behavior were stimulated by the studies of Tinbergen, Lorenz, Leyhausen, and others, and have developed since the appearance of Hamilton's path-breaking work *The Genetical Evolution of Social Behavior* in 1994 into the central problematic of a new science of behavior, founded in evolutionary biology. The science has been known since 1975 as sociobiology, after the title of E. O. Wilson's already classic treatment.[2]

And sociobiology's answer to the question of the compatibility of altruism and other forms of group-related behavior with Darwin's theory was given, in concrete form, by the theory of genetic relatedness and reciprocity.[3] According to this well-founded theory, the principle of "the good of the community takes precedence over the good of the individual" (as was also held by Konrad Lorenz) is not compatible with Darwin's evolutionary biology.[4] The fundamental unit of natural selection is neither the species nor the group nor the individual, but rather the individual genetic program, which makes use of its bearer for purposes of reproduction. The "selfish gene" is therefore not interested in either the individual or the much acclaimed survival of the species.[5] Axelrod states that: "In the end, the gene looks beyond its mortal bearer and to the potentially immortal quantity of its replicates in other

2. Edward O. Wilson, *Sociobiology: The New Synthesis* (Cambridge, MA, 1975).

3. Robert Axelrod, *Die Evolution der Kooperation* (Munich, 1991), 80ff.

4. Klaus Immelmann, Klaus R. Scherer, Christian Vogel, and Peter Schmoock, eds., *Psychobiologie, Grundlagen des Verhaltens* (Stuttgart/New York, 1988), 829.

5. Richard Dawkins, *The Selfish Gene* (Oxford, 1976), German edition: *Das egoistische Gen* (Berlin, Heidelberg, New York, 1978).

individuals. If these are related closely enough, altruism can, despite disadvantages for the individual altruist, be advantageous with regard to the reproduction of these replicates."[6]

These principles of the preferential treatment of relatives (nepotism), deeply rooted in all of life, are a first indication of the fact that closely related small groups are the basic unit of all social behavior, which includes both readiness to cooperate within the group and its reverse: lack of readiness to cooperate with, or active hostility towards, strangers to the group.

What Sociobiology Is and Is Not

Sociobiology is the science of the biological adaptability of the social behavior of humans and animals. "In describing 'survival' and 'reproduction' as evolved life principles in humans as well as animals, sociobiology helps us to understand diverse phenomena of humans' coping with existence and of cultural history against the background of biological function," as Eckhart Voland defines the aims of sociobiology in a recently published handbook.[7]

If humans take their place among all living things in the millions of years of phylogenetic development, then also their patterns of aggressive behavior must at least in part be biologically, that is genetically, based and have a determining effect on their social behavior. Investigations have shown that there exist universal behavior patterns of threat and fighting, found worldwide and evidenced in all peoples. In a study of Bushman children playing in groups, Irenäus Eibl-Eibesfeldt, in a filmed observation period of 191 minutes, recorded in a group of nine children 166 aggressive acts such as punching, throwing objects, spitting, sticking out tongue, pushing, biting, kicking, and so on—all threatening and fighting postures, which are just as well known and used by European children today.

But not only humans worldwide show these common threatening and fighting behaviors. The same are found in chimpanzees and gorillas as well. Comparative studies show, finally, that very specific situations trigger aggressive behavior in both humans and apes:

6. Axelrod, *Evolution*, 81, trans. by the author.
7. Eckhart Voland, *Grundriß der Soziobiologie*, trans. by the author (Stuttgart, Jena, 1993), 1.

- competition for food
- defending the young
- dominance fighting to establish rank order in a group
- passing on of aggression to lower-ranking animals after being subjected to aggression themselves
- perception of deviant behavior in a group member
- change of rank order, change of leadership
- pair formation
- intrusion of a stranger into the group[8]

We historians should also take note of this new science and its insights. It can provide us with important help in understanding significant questions regarding historical and political actions.

Three notes of caution should be sounded at this point:

1. As we single out in the following the particular aspect of images of the enemy from humankind's behavioral repertory and attempt to explain it on the basis of biological-genetic facts, we by no means adhere to a stance of biological determinism. There are no indications of purpose or intentions effective in evolution—neither those working out of the past nor those working out of the future. Accordingly, we speak here of the biological *function* of a behavior, which over eons of time—over millions of years—evolved and, in the sense of the life interest mentioned, was functional and adapted to the environment.

2. Such original or archaic behavior is not taken to mean "natural" behavior and thus justified as the behavioral norm. Sociobiology explains solely functional connections. It does not set up ethical norms and does not derive instructions for behavior from biology. Sociobiology tries to avoid the naturalistic fallacy, which draws direct conclusions from actual conditions to form norms of the desirable—something David Hume warned against as early as 1741.[9]

3. While human behavior is shaped by biology in certain fundamental preconditions, or limits to plasticity, it is also codetermined by cultural factors in the social surroundings and is thus revisable or "re-trainable." Taking this fact into account, the more appropriate, but less well-known concept

---

8. Irenäus Eibl-Eibesfeldt, "Stammesgeschichtliche Anpassungen im aggressiven Verhalten des Menschen," in *Aggression und Frustration als psychologisches Problem*, ed. Hans-Joachim Kornadt, 2 vols. (Darmstadt, 1981), 1: 212–18.

9. Immelmann et al., *Psychobiologie*, 820.

of *co-evolution* attempts to transcend the "nature/nurture controversy."[10] Modern people's behavior is defined by the delimiting conditions of both biological and cultural determinants. Their degrees of freedom and potential for self-determination actually increase to the degree that they become conscious of that which has molded their behavioral propensities, which they then can modify and revise.

Sigmund Freud came to insights astonishingly similar to Darwin's in his research activities, as he recognized a fundamental antagonism between self-survival and sexual instincts in humans. When Freud speaks of "instinct," he does not mean, as is so often falsely understood, reduction of all psychological processes to drive impulses and sexuality. Rather, instinct is to Freud a term on the frontier between the mental and the physical. Instinct is the psychological representative of the stimuli originating from within the organism and reaching to the mind. It is a measure of the demand made upon the mind for work in consequence of its connection with the body.[11]

In recognizing the insoluble conflict between the self-survival instinct and the reproductive instinct as a basic constant in human existence—but placing this constant within a further, new field of conflict, namely that between the psyche and the body—Freud departs from Darwin's world of closed, instinctive behavioral reactions in the animal world and goes into that which makes humankind different from the entire previous evolutionary development.

The pioneering works of Hamilton, Wilson, Dawkins, Trivers, and Alexander opened up an expanded approach to understanding human behavior in the light of biological and cultural coevolution.[12] In the German-speaking realm, Christian Vogel's publications

10. See, for example, Elmar Holenstein, "Koevolutionäre Erkenntnislehre," in *Evolution und Selbstbezug des Erkennens, Mit Beiträgen von Rupert Riedl, Gerhard Vollmer, Herta Nagl-Docekal, Bernhard Irrgang, Elmar Holenstein, Herbert Hrachovec,* ed. August Fenk (Vienna, Cologne, 1903), 107–23.

11. Sigmund Freud, "Triebe und Triebschicksale" (1915), in *Gesammelte Werke*, 17 vols. (London, 1940–87), 10: 214, English edition: "Instincts and Their Vicissitudes," in *The Standard Edition of the Complete Psychological Works of Sigmund Freud,* trans. from German under the general editorship of James Strachey, 24 vols. (London, 1957), 14: 121f.

12. William D. Hamilton, "The Genetical Evolution of Social Behavior," *Journal of Theoretical Biology* 7 (1964): 1–16 and 17–52; Wilson, *Sociobiology*, 1975; Dawkins, *Selfish Gene;* Richard D. Alexander, *Darwinism and Human Affairs* (Seattle and London, 1979); Robert Trivers, *Social Evolution* (Menlo Park, CA, 1985).

are of particular importance with regard to the connections considered here.[13]

Images of the Enemy

From the beginning, the enemy has shaped the structure of relationships in all of living nature, in the form of rigorous fighting for territory, food, and reproductive partners. During the course of evolution, only those life forms could develop which—in ways however primitive—were able to distinguish between survival-enhancing factors in their environment and survival-endangering factors and to respond to these appropriately. Such factors were light or temperature conditions, abundance or scarcity of food, reproductive partners or competitors for territory, or resources. *The fundamental schema of friend/foe proves to be an elementary aid to orientation in the evolutionary fight for survival.* This basic thought pattern is so elementary that in humans a tendency to fall back into this digital schema has survived.

Since the development of modern means of mass annihilation on the one hand, and since recent, new eruptions of old ethnocentrism and the many demonstrations of the destructive powers of concepts of the enemy on the other, it has become ever more imperative that behavioral and perceptual patterns be revised which may have been adaptive at the time of the Paleolithic hordes of hunters and gatherers. Today, however, with the increasing demographic density of the rapidly growing human population, these patterns represent a dangerous powder keg.

Images of the enemy are based, in humans as well, on a perception of the unfamiliar, or strange, which is evaluated only negatively. Concepts of the enemy thus evoke feelings and reactions such as fear, aversion, aggression, and hate. In a general form, these reactions may be described as a syndrome. The following characteristics belong here:

1. *Negative anticipation.* All acts of the enemy in the past, present, and future are attributed to destructive intentions towards one's own group ("Everything the enemy does is either bad or—when it appears reasonable—stems from

---

13. Christian Vogel, *Vom Töten zum Mord, Das wirkliche Böse in der Evolutionsgeschichte* (Munich and Vienna, 1987), particularly Ch. 2: "Evolutionsbiologie und die 'doppelte Moral,'" 38–58.

dishonest motives.") Whatever the enemy undertakes, it is meant to harm us.

2. *Putting blame on the enemy.* The enemy is suspected of being the source of any stress factors impinging upon the group. ("The enemy is guilty of causing the existing strain and current negative conditions.")

3. *Identification with evil.* The system of values of the enemy represents the negation of one's own value system. ("The enemy embodies the opposite of that which we are and strive for; the enemy wishes to destroy our highest values and must therefore be destroyed.")

4. *Zero-sum thinking.* ("What is good for the enemy is bad for us," and vice versa.)

5. *Stereotyping and deindividualization.* ("Anyone who belongs to the enemy group is *eo ipso* our enemy.")

6. *Refusal to show empathy.* There is a refusal to empathize with all members of the enemy group in their particular situation. Consideration for one's fellow being is repressed through strong feelings of opposition. ("There are no things in common binding us with our enemies; there are no facts or information that could alter our perceptions; it is dangerous, self-destructive and out of place to have feelings of human consideration and ethical criteria with regard to our enemies.")

Perceptual evaluations such as these are in their essence subjective and deeply rooted in the prerational realm. For this reason, we must from the start be prepared to accept that purely explanatory appeals for more empathy will not reach the real roots of concepts of the enemy and have little chance of success.

In-Group/Out-Group

Closely tied to the friend/foe schema is the elementary distinction observed worldwide between "in-group" and "out-group."

Feelings and acts of care, love, support, help, and so on are first of all reserved for one's own family, and then in decreasing intensity also spread to include those persons who in some way can be regarded as members of one's own group and identified on the basis of common characteristics ("badges"). What one has in common can be based upon completely different contents such as, for example, being the products of a particular history, speaking a common special language, adhering to a certain religion. The basis is made up of common interests in the largest sense of the word, especially—over the longest periods of evolution with accordingly lasting effects—the optimization of reproduction chances. Or, in other words, common basis is kinship selection or reciprocal altruism, which gives the group members as much as they can, on another occasion, expect to receive, under the condition of the lowest possible danger of betrayal.[14]

On the other side of the feeling of belonging to the extended group, as the broadest application of solidarity feelings to all individuals one knows personally, lies the large middle field of indifference: the mass of persons and groups of whose existence we theoretically know, but with whom we have no contact at all. Finally, at the other end of the relationship scale, we find enemy group(s), towards whom we feel strongly negative emotions. These are groups and individuals who for some reason or other are held to be a threat, or competitors, rivals, opponents, and enemies. Concepts of the enemy are therefore the reverse side of cooperative feelings of belonging.

The Double Moral Standard

The conspicuous contrast in human social behavior between treatment of in-groups and treatment of out-groups has long been a concern to social scientists and, of course, moral philosophers. Peter Kropotkin—the Russian aristocrat and anarchist, who in his book *Mutual Aid: A Factor in Evolution* (1902) presented the principle of cooperation as a forming basic principle of evolution, as a counter to Darwin—complained of the "double standard":

> Already the lives of the so-called savages appear in two different ethical forms: the relationships within the tribe and the relationship to outsiders; and inter-tribal justice deviates (as does our international law) greatly from common justice in the tribe. Thus if war breaks out, the most horrifying atrocities elicit the tribe's admiration. This double moral standard is seen throughout the entire development of humanity and has been maintained up to this day.[15]

14. Kinship selection and reciprocal altruism are presented in short form in Andreas Phocas, *Biologische Aspekte politischen Verhaltens* (Munich, 1986), 59–89.

15. Peter Kropotkin, *Mutual Aid, A Factor in Evolution* (New York and London, 1902), cited in: *Psychobiologie*, ed. Immelmann et al., 832, paraphrased by the author.

Christian Vogel, an anthropologist in Göttingen, comments that in all human cultures and all human societies, willingness to help and solidarity are exercised in a carefully graded way, not by any means egalitarian, and, as a rule, exactly in the manner sociobiologically schooled evolutionary biologists would predict.[16] And the English philosopher Henry Sidgwick (1838–1900) formulated in his book *The Methods of Ethics* the morals generally practiced in Europe as follows:

> We are in agreement that each individual has the obligation to behave in a friendly and helpful way towards his parents, his spouse and his children as well as towards other relatives (but there to a lesser degree), towards those who have helped him and those he has embraced in his most inner circle, towards neighbors and countrymen more so than towards other people, towards members of his race more so than towards Blacks and Yellows and, generally, towards persons according to their closeness to us.[17]

This is nothing other than kinship selection and reciprocal altruism, exactly according to the predictions of sociobiology, a formulation which unfortunately comes closer to existing (Western) societal reality than the equality and solidarity postulates of the UN Charter or the UN Declaration of Human Rights and official political rhetoric.

In a critical and purposely overstated comment, the behavioral researcher Paul Leyhausen described in 1974 that which we take exception to in the double moral standard: "You must not kill any group members, but the killing of strangers is allowed, at least under certain conditions; because only we are really humans, the others merely look human."[18]

A daily glance at reports from the former Yugoslavia, Rwanda, Algeria, or Cambodia shows immediately that this repulsive formula is not an exaggeration of reality, but is rather a realistic reflection of it both today and in all past centuries.

Our ability, through the aid of reason, to transcend in thought these traditional behavioral patterns and to attempt to change our behavior accordingly is that which actually makes up our humanness, even though the gap between practice and theory, observed daily, demonstrates the tough persistence of our archaic patterns of behavior.

16. Christian Vogel, in: *Psychobiologie*, 832.

17. Henry Sidgwick, *The Methods of Ethics* (London, 1884), cf. in *Psychobiologie*, 832, and paraphrased by the author.

18. Paul Leyhausen, cf. in *Psychobiologie*, 829, paraphrased by the author.

The Role of the Brain

We humans are on the one hand the product of millions of years of ongoing biological evolution with its specific perceptual structures, but at the same time we are the product of a cultural evolution, which shares in determining our values, our knowledge, and our customs and enlightened standards. The vehicle of this development over hundreds of millions of years is the human brain.

Modern brain research has demonstrated the developmental history of hundreds of millions of years as well as the lasting, continuing effects of even the phylogenetically oldest parts of the brain upon human life. The human brain is, phylogenetically speaking, structured hierarchically: each evolutionary—that is, appearing at intervals of millions of years—formation maintaining principally its original function and developing up to today its specific activities.

The *brain stem* originates far back in our species' history. It has remained the seat of life-maintaining regulatory circuits (body temperature, total body water, sleep-wake-attention cycles, etc.). This structure originated some 500 million to 1 billion years ago.

Superimposed on the brain stem is the *diencephalon*, or so-called reptile complex, the seat of emotions, at the same time serving continuing survival by means of the reflex control of behavior. Here, impulses for joy, sadness, anger, hate, and fear originate. These impulses can be, in their spontaneity and intensity, only partially controlled. The human tendency, demonstrated in empirical investigations, to experience conflict spontaneously and to react with a win/lose attitude before any thinking takes place seems to belong to those archaic forms of reaction based in the diencephalon. Another example is the universal anxiety of infants at eight months, observed in all cultures, whereby infants react defensively to strangers. The diencephalon is some hundreds of millions of years younger than the brain stem.

The *limbic system*, also called the ancient mammal complex, is involved in social behavior, nurturance, and care of the young, and also in a variety of emotional aspects of behavior and experiencing the world: sympathy, antipathy, love, grief, joy, hate, envy, etc.

And finally, the phylogenetically most recent development is the *cerebral cortex*, or neocortex (20 to 30 million years old), where consciousness, reason, logic, and thinking first become possible. According to findings in brain research, the neocortex continues to develop and expand today. The specific human evolution of the cortex is in fact the product of only the last 4 million years. During this period, the volume of the cortex has increased threefold.

In no other life form is the cortex so extensively developed. The composition of the cortex has made possible completely new functions. All conscious and deliberate processes take place within the cortex. Consciousness, rational thinking, reasoning, morals, and ethics replace the predominant instinct-bound patterns found in the animal world and allow the development of human culture. However, the various brain parts have not become ineffective in their functions, but rather fight one another and together form a totality of continually changing moods, feelings, strivings, affects, and so on, which in the end determine our current behavior.

If we consider here the time spans mentioned, periods of two, ten, a hundred or even a thousand years are very brief compared to the developmental processes discussed. And as the emotions tied closely to images of the enemy are seated in the diencephalon and the limbic system, the persistence of archaic reactions becomes more comprehensible in view of this aspect of developmental history. The structures and ways of acting and reacting which developed and became consolidated over very long spans of time still linger in us and guide us, even if they have long since lost their former function of protection.

In escalating confrontations and the emotional processes accompanying them, we see that in almost all cases there are behavioral reactions that are based in these earlier developed stages of our nervous system. We modern humans too are shaped by an ancient "biogrammar" of social behavior, which we inherit as a deeply impressed principle of order and which has the effect of forcing us to think in terms of opposites such as friend/foe, good/bad, right/wrong. This biogrammar possesses a fundamental power and strength against cultural (ethical, differentiating, reflective) influences.

In addition to the ancient biogrammar, however, the new possibilities within the cortex have created in a quantum leap undreamed of prerequisites, as learning and adaptation processes in genes (via mutation and selection) can be shifted to the brain (and thus to rapidly occurring cerebral processes). With this, ever more closed behavior and perception programs could be opened up through the development of consciousness and language, through the exchange of thoughts and other forms of complex social contacts, and also through the possibility of communicating and passing on experience. With these new abilities, the tempo of adaptation to the environment increased enormously. The result was a shortening of time required for an adaptation from millions of years to only days or hours!

With this as well, however, the conflict began between biological inheritance and human culture—a conflict which continues to give us pause and yet receives too little attention. For as mentioned, phylogenetically older parts of the brain have not lost their functions, but rather continue to interact and form a fluctuating sum of moods, feelings, strivings, affects, etc., which in the end determine our current behavior. Our brain—organized in a controlled chaotic way—is apparently in a continuously unstable state. Its behavior is not any more predictable than the long-term course of weather patterns.[19]

We can, however, predict that under stress, fear, and threatening conditions, older drive and reflex reactions will be the stronger reactions and predominate over more recently evolved, culturally shaped behaviors such as reason, analysis, and insight. Our rational abilities do not then become turned off, but they are placed at the service of the more primitive and undifferentiated perceptual and behavioral patterns, a situation comparable to the rider who has lost control over his horse and must simply go where his horse leads him. On the outside, however, this is not always apparent; in other words, even an extremely emotional or biased reaction to a supposed opponent can be presented very intelligently. This often makes it difficult to recognize the fact that deeply regressive perceptual and emotional patterns lie hidden behind the reaction.

Cultural or Psychological Shaping Influences

While every person, every newborn child, goes through the long phylogenetic developmental process, which lasted for hundreds of millions of years, in the course of fetal development and early childhood automatically and according to an identical time plan, the complex achievements of information processing which have become possible in the cortex and have made us viable must be newly acquired by each individual independently.

Human culturally determined emotional and cognitive abilities are formed in the course of *individual* development, through continual interaction with other people in one's environment.

19. John Briggs and F. David Peat, *Die Entdeckung des Chaos*, trans. from English by Carl Carius (Munich, Vienna, 1990), 96.

These others bring to the child, not only as transmitters of the symbolic contents of important group meanings, but rather strongly codetermine, by means of their specific *affective* reactions, individual psychological structure. The diversity of human ways of existence, which in part seem incompatible, and also the most diverse perceptual, experiential, and behavioral orientations of people even within the same culture, can be explained by the fact that development is *ontogenetic* and shaped by individual biography. Differences in the acquiring of phylogenetic (automatic) and ontogenetic (individual) characteristics explain the paradox in the fact that what can be said generally about humans as a species is more easily grasped than general statements about all members of a specific culture.

Psychological Aspects

Based upon Sigmund Freud, modern object relations theory has proved empirically that the capacity for perceiving oneself and others and the development of a feeling of belonging to a group, as well as the capacity to feel for or with others, are all the results of a complex process of relating and interaction between the child and its first and closest environment.

Object relations refer to internal mental experiences which are created primarily through emotional experience of the relationship of self to other persons and things. These representations, which become the inner life of a person, are formed within the mother-child matrix, which from the very first day of life is important not only for physical survival, but for psychological survival as well. Within this matrix, quite specific experiences and tasks as well as sequences of development must take place in order for the child to move successfully from a state of being embedded within the symbiotic matrix to the achievement of a stable, individual identification, thus becoming an autonomous human being capable of perceiving others realistically and forming human relationships. In other words, the ability to form object relations is a developmental acquisition that cannot be taken for granted. In the child's personal relationship to the mother—and later to the father as well—the child acquires the basic elements of the capacity for object relations and with it, the basic elements of social behavior.

In acquiring these abilities, the emotional life of the child passes through distinctive stages of development. Perception of oneself and of others—which is of great importance in relation to the subject of images of the enemy—develops through four stages which form, extend, and differentiate the potential for emotions and perceptions and create important emotional bonds between the individual and society.

In the first stage, the first weeks of a child's life make up what is known as the symbiotic phase. The child is unable to perceive any difference between inside and outside, between "self" and "non-self." This hallucinatory-narcissistic fusion with the mother can be described by the feeling "we two are one." The consequence of this non-differentiation is illusions of omnipotence. And at this stage, experience is categorized as either "good," equivalent to pleasurable, or "bad," equivalent to painful. Accordingly, islands of "good" and "bad" memory traces start to form within the infant's brain.

In the second stage ("everything that is 'non-self' is threatening"), the first noticeable differentiation takes place. The first visible sign of an incipient distinction between inside and outside is the appearance of stranger anxiety at the age of approximately six to eight months. Stranger anxiety can be observed as an ontogenetic phenomenon in all cultures. It indicates the child's achievement of differentiation among external objects. The child rejects and feels threatened by anything unfamiliar, i.e., by anything that is non-self (self at this stage meaning everything that is familiar). A peculiar feature of stranger anxiety is the fact that no direct negative experience is connected with the anxiety or rejection. The child is not reacting to real danger but much rather to the unfamiliar, the strange, which—in a trigger reflex—seems to be discriminated against as dangerous. Hence the first and most original classification of data in the emotional sphere is based upon contrasts between familiar and strange, or safe and threatening. At these elementary depths, familiar and strange have the same meaning as "good" and "evil."

In the third stage, between the first and third year of life, the child learns gradually to distinguish between itself and its mother ("there is 'I' and there is 'you'"). The child develops a sense of its own ego as well as a sense of the "you." With this, a further fundamental stage of development is underway: there is an increasing capacity for integration of the previous division between good and evil, both in the self and in the object. (Originally, the child was unable to perceive the nourishing, available mother, or good object, and the unavailable, frustrating mother, or bad object, as one and the same person.) With the integration of these contrasting representations, and with the acknowledgment that the mother, as a whole object, possesses both good and bad qualities, the child becomes able to conquer a part of reality that makes it possible for love for the mother (and for itself) to be maintained even during disappointments. The child also becomes able to endure and monitor contrasting, i.e., ambivalent feelings, and to function in the absence of a helping mother, a capacity which indicates the achievement of psychic separateness.

All this implies a considerable expansion of the emotional repertoire, emotional monitoring, and thus an increase in the capacity to cope with fluctuations in mood and with frustrations. The perception of self and object is also extended in a decisive way. Now the child experiences itself as something whole and permanent within the course of time and under changing internal and external conditions. At this stage of "I" and "you," the other person, like the "I," has received a face, an identity, regardless of whether the current relationship to this person is one of friendship and cooperation or of enmity and competition. Integrative forces have grown strong enough at this stage of development to prevent the process of splitting, which in previous stages brought about feelings of being totally overwhelmed or annihilated by the unpleasant or frustrating experience. Once resistance and defiance as well as submission out of love or fear are possible towards one and the same object (the same significant other), the child has not only an emotional knowledge of demands, prohibitions, and values, but also of guilt, power, and impotence.

The child then arrives, between the third and sixth year of life, at the fourth stage ("There is I, there is You, there is He"). Only now can the child perceive its father as independent and separate from its mother. This step is decisive in the process of socialization. The child achieves the inner capacity and readiness to form not only dyadic, but also triadic human relationships. This means that it can maintain and cope with a wide variety of human relations, including those which occur outside its own participation or group allegiance. This new capacity allows for plurality, i.e., the child is now rooted emotionally in its own identity, so that it can maintain human relationships over the distance of time and space and through conflicts. It can also accept that people can have close relationships to one another that do not involve the child without this causing fears of isolation and loss. The emotional conditions are now created which allow the child to perceive other identities as such and to accept them in their different natures.

In the third and fourth stages of emotional development, we can trace with particular clarity how extensively the individual and society are two systems of action dependent upon one another. We see how children, long before reaching the intellectual and rational capacity for reconstruction, "know" in the emotional realm about demands, values, and symbolic coding and adjust their actions accordingly. This knowledge is acquired through interaction with parents or other emotionally important figures substituting for parents, who first approach the child carrying important data and information regarding their group, long before any conscious dealing with these contents is possible. This "emotional" knowledge is thus to a large extent anchored in the unconscious and therefore outside the scope of critical examination. It is more easily accessible to manipulation than ideas gained through conscious dealing. This emotional knowledge is an important factor in the formation of the feeling of belonging to a group, but also in the capacity to feel one's way into another person. How does this come about? Object relations theory differentiates between two basic processes which are both necessary for this development: internalization and identification.

In internalization, intersubjective relations are transformed into intrasubjective imprints. This has to do with the transformation of object relations, in the sense that inner regulation now takes over the functions of living objects of the external world. For example, the father declares what is right and wrong, punishes and praises, and the punishing and praising father becomes internalized in such a way that the child feels accepted or rejected according to what it does, without the father needing to be present. In the course of this development, however, not only objects (such as the father) are internalized, but also conceptions of values, ideals, normative obligations, expectations, and so on. Thus, these demands and attitudes also become part of the intrapsychic structure, and behavior not in accordance with them triggers feelings of guilt, fear of loss of love, and of punishment. Through internalization of all these various qualities, a deeply anchored system of common values is created, which is generally not reflected upon and which prepares the ground for common action and for common interpretation and evaluation of data. This forms and determines the perception of social reality. Since—along main lines at least—one's own group can be defined only by its difference from other groups, the emotional representations of specific values distinguishing one's own group from other groups becomes an integral component of the general process of socialization, thus making a significant contribution to both individual self-conception and social identity.

To understand collective phenomena (such as images of the enemy), we need to examine yet another basic developmental process: identification. Identification is an unconscious process that is usually preceded by conscious imitation. The child's growing inner conflict between feelings of dependency and the wish to become independent develops into a drive to become the same as the loved (or feared) significant other, whom the child needs. In the process of identification, the child assimilates characteristic traits of the important other, thus changing according to the image of the other. In other words, through assimilation, the child's own inner structures become changed. However, assimilation does not mean the changing of developing inner structures by means of integration only of external elements (such as behavior or attitudes); assimilation also means acquisition of knowledge via the information contained in these elements.

Through the assimilation process of identification, the child thus acquires new inner structures and constitutes itself anew. At the same time, it assimilates information and acquires, through this unconscious osmosis of "ego-alien" characteristics, behavior, and feelings, a kind of "knowledge" about the other. Here we find the deep roots of empathy, the capacity to feel and take on the other person's perspective, as well as feelings of togetherness.

Cognitive development overlies emotional development and complements it in a way that makes human functioning possible. The cognitive functions are settled in the cerebrum and are accordingly much younger phylogenetically than the emotional reaction and orientation functions seated in the diencephalon and cerebellum.

Normal social-cognitive development progresses from an egocentric, undifferentiated standpoint to a differentiating orientation towards things and persons. Step by step, one's own *absolute* personal perspective becomes decentralized and qualified. Understanding of other viewpoints becomes developed. The ability to put oneself in the place of the other unfolds and makes human social relationships, with all their nuances, possible. In the development of human cognitive abilities lies the crucial, and often not considered, key to understanding the unfamiliar, or the ability to take the other's perspective.

Development of these abilities, however, is threatened by uncertainty, social pressures, fears, and stress of all kinds, as for example appear in times of crisis and radical change. Even already achieved capabilities can be lost under stress, either gradually or suddenly. Not only children but adult individuals as well then behave in ways that accord with the developmental stages of early childhood. In his work *Zeitgemäßes über Krieg und Tod,* Sigmund Freud presented a vivid formulation of this matter:

> For the development of the mind shows a peculiarity which is present in no other developmental process. When a village grows into a town or a youth into a man, the village and the child become lost in the town and the man. Memory alone can trace the old features in the new picture; and in fact the old materials or forms have been got rid of and replaced by new ones. It is otherwise with the development of the mind. Here one can describe the state of affairs, which has nothing to compare with it, only by saying that in this case every earlier stage of development persists alongside the later stage which has arisen from it; here succession also involves coexistence, although it is to the same materials that the whole series of transformations has applied. The earlier mental state may not have manifested itself for years, but none the less it is so far present that it may at any time again become the mode of expression of the forces in the mind, and indeed the only one, as though all later developments had been annulled or undone. This extraordinary plasticity of mental developments is not unrestricted as regards direction; it may be described as a special capacity for involution— for regression—since it may well happen that a later and higher stage of development, once abandoned, cannot be reached again. But the primitive stages can always be reestablished; the primitive mind is, in the fullest meaning of the word, imperishable.[20]

What Is the Connection to the Real Happenings?

Much of what also could be said about images of the enemy and the in-group/out-group problem has not been mentioned. For example, the significance of *social conditions* was not discussed which, as stress factors, can gain considerable importance in the escalation of conflict between groups. We also have not dealt here with various approaches to understanding, such as aggression research, the scapegoat syndrome, and the large field of research on prejudice and stereotypes. Naturally, in this introduction to the topic we could not hope to attain a complete descriptive treatment

20. Sigmund Freud, "Thoughts for the Times on War and Death," in *Standard Edition of the Complete Psychological Works of Sigmund Freud,* 14: 285f.

of the factors involved in the analysis of such a many-sided phenomenon as images of the enemy. We hope rather to have drawn attention to new possibilities which, for the historian as well, offer interesting explanations of central aspects of human behavior. Using the example of images of the enemy, we have aimed to point out that there is no expression of life which does not in some way involve individual genetic makeup in interaction with psychological and cultural shaping. Even if genes do not "determine," they do define the "limits of behavioral plasticity"[21] of our subjects—humans acting throughout history—and we are faced with the enormous task of reaching a newer and deeper understanding on the basis of the conditions of coevolution.

Perhaps we, as specialized historians, have not found the attempt superfluous to transcend the boundaries of our field and to recognize interrelation effects which may have been molded in other disciplines, but whose consequences, however, continually affect our sphere of activity.

21. Volker Sommer, "Soziobiologie: Wissenschaftliche Innovation oder ideologischer Anachronismus?" in: *Fortpflanzung*, 65.

Chapter Two

THE SOCIOLOGICAL ANATOMY OF ENEMY IMAGES

The Military and Democracy After the End
of the Cold War

Ulrich Beck

Two Distinctions, One Definition

To begin with, two distinctions: first, it is one thing to study and discuss *sociobiological* (anthropological) theories of aggression, conflict readiness, etc., in animals and human beings, and it is something different to examine *social* frontiers and conflicts based on in-group/out-group relations and stereotypes. The difference, roughly speaking, is that biological or anthropological hypotheses make statements about a basic *potential* for aggression but not about the actual *historical* or *social form* which xenophobia, racial aggression, enmity, and enemy images may take. Sociobiological research may well help to dampen optimistic hopes of increasing pacifism, especially as a product of the civilization process, but in my opinion the principles proposed by these hypotheses cannot be used to predict or explain social conflict behavior, nor can they predict who will make whom into an enemy (image) nor for what reason.

Second, it is important, especially for the analysis of historical development and causal interrelationships, to distinguish between

Translated by Dr. Susan Vogel, Essen.

heterostereotypes and *enemy images*. The distinction is not only gradual, for example, in terms of composition and presentation, but also qualitative: here the core of enemy images is revealed, namely the fact that they are closely associated with the state, nation-state, and the military, i.e., they play a role in legitimizing the state monopoly on the use of force. To put it bluntly: if someone succumbs to racial prejudices and kills, it is murder. Under the influence of enemy images and in wartime, however, killing others becomes one's "duty." In this case the same deed is evidence of bravery, and not killing or refusing to kill someone is seen as cowardice in the face of the enemy and condemned accordingly. In other words, enemy images *turn established values upside down*. The otherwise forbidden is encouraged—it becomes honorable; noncompliance has legal consequences—it becomes normal.

Enemy images are not only heterostereotypes which have been functionalized and legitimized by the state, not only ethnic or racial stereotypes staged for propaganda purposes. They also exhibit a second distinctive feature: unlike racial prejudice, they are subject to *no higher instance of authority, no arbitrator*. No one sits in judgment upon enemy images. "Rulings," ultimately, are made by the violence of war. Seen in this light, enemy images are thus the precursors of a call-to-arms. They justify armament, mobilization, military intelligence, the restriction or even revocation of democratic freedom and civil rights. In other words, enemy images permit Pandora's box to be opened—as an act of patriotism. In nationalistic ears, the word "enemy" rings with overtones of heroism and self-sacrifice to protect one's own values. It rattles the saber, not of the Ku Klux Klan, but of legitimate state authority.

All of this does not mean, however, that it is always easy to draw a sharp line between heterostereotypes and enemy images. The opposite is the case since both develop in the same way. If it is true that traditions cannot be created by administrative decree, it also holds that the public presentation of enemy images must presuppose cultural prejudices against human beings, groups, cultures. They cannot be prescribed from above, they must be nourished, formed, and dramatized by heterostereotypes and autostereotypes already generated by and existing in the culture.

In the process of functionalization, the material, the stuff is provided by culturally generated and readily available images and writings about the threat posed by other cultures and other people. Sources which enjoy high cultural credibility are especially well-suited to this task—as is made clear by the example of Bülow's letters on America. These were written by an "enlightened noble-man with a republican turn of mind" whose attitude changed, after traveling through the country, from one of admiration to one of contempt for the "American barbarians."

I would like to define "enemy images" as culturally generated (available) prejudices and heterostereotypes that have been dramatically composed, enhanced, and made legitimate and which are then used to create and expand the apparatus of state authority and the military. Enemy images—as opposed to heterostereotypes and racial prejudice—permit the transvaluation of values. They are subject to no higher instance. Enemy images provide a second source of legitimation for modern nation-states, one which is exo-democratic, non-democratic, even anti-democratic. And given the difficulties inherent in the process of reaching democratic consensus in the self-reflective modern period, enemy images are becoming increasingly attractive to state protagonists (see below).

The significance of the distinction between cultural heterostereotypes and enemy images can also be demonstrated by a recent example. In western Europe, manifold prejudices and feelings of resentment survive and have revived even since the end of the East-West conflict, in particular between Germany on the one hand and Great Britain, France, and Italy on the other. There prejudices, however, exist *within* a military alliance, NATO, and a military conflict between these allies is almost unthinkable. Conversely, the shattered Warsaw Pact and in particular the disintegration of the former Yugoslavia provide painful, bloody examples of how quickly state images of friends can be changed back into images of ethnic and military enemies.

It is only a slight exaggeration to claim that universal postmodernism governs the delineation of enemy images—anything goes! Thus, at the time of the American Revolution, the mother country England (same language, same ethnic identity, same fundamental political convictions) was the "natural enemy," but in the twentieth century the "natural ally" in two world wars. At this point we can cast a glance back at the first distinction between aggressive instincts as diagnosed by sociobiology, as opposed to social frontiers and demarcation strategies. These two perspectives must be kept strictly apart since what counts as "self" and as "other" in one specific social space, one particular era, is nothing natural. It is instead completely unforeseeable, unpredictable—in a word, chaotic.

Under the heading "The Contents of History," Gottfried Benn noted the following:

> In order to inform myself, I open up an old school textbook, the so-called little Ploetz: *Excerpts from Ancient, Medieval and Modern History*, Berlin 1891, published by Ploetz. Opening to a random page, it is page 337, it is the year 1805. Here we find: 1 naval victory, 2 ceasefires, 3 alliances, 2 coalitions, one man is marching, one enters into an alliance, one rallies his troops, one reinforces something, one is advancing, one captures, one is retreating, one is taking a camp by storm, one resigns, one makes a glorious start, one is captured, one must pay reparations to someone else, one threatens someone else, one marches on the Rhine, one through the region around Ansbach, one on Vienna, one is forced back, one is executed, one commits suicide—all of this on one single page. The whole thing is undoubtedly a case history of lunatics.[1]

It is precisely this "case history of lunatics" that makes it impossible to draw connections between a general potential for violence, as diagnosed by sociobiologists, and any particular conflict or battle array. As an example, German emigrants from the class constrictions and oppressions of Europe were on good terms with blacks in the United States, entered into mixed marriages, tolerated them, defended them—in one of the original democratic countries, one in which slavery was protected by law. No conclusions can be drawn by sociobiology that apply to the history or sociology of social heterostereotypes and autostereotypes and absolutely none that relate to the social history of enemy images.

It is also important to make a clear distinction between *enemy images* and actual *enemies* (no matter how difficult this may be in a particular case). There are not only enemy images which justify and generate enmity, as a kind of self-fulfilling prophecy (see below), but there are also enemies that generate legitimate enemy images. The most striking case of this is the image of the Nazis held by the Jews who were being systematically annihilated in concentration camps by German fascists.

Finally, there are also historical cases where societies that have been established on the basis of enemy images not only lose their enemies but even switch allegiance. The news that Moscow wants to join NATO is of this type. Soldiers of the former East German Volksarmee now serve in the German Bundeswehr. What happens, then, when enemy images break down? The answer is suggested by the collapse of East-West order: new ones arise.

1. Gottfried Benn, *Essays und Reden* (Frankfurt, 1989), 362.

Towards a Typology of Enemy Images

The German Minister of Defense Volker Rühe recently said that "Germany is encircled by friends." "Encircled" is particularly apt for the country, combining as it does the former FRG and GDR, both of which were based on enemy images of the East-West conflict, and now experiencing its new lack of enmity and enemies as a source of deep insecurity. Up until now there has hardly been any public mention, let alone discussion, of what the end of the enemy image "GDR" really means for the new Germany; instead, new threatening "enemies" are being sighted everywhere, with the active assistance of intellectuals of every political persuasion.

A lack of enemies, thus, does not mean a lack of enemy *images*. On the contrary, an insatiable need for new enemy images seems to arise. These are the paradoxes of the victory crisis of the West: without enemies there is no funding, no legitimacy, perhaps even no nation-state integration and legitimation, no unity within, for example, the conservative parties, which were actually glued together by their shared anti-communism. The daily press reveals that an army without enemies is a kind of long-term unemployed service. The institution is desperate in its search for new tasks— now, after dealing with drug dealers and refugees, the army may be called in to regulate traffic problems.

My observations indicate that following the demise of East-West enemy images, three new types of enemy images have emerged. These progress from the *specific* to the *interchangeable* to the *general* enemy.

First, when the archenemy is gone, individual enemies, *specific*, *changing*, and *mobile*, become a threat, e.g., Saddam Hussein or now the Serbs in Europe, and in the foreseeable future the new "Russian Hitler" Shirinowski. Looking back, it becomes clear that the Cold War provided an order for denationalized nation-states. In a certain sense, the natural law of nation-state anarchy was kept in check by the two blocs and their nuclear stalemate. Hence, with the collapse of the East, renationalization as well as a return to the anarchical international system are the trends that result.

In his book *The Empire and the New Barbarians*, the French political scientist Jean Christophe Rufin goes a significant step further. He compares the situation after the end of the Cold War to the Roman defeat of Carthage in 146 B.C. Then, too, a global enmity came to an end, or rather, was replaced by new ones. The Romans, now without enemies, disassociated themselves from the barbarians to the north and in Asia. In the U.S. and Europe, too, a new empire is beginning to fence off its boundaries, the north against the "barbarians" in the south—Latin America, Asia, Africa. New enemy images are appearing, ones which are varied and collective, such as Islamic fundamentalists and the countries or parts of the world where poverty combines with overpopulation to produce, it is argued, ecological disaster.

But here we have reached the second type of new enemy image: the *collective* or *abstract* enemy. Whereas in the first type specific persons, states, and governments are targeted, abstract enemies consist of diffuse collectives (North-South, rich-poor, even refugees, immigrants or illegal aliens) and general anomies of the modern period (drug addiction, drug dealing, organized crime). Amalgamations between mobile and abstract enemies can be found in areas where civil and military risks intersect (i.e, smuggling plutonium or military threats to atomic power plants).

Finally, a temporary lack of enemies can be remedied in a third way, by regarding enemies and enemy images as absolutely indispensable in one way or another. Quite a range of different theories belong here: for some, enmity is seen as a basic anthropological fact, for others, the continuous process of opening up society forces enemy images into being as a "lesser evil."

"But why are such borders necessarily those of a nation state?" asks Karl-Otto Hondrich. "The answer is as simple as it is sobering: because there are no other borders that can achieve nearly the same result, to demarcate an area where the state monopoly on the use of force coincides with feelings of belonging together. On the one hand, without the inner lining of sentiments of solidarity, states are only arbitrarily constructed outward shells of authority which collapse under pressure. On the other hand, without the protection of a legitimate monopoly on the use of force, cultures and the peoples who constitute them are prey to humiliation and annihilation."[2]

Theoretical Positions

Considering the fact that the West, which has, after all, *lost* its archenemy, now seems to be suffering from enemy overflow, a range of questions emerges, questions that a sociology of enemy images

2. Karl-Otto Hondrich, "Grenzen gegen die Gewalt," in *Die Zeit*, no. 5 (28 January 1994), 4.

must address. To put it bluntly: are enemy images essential for integrating societies, in particular in the late modernity? Instead of being a reaction to primarily *external* threats, do enemy images arise from the *internal* demands for power and functionality that are raised by a self-reflective modern period which is in the process of destroying its own foundations?

Is the creation and activation of enemy images perhaps one tool—or even the primary tool—used by states to reintegrate a society where solidarity is on the wane? At what point does an increase in individualism and worldwide networks overwhelm a culture's readiness to fight in an emergency? At what point does thinking in terms of friends vs. foes rule out all individualism?

These questions cannot be fully answered here. I only want to present and summarize a range of arguments that indicates the horizon of possible answers. I will present my own theory of the militarily bisected modernity with reference to four groups of theories: 1) pacifistic capitalism, 2) military capitalism, 3) political nationalism and constitutional patriotism, and 4) modernization of aggressiveness.

Theories of Pacifistic Capitalism

These are not based on the moral conviction that capitalism is pacifistic. On the contrary, capitalism is seen as the superior means of conquering the world. With the victory of the capitalistic economy, conquering the world becomes civilized and potentialized into conquering the world market. There are two kinds of conquest, argues Auguste Comte—either the subjugation and exploitation of nature by industry or the subjugation of foreign peoples. The former costs money, the latter makes it. For this reason, Comte concluded, the development of industrial capitalism will cause war to wither and die out.

Earlier, warring states subjugated commerce and trade, now it is the other way around. Since economic conquest is superior to military conquest, capitalism is "essentially non-belligerent" (Josef Schumpeter). This position has been elaborated by liberal theorists from Kant to Talcott Parsons and Jürgen Habermas. Interestingly enough, Engels also advocated the theory of pacifistic cost-cutting: weapons are not only destructive but also unproductive. Modernizing them makes them "overly expensive and at the same time useless for the purposes of war." He also predicted that "the army

of the princes will change into an army of the people," thus causing militarism to collapse.

The theory, first proposed by Comte, that industry is superior
to war—in the long run—as a means of world conquest is challenged (refuted?) by the coexistence of war and industry up to the
present. Industry serves and profits from war and vice versa: war
has served industry. Factories produce the weapons that guarantee industrial nations their markets and their raw materials. The
evidence contradicting this theory, however, is overwhelming:
two world wars, fought not between underdeveloped but
between highly developed industrial nations.

One simple historical example is revealing: all of the supposedly
bellicose preindustrial political bodies of the Middle Ages ex-
pended only a fraction of the sum for weapons and warfare that is
seen as self-evident in the "essentially non-bellicose" (Schumpeter)
democratic capitalist states, with their horrendous budgets for military spending. And in terms of being peace-loving, the communist
states (in terms of their military budget) outdid them all.

Theories of Military Capitalism

The opposite position, that capitalism is necessarily military, claims
that capitalism may not have invented war, but it has adopted
war, so to speak, and brought it up. War is merely the culmination
of the inherently destructive force of competition which affects all
areas of life in a capitalistic society. War destroys surplus production and opens new markets. War, the military, and armament are
integral parts of industrial capitalism.

But this primarily neo-Marxist criticism remains one-sided. It
overlooks what Martin Shaw, in his book *Dialectics of War*, calls the
socialism of total war:[3] not only are all traditional variants of socialism militarily open, in one way or another, but also the forms
of the state and the social organization they represent or strive to
achieve are closely tied to the epoch of mass militarism—and will
collapse along with it.

Political Nationalism: Max Weber

The fact that military capitalism and military democracy can exist
at the same time as military socialism and military communism

3. Martin Shaw, *The Dialectics of War* (London, 1988).

points to a common denominator: the nation-state, i.e., the state characterized by the monopoly on the use of force which is organized and legitimized by friend-foe demarcations. In the first half of this century, a debate took place in sociology which is highly relevant again today. It can perhaps be characterized by the distinction between "state nation" and "civic nation." The range of positions can be seen in the work of Max Weber and Talcott Parsons.

Max Weber (and to an even greater extent his student Carl Schmitt) developed a complex concept of political nationalism in which the concepts of community and society are combined and embedded in political constructivism. In his opinion, ethnic identity is a constructed "subjective belief in a community of common origins," which is necessary but hardly sufficient for a nation in the sense of a political community. According to Weber, a political community is primarily characterized by its willingness to use force. "A political community is understood as one in which community action proceeds as follows: a territory (not necessarily an absolute constant one with fixed boundaries but at least a territory delimited in some way) in which well-ordered rule is maintained (and further territories may be acquired) by the permanent and temporary residents, if need be by physical force, normally armed force."[4]

Building a nation thus requires both potential and actual use of force directed both inward and outward. In this context Weber refers to the mechanism whereby identity is generated by memories of wars in the past. Nation, to Weber, is state nation. It combines ethnic identity, political community, the readiness to use force, and the state monopoly on the use of force.

"Civic Nation" and Constitutional Patriotism

The "civic nation" as the counterpart to the "state nation" and the transition from the one to the other can be reconstructed from the early and late writings of Parsons. Like Max Weber, the early Parsons (1942) regarded nationalistic conflicts as a source of solidarity in that aggression directed outwards also serves as an appeal to the "infranational sentiments" of the nation as an informal group.[5] In addition, aggression is a source of internal unity in that

4. Max Weber, *Wirtschaft und Gesellschaft* (Tübingen: Mohr, 1968), 514.
5. Talcott Parsons, "Certain Primary Sources and Patterns of Aggression in the Social Structure of the Western World," in Talcott Parsons, *Essays in the Sociological Theory* (1949, rev. ed. New York, 1964), 318.

"hostility to the foreigner has thus furnished a means of transcending the principal, immediately threatening group conflicts, of achieving 'unity.'"[6] The nation is thus, for the early Parsons, a special value-laden phenomenon that can channel aggression, on the one hand, and on the other hand, imply superiority or the right to accuse other nations due to their supposedly illegitimate claim to superiority.

A change occurred in Parson's thinking in the 1950s: from then on he speaks of the "societal community." Here he is making use of the English sociologist Thomas H. Marshall, who, writing in the late 1940s, had suggested that the decisive foundation of modern Western society was the development of citizenship.[7] He further postulated that citizenship would be impossible without the existence of a bond between members of the community to express their loyalty to a shared civilization.[8]

It is just this bond that Parsons thought he had found in the concept of societal community: "[T]he concept of citizenship, as used here, refers to full membership in what we call the *societal community*. This term refers to that aspect of the total society as a system that forms a 'Gemeinschaft' which is the focus of solidarity or mutual loyalty of its members, and which constitutes the consensual base underlying its political integration."[9] The acceptance of the concept of citizenship, which in modern society is no longer restricted to particular groups, is directly coupled, according to Parsons, with loyalty to the "Gemeinschaft" or community.

The problem of inclusion is no longer cast in particularistic terms but ordered by the modern societal community of citizens. The line drawn between an emotionally charged, particularistic nationalism based on common origins and a universalistic concept of nation continues to exist today: it serves to identify "good" as opposed to "evil" nations.

The concept of "constitutional patriotism," developed by Dolf Sternberger and Jürgen Habermas, picks up this idea and elaborates on it further. Even the "good" civic nations, however, seem to need enemy images, as is shown by the example of France marching against "barbarism" under the flag of "civilization."

6. Ibid., 319; see also Dirk Richter, "Der Mythos der 'guten' Nation," *Soziale Welt* 3 (1994): 304–21.

7. Thomas H. Marshall, *Citizenship and Social Class* (New York, 1950).

8. Ibid., 92; *The Condition of Citizenship*, ed. B. v. Steenbergen (London, 1994).

9. Talcott Parsons, "Full Citizenship for the Negro American?" in Talcott Parsons, *Sociological Theory and Modern Society* (New York, 1957), 423.

Modernization of Aggressiveness

With the renewed flare-up of violence and wars in Europe, one final set of theories has acquired new significance. These turn the previous arguments upside down in that they regard the increase in freedom and modernity as a source of violence and aggression. "The fateful question for the human species," writes Freud in *Civilization and Its Discontents*, "seems to me to be whether and to what extent their cultural development will succeed in mastering the disturbance of their communal life by the human instinct of aggression and self-destruction. It may be that in this respect precisely the present time deserves a special interest."[10]

In his essay "The Idea of Peace and Human Aggressiveness," Alexander Mitscherlich develops this idea further. He argues that aggressive tendencies are not only inborn but also created and exacerbated by societal contradictions and the frustrations they produce. In modern society, at the same time that frustrations are increasing, outlets or sublimations (e.g., work or even family values) are on the decline. The result is that the opening up of society also opens the vents of aggressiveness and violence. "It is not only the case that prejudices come to power or are used to protect the dominant group. The society must also find alternative solutions via its political institutions to channel rising sentiments of hatred, envy and the need for aggression. If not, it will sink into civil war. In this process, at least in the past, shifting the blame to one's neighbor—as an easily alienated object of hatred, envy, anger— was an alternative solution that seemed to be the lesser evil."

Looking back, it is striking that all these different theories of the state, from both the political left and right, presuppose some kind of enemy image. The idea of an "enemy-free" state seems an analytical impossibility.

Against this background of heterogenous explanations—1) pacifistic capitalism, 2) military capitalism, 3) political nationalism and the civic nation, and 4) the liberation of aggressiveness as a product of modernization—I would like to introduce my notion of the militarily bisected modernity. It picks up on various arguments, rejects others, and represents a special combination of perspectives. I maintain that we are living in a stage of the modern period which has not yet been fully grasped—I call it the *globale Risikogesellschaft* or global risk society, in which the borders and categories of industrial society and nation-states are being questioned both internally

10. Sigmund Freud, *Civilization and Its Discontents* (New York, 1961), 92.

and externally. As a result of global interdependencies caused by modernization processes, the entire model of nationally organized industrial capitalism has begun to collapse, and a "new" modernity appears. Sociological concepts and theories as well as political institutions remain to be developed for this new era.

The Sociological Anatomy (Theory) of Enemy Images

Looking back, the architecture of industrial society can be seen as a modernity that is cut in half, bisected—in this context—by the military. The move into modernity, i.e., the elimination of rigid class-based hierarchies, the replacement of divine providence with human order—parliaments, the separation of powers, governments that can be voted out—saw all these achievements introduced side by side with the extension of military duty to all citizens. Universal suffrage and universal conscription (both for men) are twins, born at almost exactly the same time. Industrial development also proceeded hand-in-hand with the industrialization of warfare. Arms production becomes mass production. The setting up of transport systems serves both civil and military ends. The contradictions between political (democratic) and military mobilization are cancelled out by the internal presence of an external agency: enemy images.

An enemy image, presented as a counteractive "reaction" to enemy violence, derives its legitimacy from the violence of the enemy. The threat of the enemy, however, is depicted by the image itself. It thus creates delusions of power that limit democracy, bisect it, with democratic approval. If we refer to this as a vicious circle of power, in which state power is derived from enemy images, the question arises: how can the anatomy of enemy images which generate power be reconstructed and explained?

Existential Exclusion

First of all, the special characteristic of exclusion, of either/or thinking, is that it can be used to create a consensus on empowerment. By means of their existential violence, enemy images force the issue of the ultimate simplification: either for or against. Enemy images eliminate the possibility of neutrality, not in terms of intention but as a presupposition. The confrontational schema already created by the threat of violence turns the role of bystanders—irrespective of their own awareness of the situation, their willingness or ability to participate—into that of passive accomplices. When the relationship between enemies worsens, third parties, the neutrals who live and think on both sides, are destroyed.

External and Internal Enemies

The way this happens is remarkable. It develops out of the consensus which springs from the need for self-defense, and it represents a collective answer to a collective threat. Since *all* are threatened, warding off the threat can count on the consent and even the active resistance of *everyone*. This leads to the second aspect: the enemy enforces a form of counteraction that channels all efforts, all decisiveness, so that doubt, reservation, or disinterest is already seen as weakening the group and hence as support for the enemy. The principle of mutual exclusion—either friend or foe—eliminates differentiation. It springs from an imputed, general and collective threat to existence, leads to consensus among the threatened, and permits the *noncommitted to become externalized*. These unfortunates are seen as promoting the cause of the enemy, at best unwittingly, from within. According to the ideology, hesitation and criticism come to be seen as signs of inner weakness. They are, therefore, part of enemy activity and must be fought against with different, i.e., internal and domestic, weapons.

In other words, enemy images permit (and almost force) a distinction between *external* and *internal* enemies. The non-committed neutrals, the undecided, and the critics are declared to be internal enemies (against their own will). They fall (with the blessings of the defense consensus) into a gray area at best, and often into the purview of the FBI, the CIA, and military intelligence.

It is not a delusion: this classification seems to be arbitrary, against all the rules of a constitutional state, obeying only the logic of power. But this "arbitrariness" derives its legitimacy from the consensus of defense. This—it might be better to say—"reflex," cultivated and mobilized by means of enemy images, constitutes and creates its own legitimacy. And, should parliamentary democracy become weakened or suspended—or rather, especially when this is the case—claim can be made to the "higher" legitimacy of defense against the actual or potential attack of the enemy. This game, of course, can be overplayed, and it often is, as is shown by the many unsuccessful attempts by what are later

referred to as "dilettante" insurgents, e.g., in Third World countries or in 1991 in the former Soviet Union. It always depends on
how real the threat is *believed to be,* how *realistic* the threat is *made
to be.* Only then can the political potential of the defense consensus be fully utilized.

When the "reality" of the enemy is successfully created, a reality that permits no doubt and no more hesitation, then (and only
then) can the defense consensus become a source of legitimacy for
the license to treat all intermediate positions, all shades of the
political spectrum, as sabotage. This ability to turn neutral third
parties into "internal enemies" is an additional license which state
protagonists can receive from the defense consensus. These are
not to be treated better than external enemies, indeed they are
treated all the more brutally since they have betrayed the cause.
The twin brother of the enemy in one's own ranks, the internal
enemy, is just as much a "man with no distinctive features" as the
enemy himself. The characteristics attributed to him—extremist,
radical, terrorist, left-wing or right-wing—are generalized fact
files or wanted posters that call for general punishment, punishment for all. There are degrees within this construct of the internal
enemy, but once someone comes close, infringements that cut to
the core of civil rights are legitimate. Whoever falls into this category, falls: they become victims of the machinery of power that is
trained against enemies both within and without.

All of this can happen in the context of a parliamentary democracy. When a defense emergency threatens, a tidal wave of consensus threatens to wash away all those who doubt and find
fault, even in the government—if not immediately, then in the
next election. "Unpatriotic" is a term closely followed by depor-
tation, emigration.

Top Priority in Conflict

Enemy images enjoy the highest esteem and have top priority in
conflicts. When enemies threaten, all other problems and conflicts
are stifled. Enemies may be cruel. In one way, however, they are
useful (and are cherished by their "co-enemies" with almost
brotherly love): they drive off the flea-like problems that otherwise torment a society (or they at least soothe the itching). The
variety of crises and struggles that afflict a society, particularly in
the modern period, melt in the heat of this supracontradiction that
wraps all others in silence.

Enemy images spark, fan the flames in which a society can be melted into one. More precisely, they provide the ruling elite with the tools, the license to paint over strife. This side effect of enemy images—the reduction or, in extreme cases, elimination of conflict (class conflicts and corresponding conflicts between political parties, differences between men and women, young vs. old, unemployed vs. employed, producers vs. consumers)—is also a product of the defense consensus. Class conflict *polarizes*, defense consensus *harmonizes* (internally).

Cultivating enemy images enables a society or a state to draw on a primary—and perhaps the last—source of overriding consensus. Especially in modern individualistic societies on the edge of norm chaos, the defense consensus enjoys a monopoly on this overriding consensus: it integrates enemies.

This old, simple truth has been enormously significant for modern societies that have used up all other reserves of integration and suffer from a chronic lack of consensus. Its true range of implications, however, has not been fully recognized. One reason, perhaps, is that an abundant supply of enemies has been available as a natural resource for consensus throughout history—particularly in the modern period. Hence, it has been most plausible and profitable to do business with the mutual reinforcement provided by enemy images.

It may be somewhat painful, but none the less accurate, to realize that in the advanced stages of the modern period, Western democracies have been held together neither by Western traditions of Christianity nor by civil beliefs in democracy—and certainly not by inner ties and achievements. Instead, at least until 1989, they were tied together *externally*, in united opposition to the archenemy communism and its military threat. Integration, borrowed from the enemy and carried, so to speak, on its shoulders, has had one disadvantage: the degree of integration has also been in enemy hands. Soviet missiles (used to?) integrate the West: No threat, no integration.

Communism, both in and of itself and measured against its own standards, may not have proved very positive. As an actual living enemy, however, it met the most stringent requirements—in terms of size, virulence, and stability (until shortly before the end). Its reliably hostile stance has been a fountain of health for the West. Its highly visible, easily comprehensible threat was a constant source of fresh waters of consensus flowing westwards, a mineral spring to heal the wounds of internal strife.

One Enemy Creates Another: The Power of Self-Generation

Enemies and enemy images have two further characteristics: they appear only in the *plural* (normally in pairs, sometimes in packs) and *corroborate each other*. The idea of one enemy aimless and alone is amusing but unreal. The enemy as a singular being, as Homo clausus, is absurd, inconceivable. Enemies are social, or rather asocial, antisocial beings, who share in common the desire or need for mutual destruction. Enmity is murder—mass murder, not suicide, although in the age of nuclear obliteration the two can no longer be separated.

Enemies do not have to agree to their status. One enemy is enough. One creates the other. Even if someone does not want to be an enemy, the self-definition of the other as an enemy turns him into one, too. Being an enemy, therefore, can be a singularly one-sided relationship, even if the threat is seen as mutual. And even those who do not want to be enemies but want to live in peace with themselves and others can be made into enemies by the mere fact that others regard them as such.

Enmity can be produced by one side alone—unless the other is prepared to give up and surrender to the will of the enemy.

Enmity creates enmity: be it by projecting someone into the role of the enemy and rekindling old memories and fears, re-opening old wounds from wars of the past, or be it that aggression sets off a spiral of counteraggression. Enmity and enemy images have a special power, perhaps unique in strength, to create the reality they insinuate. Enemies are not born—they are created by enemy images.

Enemies can be conjured up: enemy images injure, target, needle, beget fear; they prepare for violence, equip, and align their troops until even friends draw their weapons—be they swords or missiles. Enmity is a social relationship that is extremely hazardous to a society—it can force its acceptance, and it tolerates no resistance. It has the dreadful power of self-fulfillment, both figuratively and literally, since it produces a mechanism of defensiveness and defense and feeds the flames of fear by the mere anticipation of fear. Enemy images thus create the perception that threat is mutual, atrocities are reciprocal, and this leads, paradoxically, to their acceptance by both sides. "In the beginning was the Word"— this Biblical sentence was never so cruelly accurate as in the world of violence created by the word "enemy."

The Active-Passive Substitution

Enemies—and this is a crucial source of their legitimacy—are always forced into their role by others. Enemies are "little innocents" whose aggression is determined by the existence of the other. Enmity is always *against one's own will*. The attacker, too, cherishes the role of the victim.

An enemy image accomplishes something that is otherwise impossible: the creator of the enemy image takes the active role but can pass off responsibility for all activity onto the "victim." The result is that enemy images tend to be not only self-fulfilling but also self-justifying: enemy images give one the "right" to justify and return enmity.

At this point the terrible force that enemy images possess becomes clear—they create their own reality. "Hell is us," says Sartre. Perhaps we should be more precise: Hell is the enemy image we make of each other.

The Archaic Anarchy of Enemy Images

Enemy images possess the power to create enmity and put it into words, but where does this power come from? A comparison with intrasocietal prejudices points to a special feature of enemy images in interstate relations. When antipathy between neighbors escalates into disturbance, molestation, or attack, it is reported to a mediating authority, the police, or, if necessary, is fought out in court. These higher instances of authority are not available to quarreling neighbor states that have developed enemy images as a result of their enmity. If appropriate supranational institutions do exist (the European Court of Justice, the U.N.), they do not yet have sufficient power to impose sanctions. Conflict between nations and its intensification—enemy images—cannot be settled by independent courts or by calling in a supranational police force. Each partner in the conflict, instead, plays all the roles at the same time; perpetrator, prosecutor, judge, and executioner of an inevitably biased judgment (prejudice).

Conflict relationships between states are *archaic*. First, they demand the complete negation of the principle of the separation of powers that is an integral part of democracy. Enmity does not gain its executive power, at least not exclusively, from its power to create its own reality, but from the dominant position, the insidious, violent, evil intentions of the "neighbor." It also derives its strength from the fact that the internal model of the separation of powers corresponds, between nations and states, to the model of absolutist rule. Here, perpetrators, prosecutors, judges, and executioners are one, combined into a sole image of sovereign power, possessing exclusively the monopoly on the legitimate use of force.

The Bisection of Democracy

The bisection of democracy, thus, refers to both internal *and* external state relations: each substantiates the other, and together they constitute the core of state sovereignty. Since interstate relations are governed by the opposite of democracy—absolutism and anarchy—and because states do not recognize any higher authority than themselves, and, further, since states are uninhibited in playing out their prejudices and interests (now raised to the status of "national interests") against each other, democracy must be limited internally, too, by the military and by force. The nonseparation of powers exhibited by unruly states is what makes their friend and enemy images, their egoism inflated into national interest, so powerful, so dangerous, so bellicose, so real. This is because there is nothing—no judge, no interstate enforcer of supranational law—that can check the archaic force of self-interest, tame it, rein it in, bring it back to "reason" in the cold impartial light of legal proceedings in a higher court.

The power of enemy images to create their own reality is thus the other side of the coin of state sovereignty. States, or to be more precise nation-states, are, in other words, all in one: perpetrators, judges, executors of the judgments they pass on each other, subject only to what is permitted by existing power relationships. Seen in this light, nuclear states, where deployment also threatens to destroy the victor, are a "taming" influence: they are forced to find other ways to resolve conflicts.

Love Images, Enemy Images

A comparison with love and marriage, now freed from traditionalism, is quite striking: it is now free, too, from any higher authority. If someone loves rightly or wrongly, or not at all, no court, no law, no priest, hardly any moral principle is responsible—only those who love or no longer love. Love images, like enemy images, are subject to no higher jurisdiction. Love, like national friendship, can be withdrawn one-sidedly, leading to negative self-images and, as with enemy images, spirals of self-destruction. Love images are also, like enemy images, highly susceptible to interpretation. Even slight communication disturbances can have devastating consequences when a conflict recognizes no higher authority, no set of overriding rules. In interstate conflicts this is exacerbated: not merely the fate of individuals but of entire nations is at stake, and both combatants have military force at their disposal. Also, the deployment of the "private monopoly on the use of force," which grows out of mutual intimacy and intimate knowledge of the other, can cause dramatic injury and destruction. The only major difference between private marital "wars" and interstate enemy images is that nations are armed and legitimized by everything that state power and legitimacy has to offer: laws, parliament, approval of the churches, unions, associations, corporations. In interstate conflict, violence and the threat of violence are *internally* legitimized on *both sides*. Thus it is the national organizations of perpetrators that reserve the right to deploy their enemy images against each other, justified by their legitimate power—power which tolerates no internal resistance. This is why elite groups are so important, along with groups of counterelites who are needed to keep the former in check.

Thus, the self-justification or—one almost has to say—self-executive power of enemy images is not only a result of the fact that there are no supranational institutional authorities that can bindingly regulate interstate conflicts. Since it is based on all sources of national legitimacy, law, and morality (including the church, the unions, the scientific community, etc.) the legitimate, archaic force of enemy images can also be mobilized.

Individuation and the Cultural Decomposition of Enemy Images

But unless they are so perceived, enemies as such are not enemies. The threat comes always and only from perceptions or depictions of threats—from enemy *images*. If more and more people and cultures were to dismantle their enemy images of one another, it might be possible that aliens from Mars or other extraterrestrial beings could suddenly attack them and subject them to their rule and laws. Cultures without enemy images would never be able to raise their weapons: no enemy image, no war.

Only societies and cultures in which enemy images are culturally transmitted, kept alive, in which they determine human thought and action, only those are ready and willing to fight in a state of emergency. In other words, the degree to which a culture's enemy images fade or dissolve, or the prerequisites for their transmission and socialization decompose, correlates with the degree to which a society becomes unwilling, incapable of waging war—be it ever so well armed and militarily well organized. Increasing *individuation*— that is the thesis here—*calls a halt to the cultural reproduction of enemy images*. A kind of involuntary *civil inhibition of the biting instinct* develops in society, even if it is still armed to the teeth. This is not because members are convinced pacifists or a group suffers from a lack of military equipment or technological know-how. Rather, it is because, during the course of the process of individualization, which—to borrow a phrase from the machine tool industry—has been "incised" into life by the "mechanics" of welfare-state modernization, thinking in terms of large group categories—be they social classes, strata, or enemies—has lost its historical foundations.[11]

To recapitulate, in all democracies up to now, there have been two types of authority: one derived from the people, the other from the *enemies*. Enemy images integrate. Enemy images empower. Enemy images have top priority in conflict. They permit all other social oppositions to be covered up, limited by force. Enemy images are, so to speak, an alternative source of energy for the modern period with its dwindling supplies of the raw material of consensus. They allow democracy to be freed from democracy, with democratic approval. The military, the state of emergency are not only concepts of geostrategy and foreign policy but are also aimed towards establishing an internal, nonmilitary organizational form of society that conforms to the military. This can be found in all facets of society: production, labor, law, the arts and sciences, domestic policy, public relations. In other words, all democracies are militarily bisected. Military consensus delimits democratic consensus and vice versa: if one were to enforce true democracy, conflict readiness in a state of emergency would be impossible.

Unbounding Modernity

Thinking in terms of friend vs. foe is the most radical simplification with which world diversity can be defeated and destroyed. In

---

11. This argument has been developed in Ulrich Beck, *Risk Society: Towards a New Modernity*, part II (London, 1992), 91–138; for discussions see *Riskante Freiheiten*, ed. Ulrich Beck, E. Beck-Gernsheim (Frankfurt, 1994).

the canon of the sociological theory of institutions (Gehlen, Schelsky, etc.), there is a marked predilection for the usefulness of simplifications. This preference has had a profound effect on all sectors of theoretical and political thought. The more drastic the simplification, the more useful, functional it is. Following this argument to its logical conclusion, it would seem most efficient to direct all one's theoretical attention and research energy into implementing enemy images. Action, which threatens to be choked to death by available options, can choose between clear alternatives. And these are even sanctioned by the choice between life and death. The Greatest Conceivable Simplification (GCS) is not only created by thought processes but also by a short-circuit with action itself. All of this provides security, clearly marked borders and their fortification, armament.

In summarizing all of the functional achievements of enemy images, which—as we now know—integrate societies, in particular modern ones, and provide a source of self-empowerment of the powerful, etc., the *(modern) contramodern character* of enemy images now emerges. These are modern products and constructs which *contradict* the modernity and radically *counteract* its tendency toward self-destruction.[12]

Increasing modernization produces a double effect: the prerequisites for the cultural transmission of traditional enemy images are weakened, eliminated. Internally, this means that various types of mobility affect one's identity—regional, national, individual—and it becomes unclear, questionable, confused. Externally, supranational and international networks have become established—from the economy to information networks, telecommunications, and questions of environmental devastation or the movement of toxic substances in the air, in water and food, movement that ignores all frontiers.[13]

Defining identity, in particular, becomes increasingly difficult, and evidence of this is provided by the process of individualization now in high gear. This means that the sense of having a culture of one's own is shattered. Born in Topeka, a woman may go to school in Kansas City, work in Dallas, get married and move to Atlanta, while her husband works in Nashville; they spend their

12. Ulrich Beck, *The Renaissance of Politics* (Cambridge, 1996), Ch. 3: "The Other Side of Modernity is Manufactured: Counter-Modernization."
13. This theory of reflexive modernization is discussed in Ulrich Beck, Anthony Giddens, and Scott Lash, *Reflexive Modernization—Politics, Tradition and Aesthetics in the Modern Social Order* (Cambridge, 1994).

vacation in Florida and have international business contacts. This means that the individualized individual is tied to the mobile existence of the nomad—across and throughout the course of life. What Georg Simmel understood as the characteristic feature of the "other," "the wanderer who comes today and goes tomorrow," is about to become, in the age of individualization, the normal way of life. In other words, the global risk society has generalized the concept of the other: one of its central features is universal "otherness." More and more individuals are losing their clear social identity in terms of origins and status.

Nonetheless, enemy images are obviously not disappearing. Instead, they develop somewhat differently. In place of *traditional* hereditary enemies (always a construct), we now find enemy images that are an *(admittedly) political* construct. To be more precise: these are mobile, abstract, generalized enemy images in which various types of threat are combined and become highly combustible. When social constructs of the self and the other are preserved in fewer and fewer traditions that are taken for granted, they become a political issue. Individuals, set free from strong cultural ties, construct their own concepts of self and other—in a manner that tends to be more arbitrary, temporary, and variable, more determined by competition for advantages and resources, and more concerned with the implementation of force and terror than guided by the degree of cultural self-evidence and historical recollection.

The Future: International Networks

Behind the political boom in ever changing enemy images is a problem which must be taken very seriously: *how much disintegration can human beings stand*? Or, to put it more strongly, *how much enlightenment can they take*? The extraordinary energy devoted to the search for and addiction to structures that can provide order is evident here. One relatively common error can be corrected with the help of the theory of the bisected modernity: not only national identity, based on enemy images, can provide order. In the case of ecological morality, we seem to be dealing with a kind of cultural Red Cross or rescue squad mentality. As the example of the current concern about toxic waste clearly shows, however, this consciousness can be very motivating and integrating, or can at least be used as such; and it is supranational, even global, in its orientation.

In highly developed societies, thus, everyday life has evolved an ecologically moral consciousness along with the corresponding calls for action, calls which do not draw their authority from identifying an enemy but from targeting false means of production, false nutrition, false ways of life. This awareness, by the way, ties the most intimate issues of lifestyle to the most general issues of worldwide technological and industrial policy. The crucial point, however, is that this simultaneously personal and global identity has yet to receive an institutional form, one that would provide it with durability, increased stability, and order.

The breakdown of enemy images—if you will permit me to point out this light at the end of the tunnel—must therefore be accompanied by the creation and fortification of supranational networks, institutions, and identities. The ecological issue is just one example. These international networks are growing, as political scientists have noted. Ultimately, economic interdependencies and, as a result, the old theories of "pacifistic capitalism" will gain in significance. It may be that all of this will happen quickly enough to counteract the current flight, both in Europe and other parts of the world, into old and new enemy images. We can only hope that this will be the case.

PART II

THE AMERICAN REVOLUTION AND ITS AFTERMATH

Chapter Three

THE IMAGE OF AN ENGLISH ENEMY DURING THE AMERICAN REVOLUTION

Jürgen Heideking

T he age of the Enlightenment is commonly associated with the concept of reason, with the victory of rationality over superstition. In the meantime we have learned, however, that this was only partly true, that the Enlightenment, while overcoming traditional ways of thinking, created its own forms of superstition and irrationality, mainly in the guise of secular ideologies. Therefore, medieval and early modern enemy images or negative stereotypes based on religious beliefs did not completely disappear but were transformed and adapted to the requirements of the new era. This process of change and adaptation can be studied quite well in the case of the estrangement between Great Britain and its North American colonies that, during one generation, led to revolution and caused two wars.[1]

When we think of Great Britain and the United States, the positive image of a "special relationship" immediately comes to mind, a close political and cultural association of two Anglo-Saxon nations that helped to shape the history of our century. Things were

1. The following is a revised version of my article "Das Englandbild in der nordamerikanischen Publizistik zur Zeit der Revolution," in Franz Bosbach, ed., *Feindbilder: Die Darstellung des Gegners in der politischen Publizistik des Mittelalters und der Neuzeit* (Cologne, 1992), 179–99.

different, however, during the first 125 years of American independence: the British Empire, the monarchy, the English governments and parliaments, and at times even the English people were considered by many Americans as enemies or at least as archrivals in political, economic, and military affairs. How could that happen, and why did this enmity last for such a long time? To answer this question is of special importance because of the very close links that have existed between England and North America since the founding of the first colonies in the early seventeenth century. It seems to be much easier, for example, to explain the hostility between ethnically and religiously different neighbors such as Germany and France, or between Poland and Germany and Poland and Russia, than to account for the deep animosity, aggressive feelings, and violent behavior of Americans towards Englishmen and vice versa.

This chapter concentrates on the Revolutionary period from the 1760s to the end of the eighteenth century when the image of an "English enemy" was created; special attention is given to its origins, its various elements, its nature and character, and its political functions. With regard to the transformation of this enemy image in the early national period, its impact on American foreign relations in the nineteenth century, and its survival well into the twentieth century, only a few brief and more or less speculative comments will be given.

There can be no question that from the point of view of the American Revolutionary generation the image of an English enemy was more than just an invention of radical nationalists and propagandists who used it as a tool for achieving independence from the mother country. Modern historical research has shown that British imperial policy after the victory in the French and Indian War in fact aimed at limiting the political and economic autonomy of the North American colonists.[2] During the 1760s and early 1770s, the authorities in London from time to time made concessions to colonial demands, but they never offered a compromise in matters of principle, such as the unlimited right of Parliament to tax the colonies; this basic attitude, and not just "mutual misunderstandings," contributed significantly to the escalation of the conflict between the colonists and the mother country. In 1774, King George III and his advisers, not the Americans, decided to solve the imperial crisis

2. The best general survey is Robert Middlekauff, *The Glorious Cause: The American Revolution, 1763–1789, The Oxford History of the United States*, vol. 2 (New York and Oxford, 1982).

with military means; they were the first to systematically use force in order to stamp out what they considered to be a "rebellion" instigated by a few radical agitators. This decision provoked the final break between the colonies and the mother country; it led to the Declaration of Independence and to six years of fighting that caused considerable destruction in many parts of the country and exacted a heavy price from the Americans: at least 5 percent of all free white males aged sixteen to forty-five died in the war; in terms of present-day population figures this would mean a death toll of 2.5 million Americans. In addition, Congress estimated the cost of the war between $158 and $168 million.[3] After the Treaty of Paris was signed in 1783, the British government continued to seriously damage American trade by closing the Caribbean islands to most American products; at the same time British troops continued to occupy—contrary to the stipulations of the peace treaty—several forts in the Ohio region, which allowed them to block the westward migration of American settlers. Leading English politicians made no secret of their hope that this combined pressure would help to undermine the American experiment in self-government and push the colonists back into the arms of the mother country.[4] In the next two decades, when revolutions swept through the European continent and Britain and France fought for hegemony, the Royal Navy again obstructed American trade relations, disregarding commonly accepted neutrality rules, confiscating American property, and even kidnapping American sailors from American ships.

For a number of reasons, therefore, the Americans' disappointment, frustration, and anger were based on facts and may be seen as understandable reactions to British arrogance and provocation. These conflicts of interest and objective difficulties cannot, however, fully explain the deep hostility that had already erupted during the Stamp Act crisis in 1765, a sense of hostility that was fueled by what the historian Arthur M. Schlesinger Sr. has called an American "newspaper war on Britain,"[5] and that began to separate two

3. E. James Ferguson. *The Power of the Purse: A History of American Public Finance, 1776–1790* (Chapel Hill, NC, 1961). This equals $15 to $16 billion in 1990 dollars.

4. Cf. the pamphlet published in 1783 by the Earl of Sheffield (John Baker Holroyd), *Observations on the Commerce of the American States with Europe,* which convinced many Americans that the British government intended to regain political influence by stirring up rivalries between the American states.

5. Arthur M. Schlesinger Sr., *Prelude to Independence: The Newspaper War on Britain 1764–1776* (New York, 1957); cf. Kenneth Silverman, *A Cultural History of the American Revolution, 1763–1789* (New York, 1987), 72–81.

peoples who, for over a century, had seen themselves as common subjects of the British Crown, as part of one single nation, as members of one big family. Only a few years earlier, in 1760, all the colonial cities and towns from New England to Georgia had staged enthusiastic celebrations on the occasion of King George III's accession to the throne. In this sudden change of perceptions and images, modern historians detect a kind of emotional, irrational surplus, an exaggerated, overheated, and sometimes even hysterical excitement, which allows us to speak of an "enemy image."

On the other hand, the change was less abrupt than it seems. In reality, a highly critical and negative view of England had emerged long before the outbreak of the War for Independence, and the war itself only helped to fix this negative point of view in the minds of the American people. Seen from this perspective, disseminating the image of an English enemy was part of a fundamental change in the mentality of the colonists, a change remembered well and vividly described by one of the leading Revolutionaries. "What do we mean by the Revolution?" John Adams asked in a famous letter written to Thomas Jefferson in 1815. "The war? That was no part of the Revolution. It was only an effect and consequence of it. The Revolution was in the minds of the people, and this was effected, from 1760 to 1775, in the course of fifteen years before a drop of blood was drawn at Lexington." And three years later Adams recommended that historians should more thoroughly investigate "by what means this great and important alteration in the religious, moral, political and social character of the people of thirteen colonies, all distinct, unconnected, and independent of each other, was begun, pursued, and accomplished."[6]

Even if we do not fully agree with Adams's definition of the American Revolution, we must admit that the Americans' perception of themselves and of their English counterparts changed drastically in the years between the French and Indian War and the War of Independence. This is confirmed by the work of Bernard Bailyn, Gordon S. Wood, and others, who have studied the public debate of the late colonial period and made available most of the relevant historical sources. From these writings, three conclusions can be drawn concerning the image of an English enemy. First, the

6. John Adams to Thomas Jefferson, 24.8.1815, The Adams-Jefferson Letters, ed. Lester J. Cappon, 2 vols. (Chapel Hill, NC, 1959), 2:455; John Adams to Hezekiah Niles, 13.2.1818, The American Enlightenment: The Shaping of the American Experiment and a Free Society, ed. Adrienne Koch (New York, 1956); cf. Michael Kammen. A Season of Youth: The American Revolution and the Historical Imagination (New York, 1978),18–19.

hostility towards England was primarily motivated by ideological beliefs and convictions; one could even argue that the American image of an English enemy was the first ideological enemy image in modern history. Second, the nature of this enemy image was to a large extent defined by the colonial situation, by the contrast between, in present-day terms, imperial center and colonial periphery. This accounts for the rhetoric of liberation and emancipation, but it also accounts for a lot of confusion and ambivalence: the European origins of the settlers and the close bonds that connected colonies and mother country made it difficult to draw a clear line between Americans and Englishmen/women, and this, in turn, created grave domestic problems for the colonies and later for the United States. Since some Americans always remained loyal to the crown and sought to cultivate a positive image of England and the British Empire, the enemy image was in part directed against an internal enemy; it affected not only the external relations but also the domestic affairs of the United States. Third, the image of an English enemy is closely related to American nationalism and the Americans' quest for national identity. By constructing and disseminating this enemy image, the American patriots in a way anticipated the formation of a separate American nation. In that sense, the enemy image helped to create and construct a separate national identity, because it acted as a unifying force in the face of all the existing diversity and fragmentation in and between the states. This underlines the close and problematic connection between enemy images and modern nationalism, which is well documented in the European context.[7]

The Ideological Nature of the Image of an English Enemy

Are we really justified in speaking, in the case of the Anglo-American relationship, of an ideological enemy image, a *Feindbild* motivated by and steeped in ideological beliefs? The answer

7. One of the most interesting examples of recent scholarship in this field is Michael Jeismann, *Das Vaterland der Feinde: Studien zum nationalen Feindbegriff und Selbstverständnis in Deutschland und Frankreich 1792–1918, Sprache und Geschichte,* vol. 19 (Stuttgart, 1992). Jeismann's thesis of "the formation of the modern nation through enmity" captures quite well the tension between constructive and dangerous elements contained in most enemy images, a tension which can be observed in the American case, too.

can be found in Bernard Bailyn's influential book, *The Ideological Origins of the American Revolution*.[8] In accordance with a general trend in the social sciences, Bailyn uses a fairly broad definition of "ideology": he describes it as a coherent world-view, a structured belief system, rooted in secular as opposed to religious concepts. As he shows, the pamphlets, newspaper articles, letters, diaries, etc., written during the imperial crisis prove that the American patriots were heavily influenced and inspired by the English opposition literature of the early eighteenth century. In essence, this opposition literature was a radically conservative, anti-modernist critique of and protest against English politics, economic development, and social change in the age of prime minister Robert Walpole. Most of the central ideas originated in Renaissance Italy, from where they spread to seventeenth century England through the mediation of some republican writers, especially James Harrington.

In the first decades of the eighteenth century, the "opposition language" was used by radical Whigs such as William Gordon and John Trenchard in their famous *Cato Letters* as well as by conservative Tories, the most prominent being Henry St. John, Viscount Bolingbroke. Radical Whigs and Tories met in their rejection of the new commercial way of life which they contrasted with a lost "golden age," an agrarian utopia of free and independent farmers. This opposition "discourse" was characterized by a particular style and terminology, by certain recurrent themes and maxims, often condensed in political slogans such as "annual elections," "rotation in office," "no standing army," etc. Central to an understanding of this literature is the concept of classical virtue, personified in the republican citizen who is ready to sacrifice himself for the common good. Comparing their own time with the classical ideal, the opposition writers perceived the modern history of England in terms of growing decadence, as a decline or loss of virtue, a degeneration, a deviation from traditional values, from the ideal "ancient constitution" of England. In their books, pamphlets, and articles, eighteenth-century England appears as the opposite of a virtuous commonwealth: it is being overwhelmed by the forces of vice and corruption; its leaders are selfish, immoral, and incompetent, and its people are, in the angry words

8. Bernard Bailyn, *The Ideological Origins of the American Revolution*, 13th ed. (Cambridge, MA, 1976); cf. Jack P. Greene, *The Intellectual Heritage of the Constitutional Era: The Delegates' Library* (Philadelphia, 1986).

of James Burgh, "wallowing in luxury, infidelity, dissipation, perjury, idleness, drunkenness, and lasciviousness."[9] From the perspective of a modern historian, this judgment sounds quite extravagant and out of proportion; in the 1740s, however, it had become the standard argument of a group of disaffected politicians and intellectuals, the so-called Country Party (as opposed to the governing Court Party). In Bailyn's view, the writings of this group are sufficiently coherent and systematic as to justify the term "Country ideology."

Whereas in England itself this pessimistic world-view and cultural criticism slowly gave way to a more liberal, individualistic understanding of politics and society, the Country language of "virtue versus corruption" became more and more popular in eighteenth-century America. This was probably due to the economic backwardness of the colonies, where the agrarian way of life was still unchallenged. To many Americans who visited England, the mother country appeared like a modern-day Babylon. A letter written in 1754 in London by the young Pennsylvanian John Dickinson gives a good example. Dickinson describes the atmosphere surrounding that year's parliamentary elections:

> It is astonishing to think what impudence and villainy are practiced on this occasion. If a man cannot be brought to vote as he is desired, he is made dead drunk and kept in that state, never heard of by his family or friends till all is over and he can do no harm.... Bribery is so common that it is thought there is not a borough in England where it is not practiced.... It is ridiculous and absurd to pretend to curb the effects of luxury and corruption in one instance or in one spot without a general reformation of manners, which everyone sees is absolutely necessary for the welfare of the kingdom. Yet Heaven knows how it can be effected. It is grown a vice here to be virtuous.[10]

The Country ideology provided the colonists with a mental pattern or framework for interpreting all the information they could gather about their mother country. Central to this framework was a negative image of modern, commercial England; this negative image remained latent until the 1760s, but its existence helps to explain why the colonists reacted so vehemently to the

9. James Burgh, *Britain's Remembrancer: Or, the Danger Not Over* (London 1746; reprinted in Philadelphia, 1747 and 1748; in Boston, 1759).

10. Quoted from Bernard Bailyn et al., *The Great Republic: A History of the American People* (Boston and Toronto, 1977), 222.

strengthening of imperial controls after the French and Indian War, and why admiration and friendship could turn so quickly into hostility when the question of taxation became acute with the Stamp Act.

What happened between 1765 and 1776 can be described, therefore, as the activation and transformation of a latent negative image into the actual image of an English enemy. Because of their ideological predisposition, the patriots tended to interpret every single measure of the British government as part of a great conspiracy, or, as Thomas Jefferson put it in 1774, as part of "a deliberate, systematic plan of reducing us to slavery."[11] The fact that this conspiracy theory was widely accepted in the colonies can be understood only in light of the almost general acceptance of the principles and maxims of Country ideology.[12] In their writings, speeches, and symbolic acts, the American Revolutionaries, following the lead of the Country writers, portrayed England as the counterimage of a virtuous commonwealth, as a country in moral decline, unable to defend the liberty of its own people and intent on enslaving others. At the same time, they praised the colonies as defenders of republican virtues and ideals, as guardians of the "sacred flame of liberty" enshrined in the ancient English constitution, and as bulwarks against British vices and corruption.[13]

In this process of activating the enemy image, different stages can be distinguished. At first, the criticism was directed only against some advisors and ministers of the king, such as the Earl of Bute and Lord Grenville. Then Parliament became the enemy, but for a certain time it was seen as a body that did not really represent the nation; again and again the patriots expressed hope that there must be some virtue left in the English people or that at least the "mercantile interest" would lobby in their favor.[14] When this

11. Thomas Jefferson, *A Summary View of the Rights of British America* (1774), quoted from Bailyn, *Ideological Origins*, 119–120. John Adams was convinced that the British government followed a "settled plan to deprive the people of all the benefits, blessings, and ends of the contract, to subvert the fundamentals of the constitution, to deprive them of all share in making and executing laws." *Novanglus* (1775), quoted from John R. Howe Jr., *The Changing Political Thought of John Adams* (Princeton, NJ, 1966), 43.

12. For a more detailed analysis of this phenomenon see Gordon S. Wood. "Conspiracy and the Paranoid Style: Causality and Deceit in the Eighteenth Century," *William and Mary Quarterly* 39 (1982): 401 passim.

13. Cf. Peter Shaw, *American Patriots and the Rituals of Revolution* (Cambridge, MA, 1981).

14. Cf. Alison G. Olson, "The London Mercantile Lobby and the Coming of the American Revolution," *Journal of American History* 69 (1982): 21–41; Pauline

hope faded in the early 1770s because of the Boston Massacre and the harsh British reaction to the Boston Tea Party, the king for a while remained the last positive symbol of the Empire relationship; but this symbol was being demolished in 1776 by Thomas Paine's pamphlet *Common Sense*. Now, finally, the imperial conflict took on the quality of a struggle between two different or even contrary political and social systems, republicanism versus monarchy.[15] The Declaration of Independence accused the king of a breach of the social contract, but for Jefferson and the Continental Congress the English people as a whole shared responsibility for the events that had led to separation. In his first draft of the Declaration, Jefferson denounced them as "unfeeling brethren"; Congress deleted these words from the final version, but another sentence remained, stating that the Americans would treat the English people no longer as relatives but, like the rest of humanity, "as enemies in war, in peace friends."[16] The war itself, which had already begun at that time, confirmed and strengthened this hostile attitude. From now on the patriots referred to the common history only in order to emphasize the special cruelty of the former English "relatives" who had turned against their own kind.[17]

What should be stressed in this context is the secular, ideological character of the evolving enemy image. Religious matters played a certain role in the conflict between the colonies and the mother country, for example when the American clergy condemned the concessions made to Catholics in the Quebec Act of 1774, or when they opposed the English idea of naming an Anglican bishop for the colonies. But in this case religious problems only supplemented and sharpened the basic ideological division. Contrary to all the major conflicts from the Reformation to the

---

Maier. "John Wilkes and American Disillusionment with Britain," *William and Mary Quarterly* 20 (1963): 373–395.

15. Cf. Bernard Bailyn. "Common Sense," in: Library of Congress Symposia on the American Revolution. *Fundamental Testaments of the American Revolution* (Washington, D.C., 1973) 7 passim.

16. Cf. Gary Wills, *Inventing America: Jefferson's Declaration of Independence* (Garden City, NY, 1978), 307 passim, 378.

17. After the first attacks of the Royal Navy against New England coastal towns, Benjamin Franklin wrote to a member of Parliament: "You have begun to burn our towns and murder our people. Look at your hands! They are stained with the blood of your relations! You and I were long friends. You are now my enemy as I am yours." Quoted from Barbara W. Tuchman, *The First Salute* (New York, 1988), 46. On the other side, a British military commander in America complained that he had to fight "a most savage, inveterate, perfidious, cruel enemy." Ibid., 208.

French and Indian War, the American War of Independence was not fought on the basis of religious enemy images. In 1755, when British and French interests clashed in Europe and in North America, public opinion on both sides had been mobilized in the name of "true religion" versus the "Anti-Christ." Twenty years later, this traditional millennial, eschatological, and apocalyptic language was still being used by a number of Americans, particularly New England clergymen, but in the political arena it had given way to secular, ideological distinctions.[18] The image of an English enemy had been borrowed from the English Country party and transformed into a republican, anti-colonial propaganda weapon. The enemy was no longer defined in terms of ethnicity or religion, but in an ideological way as an adherent or subject of a monarchical system of government that, after having corrupted its own people, now intended to destroy republican liberty and self-government in the rest of the world.

The Domestic Dimension of the Enemy Image

At the time of the Declaration of Independence a fully developed ideological enemy image existed in the patriot press, but one can only speculate to what extent and by how many people it was accepted. We know, on the other hand, that a sizable minority in the thirteen states openly rejected the radical propaganda aimed at the mother country and remained loyal to the British crown. These loyalists or Tories, as they were called by the patriots, clung to the traditional positive image of England as the country of liberty and prosperity, a well-ordered society, whose social peace and happiness, according to the Baron de Montesquieu, was guaranteed by an ideal "balanced" constitution.[19] In the public debate which continued well into the war, the loyalists outlined a conservative counter ideology based on notions of authority, order, and

18. Cf. Ernest L. Tuveson, *Redeemer Nation: The Idea of America's Millennial Role* (Chicago, 1968); Nathan O. Hatch, *The Sacred Cause of Liberty: Republican Thought and the Millennium in Revolutionary New England* (New Haven, CT, 1977); idem, "The Origins of Civil Millennialism in America: New England Clergymen, War with France, and the Revolution," *William and Mary Quarterly* 31 (1974): 407–30; Ruth Bloch, *Visionary Republic: Millennial Themes in American Thought, 1756–1800* (Cambridge, MA, London and New York, 1985).

19. A first translation of Montesquieu's *De l'esprit des lois* from 1748 had come out in the colonies in 1760. Paul Spurlin, *Montesquieu in America, 1760–1801* (Baton Rouge, LA, 1940).

deference. From their perspective, monarchy alone could check the dangerous passions of the people, whereas republicanism meant economic decline and political anarchy. The separation from the mother country was condemned as a rebellion against any kind of legitimate authority, in the final analysis as a negation of the divine order.[20]

In the course of the War of Independence loyalism disappeared as a political force, since most of its spokesmen left the United States or were driven out by the patriots. The positive view of England as a country of political order and economic prosperity, however, which the loyalists had tried to cultivate, survived the war and, from the 1780s on, coexisted in a precarious way with the image of an English enemy. During the so-called "critical period" from 1783 to 1787 it served as a rallying point for all those who became disappointed and disillusioned by the realities of independence. The political campaign, led by Alexander Hamilton, to replace the Articles of Confederation with a more centralized national or "federal" constitution, was at least partly motivated by a desire to move closer to the English ideal of a "balanced" system of government.[21] When the French Revolution turned violent, the internal and external enemy images became again dangerously intertwined. The governing Federalists, at least after the execution of the French King in 1791, sympathized with British efforts to isolate or stamp out the revolution, since they feared that the French example might encourage the American "Jacobins" to overthrow the Constitution and to turn the "mob" against the propertied classes. On the other hand, most Jeffersonian Republicans enthusiastically supported the revolution and suspected a conspiracy involving their Federalist opponents and the British with the aim to reestablish a monarchical system not only in France but also in the United States. When Jefferson was elected president in 1801, Federalists predicted a social upheaval comparable with recent events in France, and they again looked to Britain for assistance.[22] During the

20. In addition to Montesquieu, the loyalists used Locke, Hume, Grotius, and Vattel as their main authorities. Mary Beth Norton, "The Loyalist Critique of the Revolution," in: Library of Congress Symposia on the American Revolution, *The Development of a Revolutionary Mentality* (Washington, D.C., 1972), 127–44.

21. Cf. Jürgen Heideking, *Die Verfassung vor dem Richterstuhl: Vorgeschichte und Ratifizierung der amerikanischen Verfassung, 1787–1791* (Berlin and New York, 1988).

22. Cf. Jürgen Heideking, "Amerikanische Einflüsse und Reaktionen auf die Französische Revolution," Heiner Timmermann, ed., *Die Französische Revolution und Europa, 1789–1799* (Saarbrücken, 1989),117–31; Roger G. Kennedy, *Orders from France: The Americans and the French in a Revolutionary World, 1780–1820* (New York, 1989).

Napoleonic Wars Jefferson and Madison tried to remain neutral, but Republicans in general felt much more offended by unfriendly acts committed by the Royal Navy than by similar French violations of the neutrality rules. In 1812, when Congress finally declared war on Britain, the old enemy image resurfaced in full force. This time, New England Federalists, who opposed the war on economic and ideological grounds, played the role of the loyalists of 1776. Instead of accepting the image of an English enemy, they considered the Republican war hawks in the South and in the West as their real enemies. From the Republican point of view, such an attitude, combined with talk about a possible secession of the New England states from the Union, was tantamount to treason. Fortunately, both sides were too weak to risk a civil war. The outcome of the war against England, then, strengthened the Republican party and practically eliminated Federalism as a political force.[23]

Looking over the whole Revolutionary era, one can see that for almost half a century enemy images not only influenced American attitudes toward the outside world but also had an impact on party politics, sectionalism, and domestic affairs in general. Beginning with the War of Independence, it became almost a habit to identify one's political opponent with a hostile foreign power and to insinuate that internal and external enemies were acting in collusion. In this respect enemy images tended to polarize domestic conflicts and to ideologize foreign relations in a dangerous way. On the other hand, the image of an English enemy never completely dominated American politics and thinking. Especially during the French Revolution, the image of England became highly ambivalent. Different groups of Americans associated very different things with the word "England": for Republicans it meant monarchy, colonial tyranny, reactionary politics, and counterrevolution; for Federalists it meant stable government, a well-ordered society, secure property rights, and growing trade and industry. Obviously, both the extreme polarization and the ambivalence grew out of the colonial relationship: the enemy image helped to justify the break with the mother country, but it could not completely erase the sense of common origins and the memory of one and a half centuries of generally profitable colonial dependency.

23. Cf. Richard Buel Jr., *Securing the Revolution: Ideology in American Politics, 1789–1815* (Ithaca, NY and London, 1972); J.C.A. Stagg, *Mr. Madison's War: Politics, Diplomacy, and Warfare in the Early Republic, 1783–1830* (Princeton, NJ, 1983); Reginald Horsman, *The Diplomacy of the New Republic, 1776–1815* (Arlington Heights, IL, 1985).

The Image of an English Enemy and American National Identity

This leads to the third point, the connection between enemy images and national identity. It has often been observed that nationalism grows out of the desire of a certain group of people to set themselves apart from ethnically, religiously, or in some other way different groups of people. This process of delimitation seems to be indispensable for community and nation building, but it also tends to produce full-scale enemy images which in turn can be used to intensify and escalate any given conflict. The American case is complicated because of the close relationship that existed between the colonies and England, a relationship which found expression in the family metaphor of a mother country being responsible for the colonies as parents are for their children. In terms of ethnicity, religion, language, and culture, the colonists were so close to the people of England that it became extremely difficult for them to draw a dividing line. To a certain extent, early American nationalism seems to have been a reaction to the growth of nationalism among the middle classes in England, which was stimulated by economic modernization and imperial expansion. It was the confrontation with this kind of "exclusive" English nationalism during and after the Seven Years' War that created a feeling of "otherness" and alienation in the colonies and which helped the patriots to draw a line between themselves and the imperial center.

To achieve their goal, the patriots used two different but complementary strategies: on the one hand they exaggerated the ideological differences between themselves and the British, and on the other they invested the United States with a special mission which it had to fulfill in the historical process. The first strategy resulted in what I have characterized before as an ideological enemy image: the Americans not only claimed to preserve the ancient "English liberties" which supposedly had been lost or betrayed by the English people, but they imagined a "new science of politics," a republican system of government diametrically opposed to the British monarchy, built on natural rights and based on a written constitution. Instead of a return to the "golden age," the Revolution came to be seen as a departure into a new republican future: "We have it in our power to begin the world over again," proclaimed Thomas Paine in *Common Sense*. Everybody who declared him or herself in support of republican principles and values was accepted as an American; everybody who opposed them was excluded as a Tory or a foreigner. In 1776 ideology, not ethnicity, language, or religion, had become the touchstone of national identity.

The second strategy aimed at shaping a kind of reverse image of the enemy image: it sharply contrasted the old, corrupt, and declining mother country with a young, virtuous, and vigorously rising American nation or even American empire. To this end the patriots could draw arguments from many sources: from the Puritan idea of a chosen people and a new Jerusalem in the wilderness; from cyclical concepts of history that postulated an organic life of nations and civilizations "from infancy to maturity, to old age and dissolution." (Needless to say, the patriots saw the American nation at the beginning, the British Empire at the end of such a cycle.)[24] Other sources of this missionary self-consciousness included the idea of a westward movement of the great empires in the course of history, and finally the modern, enlightened understanding of progress based on rational inquiry and scientific knowledge. When the French Revolution "degenerated" and collapsed, many Americans saw their own country as the last bulwark of republican liberty, and they felt that from now on the survival of the idea of self-government depended wholly on their example.[25]

This complex of ideas, which confirmed a sense of American "exceptionalism," has been described fairly often in histories of the Revolutionary period. What most historians overlook or fail to mention, however, is the interesting fact that the patriots in their writings and speeches anticipated the formation of an American nation and national identity. In reality, such an American nation did not exist before the early nineteenth century, and even then it

24. The following passage from an oration delivered in 1780 by James Bowdoin, the governor of the state of Massachusetts, exemplifies this organic and cyclical world-view, which was mostly taken from the Greek philosopher Polybios: "It is very pleasing to recur back to the early ages of mankind, and trace the progressive state of nations and empires, from infancy to maturity, to old age and dissolution:— to observe their origin, their growth and improvement ..., to observe the rise and gradual advancement of civilization, of science, of wealth, elegance, and politeness, until they had obtained the summit of their greatness:—to observe at this period the principle of mortality, produced by affluence and luxury, beginning to operate in them ... and finally terminating in their dissolution ... In fine—to observe, after this catastrophe, a new face of things; new kingdoms and empires rising upon the ruins of the old; all of them to undergo like changes, and to suffer a similar dissolution." Quoted from John R. Howe Jr., *The Changing Political Thought of John Adams* (Princeton, 1966), 33–34; cf. Charles P. Hoffer, *Revolution and Regeneration: Life Cycle and Historical Vision of the Generation of 1776* (Athens, GA, 1983).

25. Cf. John C. Rainbolt, "American's Initial View of Their Revolution's Significance for Other Peoples, 1776–1787," *Historian* 35 (1973): 418–33; Buel, *Securing the Revolution*.

lacked the coherence and homogeneity of traditional European nations.[26] One of the main functions of the image of an English enemy, therefore, seems to have been to make possible the intellecutal construction of a separate American identity which only at a later stage became the actual national identity of the American people. This is similar to what happened during the Napoleonic Wars in Germany, when the violently anti-French propaganda of the freedom movement anticipated the birth of a German nation. The step from an imagined to a real nation was a difficult one in both cases, since French culture was as dominant in the Germanic states as English culture was in all aspects of American life. The American patriots had to realize that it was much easier to establish national symbols and to proclaim a national identity and a national culture, for example, in the course of the great Federal Processions of 1788 on occasion of the ratification of the Constitution,[27] than to really emancipate the United States politically, economically, and culturally from a still very powerful Great Britain. In Germany, it took another two generations before the national aspirations of the patriots were fulfilled, again after going to war with France. One should not overemphasize the parallels between the so-called Franco-German *Erbfeindschaft* with the American image of an English enemy. It seems safe to say, however, that enemy images played an important role in the process of American as well as German self-definition.

The Career and Transformation of the Enemy Image

In the United States, Andrew Jackson understood the War of 1812 against Great Britain as the "Second War of Independence" which had to be fought in order to affirm the American "national character."[28] For John Quincy Adams, secretary of state under James Monroe and later president himself, Great Britain remained the

26. Cf. Richard L. Merritt. "The Colonists Discover America: Attention Patterns in the Colonial Press, 1735–1775," *William and Mary Quarterly* 21 (1964): 270–87; idem, "The Emergence of American Nationalism: A Quantitative Approach," *American Quarterly* 17 (1965): 391 passim; idem, *Symbols of American Community, 1735–1775* (New Haven, CT, 1966).

27. Cf. Jürgen Heideking. "The Federal Processions of 1788 and the Origins of American Civil Religion," *Soundings* 77:3–4 (1994): 367–87.

28. Quoted from Bailyn et al., *Great Republic*, 383. The topic is sensibly dealt with by several authors in *Beyond Confederation: Origins of the Constitution and American National Identity*, ed. Richard Beeman, Stephen Botein, and Edward C. Carter II (Chapel Hill, NC and London, 1987).

"natural enemy" of the United States in the Western Hemisphere. Although in the course of the nineteenth century the diplomatic and economic relations between Great Britain and the United States became closer, the image of an English enemy could be revived on several occasions, most significantly in the 1840s during the struggle for Texas and Oregon. The diplomacy of the Lincoln administration was dominated by the fear of a British intervention in the Civil War on the side of the Confederate States. One generation later, on the occasion of the Venezuelan crises in 1895 and 1902/03, the American press was still able to whip up anti-British emotions and to create a real "Anglophobia" by using the same old clichés and stereotypes.[29] And even in our century the enemy image from time to time resurfaced, most notably in the form of anti-colonialist rhetoric directed against the British Empire and the Commonwealth.

American nationalism, therefore, seems to have been fueled for a long time by a strong sense of enmity towards and rivalry with Great Britain. But here, too, one has to account for a high degree of ambivalence. There always existed a much closer connection between American self-images and anti-British stereotypes than most Americans realized or would have admitted. At least during the first century of American-British relations, positive self-images and negative stereotypes formed two sides of the same coin. On the one hand, Americans found their national identity and defined their national character in contrast to what they understood as typically English. Even more striking, however, is the fact that the image of an English enemy clearly corresponded with what may be called the dark side of the American ego. This comes out very clearly in a certain type of literary sources, namely the sermons preached by American clergymen during the Revolution and well into the nineteenth century. Especially in times of crisis, when the sermons took on the form of a jeremiad, all the negative traits normally attributed to the English enemy were detected in the American character itself. Like a litany, these sermons enumerated and tried to exorcise the dangers that threatened the American experiment from within: loss of virtue, lack of religious faith, political corruption, moral decline, etc.—the very same dangers which supposedly had forced the Americans to separate from the mother country.[30]

---

29. Cf. Ragnhild Fiebig-von Hase, *Lateinamerika als Konfliktherd der deutsch-amerikanischen Beziehungen 1890–1903* (Göttingen 1986).

30. Cf. Sacvan Bercovich, *The American Jeremiad* (Madison, 1978).

In a certain way, therefore, the image of an English enemy functioned like a mirror in which the Americans saw the negative, suppressed part of their own nature. The ambivalence that characterized American-British relations for such a long time may well have originated in this psychological mechanism of suppression and projection that causes mixed feelings of aggression and admiration, envy and fear. From the days of the Declaration of Independence on, Americans saw their nation as the rightful heir and successor to the British Empire. The recurrent attacks on British imperialism during the nineteenth century seem to conceal, at least to a certain extent, their own desire for economic domination and political leadership. It is certainly no accident that the improvement of Anglo-American relations and the fading away of the image of an English enemy went hand in hand with the decline of British power, the dissolution of the British Empire, and the rise of the United States to superpower status. As imagined by the Revolutionary generation, the American Republic moved from the periphery to the center of the world system, thereby relegating Great Britain to the semiperiphery. Parallel to this change in the balance of power between the two nations, the ideological basis of the enemy image disappeared when Great Britain, while retaining the institution of the monarchy, moved ever closer to a democratic system of government. These historical developments made it possible to supplant the enemy image with the positive image of a "special relationship."[31] However, in a different shape the enemy image lives on: since World War II it has been constantly used by Americans not against the British, but against their own government and nation, as the Puritan clergy used the jeremiad to criticize the real or imagined shortcomings of their fellow citizens. The modern, secular jeremiad aims at the "arrogance of power" toward the Third World, at the corruption and abuse of power at home, and at the general "decline" that now seems to threaten the United States and its "overextended" American empire.

---

31. David Dimbleby and David Reynolds, *An Ocean Apart: The Relationship Between Britain and America in the Twentieth Century* (London, Sydney, Auckland and Toronto, 1988); William Roger Louis and Hedley Bull, eds., *The "Special Relationship": Anglo-American Relations Since 1945* (Oxford, 1986); David Reynolds, "A 'Special Relationship'? America, Britain and the International Order Since the Second World War," *International Affairs* 62 (1985/86): 1–20.

Chapter Four

THE ENEMY IMAGE AS NEGATION OF THE IDEAL

Baron Dietrich Heinrich von Bülow (1763–1807)

Volker Depkat

The description of the United States that flowed from the quill of the Prussian baron Adam Dietrich Heinrich von Bülow did its share in shattering the enthusiasm for America among the enlightened-liberal, educated classes in the Germany of the 1790s. He traveled to the U.S. and lived there from 1791 to 1792 and again from 1795 to 1796. He cherished hopes that he would find material success as well as the dream of the enlightened state come true. But not only did his trade with Bohemian glassware, on which he had wanted to base his livelihood, turn into a grandiose failure: his business disaster was accompanied by the destruction of his utopia. Bülow's ideal of America was shattered by American reality, but eventually Bülow became the victim of his own mirage. In fifteen letters and in the two-volume *Der Freistaat von Nordamerika in seinem neuesten Zustand,* the Junker digested his American experience.[1] This chapter is based on Bülow's letters, which he wrote during his second stay in the U.S., and which were

---

1. The letters were published as: Dietrich Heinrich von Bülow, "Briefe eines Deutschen in America," in *Minerva: Ein Journal historischen und politischen Inhalts* (1796), 2:73–103, 486–517, 4:385–424, and (1797), 1:105–113. The monograph appeared as: Dietrich Heinrich von Bülow, *Der Freistaat von Nordamerika in seinem neuesten Zustand,* 2 vols. (Berlin, 1797).

published in the renowned Hamburg-based magazine *Minerva: Ein Journal historischen und politischen Inhalts* while he was still abroad.[2] Their contents mirror the process of Bülow's growing disappointment in its different stages much more directly than the monograph which he wrote after his return to Germany. The image of America presented in the book was only the result of the process revealed by the letters.

However, both works hit enlightened circles in Germany like a bombshell. For the first time, central beliefs about the U.S. among the enlightened-liberal parts of the educated classes were radically challenged by someone who seemingly had shared them before. The insulting arrogance with which Bülow defended his theses, dismissing his opponents as "Americomaniacs" without further ado, added to the stir he caused.[3]

Historians have noticed Bülow, to be sure, but they have not fully appreciated him. Eugene Edgar Doll's study "American History As Interpreted by German Historians from 1770–1815," published in 1948, is still the most extensive piece of work on Bülow.[4] Doll focused primarily on the academic treatment the U.S. received from German scholars. To him, Bülow was the great opponent of Christoph Daniel Ebeling (1741–1817), the leading specialist in American studies in his time. Ebeling was at the center of Doll's attention, and he did not so much care for the intrinsic value of Bülow's description. Finally, one cannot grasp the Bülow-Ebeling controversy's dynamism by interpreting it as a scholarly debate. Rather, it was a heated political discussion about the possibility and desirability of a state and society organized on the basis of freedom.

2. One finds access to this magazine only through biographical studies about its editor Johann Wilhelm von Archenholtz. Despite the fact that he was one of the leading journalists of his time, Archenholtz has not received much attention from historians. The only extensive study is: Friedrich Ruof, *Johann Wilhelm von Archenholtz: Ein deutscher Schriftsteller zur Zeit der Französischen Revolution und Napoleons (1741–1812)* (Berlin, 1915). The embarrassing situation of Archenholtz scholarship is revealed by the fact that Ruof's dissertation was reprinted fifty years after it first appeared (Vaduz, 1965). Short versions were incorporated into compilations about German publicists. Friedrich Ruof, "Johann Wilhelm von Archenholtz (1741–1812)," in *Deutsche Publizisten des 15. bis 20. Jahrhunderts*, ed. Heinz-Dietrich Fischer (Munich, Pullach, Berlin, 1971), 129–39; see also Michael Maurer, *Anglophilie und Aufklärung in Deutschland* (Göttingen, Zurich, 1987), 182–217.

3. Bülow, *Der Freistaat von Nordamerika*, vol. 1, 296.

4. Eugene Edgar Doll, "American History As Interpreted by German Historians from 1770–1815," *Transactions of the American Philosophical Society*, N.S., 38/5 (1948): 421–534.

Horst Dippel drew his study about the American Revolution's reception in Germany to a close with a short discussion of Bülow's work. He stressed the devastating blow Bülow gave to the enthusiasm for America. According to Dippel, Bülow must be given credit for having held "a more realistic picture of the United States" against the background of the "German bourgeoisie's greatly idealized views of it."[5] This chapter, however, will argue that Bülow's account did not offer a "more realistic picture" of the U.S., but simply exchanged the ideal for the nucleus of an enemy image instead. The critique of the U.S. was as boundless as its idealization had been before, and the real cause is hidden in the fact that, no matter how much imaginative power America itself evoked, the positive as well as the negative image of it was always generated and functionalized within the framework of an overall German enlightened-liberal Weltanschauung—the discussion was not so much about the U.S. itself.

When I speak of images of America, I define them generally as perceptions, notions, and mental concepts referring to the reality of the U.S. Images can thus be defined as intellectual constructions characterized by a complex structure of cognitive, emotional, and pragmatic elements. The knowledge of the U.S. is inseparably tied to an emotional value judgment. As such, images function within cultural contexts as vehicles for individual and group-specific sympathies and antipathies.[6] Not every negative image of the U.S. is also an enemy image. I define an enemy image as a specific negative image which matches Kurt and Kati Spillmann's bundle of characteristic features.[7]

This understanding of enemy images as complex intellectual constructions that function within a specific historical situation

5. Horst Dippel, *Germany and the American Revolution 1770–1800: A Sociohistorical Investigation of Late Eighteenth-Century Political Thinking* (Wiesbaden, 1978), 321.

6. In this definition images border on stereotypes. However, I do not take the content of images to be as firmly fixed as that of stereotypes. Also, images differ from stereotypes in the higher status they grant to the cognitive factor as opposed to the emotional component. Adam Schaff, *Stereotypen und das menschliche Handeln* (Vienna, Zurich, Munich, 1980), 27–106; Helge Gerndt, "Zur kulturwissenschaftlichen Stereotypenforschung," in *Stereotypvorstellungen im Alltagsleben: Beiträge zum Themenkreis Fremdbilder—Selbstbilder—Identität: Festschrift für Georg R. Schroubek*, ed. Helge Gerndt (Munich, 1988), 9–12; Ulrike Six, "The Functions of Stereotypes and Prejudices in the Process of Cross-Cultural Understanding: A Social Psychological Approach," in *Understanding the USA: A Cross-Cultural Perspective*, ed. Peter Funke (Tübingen, 1989), 42–62.

7. See Kurt R. and Kati Spillmann's chapter in this volume, "Some Sociobiological and Psychological Aspects of 'Images of the Enemy.'"

offers a possibility of combining the two diverging theoretical approaches that are presented by Ulrich Beck and the Spillmanns in this volume. Bülow's individual experience of America can best be analyzed along the social-cognitive and psychological categories which the Spillmanns focus on. Seen from this perspective, Bülow's image of America was the result of an ongoing dialogue between his preexisting mental concepts and his personal confrontation with American reality. The images of America that Bülow had in mind when he first boarded the ship set the cognitive patterns which regulated his discussion of the young republic across the Atlantic.

For the analysis of the reception of Bülow's work in Germany one can draw upon Beck's theoretical approach. To fit the historical situation in Germany between 1789 and 1830, however, Beck's definition of enemy images has to be modified. While I agree with Beck on the *social* and *situative* nature of enemy images, I would not want to link them too closely to legitimizing the power monopoly of the nation-state and the historic force of nationalism. In the process of its reception, Bülow's work was functionalized to defend a monarchic order and a hierarchically structured society against an alternative model of state based *solely* on freedom and equality. This debate, however, was not *primarily* regulated by a nationalistic mindset or the question of the power monopoly of the nation-state. It was a lot more diffuse and much more geared to defending monarchy and the need for social differentiation in the light of a radical alternative that proved to be a complete negation of these basic ideological positions. Yet, within the frame of reference characteristic of the historical situation between 1789 and 1830, some circles in Germany used Bülow's image of America as an outspoken enemy image that functioned along just the lines that Beck discusses in his chapter.

Thus, Bülow's description of the U.S. and its reception in Germany to about 1830 can be taken as a case study that offers the opportunity to show the genesis of an enemy image in its interaction with the given and changing historical conditions. I will examine how German contemporaries perceived the U.S.; how they integrated these perceptions into their own value system; and how these images of the U.S. functioned within the political, social, and cultural situation in Germany between 1789 and 1830.

To do so, I first want to describe the Prussian nobleman and glass merchant's ideal image of America as the outcome of a Weltanschauung centering in enlightened values and norms which was characteristic of the educated elite at the close of the eighteenth century. Then I want to move to the individual level to show the inherent tension between this enlightened ideal of America and Bülow's consciousness of his noble status as well as his political convictions. The analysis of Bülow's confrontation with American reality follows. Finally, I will characterize Bülow's reception and effect on German thought up to about 1830 in broad outline to show how the negative image of the U.S. that he depicted in simply negating the ideal was reduced to an outspoken enemy image as the political struggle intensified in Germany and partisanship started to polarize the political spectrum in the wake of Napoleon's reign.

The U.S. As a Group-Specific Utopia of an Enlightened-Liberal Ideal State

In traveling to the U.S., Bülow renounced Europe and turned toward an ideal world. In his particular case, this process was perhaps so pronounced because he was an outsider in his own culture. He fell between the worlds of nobility and bourgeoisie, as his biographical development will demonstrate.

Indeed, Baron Adam Dietrich Heinrich von Bülow was an enigmatic character; for Karl Ludwig von Woltmann he was even among "the most interesting people in the Prussian states." Julius von Voß characterized him, however, as "an interesting eccentric."[8] He was probably born in 1763 as Baron Friedrich Ulrich Arwegh

8. There are few biographical sources for Bülow, and for the most part they are marred by legends. The most extensive biographical sketches were written fifty years after his death: Karl August Varnhagen von Ense, *Leben des Generals Grafen Bülow von Dennewitz* (Berlin, 1853), 15–17; Paul von Bülow, ed., *Familienbuch der von Bülow: Nach der im Jahre 1780 herausgegebenen historischen, genealogischen und kritischen Beschreibung des Edlen, Freiherr- und Gräflichen Geschlechts von Bülow von Jacob Friedrich Joachim von Bülow ... bearbeitet und bis auf die Gegenwart fortgesetzt* (Berlin, 1858), 288–89. Both sketches are based on the only biographical description which was published while Bülow was still alive: [Julius von Voß], *Heinrich Bülow: Nach seinem Talentreichthum sowohl, als seiner sonderbaren Hyper-Genialität, und seinen Lebensabendtheuern geschildert* (Cölln, 1806); Karl Goedeke identified Julius von Voß as the author. Karl Goedeke, ed., *Grundriß zur Geschichte der deutschen Dichtung aus den Quellen*, 2d ed. (Dresden, 1893), 5: 537; Voß's characterization of Bülow on p. 3. Besides this work there is a second biographical source which was written shortly after Bülow's death. In the anonymously published *Gallerie preußischer Charaktere* a friend and admirer of Bülow, who had known him personally, gave a short sketch of his life: [Karl Ludwig von Woltmann] "Heinrich von Bülow," in *Gallerie*

von Bülow's fourth of five sons in Brandenburg's Altmark. His father, lord of the manor of Falkenberg, was deeply in debt. Like his brothers, Dietrich Heinrich von Bülow received his education from private tutors in his father's household. At the age of fifteen he left Falkenberg for the military academy in Berlin and joined the Marwitzian regiment of cuirassiers in 1783, but left the army for good at the rank of cornet two years later. The day he left the army, he was in a precarious situation socially as well as materially. In 1791 he went to the U.S. for the first time, but nothing is known about his experiences there. When he returned to Germany one year later he tried to make his fortune by assembling a troupe of actors, but this enterprise turned into a financial disaster even before the first performance had taken place. Meanwhile Bülow, hoping finally to achieve material security, had talked his brother Karl Ulrich into investing their paternal inheritance in Bohemian glassware to fill a supposed gap in the American market. In 1795 the brothers sailed to the U.S. to make their fortune, but things turned out quite differently than they had expected: obviously unfamiliar with a capitalistic market economy, they were broke within a year. Bülow never said what exactly became of their glassware.

After his second return from America in 1796, Bülow was without a job or regular income and decided to become a writer, more out of necessity than conviction. He made his debut with *Der Freistaat von Nordamerika in seinem neuesten Zustand* without ever appearing as an "expert" on the U.S. again, apart from short articles with which he defended his theses.[9] Rather, he engaged in writing about military matters and became one of the most radical critics of Prussia's army establishment. As a result he was imprisoned in 1806 and died in captivity one year later.

---

preußischer Charaktere (Germanien, 1808), 381–414. Eduard von Bülow identified Karl Ludwig von Woltmann as the author. Eduard von Bülow and Wilhelm Rüstow, eds., *Militärische und vermischte Schriften von Heinrich Dietrich von Bülow: In einer Auswahl mit Bülow's Leben und einer kritischen Einleitung* (Leipzig, 1853), 39. Woltmann's characterization of Bülow on p. 413.

9. In short articles he defended his theses after they were published: Dietrich Heinrich von Bülow, "Noch ein paar Worte über America," *Minerva* (1797), 4: 540–51. He also published a letter of his brother Karl Ulrich in: Dietrich Heinrich von Bülow, ed., "Fragmente eines Briefes aus Lancaster in Pennsylvanien, vom 16ten May 1798," *Minerva* (1798), 3:166–77. Cf. also: Bülow, "Über die politische Lage von America," *Minerva* (1798), 3:536–50. Christoph Martin Wieland's and Karl August Böttiger's *Der Neue Teutsche Merkur* also offered Bülow a forum for the defense of his work. Dietrich Heinrich von Bülow, "Ueber Amerika," *Der Neue Teutsche Merkur* (1798), 1:94–98, and Bülow, "Ueber Washingtons Briefe und N. Amerika," *Der Neue Teutsche Merkur* (1798), 2:129–36.

Although Bülow was socially speaking an outsider, one can observe certain traits in his ideal image of the U.S. which were shared among large portions of Germany's enlightened-liberal educated classes. Within a broader political public, America functioned above all as a projection surface for vague as well as constitutionally undefined conceptions of an enlightened-liberal ideal state and society. The political thinking of even the most progressive parts of the developing political spectrum in Germany did not match the constitutional radicalism of the American example. Thus, the idealization of the U.S. reveals above all the tensions and contradictions in the political consciousness of the educated at the end of the eighteenth century.

The young republic across the Atlantic had become a bourgeois utopia for Germany's educated classes by 1790, and this could happen only because the general relationship between Europe and America was perceived in terms of continuity.[10] The Enlightenment's universal categories, "reason," "humanity," and "freedom," as well as the philosophical interpretation of history which identified progress and emancipation as the forces behind all historical development, made it possible for the contemporaries to relate the Old World to the New on an overall continuum. Characteristically, those participants in the German debate who idealized America ostentatiously took up the attitude of a "friend of humanity" or "cosmopolitan."[11] Thus, the U.S. was not understood as the "other" or the "foreign." It appeared as the continuation of Europe under better conditions. There, it was felt, Enlightenment had become common practice. There, reason was the only maxim for the organization of state and society. The *Berlinisches Journal für Aufklärung* commented in 1789 on the constitutional guarantee of religious freedom in Virginia:

10. Dippel provides the most extensive documentation on the evolution of the German notion of an American bourgeois utopia. He interpreted it as one result of the American Revolution's reception in Germany. The young republic's idealization was directly related to its being contrasted with the French republic. Dippel, *Germany and the American Revolution*, 279–306. A more recent essay which analyzes this interaction is by Gonthier-Louis Fink, "Die amerikanische Revolution und die französische Revolution: Analogien und Unterschiede im Spiegel der deutschen Publizistik (1789–1798)," *Modern Language Notes* 103 (1988): 540–68.

11. "Nachrichten aus verschiedenen Ländern in Nord-America," *Historisch-Politisches Magazin nebst Litterarischen [sic] Nachrichten* 10 (1791): 686; Friedrich Gentz, "Ueber den Einfluß der Entdeckung von Amerika auf den Wohlstand und die Cultur des menschlichen Geschlechts," *Neue Deutsche Monatsschrift* (1795), 2:273; "Durchflüge," *Der Neue Teutsche Merkur* (1798), 1:236.

"Oh victory of reason!... do I finally find you across the sea, in the Fatherland of the savages, after I have vainly spent so much time looking for you in Europe, home of culture and Enlightenment."[12] That a model of continuity formed the basis of this statement is beyond doubt: geographically speaking, Enlightenment and culture originated in Europe, but in the New World the historical process of emancipation, which coincided with reason unfolding its power, had reached its goal. There, what in Europe was still within the realm of theory had been translated into everyday reality. In this way, America provided for Germany's enlightened-liberal circles the empirical evidence of the feasibility of their own ideals. Seen from the point of view of the philosophy of history, America marked the "end of history," which under Europe's present conditions could only be anticipated as the future.

Yet the functionalization of this ideal of America in the political discourse of the day remained strangely removed from concrete constitutional questions. In incorporating the ideal image of America into their own Weltanschauung, vast parts of Germany's educated elite concentrated upon the "new mankind," defined through moral and ethical categories, which had developed across the ocean due to the fact that Enlightenment was the foundation of the American order. In this context the principles of freedom and equality established by the American Revolution were not ends in themselves, but rather the means to an end that was much more important to enlightened Germans, that is, the ethical and moral improvement of society. In 1796, when Bülow was still in America, the audience of the *Berlinische Monatsschrift* could read the following statement from Justus Erich Bollmann about the U.S.: "Wealth, independence, greatest possible equality, freedom, and what only comes of it: these are morally speaking ... the most striking, shining features when looking at this country."[13]

Bülow's expectations, too, were primarily morally conditioned. He traveled to a republican state and expected to find a republican society. In his thinking such a society was characterized by "social

<hr>

12. "Akte, wegen Festsetzung der Religionsfreyheit, wie selbige in der Versammlung in Virginien zu Anfange des Jahres 1786 zu Stande gekommen ist," *Berlinisches Journal für Aufklärung* (1789), 2:179.

13. Justus Erich Bollmann, "Auszug eines Schreibens von Doktor Bollmann aus Philadelphia den 20. Juni 1796," *Berlinische Monatsschrift* 28 (1796): 464.

virtues," "patriarchal simplicity," "morality," and "innocence."[14] Roman antiquity served as an important point of reference for this ideal of a republican society. Especially the conduct of George Washington, who, besides Benjamin Franklin, appeared as the outstanding symbol of the republican America, repeatedly gave rise to comparisons with Roman examples. Above all, the fact that Washington had willingly resigned power twice, first as general at the end of the Revolutionary War, then at the end of his second term as president, provided ample evidence of his republican virtue, letting him appear as the new Cincinnatus.[15] The contemporaries understood Washington and Franklin as personifications of the American society. They saw Americans primarily as the "hopeful fellow citizens of a Franklin and Washington."[16] The characteristic features of the "new mankind" corresponded in large measure to the ideal of the Roman republicans, and it was not for nothing that Bülow's biographer, Julius von Voß, referred to Bülow's motives for emigration to the U.S.: "In Europe ..., Bülow thought,... mankind is too profane, away to lovely North America! There holy freedom sits enthroned. There the better citizen, filled with Roman spirit, walks under its plane trees and catalpas."[17]

These remarks show that in idealizing America as the enlightened state, the majority of Germans did not let themselves be guided by the example set by the U.S. itself. Rather, they simply projected onto the U.S. the ideal of a republic nourished by models from antiquity.

14. Bülow, "Briefe," *Minerva* (1796), 2:511.

15. Washington's *Farewell Address* was one of the few American documents that some German magazines published in unabridged translation. It provoked positive comparisons with the Roman example. "Washington's Adresse an das Volk der Vereinigten Staaten in America," *Minerva* (1796), 4:489–525; "Adresse des Präsidenten Washington bei seiner Resignation an das Volk der vereinigten [*sic*] Staaten vom 16. Sept. 1796," *Deutsches Magazin* 13 (1797): 174–206; "Georg Washington an das Volk der Vereinten FreiStaaten [*sic*] von NordAmerika [*sic*], bei Niederlegung seiner Stelle eines Präsidenten (Mit einer Einleitung)," *Europäische Annalen* (1796), 4:156–80. Burckhausen drew an explicit comparison to Cincinnatus in his biographical sketch: Count K. J. A. von Burckhausen, "Washington," *Minerva* (1796), 1:399. There is a good compilation of sources, including references to Franklin, in: Fink, "Die amerikanische Revolution," 548–52.

16. "Durchflüge," *Der Neue Teutsche Merkur* 1 (1798): 236–37; cf. also Dippel, *Germany and the American Revolution*, 248–56; Horst Dippel, "'Eripuit coelo fulmen sceptrumque tyrannis': Benjamin Franklin als die Personifizierung der amerikanischen Revolution," *Amerika-Studien* 23 (1978): 19–29.

17. Voß, *Heinrich Bülow*, 15–16.

The Tension of Enlightened Bourgeois Values and the Absolutist Conception of the State in Bülow's Weltanschauung

It is only too revealing of the ideal's constitutional vagueness that Bülow, who had grown up in an aristocratic environment, could share the basically bourgeois notion of an enlightened state across the Atlantic. The Junker's idealization of the U.S. did not have any consequences either for the consciousness of his noble status or his absolutist conception of the state. Nobility, Enlightenment, and absolutism lay tensely side by side in Bülow's individual Weltanschauung.

In Dietrich Heinrich von Bülow we witness a Prussian who was aware of his noble birth, and for whom the consciousness of being educated and enlightened was a very important element in his self-image. He took the level that culture and education had reached in Europe as a measure for judging American reality. Looking at the social habits of the Americans as well as their cultural and educational standing, he refused to concede to them any aesthetic refinement. In the field of music he considered them to be "true barbarians," and in any case the level of culture was generally "much lower than in Europe."[18] As a Prussian baron he despised the American "moneyed aristocracy" as upstarts, and in many anecdotes he ridiculed the conduct of the American "rabble."[19] George Washington, he wrote, was idolized by Americans, but they did so not because they acknowledged his achievements, but rather because they simply needed someone to idolize. Bülow found such behavior typical of the "rabble" and contrasted it with that of the nobility. "Such has always been the rabble's way, and to be sure the lowest-class's rabble, and not that of the courtiers because they pretend to worship their prince while they deride him in their hearts."[20]

His awareness of being enlightened, however, was closely confined to the fields of culture and education, thus remaining without consequences for his political thinking. His pronounced efforts to comprehend the U.S. in appropriate political terms is striking. In his letters, the words "republic," "sovereignty of the people," and "freedom" were ubiquitous; however, they referred only to the

18. Bülow, "Briefe," *Minerva* (1796), 2:507, 512.
19. Ibid. (1796), 2:504.
20. Ibid. (1796), 2:516.

ethics of state and society. In all that, Bülow's thinking was characterized by an almost manic fixation on the "common good," which was the focus of his reflections on state and society. This common good, however, was identified with the abstract welfare of the state, separate from the individual's interests and rights. In this fixation on an abstract common good, Bülow was the child of Prussian state theories—and in his analysis of the U.S. he never stepped out of this frame.

The common good was to guide the behavior of both the rulers and the ruled. The term "republic" described, according to the Prussian Junker, the "public cause" or "the common interest." In this very general definition the term referred to the quality of government policy independently of the type of state. Everything that served the common good was republican. He wrote: "Every government whose decrees promote the common good which results from the accumulation of the individual good is to be called republican, whatever the type of state." Consequently, he reasoned that even a despot could be a republican as long as he reigned in accord with the common good.[21]

Consequently he defined the term "sovereignty of the people" only along these lines. He saw it realized whenever the individual members of a society understood themselves as being a part of a larger whole, thereby subordinating their personal inclinations, desires and interests to "the common central point, the common good" without "making themselves the egoistic center." If this condition was met, "sovereignty of the people was in existence in all types of states."[22]

It is hardly surprising, then, to hear that "freedom," too, was nothing else than the "love of the good," and that "the good" was nothing more than the common best. Individuals achieved their freedom by serving the public good, and they became unfree the moment they made private interest the guiding principle of their conduct, thus becoming "slaves of their desires."[23]

This definition of republican terminology missed the central principles of American constitutional thought. In the founding fathers' republican theory there was no room for the identification of the individual good with the common good, the common good

21. All quotes ibid. (1796), 2: 87–88. To be sure, in this passage he defines the common good as an abstraction of the individual good. He leaves open, however, how this abstraction is achieved, and especially who defines the common good.

22. Ibid. (1796), 2:94.

23. Ibid. (1796), 4:385.

with the welfare of the state, or the government with the common good, as Willi-Paul Adams has stressed.[24] Small wonder that Bülow and an American gentleman he quoted talked at cross-purposes in their political dispute, which in turn had serious consequences for the way the German judged the American order:

> An American gentleman at a reception recently made a comment to the effect that the principle of republics was interest, that of monarchies vain honor. I replied that monarchies also loved their interest, believing he was referring to the interest of the state. However, I was surprised to find out that he had in mind the citizens' private interests, and he declared it to be the basic law of republics that every individual should do as little for the common good as possible.[25]

This passage reveals in condensed form the different levels of communication: to Bülow the common good was identical with the interest of the state that was defined by the monarch. In the U.S., this authority was missing, although it was theoretically possible for it to exist even in a republic if its citizens submitted themselves willingly to the service of the overriding common good. To fulfill the function of a state, a republic needed to be sustained by a society conditioned to serve it. In the group-specific ideal of America and the cornerstones of the individual Weltanschauung we thus have the most important prerequisites for Bülow's understanding of the U.S. when in 1795 he embarked on a ship to the New World for the second time.

The Negotiation of the Ideal in the Confrontation with Reality

In the confrontation with American reality, the tensions and contradictions at the core of the ideal become obvious to today's observer. Bülow's description of the republican society's reality can be read as a continuous dialogue with his ideal. This dialogue produced an image of the U.S. that was diametrically opposed to Bülow's own values, norms, and interests.

24. Willi-Paul Adams, *Republikanische Verfassung und bürgerliche Freiheit: Die Verfassungen und politischen Ideen der amerikanischen Revolution* (Darmstadt, Neuwied, 1973), 132. See also Timothy H. Breen's remarks about American conceptions of state power at the Krefeld Symposium. Hermann Wellenreuther and Claudia Schnurmann, eds., *Die amerikanische Verfassung und deutsch-amerikanisches Verfassungsdenken: Ein Rückblick über 200 Jahre* (New York, Oxford, 1990), 177–8.

25. Bülow, "Briefe," *Minerva* (1796), 2:504–5.

Things had not even started out that badly. The first breakfast in Philadelphia's City Tavern was good and filling. But while Bülow used this experience initially to refute Buffon's theory that, due to climatic conditions, nature—and thus the food, too—had degenerated in America, his willingness to defend the Americans against their critics soon turned into the direct opposite.[26]

As could hardly be expected otherwise, the Prussian baron focused in his description primarily on the "national character" of the Americans. To discover it, however, he did not travel very extensively but apparently confined himself to the regions around Philadelphia and Lancaster.[27] He seems not to have advanced to the wealthier circles, as Friedrich August Mühlenberg later revealed. The first speaker of the House of Representatives wrote: "What came to be well known of him here was that he was very proud of his aristocratic status, and that his most distinguished companions were his hounds and pointers which made him a burden to everyone."[28]

In Bülow's description the Americans were transformed from a "people of philosophers" into a people of egotists wallowing in the "mud of their desires" with the sole motivation for action being the satisfaction of their private passions.[29] A "systematic material egoism" was commonly practiced, Bülow wrote, contrasting this observation with his expectations: "One could expect this of the Jews but one really wonders about people who are believed to be exemplary republicans in Europe."[30]

Yet his description went beyond simply contrasting isolated observations to the image of his ideal. He integrated them into a whole network in which the political and economic system as well as the character of a society were interrelated. Out of this causality grew the vicious circle. The Americans were neither virtuous nor moral since they were the offspring of European immigrants who had not been so either. "How can one possibly expect the Americans to be such great heroes of virtue since they

26. Ibid. (1796), 2:77, 79–80. Gerbi's book is standard for the history of the degeneration hypothesis: Antonello Gerbi, *La Disputa del Nuovo Mondo: Storia di una Polemica 1750–1900* (Milan, Naples, 1955), English translation: *The Dispute of the New World: The History of a Polemic 1750–1900*, trans. Jeremy Moyle (Pittsburgh, 1973).

27. All his letters were sent from these two cities.

28. Christoph Daniel Ebeling, ed., "Einige Briefe aus Amerika, Herrn D. von Bülows Nachrichten, den nordamerikanischen Freistaat betreffend," *Der Genius der Zeit* 15 (1798): 127–76, 279–91, quotation, 281.

29. Bülow, "Briefe," *Minerva* (1797), 1: 109.

30. Ibid. (1796), 2:505–6.

have descended from Europeans who, to say the least, were not better than their brothers who remained in Europe," Bülow asked. Here the lines of continuity were suddenly drawn on a different level. By emigrating to America, the Europeans of the lowest class had remained Europeans of the lowest class, and had been left to themselves. An authority which could have promoted their refinement had been missing in America. Quite the reverse, the liberal economic system had corrupted them further because due to it, they were in a position to indulge in their private desires. Bülow made commerce responsible for the fact "that the people, totally sunk in the mud of desires, make the satisfaction of their dirty egoism the sole motivating force behind their miserable actions."[31]

In order to let a republic function, however, the Americans should have been moral and virtuous. Yet the way things were in the U.S., the republic was, according to Bülow, put solely to the service of private passions. He argued that generally only the aristocracy of wealth profited from Congressional legislation.[32] After all, Bülow reduced the political controversies between the Federalists and the Jeffersonian Republicans to a simple clash of conflicting material interests. "Indeed, I do believe that one is not mistaken if one boldly claims that each of these parties has in mind only its own benefit just as well as within each party every individual has his." This egoism, however, appeared to Bülow to be caused not by the lust for power, but rather by the lust "to own the goods of this world."[33] In turn, this lust perverted in Bülow's view the purpose of every state, namely serving the common good. Instead of the common good, private passion reigned in the U.S., and the republic perpetuated the status quo. In America an authority defining the common good was missing, and therefore the Americans were corrupt; they had always been so and would continue to be so. On balance, the conclusion he drew was the following:

> If the people are corrupt, no law, in case the people have the power of legislation due to the constitution, will ever be the expression of the common will but the result of egoistic private passions which destroy the common good and as a consequence also the common will.[34]

31. Ibid. (1796), 2:488–90.
32. Ibid. (1796), 2:90–91.
33. Ibid. (1796), 2:488.
34. Ibid. (1796), 2:94–95.

At this point the U.S. became the epitome of a political and social order that was diametrically opposed to Bülow's ideological principles. The ideal had turned into the germ of an enemy image, which already bore some of the traits mentioned by Kurt and Kati Spillmann in this volume, namely stereotyping the Americans and identifying their order with evil. The elements missing to match the Spillmanns' definition are negative anticipation and a feeling of threat. Bülow's disappointment did not cause him to feel threatened. Quite the contrary, in the end he still hoped that the Americans would reform their manners to live up to the republican ideal he still had in mind. "Americans!" he shouted to the inhabitants of the New World when he was back in Germany, "I have told you bitter truths because I love you."[35] In a similar statement in one of his last letters from America he had proclaimed his hope "that they may better themselves, change their habits and become true republicans which they now are certainly not."[36]

However, in his description of the U.S. Bülow already drew new lines of continuity between the Old and the New World which amounted to the basic thesis that, at the present state of humanity's historical development, a republic was not possible. Thereby, he functionalized his image of America for legitimizing the feudal-absolutist structures in Germany. His description reached its climax in the statement: "tout comme chez nous"—everything just as corrupt as in Europe.[37] With this sentence America was once again seen within a European continuum, this time, however, under reversed circumstances. Bülow commented with resignation:

And so the flourishing American freedom is already wilted in its young blossom! And hopes that a numerous people under the guidance of a wise government and in the bosom of peace, virtue, and innocence, would make unheard-of progress in the cultivation of man and nature has painfully been disappointed here *also*.[38]

After the escalation of the French Revolution into the *Terreur*, which was a shocking experience for the largest part of Germany's educated classes, humanity not only in Europe but also in America appeared unready for the realization of enlightened-liberal principles. Bülow's remarks must have reverberated badly in the ears of his contemporaries. To the degree that they had turned

35. Bülow, "Über die politische Lage von America," *Minerva* (1798), 3:544.
36. Bülow, "Briefe," *Minerva* (1797), 1:551.
37. Ibid. (1796), 4:424.
38. Bülow, "Über die politische Lage von America," *Minerva* (1798), 3:542–43.

away from the French Revolution in dismay, many of them had resorted to the U.S. as the last repository for their enlightened hopes.[39] Reading Bülow's work, suddenly the only imagined empirical proof of the feasibility of their ideals seemed to fade away. After the tremor caused by the earthquake of the French Revolution, the enlightened-liberal certainty of salvation was exposed to an—albeit much weaker—aftershock as the reception of Bülow's works in Germany will show.

The Enemy Image "America" As Legitimization for the Monarchical-Absolutist Political Order: The Reception of Bülow's Work Up to 1830

Up until 1830, the negative image of the U.S. drawn by Bülow was condensed into an outspoken enemy image, especially within the conservative-reactionary camp. All it took was a progressive differentiation and polarization of the political spectrum in Germany. Beginning in the Napoleonic reign, and increasingly so after the wars of liberation, the camps of the reactionary forces and that of the liberal reformers were drifting apart. The liberal answers to the question of how to give a new definition to the relationship between the rulers and the ruled were increasingly shaking the foundations of the monarchical-absolutist order itself. As this happened, the defenders of the status quo resorted to repressive measures. The decrees of Karlsbad were an attempt to stop public discussion about alternative models of the state. This policy was accompanied by the development of monarchist ideology: the absolute monarchy, which was founded in religion and dynastic legitimacy, served as ideological glue for the Holy Alliance shaped by Prince Klemens von Metternich. In this repressive political climate of the 1820s, Bülow's negative image of the U.S. was increasingly turned into an enemy image by the supporters of the status quo. At the same time, the discussion about the U.S. in Germany's liberal camp did not develop the radicalism necessary to set an undiluted ideal of America against the enemy image of the reactionary camp. Quite the contrary, elements of Bülow's image of the U.S. spread widely in liberal circles. Thus, until 1830, negative images of the U.S. were primarily used in the political discourse of Germany's magazines for legitimizing the monarchical order.

39. Dippel, *Germany and the American Revolution*, 289–301; Fink, "Die amerikanische Revolution," 558–64.

It is an expression of Bülow's typicality that his writings on the U.S. were taken seriously in the Germany of the 1790s, very seriously indeed. The effort of Christoph Daniel Ebeling, the age's leading expert in American studies and apologist of the ideal state across the ocean, to refute Bülow's theses is striking. He sent a few copies especially to the Mühlenbergs in the U.S. together with a request for comment. Ebeling immediately published the answers he received from Heinrich and his brother Friedrich August in the magazine *Der Genius der Zeit*, edited by August Hennings.[40] Before he could do this, however, he had already launched an attack against Bülow with his own writings.[41]

It is only too characteristic that as a theoretician Ebeling, though he had an intimate knowledge of the American Constitution, communicated on a level that was simply irrelevant to Bülow's line of argument. Ebeling had an easy job exposing the vague and contradictory terms in Bülow's theory of the state as complete nonsense. He revealed convincingly Bülow's lack of knowledge and understanding of the American Constitution, laws, and history. Yet where Bülow talked about morality, virtue, and national character, Ebeling spoke of constitutional law and judicial principles. Thus Ebeling doubted the violence against the Indians, which Bülow wrote on in his monograph although not in his letters, and remarked as a counterargument that the colonies had passed legislation "to the benefit of the Indians."[42] The intentional bankruptcies that Bülow claimed to be fairly common were forbidden by law, Ebeling wrote.[43] Due to this retreat to a bookish and judicial line of argument, Ebeling was less convincing when it came to the question of concrete social realities. Here, he contented himself with the statement:

> How exactly he [Bülow] has observed the *general* morals, judgments, and opinions, the manner of social interaction, the *general* taste etc., having only traveled in one part of the middle states, this can only be decided by those who have extensively traveled through all states.[44]

The debate developed into a dispute between practicians and theoreticians. Even the Mühlenberg letters could only weaken Bülow's image in part, not really erase it completely. The Mühlenbergs

40. Ebeling, "Einige Briefe aus Amerika."
41. [Christoph Daniel Ebeling] "Ein paar Rezensionen, Amerika betreffend," *Americanisches Magazin* (1797), 4:170–84.
42. Ibid., 176.
43. Ibid., 180.
44. Ibid., 175. Emphasis in the original.

were right in defending themselves against the undifferentiated generalization of Bülow's observations. One could not judge a whole nation by the actions of a few individuals, Heinrich Mühlenberg commented.[45] However, even the Mühlenbergs could not dispute the rampant materialism that corrupted the morals. Even the frequency of business fraud was not denied. "Yes," Heinrich Mühlenberg conceded, "fraud is widespread and is very much deplored by every honest American."[46]

Other contemporaries who, in contrast to Ebeling, were not outspoken experts on America were initially quite confused by Bülow's work. In 1797 Archenholtz emphasized in a review the contradictions in the Junker's description without really coming to a final judgment about American national character. That all Americans were supposed to be swindlers appeared to him to be a malicious generalization, especially with the U.S. trade balances in mind. "It would be strange that the trade of such a nation is still booming," he wrote incredulously.[47] Bülow's account of widespread egoism, too, did not accord with the events during the Revolutionary War, when the Americans had selflessly committed themselves to the common cause in patriotic devotion. All in all, Archenholtz did not want to condemn Bülow's work completely, but it was "comforting to him that he was able to doubt a good many of the things he read in it for many reasons."[48] A few months later, Bülow's work already appeared to Archenholtz in a more favorable light. All that Archenholtz still criticized was its insulting tone and Bülow's hasty writing, relying only on questionable sources. Apart from that, however, it offered many new insights and "very interesting information, and many deep, partly astute remarks."[49]

Der Neue Teutsche Merkur, next to the *Minerva* one of the most popular journals in those days, took the same line. To be sure, one did not believe everything Bülow said and considered his generalizations to be quite inappropriate, but this author, too, agreed with Bülow that "in the case of most North Americans business egoism has devoured all nobler inclinations."[50]

45. Ebeling, "Einige Briefe aus Amerika," 137.

46. Ibid., 157.

47. The review was published in *Beyträge von Gelehrten Sachen* which was a supplement to the *Hamburgische Neue Zeitung*, 1 February 1797. Ebeling reprinted it in his *Americanisches Magazin*, "Ein paar Rezensionen," 171.

48. Ibid., 172.

49. Archenholtz, "Miscellen," *Minerva* (1797), 3:186.

50. "Filadelphia: Literatur und Vergnügungen der Nordamerikaner," *Der Neue Teutsche Merkur* (1797), 2:169.

Thus, the promise of a "new mankind" on the other side of the Atlantic had been shattered by the end of the 1790s. Bülow alone did not extinguish the fiery enthusiasm for America in Germany. He had this effect because similar news which seemed to support his view increasingly made its way into the German press.[51] All in all, the change in opinion about America among large parts of Germany's educated classes did not end the preoccupation with America, but it did allocate a different status to the U.S. in the overall Weltanschauung. It soon became a widely shared belief that the U.S. had very little to offer to the educated. For the poorer classes as well as for those who hoped to gain material wealth through their own hands' work, it had still many opportunities in store, but not so for the people "of education and taste."[52] Yet some enlightened-liberals were not willing to abandon the hopes connected with the U.S. completely. However, they projected their hopes into the future, far away from their own age. Archenholtz thus allowed for a possible change to the better, but it was no longer a concern with regard to the present "Philosophical Century." It could be, he wrote, that perhaps in the twentieth or twenty-first century it would be "very nice to live in America even for the most distinguished Europeans," but at the moment there were not many signs pointing in this direction.[53]

The controversy at the end of the 1790s was largely a debate among men of the eighteenth century. Their political consciousness had been molded during the golden age of Frederick the Great's Prussia after the Seven Years' War. Their political demands did not really put them outside the existing absolutist order. The generation whose politicization was deeply rooted in the experience of Germany's wars of liberation and the following period of political repression brought about a change in the

51. Archenholtz mentions in this context a lecture of Talleyrand's at the National Institute in Paris; the experience of a certain Delius, merchant from the city of Bremen; Count Burckhausen's article about George Washington (see note 15) in the *Minerva*; as well as an article in *Der Neue Teutsche Merkur*. Archenholtz, "Miscellen," *Minerva* (1797), 3:186–88. Talleyrand's lecture was published in the *Minerva* in 1812. "Talleyrand's Bemerkungen über die Handelsverhältnisse der Vereinigten Staaten von Nordamerika mit England," *Minerva* (1812), 2:243–79. For the article in *Der Neue Teutsche Merkur* quoted by Archenholtz see note 50.

52. Benjamin Franklin's thoughts on emigration had laid an authoritative basis for the further development of this opinion. They were published by Archenholtz as: Benjamin Franklin, "Nachricht für diejenigen, die nach Nordamerika sich begeben und alldort ansiedeln wollen," *Neue Litteratur und Völkerkunde* (1790), 2:138–54.

53. Archenholtz's comment in: Burckhausen, "Washington," 395; see also note 15.

idealization of America. The terms "freedom" and "republic" were increasingly defined along constitutional lines, and the change in the idealization of America corresponded to this development.[54] At the same time the notion of all-encompassing progress as the moving historical force was retained. However, the constitutional guarantee of human rights and the principles for the organization of state and society generated by them were increasingly taken to be the real manifestations of progress. Ludwig Börne's journal *Die Wage* [sic] thus commented in 1818: "The political development of humanity has reached a level in the New World which in this splendor can be seen nowhere else in the world." The author singled out the "political institutions based on natural human rights" as the main reason for America's much-admired progress.[55] After the wars of liberation, the enlightened ideal of America of the 1790s was increasingly politicized in ever more concrete constitutional terms within the context of a liberal agenda of demands.

The formation of a liberal platform in Germany after 1815, however loosely held together it may appear in light of the events after 1830, corresponded to a hardening of the feudal-aristocratic position. For them, the image of America presented by Bülow fitted nicely when it came to defending the supremacy of the aristocratic elite against liberal models of state and society that were becoming increasingly dominant. Bülow had already seen the landed gentry as the only guardian of the common good in a monarchy,[56] and now the negative image of America was reduced to an outspoken enemy image within the conservative discourse, since the U.S. was explicitly addressed as the "land of the third estate," thus representing evil incarnate. Johann Georg Hülsemann, referring to Bülow in 1823, stressed "that the higher interests of a human being cannot be protected without the existence of a true church and a hereditary nobility," and that was why he thought he had to deplore

54. Looking back in 1821 a reviewer gave a short sketch of the history of the idea of freedom. He said that before the French Revolution freedom in Europe had not yet been defined as "general rights of the people,... popular participation in legislation and government ... and the limitation of the sovereign's power through it." The American Revolution, so the reviewer continued, had for the first time defined freedom in this way, and had transformed this abstract theory into reality. Q. B. O., "Das positive Staatsrecht der europäischen Völker: Gemeinschaftliche Darstellungen und Sammlungen," *Hermes* (1821), 2:13, 15.

55. M., "Der europäische Staatenbund und der nordamerikanische," *Die Wage* [sic] (1818), 3:105–6.

56. Bülow, *Freistaat von Nordamerika*, 1:94–95.

"the absence of them, wherever it might be."[57] Hülsemann did not confine himself merely to lamenting. He also felt threatened by the American order and thus another feature of an enemy image, listed by the Spillmanns, was added to Bülow's description. To Hülsemann, the relationship between America and Europe appeared to be "distinctly hostile" since America questioned not only the foundations of the feudal-aristocratic order that were defined as the integral part of "the European," but also played an active role in overthrowing this very order.[58] "The liberals in France, the radicals in England are to be understood as the spearheads of this transatlantic battle formation." Hülsemann, later a diplomat in Metternich's service, continued: "We may already take it as a portent of victory if we are able to drive back the advanced lines of the enemy and to shift the theatre of battle to his territory."[59]

Yet Bülow's image of America went far beyond the conservative-reactionary discourse of the 1820s and penetrated deeply into liberal circles, which eventually led to a new consensus within Germany's political spectrum. The dispute about the social prerequisites of a republican state remained a central topic in Germany's debate about America. A strange ambivalence was the result: positive and negative aspects lay side by side, and the dividing line ran not only between the developing political camps but also right through them.

Those who supported the monarchy, whether from an enlightened-liberal or reactionary point of view, used their image of American reality to prove the basic assumption that republican and democratic principles led inevitably to the dissolution of all social order. "Unfortunately it is proven every day," a correspondent from the U.S. wrote in Johann Friedrich Cotta's *Morgenblatt für gebildete Stände* in 1821, "that the feature distinguishing monarchies from democratic republics seems to be that the former guarantees tranquillity and security whereas the latter guarantees freedom and

57. Johann Georg Hülsemann, *Geschichte der Democratie in den Vereinigten Staaten von Nordamerika* (Göttingen, 1823), xvii-xviii. For a biographical sketch of Hülsemann (1799–1868), who was lecturer in law at the University of Göttingen when he published his book on America, see the article "Hülsemann, Johann Georg," in *Deutsches Biographisches Archiv*. The references listed there are very vague, only dealing with the time from 1799 to 1830. See also Eckhart G. Franz, *Das Amerikabild der deutschen Revolution von 1848/49: Zum Problem der Übertragung gewachsener Verfassungsformen* (Heidelberg, 1958), 4–7. On p. 5, note 9 one finds additional literature concerning Hülsemann.

58. Hülsemann, *Geschichte der Democratie*, viii.

59. Ibid., xii.

equality." In the U.S., he understood the social hierarchy as well as domestic peace to be in a process of dissolution, and he drew the conclusion: "Thus it goes in republics without republican virtue."[60]

The social consequences of freedom and equality remained a problem for liberal contemporaries. In the U.S., or so it appeared to many German liberals, the individual's autonomy seemed to have gotten completely out of control and had resulted in the total destruction of all ties that bound the individual to a common cause. This perception in turn gave new impetus to the deep-rooted fears about the potential consequences of their own principles; fears which the German liberals had harbored ever since the French Revolution. This fear induced them to accept the fundamental premises of the monarchical order. In 1823 the *Morgenblatt für gebildete Stände* published the remarks of a Swiss emigrant to the U.S.:

> It [the U.S.] is like feverish wanderings come true. At one moment one rejoices at the magnificent lot of becoming a citizen of this magnificent country, and being allowed to live under such a just and wise constitution and government, with such an unprejudiced, moral, and educated people, and the next moment one wants to escape to an empty desert. In the constitution one detects only the principle of eternal anarchy, legislation only seems to support horror; in the people one sees but a crowd of riff-raff which has lost every feeling for virtue, order and respectability; one no longer finds pleasant, gentle education but only animal self-satisfaction.[61]

Letters like this prove that contemporaries in the 1820s were still thinking about America in the categories of Bülow's imagination. Even the liberal journalist Eduard Widenmann, who had accused Hülseman of having "collected all the bad news about it [the U.S.] in the good Göttingen library" for his history of democracy in America, wrote in 1826:

> Whoever is attracted by the term republic may go there [to the U.S.] and see for himself, but he will not find much of a republic's essence in the minds of the inhabitants; not even the most biased traveler has ever called them magnanimous republicans capable of great sacrifice. Although many things have changed and improved over the past twenty-eight years, Bülow's work can still be taken as the basis for an accurate view of North America.[62]

60. "Korrespondenz-Nachrichten: Bruchstück eines Briefs aus Philadelphia vom 20. April 1820," *Morgenblatt für gebildete Stände*, no. 4 (1821): 16.

61. "Amerikanische Anekdoten," *Morgenblatt für gebildete Stände*, no. 29 (1823): 115.

62. Eduard Widenmann, *Die nordamerikanische Revolution und ihre Folgen* (Erlangen, 1826), 191; his criticism of Hülsemann is on p. 258. There is a very informative

Thus, the general ambiguity in the attitudes toward America which was characteristic of the controversy in the 1790s remained an integral part of the German discourse. The admiration for the realization of an enlightened-liberal order of state and society in America was time and again frustrated by looking at the social realities there. The real reason for this kind of thinking, however, was still the same as in the case of Baron Adam Dietrich Heinrich von Bülow: the German debate on the U.S. always developed into a confrontation with the abstract ideal of a republic, which was generated from a specifically German Weltanschauung and from references to antiquity. American reality was measured according to the ideal, and it comes as no surprise that the results were mixed. In its most extreme form, this discussion produced out-spoken enemy images, in its weaker form ambivalent images of the U.S., but in any case America remained a controversial issue up to 1830, and Bülow had contributed substantially to this development. Even in 1830, Ernst Ludwig Brauns wrote: "Primarily, the eccentric and effusive Bülow is to blame for the many wrong ideas about America." With a sharp analytical view, the liberal Brauns revealed the fateful mixture of noble status consciousness, disappointed hopes, and especially business failure which had all interacted to produce Bülow's image of America. "If Bülow had really managed to rise above his prejudices that he had absorbed since his birth," Brauns commented, "and if he had not been deprived of a very large part of his fortune due to his carelessness and his ignorance of America's world of commerce, truly his work would have turned out quite differently."[63]

Conclusion

Images of America, that is, perceptions, notions, and mental concepts about American reality, did not stand isolated for themselves,

---

review of Widenmann's book in: "Die nordamerikanische Revolution und ihre Folgen. Ein Versuch von Ed. Wiedeman [*sic*]. Erlangen, Palm und Enke. 1826," *Blätter für literarische Unterhaltung*, no. 239 (1827): 953–55. There is very little biographical information on Widenmann. The *Deutsches Biographisches Archiv* does not list an entry. Franz characterizes Widenmann as a "liberal journalist" who later worked for Cotta's magazine *Das Ausland*. Franz, *Amerikabild*, 7, note 25.

63. Ernst Ludwig Brauns, *Skizzen von Amerika: Zu einer belehrenden Unterhaltung für gebildete Leser und mit besonderer Rüksicht [sic] auf Reisende und Auswanderer nach Amerika* (Halberstadt, 1830), 60–61.

no matter whether they transported a positive or a negative attitude, or whether they were even reduced to an outspoken enemy image. They were not autonomous categories, reproductions of a given situation, or simple expressions of an individual experience. Rather, they were embedded in an overriding system of time-specific values and norms, emotions and mentalities, interests and ideologies, as well as social and political developments. Images of America were thus always part of a Weltanschauung which created identity on an individual as well as on a group level.

The case of Bülow has shown that even contradictory images of America, ideal as well as developing enemy images, were the product of one and the same Weltanschauung. At one level, Bülow's American experience was an individual affair, of course, but simultaneously in its dynamics it was typical of the time and cannot be divorced from widely shared perceptions of and notions about the U.S. among Germany's educated classes. The immediate cause for Bülow's negative description of the U.S. is to be found in the economic disaster he and his brother experienced with their Bohemian glassware. In his letters, however, he painstakingly avoided mentioning this fact. He is silent about his private failure in the capitalistic market economy. But this alone does not sufficiently explain his attitude towards the U.S. Bülow did not belong to the group of really original thinkers of the Enlightenment, and yet he was inspired by an enlightened feeling of dissatisfaction with regard to his social, political, and, first of all, cultural environment; a feeling which was fed by the belief in an objectively possible better future. In this context, a whole bundle of vague and all-encompassing hopes was projected onto the U.S. Bülow's political thoughts did not excel in theoretical clarity, let alone inner coherence. Ostentatiously, he insisted that he was measuring the U.S. in appropriate categories, and yet he was never *willing* to transcend an enlightened but absolutist, and therefore contradictory, theory of the state. This makes him an instructive example of the reception of enlightened thought within a broader community. At the level of journals, ideas, values, and norms originating in enlightened philosophy had, in a sense, become hollow. They circulated in the educated classes' sphere of communication, and they were condensed into an attitude toward life that was fashionable, although laden with tension. In the case of Bülow, too, the certainty of being ahead of his contemporaries with regard to education and a belief in Enlightenment had become a pose. The status consciousness of the nobility and enlightened-bourgeois values were ambiguously combined. Confronted with American reality, the ideal became the victim of its own contradictions.

In their concrete formation, images, and thus enemy images, too, are not anthropological constants, although their contents might show an astonishing longevity. They originate and develop within contingent historical contexts. The analysis of Bülow's reception in Germany up to 1830 has given us the opportunity to understand the genesis of an outspoken enemy image, "America." It resulted from the continuing polarization of the political spectrum in Germany. Only after the political and socioeconomic program of the liberal camp had taken shape to a degree that it was perceived as a threat to the status quo did the actual enemy image "America" come into being. That the conservative-reactionary fears do not stand up to a critical examination from today's perspective was demonstrated by the way liberal participants in the discussion viewed the U.S. Their discourse about America at no point reached the systematic radicalism of the American model. Until 1830, most German liberals were susceptible to the fears that helped to generate the enemy image "America."

PART III

ETHNIC ISSUES

Chapter Five

GERMAN IMMIGRANTS AND AFRICAN-AMERICANS IN MID-NINETEENTH CENTURY AMERICA

Hartmut Keil

This chapter is part of a larger study that intends to explore the relationship between German immigrants and African-Americans in the antebellum period. Traditionally, racial and ethnic relations in mid-nineteenth century America have been described as dominated by racial antagonism, hatred, and violence that often erupted into mob action, lynching, and murder of black Americans. The standard explanation for this hostile record has been that these groups had similar socioeconomic status and competed for the same jobs in the labor market. Previous joint exploratory research by James Horton and myself[1] implies that this stereotypical view was largely shaped by studying the Irish as the largest and most visible immigrant group. It has raised substantial doubt, however, as to the applicability of this model to the second largest immigrant group, i.e., the Germans, arriving before the Civil War. Although German immigrants also subscribed to the ideology of nineteenth-century racism, it often

1. James O. Horton and Hartmut Keil, "African Americans and Germans in Mid-Nineteenth Century Buffalo," in *Free People of Color: Inside the African American Community,* ed. James Oliver Horton (Washington, D.C. and London, 1993), 170–83.

found different and less confrontational expression among them than among the Irish. Filiopietistic evaluations of German immigration have indeed emphasized the opposition of German immigrants to slavery. They pointed out that these immigrants formulated protests, petitions, and resolutions against the institution; contributed substantial membership to the Republican Party; and supported John Frémont as the most consistent opponent of the "peculiar institution." These interpretations contributed to the myth that German votes were decisive in electing Lincoln to the presidency.[2]

The myth about the Germans and the stereotype of the Irish both need to be revised. This study intends to do so for German immigrants. Their relationship to African-Americans has been largely ignored, not only with respect to the period under consideration here. As Randall Miller summed up the current debate six years ago: "Although the literature on inter-group relations and conflict has been growing of late, no study of black-German perceptions, relationships, or conflicts exists. To date scholars have yet to map the geographical, much less the cultural, social, economic, or political linkages between Germans and blacks in America."[3]

Focusing on selected cities from the Northeast, Midwest, and South, the study will explore the following hypotheses:

1. German cultural and political traditions, relative numerical strength of both groups in specific local settings, the near absence of direct occupational competition coupled with a difference in class status, and specific patterns of spatial proximity in the neighborhoods molded social relations in ways that tended to alleviate racial tensions.

2. Racism as practiced in the United States was not automatically adopted by immigrants when they stepped ashore but was a gradual learning process and an integral part of, or even precondition to, becoming integrated into American society. For the German immigrant community it seems as if this process took place at an accelerated pace in the decades following the Civil War.

2. Cf. Frederick Luebke, ed., *Ethnic Voters and the Election of Lincoln* (Lincoln, Nebraska, 1971); Jörg Nagler, *Fremont contra Lincoln: Die deutsch-amerikanische Opposition in der Republikanischen Partei während des amerikanischen Bürgerkrieges* (Frankfurt, 1984).

3. Randall Miller, "Preface," in *States of Progress: Germans and Blacks in America over 300 Years*, ed. Randall Miller (Philadelphia, 1989), xi.

Within this larger framework this chapter will isolate the specific issue of mutual intellectual traditions and a common philosophical heritage that may account for sympathy for abolitionism and anti-slavery sentiment among parts of the German immigrant population. I suggest that European and American Enlightenment thought evolved not in isolation, but through an intense exchange of ideas that crossed the Atlantic in both directions. Between the German states and North America a transatlantic intellectual network evolved in the process of emigration from Germany from the 1820s onward that was nourished by personal contact, travel, intellectual exchange of letters, books, and the leading contemporary German-language journals and papers in both the United States and in Germany so that a sophisticated level of information emerged, as evidenced in a variety of publications on the United States. I will pay close attention to Alexander von Humboldt as an embodiment of the enlightened scholar and humanist in Germany, who had a tremendous impact on German immigrants, and to Ottilie Assing as a journalist intellectual closely involved in the abolitionist cause who influenced important intellectual circles in Germany through her reports.

European Enlightenment Thought and the American Example

The European and American Enlightenment were connected in a mutually reinforcing way.[4] Paradoxically, it was on the North American continent that the Enlightenment tradition first went beyond intellectual circles, left behind purely philosophical implications, and assumed an immediately practical impact. Europeans saw the Declaration of Independence and the American Revolution as a victory of Enlightenment thought as it had emerged on the old continent. Even before the Fourth of July, 1776, the German educated public closely followed developments in England's North American colonies. One of Germany's major newspapers, the *Leipziger Zeitung*, declared that "the conflict between England and its colonies is at present the most important event of all public affairs. Everyone takes close interest in it, and everyone takes a

4. Cf. Robert R. Palmer, *The Age of the Democratic Revolution: A Political History of Europe and America, 1760–1800*, vol. 1: *The Challenge* (Princeton, NJ, 1959); Otto Vossler, *Die amerikanischen Revolutionsideale in ihrem Verhältnis zu den europäischen untersucht an Thomas Jefferson* (Munich and Berlin, 1929).

stand."[5] With differing degrees of intensity, Europeans kept informed of the progress of the war and of American independence. However, theirs was a particular perception guided by aspirations they had for their own societies. Their interpretation of the American Revolution thus did not mirror the reality of American institutions and life but rather universal ideals to be aspired to in the European context of the Napoleonic era and the wars of liberation.

In the case of the German states where the beginnings of a viable liberal opposition were barely evident at that time and mostly confined to cultural expressions anyway, American independence was a tremendous boost for suppressed longings to be freed from the despotism and tyranny of feudal domination and absolutist monarchy.[6] Public discussion quickly assigned the American Revolution an idealistic and utopian quality. The historical event of American independence was rationalized into an ideological symbol of the universal aspirations of humanity.[7] The considerable and increasing number of publications on the topic were uninformed by firsthand experience and remained theoretical for the most part. Actual social developments and the important constitutional debates of the 1780s were widely ignored by the German bourgeoisie. Instead the American Revolution appeared to them as a free-floating, intellectual, even philosophical phenomenon proving the validity of their enlightened vision. An important result of this "theoretical and contemplative"[8] reception was the

5. *Leipziger Zeitung*, 6 February 1776, quoted in: Horst Dippel, *Germany and the American Revolution 1770–1800: A Sociohistorical Investigation of Late Eighteenth-Century Political Thinking* (Chapel Hill, NC, 1977), 206.

6. For a general introduction to the literature see Hildegard Meyer, *Nordamerika im Urteil des deutschen Schrifttums bis zur Mitte des 19. Jahrhunderts. Eine Untersuchung über Kürnbergers "Amerika-Müden." Mit einer Bibliographie* (Hamburg, 1929); Paul C. Weber, *America in Imaginative German Literature in the First Half of the Nineteenth Century* (New York, 1929); Rolf Engelsing, "Deutschland und die Vereinigten Staaten im 19. Jahrhundert. Eine Periodisierung," *Die Welt als Geschichte* 18 (Stuttgart, 1958): 139; Günter Moltmann, *Atlantische Blockpolitik im 19. Jahrhundert: Die Vereinigten Staaten und der deutsche Liberalismus während der Revolution von 1848–49* (Düsseldorf, 1973), 39.

7. Ernst Fraenkel, ed. *Amerika im Spiegel des deutschen politischen Denkens: Äußerungen deutscher Staatsmänner und Staatsdenker über Staat und Gesellschaft in den Vereinigten Staaten von Amerika* (Köln and Opladen 1959), 20; Meyer, *Nord-Amerika*, 10; Engelsing, "Deutschland und die Vereinigten Staaten," 141.

8. Horst Dippel, "Die Wirkung der amerikanischen Revolution auf Deutschland und Frankreich," in *200 Jahre amerikanische Revolution und moderne Revolutionsforschung*, ed. Hans-Ulrich Wehler, *Geschichte und Gesellschaft*, Sonderheft 2 (Göttingen, 1976), 101–21.

replacement of England as the country that had served as an example of a liberal free order. In its stead, the United States became the model for those in search of a better world.[9]

This enthusiasm for the new world found expression in the adulatory poems of the *Sturm und Drang,* a literary tradition that idealized and romanticized American republicanism as a new stage in the progress of humanity, projecting central principles of European Enlightenment thought onto the new society in North America in heroic and abstract verse.[10] The heroes of the Revolution, above all George Washington and Benjamin Franklin, were idolized in similar terms. Franklin represented to Europeans the ideal union of the enlightened and searching individual, public man, and practical mind.

The emerging political liberalism in the repressive restoration period centered its attention on the American Constitution. In the opinion of liberals, it had transformed their own as yet unattained ideals of personal and political rights and freedoms into a practical reality. The United States, therefore, became the symbol of political freedom; thus, during the Hambach Festival in 1832, which united diverse radical groups in a common demonstration for national unity and political rights, cheers were voiced on "the united free states of Germany" in obvious reference to the United States of America.[11] The radical democrats of the Young Germany movement, sometimes living in exile in France and Switzerland, helped popularize republican ideals in rousing poems and songs that often were but thinly veiled calls for action, like the poems of the *Vormärz* period. Thus, a general and basically uncritical enthusiasm for America's "great democracy"[12] prevailed among radical democrats as well as among liberals during the revolution of 1848/49. At democrats' and workers' mass meetings, the Stars and Stripes was always displayed alongside the tricolor and the revolutionary red flag.[13] It was especially the democratic left that pointed to the American federal system as an example to be followed, asking for

9. Palmer, *Age of the Democratic Revolution,* vol. 1, 282.

10. Hartmut Keil, "Die Auswirkungen der amerikanischen Revolution auf Europa," in *Die französische Revolution. Wurzeln und Wirkungen,* ed. Venanz Schubert, *Wissenschaft und Philosophie. Interdisziplinäre Studien,* vol. 7 (St. Ottilien, 1989), 73.

11. Meyer, *Nord-Amerika,* 33f.; Engelsing, "Deutschland und die Vereinigten Staaten," 146.

12. The term was used by historian Friedrich von Raumer; as quoted in: Meyer, *Nord-Amerika,* 44.

13. Cf. Eckhart G. Franz, *Das Amerikabild der deutschen Revolution von 1848/49: Zum Problem der Übertragung gewachsener Verfassungsformen* (Heidelberg, 1958), 105.

a new German federal state with a "constitution along the lines of North America with accompanying republican institutions."[14]

Parallel to this liberal-republican debate ran a current of popular enthusiasm for the American Republic, grounded less in constitutional and political ideals than in hopes of material reward. Surpassing idealistic motives in importance in its long-term consequences, material ambition led to mass emigration from Germany in the middle of the century at the very moment when liberal aspirations had been shattered. In this situation other types of literature began to appear which took more realistic note of American society. These were the burgeoning travel literature and immigration guidebooks written mostly by Germans who had visited North America or by German-Americans who had emigrated and related their experiences to prospective German immigrants.[15] After the 1820s, pamphlets and books kept appearing in rapid succession. Between 1842 and 1852, for example, 308 guidebooks for immigrants were published in the German language and offered on the German book market.

Since precise information and practical advice were essential to fulfill the basic needs these guidebooks were supposed to serve, they included critical evaluations of the American political system and social institutions. A more realistic perception of the United States thus became more widespread in the German states, tempering the former uncritical enthusiasm, but not to the degree that public opinion was now directed against the American democracy. On the contrary, the realistic approach was intended to help immigrants pragmatically cope with new circumstances and to channel their expectations and preparations accordingly.

The American institution accorded the harshest criticism in the guidebooks (and in the travel literature most of the time as well) was slavery. Its condemnation coincided with the emergence of a more somber view of American society in the literature of the pre-revolutionary *Vormärz* period, which contrasted America's idealistic principles as embodied in the Declaration of Independence

14. "Erster Bericht der demokratischen Partei der deutschen constituirenden National-Versammlung vom 1. August 1848," quoted in: Franz, *Amerikabild*, 106.

15. Thus, according to Rudolph Cronau, Gottfried Duden's *Bericht über eine Reise nach den westlichen Staaten Nordamerikas und einem mehrjährigen Aufenthalt am Missouri (1824–1827)*, published in 1829, triggered an emigration fever; Gustav Koerner, in his refutation *Beleuchtung des Dudenschen Berichtes über die westlichen Staaten*, published five years later, observed: "In many families it was read day by day on the eve embarking for the New World, and became an authoritative source for their information;" cf. Weber, *America*, 115–19, quotation, 117; cf. also Meyer, *Nord-Amerika*, 23f.

and the Constitution with existing shortcomings and injustices. Thus, Heinrich Heine, poignant critic of German social and political conditions, also directed his scorn at the "peculiar institution" and the treatment accorded black people. He ridiculed German immigrants with his ironic advice: "You good German farmers! Go to America! Everyone there is equal ... with, of course, the exception of several million slaves.... The brutality used in dealing with the latter is more than just shocking." Heine then substantiated this statement by recounting a heinous example of racial prejudice.[16]

Whereas Heine's judgment was motivated by humanistic idealism, prospective immigrants were not necessarily of the same mind. Guidebooks might also address the slavery issue from a moral perspective; however, foremost in their descriptions were practical considerations. Immigrants were primarily interested in acquiring farms and finding jobs where they could apply and utilize their own labor. Of course, guidebooks were aware of this dominant incentive for emigration; they strongly advised immigrants against choosing the slave states as a region for settlement, assuming that free workers and farmers could not possibly compete against bound labor. It was often out of self-interest, then, that immigrants were opposed to slavery, that they adhered to the Jeffersonian notion of the yeoman farmer as the pillar of a democratic society, and that they came to support the Free-Soilers, the Republican Party's effort at preventing slavery's expansion, and certain attractive features of that party's program, like the Homestead Act. Humanitarian concerns were well served when they could be allied with practical considerations. But this peculiar alliance also demonstrates the limits of the support for political action that needed more

16. "I believe it was in New York where a Protestant preacher was so outraged about the way the black people were being mistreated that he married his own daughter to a free Negro to spite the horrible prejudice. As soon as this true Christian deed became publicly known, the people stormed the preacher's house, and only by fleeing was he able to escape death; but his house was demolished, and the preacher's daughter, the hapless victim, was taken by the mob and forced to suffer the fury. She was ... stripped stark naked, painted with tar, rolled around in the feathers of a mattress which had been torn open for the occasion, and, thus tarred and feathered, was dragged through the town and ridiculed." Heinrich Heine, "Ludwig Börne. Eine Denkschrift," in *Heinrich Heine: Historisch-kritische Gesamtausgabe der Werke*, ed. Manfred Windfuhr (Hamburg, 1978), vol. 11: 37–38; quoted in: *German Workers in Chicago. A Documentary History of Working-Class Culture from 1850 to World War I*, eds. Hartmut Keil and John B. Jentz (Urbana and Chicago, 1988), 349.

than motivation based on self-interest alone. Alexander von Humboldt's views can serve as a telling example of how a principled humanism could have an enormous impact upon social attitudes and political action.

Alexander von Humboldt's Practical Humanism

Alexander von Humboldt's name is usually associated with his great achievements as explorer and natural scientist and with his deep commitment to liberal and humanitarian thought. Less is known of the direct effect that the latter had on Humboldt's perception of American society, of the impact of his views on the American political debate of slavery during the 1850s and especially on the German-American community's political outlook.[17]

Humboldt was thoroughly steeped in the Enlightenment tradition. His extensive travels through South America, which were the basis for his lifelong research and publications, also influenced his attitudes toward the institution of slavery and toward the United States, since upon the conclusion of his travels in 1804 he visited the island of Cuba a second time (he spent three months in Cuba for the first time from December 1800 to March 1801)[18], where he observed the practical consequences of slavery, then sailed on to Philadelphia, from where he traveled to Washington, D.C. to meet important political figures, including Thomas Jefferson, James Madison, and Albert Gallatin.[19] These encounters established continuing relationships over several years, be it by correspondence as in the case of Jefferson, and in addition by personal contact, as was the case with Albert Gallatin, whom Jefferson met again when he lived in Paris.[20] As Benjamin

17. Publications related to this issue are Helmut de Terra, "Studies of the Documentation of Alexander von Humboldt," *Proceedings of the American Philosophical Society*, vol. 102 (1958), 136–41 and 560–89; Helmut de Terra, "Alexander von Humboldt's Correspondence with Jefferson, Madison, and Gallatin," *Proceedings of the American Philosophical Society*, vol. 103 (1959), 783–806; Helmut de Terra, *Humboldt: The Life and Times of Alexander von Humboldt, 1769–1859* (New York, 1955); Richard Henry Stoddard, *The Life Travels and Books of Alexander von Humboldt*, with an introduction by Bayard Taylor (New York, 1854). I am especially indebted to *Alexander von Humboldt on Slavery in the United States*, ed. with introduction and notes by Philip S. Foner (Berlin, 1981).

18. De Terra, "Studies," 566.

19. Ibid., 561f.; *Alexander von Humboldt*, ed. Foner, 6f.

20. The correspondence is reprinted in de Terra, "Studies," 562–64; de Terra, "Alexander von Humboldt's Correspondence."

Franklin had symbolized for Europeans the enlightened American, universal scholar, and public figure in the second half of the eighteenth century, now the European Alexander von Humboldt assumed a similar role for Americans. He became the authoritative voice not only in his proper field but in many matters, including European public affairs, politics, culture, and the arts. American intellectuals traveled to Berlin in the 1840s and 1850s in order to meet Humboldt.[21] Artists arranged sessions to paint or sculpt the venerated scholar.[22] The historian William Prescott in a letter to Humboldt acknowledged his debt to the scientist's insights into Aztec civilization, writing that "in this shadowy field I have been very often guided by the light of your researches," and expressing his hope that the work which he presented to Humboldt "may receive your approbation."[23]

It was Humboldt's book on Cuba, however, that was to have the most lasting impact on the American political debate in the 1850s. The *Essai politique sur l'île de Cuba* was published in Paris in 1826; the Spanish edition, *Ensayo Político sobre la Isla de Cuba*, followed a year later. Chapter seven contained Humboldt's scathing condemnation of slavery when he attacked the brutality of the institution even under the supposedly less harsh Spanish conditions. Humboldt exposed such euphemisms as "Black Vassalage" and "Patriarchal Protection" as terms used to disguise the true character of Negro slavery.[24]

In 1856 J. S. Thrasher, a Southerner who held commercial interests in Cuba, and who was intimately involved in efforts to annex the island, published an English translation in New York City under the title *The Island of Cuba by Alexander Humboldt* without Humboldt's authorization. Significantly, this publication omitted chapter seven, i.e., Humboldt's views on slavery, which included statements like the following: "Without doubt, slavery is the greatest of all the evils which have afflicted mankind."[25] Humboldt wrote an angry letter protesting the mutilation of his work. He pointed out, among other things, that thirty years before he had written that legislation of Spain "relating to slavery was less inhuman and less atrocious to slaves" than in the

21. Stoddard, *Life Travels*, 430–82.
22. De Terra, "Studies," 572f.
23. Letter to Humboldt, 23 December 1843.
24. Cf. *Alexander von Humboldt*, ed. Foner, 19.
25. Ibid., 19 and 51.

United States.[26] His letter was published in the Berlin *Spenersche Zeitung* on 25 July 1856. An English translation was published in the *New York Times*, the *New York Tribune*, the *New York Herald*, and other papers. German-language papers in the United States reprinted the letter as well. Thus, Humboldt's indignation received the widest publicity.

Humboldt's condemnation of slavery was grounded in his basic humanist and natural rights position, as he had expressed it in volume one of his major work, *Kosmos*, published in 1845. There he wrote:

> In maintaining the unity of the human race we also reject the disagreeable assumption of superior and inferior peoples. Some peoples are more pliable, more highly educated and ennobled by intellectual culture, but there are no races which are more noble than others. All are equally entitled to freedom; to freedom which in the state of nature belongs to the individual and which in civilization belongs as a right to the entire citizenry through political institutions.[27]

Humboldt applied these principles to American society as he witnessed, and became concerned about, the increasing political tensions over slavery in the 1850s. Commenting upon the war between the United States and Mexico, Humboldt voiced his dislike of the American conquests in tropical Mexico. He wished them all bad luck for he feared that they would "expand their devilish slave system."[28] In an interview for the *Evening Post* the then eighty-five-year-old Humboldt expressed his admiration for the American political system but then added:

> In one respect, however, you are much worse off than when I was there.... For 30 years you have not made any progress about slavery. You have gone backward, very far backward in every respect. I especially refer to the law of 1850, the Fugitive Slave Act.... In Europe you will also find bad things. But I tell you you will not find anything half as bad as your system of slavery, and I know what slavery is like in your country.[29]

Republicans were quick to use Humboldt's views in the election campaigns of 1856 and 1860, especially to reach German-American voters. Humboldt obviously did not mind the use of his

26. Quoted in ibid., 20.
27. Alexander von Humboldt, *Kosmos*, vol. 1 (Stuttgart and Tübingen, 1845), 385.
28. Quoted in *Alexander von Humboldt*, ed. Foner, 23.
29. 24 March 1855; the above quote is taken from the German-language *Louisiana Staats-Zeitung*, 17 May 1855, trans. Hartmut Keil.

name and public utterances, since he had been in contact with the party's presidential candidate John Frémont, admiring his achievements as an explorer and being instrumental in his receiving the Great Golden Medal of Progress in the Sciences from the king of Prussia in 1850. In the letter to Frémont congratulating him on the award, Humboldt had also added that as a result of Frémont's "labors, California ... has so nobly resisted the introduction of Slavery."[30] This and other quotes were used in the 1856 campaign in newspapers and in leaflets. Frémont himself wrote to Humboldt and emphasized the importance of using his views in the campaign: "In the history of your life and opinions we find abundant reasons for believing that in the struggle, in which the friends to liberal progress in this country find themselves engaged, we shall have with us the strength of your name."[31] After the election Humboldt regretted that "the shameful party which sells Negro children of fifty pounds, which says that all white workers should also be made slaves—has won. Shame upon them."[32] And shortly before his death in 1859, commenting on a publication by Julius Froebel on his experiences in America, Humboldt formulated his final legacy concerning the institution of slavery. He encouraged Froebel to

> continue to brand the shameful devotion to slavery, the treacherous importation of Negroes, under the pretense of their becoming free.... What atrocities have been witnessed by one who has had the misfortune to live from 1789 to 1858. My book against slavery ... is not prohibited in Madrid, but cannot be purchased in the United States ... except with the omission of everything that relates to the sufferings of our colored fellow-men who, according to my political views, are entitled to the enjoyment of the same freedom as ourselves.[33]

Upon his death Alexander von Humboldt was honored by the *National Anti-Slavery Standard* for his consistent anti-slavery views. The "leading anti-slavery weekly in the United States and official organ of the American Anti-Slavery Society"[34] devoted

---

30. *New York Tribune*, 15 July 1856, quoted in *Alexander von Humboldt*, ed. Foner, 22.

31. Quoted in *Alexander von Humboldt*, ed. Foner, 21f.

32. Letter to Varnhagen, 21 Nov. 1856, *Briefe von Alexander von Humboldt an Varnhagen von Ense, 1827–1858* (Leipzig, 1860), 332.

33. Quoted in *Alexander von Humboldt*, ed. Foner, 23f.

34. These were the issues of 8 June 1858 and 2 July 1859. Excerpts are reprinted in *Alexander von Humboldt*, 56–58.

two issues to Humboldt, in which his compiled opinions on slavery were reprinted.

Ottilie Assing's Radical Journalism

Ottilie Assing partook of the same humanistic tradition as Alexander von Humboldt, growing up in liberal circles connected with him.[35] After her parents died in 1840 and 1842, she and her sister moved into their uncle Varnhagen von Ense's home in Berlin. Varnhagen had been married to Rahel Levin, who had established a famous literary salon. Varnhagen himself was a liberal and a critic of Prussian autocracy and repression, and he shared these views with his good friend Humboldt. In their correspondence, which upon publication received wide publicity both in Germany and the United States, the critical issue of slavery was also addressed. When Ottilie Assing reviewed the book in 1860, she characterized its reception in the United States: "Humboldt's open liberalism and his opinions on slavery and American democracy are reason enough to make conservatives and Democrats furious."[36]

Growing up as a young woman with liberal and feminist views, Ottilie seems to have been especially sensitive to her uncle's patriarchal attitude and soon left his house when differences of opinion became too strong. She took up residence in Hamburg where, through the good offices of a friend, she began writing for the *Morgenblatt für gebildete Leser*. This contact and assignment was to prove extremely important for her career in the United States, for the *Morgenblatt* was one of the highly respected journals in Germany, catering, as even its title suggested, to German intellectuals. It was published by the respected publishing house of Johann Friedrich Cotta, who also owned the *Allgemeine Zeitung*, one of the leading liberal German newspapers. Time and again this paper had fallen under censorship because of its political views and forced Cotta to look for a more auspicious location where laws

35. Cf. Tamara Felden, "Frauen Reisen: Zur literarischen Repräsentation weiblicher Geschlechterrollenerfahrung im 19. Jahrhundert," (Ph.D. diss., University of Alabama, 1991); T. H. Pickett, "The Friendship of Frederick Douglass with the German, Ottilie Assing," *The Georgia Historical Quarterly* 73 (1989): 87–105; T. H. Pickett, "Perspectives on a National Crisis: A German Correspondent Reports on America, 1853–1865," *Tamkang Journal of American Studies* 4 (1988): 6–15; William S. McFeely, *Frederick Douglass* (New York, 1991), 183–86.

36. *Morgenblatt für gebildete Leser*, 24 June 1860, 619. This and all following translations from the *Morgenblatt* by Hartmut Keil.

were less repressive. By the 1830s the *Allgemeine Zeitung* had become so well established in intellectual circles that a subscription to it was a must. The weekly *Morgenblatt* contained the reports from abroad that were also printed in the *Allgemeine Zeitung*. Thus, the two Cotta publications reached an important part of the German middle class and intellectuals and had a tremendous impact among the elite. In fact, it is difficult to overestimate the influence, especially of the *Allgemeine Zeitung*. Heinrich Heine, some of whose work was published in the paper, acknowledged that "it so truly deserves its worldwide renown as an authoritative source that one could well call it the common newspaper of Europe."[37]

Assing therefore served an influential clientele after arriving in the United States in 1853, where she continued her assignment for both the journal and the paper. Initially, she contributed only a few articles until she had settled down. She chose Hoboken, across the Hudson River from New York, as her place of residence and accepted a language teaching position. Hoboken at the time was the largest community of German liberals and radicals of various persuasion in North America including, for example, the educator and editor Adolf Douai, who published an abolitionist newspaper in San Antonio, Texas, in the early 1850s until he was forced to leave the city. Once Assing had become familiar with American conditions, she began to dominate the correspondence from the United States for the two publications so that her views became the standard interpretation at the height of the conflict over slavery and abolition from 1856 to 1865.[38] For her journalistic activities Assing was strategically placed. Already a fervent advocate of liberal causes and of feminism, she became a convinced abolitionist. She was introduced to leaders of the movement including Frederick Douglass, with whom she became close friends. There is now evidence that this friendship of the two like-minded persons lasted more than twenty years, and that it may have evolved into a sexual relationship as well. For our purposes, it is important to note the mutual intellectual impact that they had on one another. Apparently Assing introduced Douglass to some of the liberal

37. Heinrich Heine, *Werke und Briefe*, ed. Hans Kaufmann, vol. 4 (Berlin, 1961), 368, quoted in "Introduction" to *Reports from America in German Newspapers, 1828 to 1865*, ed. and trans. Maria Wagner (Stuttgart, 1985), x.

38. Thus, in 1854 only six of sixteen reports on the United States were written by Assing; by 1857 and 1858 twenty-four of twenty-eight articles were Assing's; and in 1859 and 1860 all but one were written by her.

German authors and philosophers, whereas through Douglass she in turn gained firsthand knowledge of the abolitionist movement and its activities.[39]

Assing's reports were broad in scope.[40] After all, she was commissioned to cover any matters in the United States of interest to curious intellectuals in Germany. Thus, she presented a rich kaleidoscope of America's political, intellectual, social, and cultural life, although usually from a New York City perspective, since that is where she lived. She observed cultural events, like theater and opera performances, public lectures so popular at the time, and art exhibits. She described industrial expositions, suburbs and inner city neighborhoods, street types, the rich variety of immigrant populations, urban life; analyzed the mechanism of city and machine politics including police corruption for a readership unfamiliar with such practices; vented her anti-clerical wrath against religious orthodoxy, specific denominations, religious revivals, as well as against spiritualists and spiritists. Initially concentrating her reporting on the new impressions that metropolitan New York offered her in abundance, she soon, with fine insight, tied social and political developments to the structural foundations of the American system. Assing sympathized with conditions on board immigrant ships, described immigrants' poverty and their work situation, highlighting in stark contrast the lower classes and the scandals and immorality of the New York elite. This rich mosaic was complemented by ironic sketches of the absurdities of urban life, the simple or expensive pleasures of the rich and the poor, the rampant crimes,[41] catastrophes, and newest crazes. She even reflected on the American character, observing "a flexibility of mind,

39. Thus she wrote a report on the Harper's Ferry raid that was full of inside information that she could only have received through Douglass and his associates, cf. Felden, "Frauen Reisen," 235f.

40. The following analysis is based on all of her more than 130 reports in the *Morgenblatt*. General summaries are not explicitly documented here for reason of space. Cf. however Felden's (almost complete) list of Assing's reports: Felden, "Frauen Reisen," 251–65.

41. Her description of the crime wave in New York sounds hauntingly contemporary: "The disproportionately high number of crimes, notably murders, unprecedented by any other civilized country, as well as other dangers that continuously endanger one's life, cast an ominous shadow on conditions in the United States. Although one can forget them for a few moments, some new crime, an 'accident' will recall all those horrors immediately again. Street robberies have spread this winter to a disquieting degree so that there is hardly a newspaper edition which does not contain reports of such crimes. As a result many people arm themselves before leaving home at night." *Morgenblatt*, 12 April 1857, 354.

receptivity and agility which count among the characteristic peculiarities of the American race, although the persuasiveness and
impact of this trait has not been adequately emphasized in German publications on America."[42]

After the outbreak of the Civil War, she became relentless in her
criticism of incompetent Union generals, foremost among them
John McClellan whom she characterized as "the best enemy whom
the rebels could have wished for,"[43] of corruption in the military
and the government, of what she perceived as slighting the contributions which German immigrants made to the Union cause, and
of war profiteers and the unequal share of the war's burden.

All of these topics paled, however, beside her tireless devotion
to reform movements. The women's movement certainly received
its considerable share of attention in the pages of the *Allgemeine
Zeitung* and *Morgenblatt*. Yet foremost in her mind and pen was
the anti-slavery cause, which informed her writing about national,
state, and city politics, regional disputes, individual heroes and
villains, and especially about black Americans both bound and
free. The dominant leitmotif of her reporting that became increasingly urgent was that slavery and freedom were irreconcilable.[44]

Assing was morally outraged over the result of the presidential
election of 1856, and with clear foresight she described it as the
last time that the slavery party could display its arrogance of
power on the national level.[45] To German readers she explained
the two-thirds clause of the Constitution which gave the South
the electoral majority. But she did not forget to elaborate that free
blacks were kept from voting through property clauses in most
northern and western states.[46]

In her reports Assing admirably conveyed her thorough grasp
of the structural characteristics of the "slavocracy":[47] its effects
upon the national judicial system which was biased against
blacks; the resulting lack of respect of whites for the rights of
blacks; and the abomination of the fugitive slave law.[48] She
accused the Southern states of using terror against anti-slavery
advocates in their midst and of curtailing free speech by preventing

42. 28 March 1858, 309.
43. 16 April 1862, 382.
44. Cf. *Morgenblatt*, 4 June 1861; 3 July 1861; 10 September 1861.
45. Ibid., 1 April 1857, 22.
46. Ibid.
47. Ibid., 25 November 1869, 1149.
48. Ibid., 29 November 1857; 11 July 1858; 24 January 1858.

published anti-slavery tracts from entering the South through the federal mail. At bottom lay the pervasive fear of slave insurrections surfacing in unjustified rumors of impending uprisings, as in Texas in the fall of 1860.[49]

In the years immediately preceding the Civil War, Assing perceived growing expansionist sentiment, as evidenced in William Walker's activities in 1857,[50] and she warned of efforts to revive the slave trade, pointing out that its legalization was discussed again in Southern circles, and that the practice had not been entirely abolished anyway, as the price of slaves had gone up and a fortune could be made through trading. According to her information, fifty slave ships had set out from the New York harbor in one year (1859/60) alone to engage in the slave trade, and after hostilities broke out between the North and the South, she claimed that reintroduction of the slave trade had been a major motive of secession. Accusing certain northern commercial interests of collusion and the authorities of leniency in the matter, she was glad to finally see Nathaniel Gordon, captain of the slave ship *Erie*, captured, tried, and executed in New York. She noted that it was the first time that such punishment had been inflicted.[51]

Various emigration plans for blacks preferred by advocates in the North to solve racial antagonism met with Assing's scorn, since slavery would not be abolished by such measures; quite to the contrary, the abolitionist movement would be weakened, since free and intelligent blacks who were the movement's main pillars would thereby be withdrawn; thus these plans served in reality the slaveholders' interests. Assing did not forget to mention that Frederick Douglass himself was opposed to colonization projects. In the case of Maryland, where discussion revolved around the question of making free blacks emigrate as well, she warned that these people were badly needed to do the necessary work in the fields and factories.[52]

When it came to her German immigrant compatriots, Ottilie Assing came to a relatively positive conclusion. She had no patience with the sizable group of Germans in New York who were either indifferent or sympathetic to slavery and who sided with the Democratic Party. But more important seemed to be those

49. Ibid., 26 February 1860; 27 May 1860; 3 April 1860; 25 November 1860.

50. Ibid., 9 August 1857.

51. Ibid., 30 January 1859; 10 July 1859; 25 November 1860; 5 February 1861; 16 April 1862.

52. Ibid., 30 January 1859; 28 August 1859.

workers and farmers who proved through their hard work that free labor could produce better results than the plantation system. Thus, in Texas Germans grew cotton and tobacco with great success without use of slave labor.[53] Her showcase for the argument, however, was Missouri, where in several counties German wine-growers and other farmers had totally discouraged slave owners and forced them to remove their slaves to the deep South.[54] These counties overwhelmingly supported the Republican Party, and it was in Missouri that Germans helped defend the Union after the outbreak of the war and prevented that state from joining the Confederacy. Assing noted that all educated Germans were on the side of the Republicans, and not only did she record the preference that other liberal Germans had for Frémont over Lincoln, but she also personally and strongly advocated the same choice.[55]

The political scene that Assing observed so closely was peopled by heroes and villains. She made no secret of her sympathy for Charles Sumner, Wendell Phillips, Horace Greeley, Horace Mann, and John Frémont, all of whom she saw guided by highly idealistic and moral convictions that translated into acts of courage. With Abraham Lincoln, however, Assing had not much patience. She saw him as an opportunistic compromiser who hesitated much too long with his decision to emancipate the slaves. She blamed him for disavowing Frémont when he had issued his proclamation for Missouri and for showing leniency toward slave owners.[56] Lincoln in her opinion showed poor judgment by not using emancipation as a weapon early in the war,[57] and when he finally acted, he did so out of military and political "expediency."[58] It was not primarily an "act of justice to negroes."[59]

By contrast, Frederick Douglass was for her the epitome of abolitionists, the "lion" of the movement whose intellect, rhetorical mastery, and fine stature completely enthralled her. After she had

53. Ibid., 1 August 1858.

54. "Slavery vanishes in the face of German industriousness against which the slave owner cannot compete…. As good democrats (in the German, not the American, sense of that word) they hate the aristocracy of slave holders, and as genuine free workers they love freedom and work and they detest tyranny, laziness and waste of time." *Morgenblatt*, 1 August 1858.

55. Ibid., 22 April 1864.

56. Ibid., 3 July 1861.

57. Ibid., 26 November 1861.

58. Ibid., 19 November 1862.

59. Ibid., 11 March 1865.

heard him speak for the first time, she described him in glowing terms. He was "one of the most talented speakers in the United States," carried by "fire and passion." Douglass showed a "complete command of his topic and admirable balance of judgment," and he expressed his "richness of thought" through a "masterly use of language." She concluded her report by reflecting: "Sad to contemplate what elevated position such a man should hold, if the color of his skin were lighter by some shades, whereas now he is being excluded by so-called society as a 'nigger' despite belonging to the aristocracy of the intellect."[60]

Not only was her description of the black leader very sympathetic, Ottilie Assing also devoted her attention to ordinary black people, changing the tone of reporting in the journal's pages by showing a great sensitivity for their plight and setting the record straight against pervasive stereotypes among whites. The contrast between the reports in the *Morgenblatt* at the time when she arrived in the United States and those she wrote herself is revealing. In 1853, for example, one of her predecessors wrote:

> Poor darkies: free when in the future it will be agreeable to the whites ... but they will never reach the power and influence which they dream of; they will always be a backward, oppressed people, the pariahs of society, because, with few exceptions, they lack the higher intelligence and the spiritual force of the white race.[61]

Witness by contrast Assing's following description:

> The favorable impression that I have had of colored people from the very beginning has been confirmed and has increased upon closer acquaintance. Although there is hardly a people that has been more oppressed, mistreated and kicked around, excluded from educational influences and forcibly kept ignorant, still there is so much display of natural manners and dignified politeness.

Describing a visit to a recent social event in a black church attended by ordinary working people, she observes "how quiet, mannered and decently these 'darkies' behaved," showing a "friendly natural politeness." "They even dressed in a more tasteful way and free of those ridiculously inappropriate arrangements that one usually finds among this class."[62] She also argued against stereotypical views of black people, like their alleged laziness, pointing out that slaves were "absolutely justified" in showing "a so-called aversion

60. Ibid., 19 and 26 July 1857.
61. Ibid., 26 June 1853.
62. Ibid., 4 May 1856, 431f.

to work" and in tending "to do everything in a superficial manner, since they see no reason whatsoever to exert their energy more than they need to, since this is only to their oppressors' advantage."[63] Where slaves had been emancipated, however, as in Beaufort in South Carolina, only "the most favorable news about their conduct"[64] was reported. They proved to be "industrious workers and faithful allies."[65] "They are very industrious, orderly and reliable."[66] Assing expressed the highest praise for the black soldiers who fought valiantly, like the heroic 54th Regiment that involved "one of the most spectacular armed incidents."[67]

> The black regiments ... developed a degree of bravery and discipline which would do honor to the best army in the civilized world. This is not surprising at bottom, on the contrary, it seems only natural that those who formerly had to work under the lash to the advantage of their enemies and oppressors, are now especially industrious when they can work for themselves as freedmen, and that those who now fight for their own and their families' freedom and future will make brave soldiers.[68]

When emancipation arrived in 1865, Assing declared 31 January "the greatest, most important day in this country's history since the Declaration of Independence." Only by shaking off forever "the curse of slavery" had the American people "finally entered the ranks of the civilized, enlightened nations of the world."[69] But her joy did not cloud her judgment of what lay ahead in the future. Repeating her conviction "that the abolition of slavery did not occur out of humanitarian considerations or for reasons of justice, but that it was solely an act of necessity forced upon the nation by conditions," she warned that "one must beware that the work of emancipation remain only fragmentary in the near future. The indifference toward the future of the freedmen and the remainder of the colored population of the Southern states and the aversion of the mass to grant them the civil rights so long withheld from them, are disquieting signs which point to the dark clouds at the horizon of our future. Abolition of slavery was the first step, but the great deed remains incomplete unless followed by other,

63. Ibid., 1 August 1858, 739.
64. Ibid., 2 April 1863, 334.
65. Ibid., 12 February 1862, 164.
66. Ibid., 2 April 1863.
67. Ibid., 24 December 1863, 1241.
68. Ibid., 2 April 1863, 334.
69. Ibid., 9 April 1865, 365.

equally necessary steps." But she still ended her critical evaluation
on a more optimistic note, claiming that

> there can be no doubt that we are approaching the great goal of
> total emancipation, the granting of equal citizenship to blacks ...
> equal citizenship is the logic and necessary result of that first big
> step and despite all opposition it will sooner or later be the law of
> the land, because the spirit of this century, of civilization and prog-
> ress demand it authoritatively, and because it is the prerequisite for
> this republic's greatness and permanence.[70]

Conclusion

The above analysis of Humboldt's views and Assing's reports
yields evidence that they shared a common philosophical tradition. Not only did they adhere to the same humanistic principles,
but they also nourished them in the same or similar circle of
friends. In fact, the personal linkages between Humboldt and Assing through their relationship to Varnhagen von Ense are noteworthy. The move from one side of the Atlantic to the other seems
to have been relatively unproblematic, since a community of like-
minded individuals with close ties did indeed exist on either side,
as Humboldt had found out on his short visit to the United States
almost fifty years before Ottilie Assing set foot on American shores.
And it is remarkable that Humboldt was able to influence American politics from Europe with opinions strikingly similar to those
that Assing expressed in her correspondence from America that in
turn had a considerable impact on intellectuals in Germany. These
intellectuals were presented with a radical republican perspective
by a German compatriot who had had no difficulty identifying
with such views upon her arrival in the United States, because
they corresponded so closely with her European Enlightenment
ideals. It would be a worthwhile task to find out if Assing's opinions as she conveyed them in her correspondence were in fact
identical with those of Frederick Douglass so that German elites
received a genuinely black abolitionist perspective as mediated
by Ottilie Assing's sympathetic reports.

The black abolitionist community in turn seems to have been
considerably influenced by the circle of German-American liberals
whom Douglass and black leaders met through Ottilie Assing's

70. Ibid., 24 September 1865, 930f.

contacts in that group. If this impression is correct, this would account for the favorable opinions that African-Americans expressed about German immigrants. In his lecture on German immigration in Rochester at the end of 1853, James McCune Smith gave a very favorable description of the character of German immigrants, describing them as hard working, intelligent, competent, and of higher skill levels than the average American population.[71] Frederick Douglass's views were even more positive. He noted the "many noble and high-minded men, most of whom, swept over by the tide of the revolution of 1848, have become our active allies against oppression and prejudice." And he overextended himself when he added: "A German has only to be a German to be utterly opposed to slavery. In feeling, as well as in conviction and principle, they are anti-slavery."[72] We know, of course, that this judgment was greatly exaggerated and biased but maybe not surprising, given the intimate collaboration between himself and Ottilie Assing and hence his personal experience and contact with radical German immigrants.

The functioning intellectual network that I have tried to identify by concentrating my analysis on Humboldt and Assing informed parts of the enlightened public on both sides of the Atlantic and had important practical political consequences. Another level of analysis is still needed to find out if and how this intellectual tradition translated into a pragmatic humanism in the daily lives and relationships of ordinary black Americans and German immigrants.

71. Reported in the *Tägliche Deutsche Zeitung*, New Orleans, 1 January 1854. This lecture was later published as "The German Invasion," *Anglo-African Magazine* 1 (February 1859).
72. "Adopted Citizens and Slavery," *Douglass's Monthly*, August 1859.

Chapter Six

RHYTHM, RIOTS, AND REVOLUTION

Political Paranoia, Cultural Fundamentalism,
and African-American Music

Berndt Ostendorf

On Being a Witness

It is very hard to throw away the things one has collected during one's formative years. The years from 1964 to 1965 when I was a graduate student at the University of Pennsylvania marked a turning point in my life in that I became politically conscious and active and began to participate in the dominant (political), but also in the underground (student) life. During this period I collected all sorts of things which constitute a random sample of the Zeitgeist: pamphlets of the John Birch Society, Goldwater campaign posters, underground newspapers such as *I. F. Stone's Weekly* or Paul Krassner's *The Realist*, cartoon books such as Pogo's *Jack Acid Society Black Book* (a mordant takeoff on the John Birch Society Blue Book), back issues of campus dailies, etc., stuff that usually does not merit the label "source" among hard-nosed academics. Now I am glad to have held on to this historiographical "junk," for a remarkable reversal in my own attitude towards these sources has occurred. In preparing this chapter, I found these random texts completely absorbing. What in 1966 I had considered trivial flotsam and jetsam turns out to be a precious source in order to fill in the blanks of my memory and also the blanks that are the consequences of a structural amnesia of historiography. Though I was a witness of this zany period, my memory was extremely spotty, or, rather, had, over the years, become selective. Thinking back on the early 1960s I readily remember the aftereffects of McCarthyism and the right-wing radicalism of Robert Welch of the John Birch Society. The latter's book *The Politician*, 1963, attacks Eisenhower for having been a Communist sympathizer, "Comsymp" for short. Yet, I had quite forgotten the pervasiveness and the excesses of a certain cultural fear and paranoia that characterized what Raymond Williams calls "the structure of feeling" of that epoch. That Kent Courtney of New Orleans would present as late as 1966 "An Exposé of the Leftwing Record of Richard Nixon" indicates the dimensions of political paranoia.[1]

Christian Crusades

Few people will remember the cultural rantings and ravings of one Billy James Hargis (b. 1925), director of the Christian Crusade. Though sequestered in the American Southwest, the movement was nationally active, particularly through its publishing outlet, which produced a periodical (100,000 subscribers) and millions of pamphlets and paperback books, most of which will have perished deservedly. I will look at one of these books today, probably the only extant copy in Germany.

Hargis, who traveled the country in a remodeled Greyhound bus, was, in the words of a contemporary witness, one of the most successful fundraisers on the right.[2] "Dr." Hargis, as he called himself, was ordained a minister of the Disciples of Christ (who later disowned him), and after one and a half years in school received a B.A. from Burton College and Seminary of Manitou Springs, Colorado. His honorary doctorate is from Defender Seminary in Puerto Rico; a second Doctor of Law was conferred by Belin Memorial University, Chillicothe, Missouri. All of these schools, according to the U.S. Department of Health, Education, and Welfare, are so-called degree mills.[3]

1. Benjamin R. Epstein and Arnold Foster, *The Radical Right. Report on the John Birch Society and Its Allies* (New York, 1967), 80–81.

2. Rüdiger Wersich, *Zeitgenössischer Rechtsextremismus in den Vereinigten Staaten* (Munich, 1978), 92–103.

3. John Harold Redekop, *The American Far Right: A Case Study of Billy James Hargis and the Christian Crusade* (Grand Rapids, MI, 1968), 16.

In Germany, he is remembered for having loaded hot-air balloons with Bibles (in 1953), which he then sent, winds prevailing, across the Iron Curtain, and thus became a sort of Cold War folk hero. Epstein and Foster argue that the Christian Crusade was closely allied with the John Birch Society and, like it, organized into chapters. Today I would like to investigate more closely the cultural creed of this right-wing fundamentalist movement. The most explicit articulation of this creed is found in a book authored by Dr. Hargis's executive assistant, one Reverend David A. Noebel, Dean of the Christian Crusade Anti-Communist Youth University, Manitou Springs, Colorado. Like McCarthy, Noebel was a native of Wisconsin and, if we go by his name, of German ethnic background. Formerly pastor of a Bible church in Madison, so says a blurb by "Dr." Hargis, Noebel was a doctoral student in philosophy at the University of Wisconsin when Hargis persuaded him to join the Christian Crusade. His book is entitled *Rhythm, Riots, and Revolution: An Analysis of the Communist Use of Music—The Communist Master Music Plan* (Tulsa, OK, 1966). It is 351 pages long with ample footnotes, an appendix, and a useful compilation of hard-to-find documents.[4]

The book is a sort of summa of what Hofstadter has called the "cultural fundamentalism" within the paranoid style in American politics.[5] For us today it might serve as a magnifying glass of certain "creedal passions" typically found among those whom Nixon would later call the silent majority. In his groundbreaking essay on the paranoid style, Hofstadter referred to that collection of animosities and deep-seated passions which the beleaguered and marginalized sectors of society, people who feel left out, will muster in defense of an all but lost "natural" state of national grace. From time to time these passions give rise to all sorts of conspiratorial fantasies vis-à-vis a threatening and hostile "other" which is held accountable for the national decline.[6] The structure of the book is that of a jeremiad—as it should be, coming from a fundamentalist minister—who urges his readers to return to the path of true grace before it is too late.

4. The first owner of my copy was Prof. Robert Detweiler of Emory University who will, I am sure, be surprised to see that his offhand gift bore scholarly fruit.

5. Richard Hofstadter, *The Paranoid Style in American Politics and Other Essays* (New York, 1965), 3–40.

6. Noebel's book fits the Spillmanns' typology: (1) negative anticipation, (2) blaming and scapegoating, (3) identification with total evil, (4) zero sum choices, (5) deindividualization of the alien hordes, and (6) refusal of empathy with the "other." See their contribution to this volume: Kurt R. Spillmann and Kati Spillmann, "Some Sociobiological and Psychological Aspects of 'Images of the Enemy.'"

The "other," as we know from John Higham, Richard Hofstadter, and scholars of nativism, has in the course of American history taken on many guises: Adam Weishaupt and the Bavarian Illuminati, Freemasons, Catholics; then Jewish bankers, Communists; and today cosmopolitan, liberal Jews and secular humanists. Any one or all of these were perceived at one time or another as complete, irredeemable enemies of the American idea—distillations of the negative in a Manichaean frame: immoral, anti-Christian, anti-American, anti-white destroyers of an embattled republic. We know that all of these groups figured prominently in the logbook of the John Birch Society. Though the figures in this "un-American" pantheon of "others" remained rather stable, the deviant plots, strategies, and master plans with which they aim to destroy the republic mirror particular crises of particular groups at a particular time. Hence, they may be fully explained sociologically, i.e., in their given historic context. Yet there is, as Hofstadter writes, a recognizable family resemblance of underlying angst and nativist projections. Though the biological origin of that angst (or the neurological ability to produce reactive aggressions) may be lodged in the *Zwischenhirn*, as Kurt and Kati Spillmann suggest,[7] the projections are in their actual historical performance, culturally coded along the lines of what anthropologists would call deep-seated patterns of behavior—patterns that Fernand Braudel subsumed under *longue durée*. Hofstadter writes: "The paranoid disposition is mobilized into action chiefly by social conflicts that involve ultimate schemes of values and that bring fundamental fears and hatreds, rather than negotiable interests, into political action."[8]

Noebel's Angst

With the help of Rev. David Noebel I would like to pursue a particularly intriguing, cultural layer of that angst, for Noebel identified a new incarnation of the threatening other: African rhythms.

7. Ibid.

8. Hofstadter, *Paranoid Style*, 39. Such paranoia is alive and well. Pat Robertson, presidential candidate and spearhead of a right-wing Christian renewal of the Republican Party, who commands the respect and support of Robert Dole, William Bennett, Midge Decter, and Irving Kristol, has written four best-selling books which contain all the known subplots of grand conspiracy theory: *The New Millennium* (1990), *The New World Order* (1991), *The Secret Kingdom* (1992), and *The Turning Tide* (1993); cf. Michael Lind. "Rev. Robertson's Grand International Conspiracy Theory," *The New York Review of Books*, 2 February 1995, 21–15.

He was convinced in 1966 that African-derived culture, particularly rhythmic dance, which was noticeably creeping into the American musical grammar, was going to undermine the American nation—by no means a new fear, as I shall demonstrate later.[9]

It seems as if Noebel used Hofstadter's essay or the Spillmanns' typology as a blueprint for designing the logic and rhetoric of his book. Noebel starts with a dual legitimization of his agenda, the first by Moshe Decter, who in *The Profile of Communism* admits "The communist endeavor to capture men's minds through the cultural offensive," and the second by J. Edgar Hoover, who states that the Communists "have infiltrated every conceivable sphere of activity; youth groups, radio, television, and motion picture industries; church, school educational and *cultural groups* [his emphasis]; the press; nationality minority groups and civil and political units." In short, practically everybody in that dangerous, anarchist corner: the cultural sphere. Noebel's and Hoover's antennae anticipated the success of "culture" as the synthetic paradigm of the "new" left.

The Communist use of music follows two strategies: one is to remove "the barrier between classical music and certain types of popular music by substituting perverted form, e.g., jungle noises (atonality) for standardized classical form."[10] The second strategy is "more psychological than cultural and consists of the Communist use of music directed at destroying the mental and emotional stability of America's youth through a scheme capable of producing mass neurosis."[11] The first, according to Noebel, follows Lenin's injunction to "rework culture" by establishing proletarian as against bourgeois forms of music, thus upsetting orderly hierarchies of

9. This "Africanization" was so noticeable that the showmaster Ed Sullivan refused to show the lower part of Elvis Presley's body when he appeared for the first time on his show. Paul Boyer has demonstrated that the association of rhythmic music with the anti-Christ has a long history in the apocalyptic or millennial tradition in: *When Time Shall Be No More: Prophecy Belief in Modern American Culture* (Cambridge, MA, 1992), 64, 232.

10. "Popular taste" in music has been a classic bogeyman of the ruling elite. It is a relatively new fear imported into American musical grammar, as Larry Levine suggests, by the German music establishment from the middle of the nineteenth century onward. People such as Theodore Thomas established a high cultural canon which was strengthened in the 1880s and 1890s by the cultural uplift crowd of the progressive movement. There are, typically, current ramifications of the fear in the canon debate. The embattled "great books" represent a rather recent addition to the national educational canon introduced by President Hutchins of the University of Chicago.

11. Noebel, *Rhythm*, 12.

cultural value. (Do we hear early rumblings of the canon debate?) He reprints copious quotations from several programmatic statements of "The Russian Association of Proletarian Musicians" and from the journal *Soviet Music,* all of which Noebel takes at face value, i.e., accepts both literally and seriously. Clearly, the Communists themselves have admitted their strategy of subversion by music. A symposium entitled "Art As Weapon" held in New York City in 1946 under the sponsorship of William Z. Foster (with the entire left music-making establishment in attendance) brings the conspiracy to America. Noebel names as movers and shakers Norman Corwin and Sidney Finkelstein, the former an author of radio plays, the latter an author of books on African-American music, who propose to break down the barrier between popular and classical music and smash this barrier "by inundating the American public with the music of the Negro people." And he adds: "[O]ne can be sure Mr. Finkelstein was not referring to 'Negro Spirituals' but rather to African 'beat' Music." He concludes his methodological foreword with "the sincere prayer that those concerned will take the proper action to assure a free Republic based on Christian precepts and Constitutional concepts."[12]

Sinister Enemies Use Sinister Methods

To prove that music may be used for good as well as for evil purposes Noebel first summons the authority of Plato and Aristotle, subsequently of the American composer Howard Hanson (b. 1896), who writes "it [music] can be soothing or invigorating, ennobling or vulgarizing, philosophical or orgiastic. It has powers for evil as well as for good."[13] Howard Hanson, it should be noted, was known in his time as the "great white hope" of American music.[14] And he cites both Soviet and American experiments concerning

---

12. Ibid., 15.

13. Ibid., 20.

14. On the title page Noebel places a motto drawn from Thoreau's *Walden,* not exactly a Christian fundamentalist, who writes: "Even music may be intoxicating. Such apparently slight causes destroyed Greece and Rome, and will destroy England and America." Thoreau echoes Plato, who writes in *The Republic* "for any musical innovation is full of danger to the whole State, and ought to be prohibited." Louise Ropes Loomis, ed., *Five Great Dialogues,* translated by B. Jowett (Princeton, NJ, 1942), 312. As Hofstadter notes, the paranoid right loves to base their claims on established authorities and witnesses. The Thoreau quote rearticulates a deep Platonic and Protestant fear of sinful, hedonistic music.

the effects of music on the nervous system. There emerges a curious American-Soviet consensus in that "meaningless noise ... wears people's nerves to a frazzle."[15] It is the consensus of what I would call the "fundamentalist international" made up of cultural conservatives and defenders of the cultural status quo on either side of the Cold War divide.[16] The Soviet nomenclature on the one side and J. Edgar Hoover and the John Birch Society on the other, though divided in their politics, are united in their resolve to stem the tide of corrosive modernization by way of "African rhythms," which the former blames on capitalism, the latter on communism. The common denominator, need I say, is transideological racism pure and simple, and it is in keeping with the paranoid style to blame what they fear most on a secret conspiracy of the enemy.

Noebel cites various neuropsychiatrists on brainwashing before he introduces one Edward Hunter's book *Brainwashing*[17] and J. Edgar Hoover's *Masters of Deceit*.[18] Both accuse the Soviet agents in the country of "menticide" (destruction of the collective mind) which—because it is gradual and hard to prove—is all the more hellish. It would be interesting to investigate popular fantasies in the movies of the period: for example *The Manchurian Candidate* on the fear of brainwashing, or *Dr. No*. The Chinese sounding name is at the same time a negative in English; what better name for the unspeakable other. There are innumerable grade B movies which work over popular fantasies of subversion in this period.

Noebel then treats the Communist use of hypnotism via music and repetition. He provides lengthy quotes from studies of the stimulus-response school—Soviet scholars Pavlov, Luria, and Platonov. Noebel trots out an immense scholarly apparatus, uses copious quotes, and has himself read countless scholarly books to prove that musical stimuli can produce certain effects. It is telling that Noebel, who would doubt every word of the American political or cultural elite, trusts every word of Soviet scholars and does not for a second doubt the validity or authority of Pavlovian research. But then he would, according to his zero-sum Manichaean belief, trust the power and effectiveness of the devil. As Hofstadter and the Spillmanns argue, identification with the powers of the enemy is a constituent element of the paranoid style. The

15. Noebel, *Rhythm*, 20.
16. "The ecumenicism of hatred is a great breaker down of precise intellectual discriminations." Hofstadter, *Paranoid Style*, 15, note 5.
17. Edward Hunter, *Brainwashing in Red China* (New York, 1951).
18. J. Edgar Hoover, *Masters of Deceit* (London, 1958).

gist of the Soviet-American studies is that it is possible to train people into reflex acceptance of "alien" cultural elements—that, as he calls it, nerve-jamming of children is a reality.[19] Quite often he uses the term "hypnotic induction" and parallels it to the Communist invasion of the body politic. This is of course a rich metaphor of fear, and again I remember films from the period about alien invaders of the body. And where does the enemy begin his evil work? With our youth of course. Communists "are using this knowledge of the various stages of hypnotism and music to invade the privacy of our children's minds, to render them mentally incompetent and neurotic."[20]

The fear of hypnotic induction and intrusion logically leads to infiltration of institutions. One intermediary between Soviet science and American education was Norman Corwin (a radio personality) who had close relations with record companies and music groups such as SING OUT or Young People's Records. The fear of "epidemic infiltration" was, as Frank Donner notes, typical for the mindset of the FBI as well as for Noebel: "[I]n the view of intelligence, subversion is a disease that is hereditary, chronic, incurable—and contagious. The subject, however remote his original subversive connection, taints all the groups and causes to which he subsequently becomes attached."[21]

According to Noebel, record companies who market these new records are used as Communist fronts. Noebel trots out a counterspy of the FBI, Boris Morros, who testified that "some of the fronts for Communist machinations and operations in the U.S. are certain record companies...."[22] The paranoid disposition favors as supreme witnesses "converts" along the binary belief axis, that is, people who have moved and experienced total evil, then come back to the fold.[23] From Young People's Records the network extends to include Folkways and even Columbia Records, particularly through the activities of John Hammond Sr. and Jr. (the former a Columbia executive, and his son, who promoted the careers of Bessie Smith, Billie Holiday, and many other black jazz artists). Rev. Noebel has actually listened to the records of Young People's

---

19. His anthropology is almost entirely instrumental and functional: humanity is a pliable mass of Silly Putty in the hands of scheming scientists.

20. Noebel, *Rhythm*, 26–27.

21. Frank Donner, *The Age of Surveillance* (New York, 1980), 303n.

22. Noebel, *Rhythm*, 30.

23. These are people who have moved from being completely unreliable to being completely reliable; indeed, conversion gives their testimony additional weight.

Records and has sent copies to neurologists, psychiatrists, and educators for a scientific evaluation. From our perspective it seems an odd list for Communist-inspired records, and our spontaneous lack of comprehension merely marks the latitude and dimension of Noebel's paranoia. Note the list of titles which Noebel finds so subversive: "The Chisholm Trail," "Daniel Boone," "Muffin in the City," "Sleepy Family," "The Little Fireman," "The Little Cowboy," "Out of Doors," "Tom's Hiccups."[24] If this list seems innocuous that is precisely the subversive beauty of it: the surface is innocent camouflage, the poison seeps up from deeper layers. His analysis shows that by use of different tempi, of African-derived cross-rhythms, hypnotic substitutions, subtle changes, which the average consumer might not detect, America's children are damaged beyond recall and that therefore Khrushchev's then current threat to bury the U.S. will first be realized in music.[25] For a final support of the idea of subversive music he calls on a leftist again, Bertrand Russell, who underlines the effectiveness of music in influencing children. The argument of the chapter by this failed doctoral student in philosophy is framed by Plato and Russell.

There is an unending story here: Young People's Records has subtly woven connections to the Book-of-the-Month Club, to *Good Housekeeping* and *Parents' Magazine*, to the National Council of Churches, the Southern Baptist Convention, and the Methodist Church. All these groups, innocent dupes that they are, have endorsed these seemingly innocuous educational records. In fact, the above records were given enthusiastic endorsements by the above institutions for their pedagogical freshness and singability. It is interesting and indicative of the atmosphere of fear how quickly *Good Housekeeping* and *Parents' Magazine* caved in after receiving letters from Noebel challenging them for having promoted a Communist-infiltrated Young People's Records. All, invariably, canceled their endorsement. Noebel and Hargis clearly were more powerful than we would have liked to assume.

24. Just to give you an idea of Communist content, here are the words of the song: "My name is Tom (hic)—I am so sad. Cause these old hiccups (hic)—Make me feel bad. I'd like to cure them (hic)—wouldn't you too? Cause I (hic) all day. And I (hic) all night. What can I (hic) do?" Following the hiccups, Tom gets the whistles, the stutters, the sneezes, the yawns, and the snores. The cure at the end of the record goes: "My name is Tom and I feel so grand. My voice now is wonderful, the best in the land! I sing the whole day through—That's what I do—With my snore all gone and my yawn all gone and my sneeze all gone, and my shake all gone, and my whistle gone and my hiccups gone! I feel so grand. (hic) Oh Oh."

25. Noebel, *Rhythm*, 46–47.

Communist Use of Beat Music

Noebel now turns his attention to rock 'n' roll and beat music which are subversive in their use of African rhythm, for these are both "visceral and riot-causing." Noebel quotes *Time Magazine,* which stated "The origins of rock 'n' roll go deep—Deep South, U.S.A.," and he adds: "The full truth is that it goes still deeper—the heart of Africa, where it was used to incite warriors to such frenzy that by nightfall neighbors were cooked in carnage pots! the music is a designed reversion to savagery."[26] Indeed, rock 'n' roll is basically "sexual, unchristian, mentally unsettling and riot-producing."[27] And who will help him drive this point home to unbelieving Americans? Good old Communist scholarship. "To understand what rock 'n' roll in general and the Beatles in particular are doing to our teenagers, it is necessary to return to Pavlov's laboratory." After tedious pages of substantiating evidence, he summarizes what according to the Soviets these Frankensteins of rock are all about: rock 'n' roll leads to a "scientifically induced or experimental neurosis."[28] So what we have in the rock 'n' roll craze is a conditioned reflex technique as part of a vast conspiracy of Afro-directed cultural energies in the service of communism.

> And the frightening—even terrifying—aspect of this mentally conditioned process is the fact that these young people, in this highly excited, hypnotic state, can be told to do practically anything—and they will. One can scarcely conceive of the possibility but nevertheless the method exists, wherein the enemies of our Republic could actually use television and the Beatles (or some other rock n roll or even rock n folk group) to place thousands upon thousands of our teenagers into a frenzied, hypnotic state and send them forth into the streets to riot and revolt.[29]

Is this fear of subliminal subversion so unusual? Is it limited to the right wing and lunatic fringe, or were there similar, much more accepted fantasies at large? Vance Packard's *Hidden Persuaders* was a bestseller of the late fifties, which on the basis of Ernest Dichter's subliminal induction theory argues that crafty corporations are using subliminal messages which flash invisibly

26. Ibid., 78.
27. Ibid., 79.
28. Ibid., 81.
29. Ibid., 90–91.

on the screen to make us buy things we don't need.[30] Though he was quickly challenged, the people at large believed Packard, not his critics. Have things changed? Today, people tend to believe Oliver Stone's version of the JFK assassination, not the official line. Paranoia, it seems, is much more satisfying than complex historical explanation.

The Beatles: The New Anti-Christ of Secularization

Noebel then attacks the vulgar anti-Christianity of the Beatles. Here he rightly sees the forces of modernization and secularization looming large, indicated in Lennon's offhand remark that the Beatles are more popular than Christ. Noebel actually read John Lennon's *A Spaniard in the Works*, an irreverent takeoff of James Joyce's *Finnegan's Wake*, and stumbles over a protagonist with the name Jesus El Pifco, whom Noebel quickly uncovers: "[U]nquestionably Our Lord." A guardedly positive review of Lennon's book in the Communist *Daily Worker* and in the magazine of the W. E. B. Du Bois Clubs of America makes John Lennon a Communist sympathizer. Noebel detects a Marxist double standard: crafty Communists forbid the Beatles in the U.S.S.R. and promote them in the U.S. To settle his case he quotes leftist music critic Irwin Silber, editor of *Sing Out*, who writes: "The great strength of rock n roll lies in the music of the music—in particular in the beat and in the immensely creative harmonies, counterpoints, and answer back patterns of the sound. Because it is a sound which is basically *sexual, un-Puritan, free in expression* and outside the main idiom of white middle class and upper class America, it is music *whose very form is a threat to established patterns and values.*"[31] See, Noebel shouts triumphantly, I told you so.[32] The fortieth anniversary of the Communist journal *Daily Worker* was celebrated in Carnegie Hall in 1964, where David Landsman, a young beatnik singer first sang "We Shall Overcome" and then added that the Beatles who had sung in Carnegie Hall recently had spoken up against the bomb. Contagion again: all of this puts the Beatles squarely in the Communist camp and makes

30. It is interesting that the very same Vance Packard spoke up against the "enemy from within," namely rock 'n' roll before a congressional committee. Hill, "The Enemy Within," passim.

31. Noebel's emphasis. Noebel, *Rhythm*, 103–104.

32. Here it is telling that left and right agree on the "facts" of the spread of African rhythms, but interpret these in diametrically opposed world-views.

"We Shall Overcome" a Communist hymn. Didn't Castro sing a similar song entitled "Venceremos," Noebel asks.

He then turns to the Beatles's performance and literally drools in a veritable exhibit of paranoid and pornographic *angstlust*, over the animalistic *mise en scène*, the sexual innuendoes of the lyrics, the base instincts being addressed, the savage jungle fever, the hysteria and loss of control of the audience, all of which is manipulated by Moscow.[33] His chief witness now is Jack Staulcup, president of Local No. 200, American Federation of Musicians, whose letter to Sergeant Shriver's Office of Economic Opportunity Noebel quotes that whereas the Soviet Union forbids rock 'n' roll and their delinquency rate goes down by 36 percent, the American delinquency rate since the advent of rock 'n' roll has gone up 50 percent, let alone the number of unwed mothers, victims of venereal disease, and drug users. And what or who is to be blamed? dissonant harmonies, blue notes, and alternative rhythms, all of them Communist-inspired. Support of this thesis comes again from abroad. A distinguished British music teacher, Alice English Monsarrat, writes: "Any psychiatrist knows that it is precisely this two directional pull of conflicting drives and emotions that is helping to fill our mental hospitals with broken wrecks of humanity."[34]

Noebel skillfully mixes the views of cultural conservatives from at home and abroad, of leftist music critics with old-fashioned tastes, and of fundamentalist Christians and adds it is "precisely at this point that rock n'roll and much of the modern music becomes potentially dangerous. This is because, to maintain a sense of well-being and integration, it is essential that man is not subjected too much to any rhythms not in accord with his natural bodily rhythms."[35] This was a view for which he could find a lot of support across the entire political spectrum, including a lot of parents who were disturbed by the sounds issuing from their children's rooms. But then, did not Frank Sinatra have the same effect on the teenagers a decade before? he asks rhetorically, and then calls again on composer Dr. Howard Hanson to bail Sinatra out: "The popularity of Frank Sinatra has caused his name to be mentioned frequently in connection with the deleterious effects of popular music, but I can find no evidence to support this claim.

33. It is interesting in this context that Hargis after 1970 had to keep a lower profile in the Christian Crusade after having sexually harassed his secretary.

34. Noebel, *Rhythm*, 117.

35. Ibid., 118.

Most of the music he sings is sentimental and nostalgic. He sings with sincerity and sensitivity and not infrequently artistry. If young girls are moved to squeal with delight I do not believe any harm has been done."[36] And of course we remember Frank Sinatra's unprintable comments on rock 'n' roll, a music he hated with a vengeance. Noebel creates a broad basis of cultural consent on which to build his political argument.

Noebel then turns to the Communist use of folk music. Here he is on much firmer ground, for the folk movement of 1946 was very close to if not identical with the vastly reduced Communist movement, as the books of leftists such as Serge Denisoff or Robbie Lieberman quite readily admit. To prove the Communist involvement in folk music is so easy for Noebel that a note of disappointment creeps into his report, for he is after more insidious and hidden forces: the real enemy is not the Communist singers on stage (Noebel lists them in his appendix), but the soft liberals who go to their concerts and who ought to be listed as well. Therefore, he focuses less on Communist singers than on those people who have come out in favor of People's Songs Inc. in the media or in articles or through practical support: Woody Guthrie, John Hammond Jr., Kenneth Spencer, Alec Wilder, Walter Lowenfels, Leonard Bernstein, Norman Corwin, Lincoln Kirstein, Oscar Hammerstein II, Lena Horne, Alain Locke, Dorothy Parker, Aaron Copland, Louis Untermeyer, Sam Wanamaker, Paul Robeson, Josh White, and Moses Ash; later he adds Langston Hughes, Sonny Terry, Brownie McGhee, and Huddie Ledbetter. All are associated with *Broadside Magazine*, a folk music journal, and—he does not say so, but all his readers are alert enough to notice—with few exceptions most of these subversives are either Jews or blacks. Repeatedly, he points out the close association between Jewish Communists and black rebels such as Paul Robeson or Shirley Graham Du Bois. He is careful not to repeat the mistake of a cofounder of the John Birch Society, a professor of sociology from Chicago, Revilo Oliver, whom Welch had to drop after he gave a rabid anti-Semitic talk in Boston. Revilo indeed. Though demoted by the John Birch Society, Revilo stayed on call in its wings, where Noebel promptly found him. In the acknowledgment section of his book Noebel thanks Revilo for valuable information.[37] In sum,

36. Ibid., 117.
37. Revilo P. Oliver's interpretation of the Kennedy assassination falls into line with his paranoid style: in his view Kennedy had been slack in preparing the U.S. for

the marriage between folk and "unnatural rhythms," engineered by a Jewish-black conspiracy gives him trouble: "This new marriage of beat and folk music is proving a total capitulation on the part of the U.S. record companies to the Red-infested folk field."[38]

Folk Music and the Negro Revolution

In Noebel's view "We Shall Overcome" is the "revolutionary folk song of Communism. The togetherness of Communism, folk music … SNCC, Sing Out!… and 'We Shall Overcome' is phenomenal." We witness a Communist-planned Negro revolution. Quite like the John Birch Society, Noebel considers civil rights unnecessary, even dangerous, and often refers to the "harmonious" race relations of nineteenth-century America. Noebel presents a rather good history of the genesis of the folk song movement by quoting from left-wing publications—e.g., he points out the importance of the Highlander Folk School in Monteagle, Tennessee, and its influence in the civil rights movement. "Out of the loins of this little Red School house issued forth a student and close friend of the school by the name of Martin Luther King,"[39] who—though a fellow man of the cloth—is a "wolf in sheep's clothing." This folksy image, incidentally, was J. Edgar Hoover's official FBI line on King. Martin Luther King Jr., he quotes, was referred to as a "trouble maker and rabble rouser" by former President Harry Truman and as "the most notorious liar in the country" by FBI Director J. Edgar Hoover. King was not only a student at the Highlander Folk School in Monteagle, Tenn., but also "openly welded his Southern Christian Leadership Conference to the Highlander Folk School."[40] As a fellow Christian Noebel never comes out squarely against civil rights. Though he admits that there were people of "good will" in the Selma marches, there was much evidence of cross-racial fornication, and it is primarily Jews and blacks doing it in the street. King, the wolf in sheep's clothing could well be the "key to Communist revolution in the United States."[41] Giving the vote to Negroes, he avers in an aside, will be

---

the "effective capture" by Communists, and therefore had become a political liability. Therefore, the latter shot him. *The New York Times*, 11 February 1964.

38. Noebel, 146.
39. Ibid., 181.
40. Ibid.
41. Ibid., 184.

detrimental to the social fabric.[42] At regular intervals he stabilizes his argument by trotting out witnesses from the enemy camp. He quotes TV personality Steve Allen's *Letter to a Conservative*, 1965, which, while ridiculing the idea of Beatles being Communists, admits there is a grain of truth in Noebel's allegations that American music is more "leftist."[43] Noebel jumps on this admission gladly and triumphantly adds Allen, a liberal with excellent credentials, to his endorsers.

In a chapter entitled "BOB DYLAN AND ROCK N' FOLK!" all previous caveats come together. I won't repeat his innuendoes against Dylan and his friends, Joan Baez, and Phil Ochs. But in a rousing finale he returns to the root evil, African-derived HOT JAZZ. Again he quotes the enemy, Sidney Finkelstein: "Any description of jazz must take in the great stream of music that came out of Africa, and was worked up and transformed into Spirituals, work songs, field calls, juba dances, cake walks, including *a music of talking drums prohibited by the slave owners and becoming the most intricate and vital [force] of dancing*."[44] The book ends with an evocation of the Watts riot as one consequence of uninhibited African rhythms. In August "trained revolutionists, with their disgruntled lackeys and always present dupes, destroyed acres of Watts territory with gasoline bombs and a bloodcurdling riot cry borrowed from a Los Angeles disk jockey: "Burn, Baby, Burn."[45] So much for a rare and curious book from this epoch which I was wise enough not to throw away.[46]

42. Ibid., 191.
43. Ibid., 204.
44. Noebel's emphasis. Ibid., 237.
45. Ibid., 249.
46. Noebel's paranoia concerning African-American music, which reflected a larger systemic nativist angst, did affect, dialectically, the cultural production of black America. Indeed, the cultural fundamentalism of such racist fears could be identified as one of the causes of the rise of black cultural nationalism. Ishmael Reed's novel *Mumbo Jumbo*, published in 1972, is the mirror image of the white fear of African music: a conspiratorial view of history from an Afrocentric view. The novel depicts the spread of an Afro-American music-and-dance-plague called "Jes Grew" during the time of the Harlem Renaissance. The disease emanates from Congo Square in New Orleans, and the nineteenth-century voodoo queen Marie Laveau represents the African connection. The symptoms of the disease according to a white doctor were that "people were doing 'stupid sensual things,' were in a state of 'uncontrollable frenzy,' were wriggling like fish, doing something called the 'Eagle Rock' and the 'Sassy Bump'; were cutting a mean 'Mooche,' and 'lusting after relevance.' We decoded this coon mumbo jumbo … if this Jes Grew becomes pandemic it will mean the end of Civilization As We Know It." (Preface, no page

Fears of Africa: Family Resemblances

We might be tempted to dismiss Noebel's book as an instance of lunatic fringe paranoia. And surely it is that. But all elements of his paranoia resonate in the history of American nativism and racism and are available in more or less manifest or latent form in a large body of narratives and historical records—and in the un-ending discourse on race relations to this very day. And paranoia is not only a matter of ignorance or of false degrees. There are highbrow, middlebrow, and lowbrow versions of Noebel's fear of African rhythms throughout American history. We might divide this angst into the following clusters:

(1) African rhythm and rebellion (subversion/communism)
(2) African rhythms and heathenish practices (unchristian)
(3) African rhythms and morality (perversion, sex, and moral decline)
(4) African rhythm and the Western canon (hierarchy and status quo)

There is such an overwhelming mass of evidence in the books of Dena Epstein, Winthrop Jordan, George Frederickson, and Joel Williamson,[47] which divides neatly into these four categories, that to present it all would numb us by overkill. Hence, a few nuggets from this racial minefield may suffice.

(1) A typical example of the fear that Africanism means rebel-liousness is evident in a letter from a slaveholder in Charleston, South Carolina, to the local newspaper after the Denmark Vesey plot. "None of the Negroes belonging to the Protestant Episcopal Church were concerned in the late conspiracy ... the event which gave rise to these considerations had its origin and seat chiefly in the African church."[48] One hundred years earlier Le Page du Pratz reports from Louisiana: "Nothing is more to be dreaded than to

---

number) Interestingly enough, Reed's wacky Afrocentric fantasy mirrors the para-noid text type including as dramatis personae secret lodges and conspiratorial net-works which endure through radical social and political changes. Reed, like Noebel, also makes use of footnotes and learned references.

47. Dena J. Epstein, *Sinful Tunes and Spirituals: Black Folk Music to the Civil War* (Urbana and Chicago, 1977); Winthrop Jordan, *White over Black: American Attitudes Toward the Negro 1550–1812* (Chapel Hill, NC, 1968); George Frederickson, *The Black Image in the White Mind* (New York, 1971); Joel Williamson, *The Crucible of Race: Black-White Relations in the American South Since Emancipation* (New York, 1984).

48. Epstein, *Sinful Tunes*, 195–96. In his first message to the Virginia Legislature after the Nat Turner insurrection, Governor Floyd said: "The most active incendiaries

see the Negroes assemble together on Sundays, since, under pre-
tense of Calinda, or the dance, they sometimes get together to the
number of three or four hundred and make a kind of Sabbath,
which it is always prudent to avoid; for it is in those tumultuous
meetings that they plot their rebellion."[49] Currently, the association of rap music and rioting is a well-established fear.

(2) The attempt on the part of the clergy (white or black) to
eliminate heathenish practices is so well known in the history of
Christianization that a few pointers may suffice. Reverend Le Jau
writes in 1709 that he excludes blacks from communion "if they
dance." Reverend Whitfield speaks of the profanation of the Sabbath by black dancing in 1739.[50] In 1860 an editorial of a New England weekly, *The Universalist*, chastises the loud services that have
emerged with the Baptists and Methodists (and their black adher-
ents) and categorically states: "We are a cool people." A particularly persistent object of Christian fear was the ring-shout, a
collective ritual in which the faithful would form a ring and shuffle in a circle, and, clapping their hands in complicated rhythmic
patterns, sing themselves into a state of possession. Blacks tried to
convince their white brethren that this shuffle was not a dance,
since there was no crossing of feet. The religious establishment
remained unconvinced and clearly recognized the alien, African
practice.[51] Throughout American history there has been a concerted attempt to root out this unchristian evil.

(3) One of the most persistent clusters is the association of
African rhythms and moral decay. During the emergence of what
we would today call "American" music at the height of the new
immigration (1890–1920) the collusion of Jews and blacks was
particularly frightening, and indeed there was a concerted effort
to stem this dual tide of black and Jewish music. The latter were
seen as translators of the black style. The first "Africanization" of
the musical taste on a national scale occurred during the so-called
ragtime period (1890–1910). The reaction to ragtime by established musicians in the early part of this century was related to

---

among us ... have been the negro preachers [from new African Methodist Episcopal churches] ... Those preachers ... have been the channels through which the
inflammatory pamphlets and papers brought ... from other states have been circulated among the slaves.... The public interest requires that the negro preachers
be silenced." Ibid., 229.

49. Epstein, *Sinful Tunes*, 32.
50. Ibid., 39.
51. Ibid., passim.

the pervasive feeling of decline common among the ruling classes, as expressed in Madison Grant's *The Passing of the Great Race,* 1916. From the perspective of an Anglo-Saxon ascendancy, ragtime had to appear as a pathological, immoral, patently sexual, and subversive instrument of decline, pretty much as jazz and rock 'n' roll appeared to Noebel or as rap appears to conservatives today.[52] The composer Daniel Gregory Mason thundered: "Let us purge America and the Divine Art of Music from this polluting nonsense." Hans Muck, the Swiss conductor of the Boston Symphony Orchestra, concurred: "I think that what you call ragtime is poison.... A person inoculated with the ragtime fever is like one addicted to strong drink." Others charged that it led to permanent brain damage or that it would wreck the nervous system. "Its greatest destructive power lies in its power to lower the moral standards." Walter Winston Kenilworth wrote a letter to the Paris editor of the New York *Herald Tribune* in 1913 which was later reprinted in the *Musical Courier.* It sums up negatively what the forces of destruction are:

> Can it be said that America is falling prey to the collective soul of the negro through the influence of what is popularly known as "rag time" music?... If there is any tendency toward such a national disaster, it should be definitely pointed out and extreme measures taken to inhibit the influence and avert the increasing danger—if it has not already gone too far.... The American "rag time" or "rag time" evolved music is symbolic of the primitive morality and perceptible moral limitations of the negro type. With the latter sexual restraint is almost unknown, and the widest latitude of moral uncertainty is conceded.[53]

Daniel Gregory Mason, a New England composer and music critic, concurred and, in jumbled prose that mirrors his nativist angst, continued the argument by defining the role of the Jew in this nefarious plot to destroy Aryan America:

> Ragtime is a mere comic strip representing American vices. Here is a rude noise which emerged from the hinterlands of brothels and dives, presented in a negroid manner by Jews most often, so popular that even high society Vanderbilts dance to it. All this syncopated music wasn't American, it is un-American. The Jew and the

52. The following argument depends on and uses parts of Berndt Ostendorf, "The Diluted Second Generation: German-Americans in Music 1870–1920," in *German Worker's Culture in the US: 1850–1920,* ed. Hartmut Keil (Washington, D.C., 1988), 261–87.

53. "Demoralizing Ragtime Music," *Musical Courier,* 21 May 1913, 22–23.

Yankee stand in human temperance at polar points. The Jew has oriental extravagance and sensuous brilliance. However, ragtime is a reflection of these raucous times; it is music without a soul.[54]

These apocalyptic reactions are by now familiar stuff in the history of jazz and popular music. They articulate a latent fear of instability and libidinal freedom associated with the threatening other, represented at this time by blacks and Jews.[55] Lest German readers would gloat over these WASP excesses with *Schadenfreude* let me quote a critic from Germany, Gustav Kühl, who confessed to spirit possession in 1903:

Suddenly I discovered that my legs were in a condition of great excitement. They twitched as though charged with electricity and betrayed a considerable and rather dangerous desire to jerk me from my seat. The rhythm of the music, which had seemed so unnatural at first was beginning to work its influence over me. It wasn't that feeling of ease in the joints of the feet and toes which might be caused by a Strauss waltz, no, much more energetic, material, independent as though one encountered a balking horse, which it is absolutely impossible to master.[56]

Noebel was obviously not far off the mark to summon the authority of Pavlov. On the role of Jews, blacks, and the change towards hedonism or a consumption ethic we might also consult John Higham, *Send These To Me*: "Jewish entertainers ... novelists ... and literary critics ... became leading disseminators of an urban

54. Quoted in Kenneth Aaron Kanter, *The Jews on Tin Pan Alley* (New York, 1982). See my review in *Popular Music* 4 (1984): 323–27. There is more on the theme of Jewish-Yankee opposition in music in McDonald Smith Moore, *Yankee Blues: Musical Culture and American Identity* (Bloomington, 1985); see my review in *Popular Music* 6, no. 3 (October 1987), 358–59. In that context the music of Henry Franklin Belknap Gilbert (1868–1928) is of interest. Gilbert, a classical composer, wrote a number of pieces with a ragtime inflection: "Comedy Overture on Negro Themes" (1905) and "Dance in Place Congo," (1906–08) which was rejected by Karl Muck as "niggah music" unfit for the concert hall. He then rewrote it as a ballet score, with a premiere at the Metropolitan Opera in 1918. By this time the shock of hearing Negro inflections in classical music had worn off, and reviews of his earlier works were quite favorable, but Gilbert withdrew from what he called his "Negro phase." Charles Hamm, *Music in the New World* (New York, 1983), 419–20.

55. In 1930 Mason writes: "And our whole contemporary aesthetic attitude toward instrumental music, especially in New York, is dominated by Jewish tastes and standards, with their Oriental extravagance, their sensuous brilliancy and intellectual facility and superficiality, their general tendency to exaggeration and disproportion." Daniel Gregory Mason, *Tune In America* (Westport, CT, 1930), 160.

56. Gustav Kühl, "The Musical Possibilities of Ragtime," translated by Gustav Saenger, *Metronome* 19 (March 1903): 11.

morality, which gave a new emphasis to hedonism, intellectuality, and anxiety."[57] Lew Erenberg's *Steppin' Out: New York Nightlife and the Transformation of American Culture, 1890–1930*[58] also sees the collusion of Jews and blacks, but both of them see this positively, a liberation, a loosening of the Victorian corset. The paranoid interpretation is completely logical and in line with the liberal consensus, yet the premise is vastly different.

(4) The passing of "natural" hierarchies and of the values of the "Great White Race" is an idea that is still alive and well. The fear of the destruction of a hierarchy of cultures or a hierarchy of values was recently resurrected by the late Alan Bloom, and the fact that his incoherent book became a runaway bestseller is evidence of how deep this paranoid fear is rooted and how widespread this fear still is.

One of the very first documents on black dancing by the French monk Jean Baptiste Labat regards these African dances as "déshonnêtes, indécentes, lascives, cette danse infame" and would replace them by the minuet and courante.[59] Benjamin Latrobe watches blacks dance on Congo Square in 1819:

> A man sung a uncouth song to the dancing which I suppose was in some African language, for it was not French, & the women screamed a detestable burthen on one single note. The allowed Amusements of Sunday have, it seems, perpetuated here those of Africa among its inhabitants. I have never seen anything more brutally savage, and at the same time dull & stupid than this whole exhibition.[60]

Western standards were so deeply internalized by Franklin Frazier or Gunnar Myrdal that they concluded in the 1940s that "Blacks have no culture to guard and to protect."[61] Samuel Huntington would clearly not object today, for in—of all places—*Foreign Affairs* he talks of the "Clash of Civilizations." He writes, "the world will be shaped in measure by the interactions among seven or eight major civilizations. These include Western, Confucian, Japanese, Islamic, Hindu, Slavic-Orthodox, Latin American," and

57. John Higham, *Send These to Me: Jews and Other Immigrants in Urban America* (New York, 1975), 194.

58. Lew Erenberg, *Steppin' Out: New York Nightlife and the Transformation of American Culture, 1890–1930* (Westport, CT, 1981).

59. Epstein and Foster, *Radical Right*, 30.

60. Ibid., 97.

61. Berndt Ostendorf, "Black Poetry, Blues, and Folklore: Double Consciousness in Afro-American Oral Culture," *Amerikastudien/American Studies* 20 (1975): 209–59.

then he adds rather lamely "and possibly African civilization."[62] Everyone in the U.S. understood the message in terms of domestic race relations: African culture does not really matter. This is reminiscent of John Locke's hierarchy of civilizations, which mentions some of the same groups, but ranks them in a hierarchy with European civilization at the top and with Africa clearly at the bottom. Do not most white Americans (or European) still believe this? Noebel's fears are merely the paranoid tip of a much larger and deeper angst about an American national destiny adrift in a sea of African rhythms.

62. Samuel P. Huntington, "The Clash of Civilizations?" *Foreign Affairs* 72 (1993): 2–49.

PART IV

THE WORLD WARS

Chapter Seven

GERMAN-AMERICANS IN WORLD WAR I

Mark Ellis

By the middle of this century, German-Americans, once a distinct and readily identifiable immigrant group, had become one of the most assimilated and least remarked upon ethnic components of American society. The extent to which this transformation stemmed from group and individual war-related experiences in the period from 1914 to 1920 is a matter of some debate. La Vern Rippley and Erik Kirschbaum suggest that German-American citizens of the United States and unnaturalized German aliens made sudden war-induced decisions to assimilate. In contrast, Willi-Paul Adams argues that the war coincided with the conclusion of a lengthy process of assimilationist adjustments by German-Americans, and that its effects on this process have been overstated.[1] There can be little doubt that the level of hostility and suspicion encountered by people who were identified with Germany in the years from 1914 to 1917, and the subsequent requirement, aggressively enforced, that all inhabitants of the United

---

1. Stephan Thernstrom, ed., *Harvard Encyclopedia of American Ethnic Groups* (Cambridge, MA, 1980), 406; La Vern J. Rippley, *The German-Americans* (Boston, 1976); Erik Kirschbaum, *The Eradication of German Culture in the United States, 1917–1918* (Stuttgart, 1986); Willi-Paul Adams, "Ethnic Politicians and American Nationalism During the First World War: Four German-Born Members of the U.S. House of Representatives," *American Studies International* 29 (April 1991): 20-34.

States support the war effort, created what one historian has called a "loyalty crisis" for German-Americans.[2] By the time of the Armistice, celebrations of *Deutschtum* (Germanness) were much less frequent and confident than they had been before 1914. Germans in America had been made to recognize the disadvantages of being "hyphenated," amid an antipathy which hastened their thorough assimilation as Americans.[3] To a large extent, this resulted from the way in which the German image in the American mind was transformed during the war from being largely positive to overwhelmingly negative.

In 1910, eight million people of German extraction lived in the United States (8.7 percent of the population), of whom 2.3 million had been born in Germany. They lived mostly in the Middle Atlantic and East North Central states. More than half were members of Lutheran, Reformed, or Evangelical Protestant churches; one-third were Catholics. Between the Civil War and World War I, Germans were the largest single group of first-generation immigrants, but by the end of this period they had ceased to be a significant element among new arrivals. In the 1850s and 1860s Germans constituted over a third of all immigration; by 1910 they made up less than 5 percent, and immigration was now dominated by other groups, such as Italians. Whereas 250,000 Germans and just 38,000 Italians entered the United States in 1882, the figures for each nationality were reversed by 1907.[4]

Partly as a result of the ways in which immigration was changing, a latent nativist, anti-immigrant, tendency in American society and politics grew rapidly between 1890 and 1914. This was heightened by recurrent economic problems and the expansion of the cities. Calls for immigration restriction were bound up with an ideology in which the foreigner was presented as a threat to American institutions and civilization. Thus, the reaction against German-Americans during World War I did not derive solely from their being identified with the enemy; its language and assumptions

2. Frederick C. Luebke, *Bonds of Loyalty: German-Americans and World War I* (De Kalb, IL, 1974), 327.

3. Luebke, *Bonds of Loyalty*, xv and 329; John A. Hawgood, *The Tragedy of German-America: The Germans in the United States of America During the Nineteenth Century—and After* (New York, 1940), 198–99; Rippley, *German-Americans*, 180; *Harvard Encyclopedia*, 406.

4. Phyllis Keller, *States of Belonging: German-American Intellectuals and the First World War* (Cambridge, MA, 1979), 265; *Harvard Encyclopedia*, 406, 409. In 1900, Germans were the largest foreign-born group in twenty-seven states. Hawgood, *Tragedy*, 82–83.

owed much to a preexisting high level of anti-immigrant thought. Nativists were not especially anti-German—they were much more concerned about immigrants from southern and eastern Europe, whose numbers had grown sharply since the 1890s—but the nativist tendency was always unforgiving toward any group which seemed to have reservations about becoming purely American. When German-Americans were perceived as having divided loyalties during a superpatriotic surge that swept the United States from 1915 to 1918, anything which suggested an attachment to German heritage was attacked. John Higham has argued that prewar nativism "formed a backlog of sentiment for and a bridge of transition into the greater nationalism of the war period." William Preston, while accepting much of Higham's thesis, sees the relationship more in terms of a specifically anti-radical nativism on the part of the federal government. World War I, he argues, provided "the tools to translate this desire into effective action."[5]

In a sense, then, since German-Americans were not part of the "New Immigration" of the turn of the century, and since most of them were not politically radical, they were innocent bystanders, caught in the wildly scattered blasts of the nativist forces that grew in strength as American intervention in the war in Europe became first a controversial possibility and then a fact. During 1915 and 1916, the phrase "100% Americanism" came to mean patriotic conformity, in contrast to "hyphenated Americanism." Foreign attachments of all kinds were regarded as disloyal by those who proclaimed themselves "100% American." Moreover, once the United States entered the war, the Wilson administration and its supporters condemned all criticism of the government, believing that a diverse society like the United States could only prevail in war if all doubts were silenced. By the spring of 1917, therefore, any dissenting voice, German-American or otherwise, might automatically be accused of "pro-Germanism."

During the nineteenth century, Germans had enjoyed a generally positive image in American society, one which derived from the obvious commercial, educational, and cultural contributions they made to American life.[6] While they played a major part in

5. John Higham, *Strangers in the Land: Patterns of American Nativism, 1860-1925* (New York, 1966), 195, 198–202, and 204–207; William Preston Jr., *Aliens and Dissenters: Federal Suppression of Radicals, 1903–1933* (Cambridge, MA, 1963), 3.

6. See, for example: Wolfgang J. Helbich, *"Alle Menschen sind dort gleich": Die deutsche Amerika-Auswanderung im 19. und 20. Jahrhundert* (Düsseldorf, 1988), 55, 126–28, and 132–34.

building the expanding nation, they also retained their *Deutschtum*. Indeed, since the mid-nineteenth century, German-American
intellectuals and politicians had fostered the idea of permanent
German-American biculturalism. In 1901, this urge to retain a distinct identity within the United States found expression in the
National German-American Alliance (Deutsch-Amerikanische Na-
tionalbund). It was created to encourage good citizenship, the use
of the German language, cordial relations between Germany and
the United States, and, in its own words, "for the protection of the
German element against 'nativistic' attacks."[7] By the outbreak of
war in Europe, it was the largest-ever American ethnic organization, at least on paper, claiming two million members and chapters
in forty states. It was endorsed by the German-language press and
assisted financially by the brewing industry.[8] The tone set by leadership of the German-American Alliance was chauvinistic and, in
the nativist circumstances, perhaps ill judged. In 1914, the
Alliance's support of Germany and its insistence on American neutrality was so fervent that the actual interests of the United States
seemed to be of lesser importance.[9] Guido Dobbert has argued that
German-American chauvinism, which had been growing since the
1890s, was a defensive response, not just to nativism, but also to the
temperance movement and a loss of political and social influence,
as German suburbs and towns were annexed by large cities, such
as Cincinnati. In some German-Americans, it also produced a rev-
erence for the Kaiser and support for the foreign ambitions of the
Imperial Government.[10]

7. Clifton James Child, *The German-Americans in Politics, 1914–1917* (Madison,
1939), 3.

8. Rippley, *German-Americans*, 180-2. Club membership was common among
German-Americans. In 1915, New York, Chicago, Philadelphia, and Milwaukee
each had more than 200 German clubs, *Harvard Encyclopedia*, 416–7.

9. Willi-Paul Adams, "Ethnic Leadership and the German-Americans," in
*America and the Germans: An Assessment of a Three-Hundred-Year History, Volume
One: Immigration, Language, Ethnicity*, ed. Frank Trommler and Joseph McVeigh
(Philadelphia, 1985), 157; Child, *German-Americans in Politics*, 174–9; Horace C.
Peterson, *Propaganda for War: The Campaign Against American Neutrality, 1914–1917*
(Norman, OK, 1939), 140; Higham, *Strangers in the Land*, 197. Herman Ridder, in the
New-Yorker Staats-Zeitung, attempted to rebut charges of insufficient German-
American devotion to the United States: "Whenever it has been a question between
my own country and that of my fathers, I have given wholehearted support to the
former. Only when it was a question of supporting Germany or her enemies have
I given rein to an unerasable affection for the Fatherland." Hawgood, *Tragedy*, 294.

10. Guido A. Dobbert, "German-Americans Between New and Old Fatherland,
1870-1914," *American Quarterly* 19 (1967): 663–80.

The prohibition issue was important, in that it helped to condition Americans to accept the wartime portrayal of German culture as bestial, deviant, and incompatible with Americanism. The temperance movement had long regarded beer-drinking German-Americans as its toughest opposition; German resistance to temperance had prevented the passage of state prohibition laws in Pennsylvania, New York, Ohio, Wisconsin, Indiana, Illinois, and Iowa. Long before the United States itself declared war, the temperance movement began to exploit the European conflict to attack Germans and, by association, the trade in alcohol. German-Americans were denounced as spies, while atrocities in Belgium were blamed on drink-crazed soldiers. Surreal characterizations of the German people flourished. One leading prohibitionist regarded the failure of diplomacy as only a marginal cause of the war:

> The primary and secondary and all-compelling cause is that a race of people have arisen who eat like gluttons and drink like swine— a race whose "God is their belly," and whose inevitable end is destruction. Their sodden habits of life have driven them constantly toward brutality and cruelty until they were prepared to strike for universal conquest, though millions of lives and oceans of blood was to be the price of reaching that unholy ambition. Beer will do for a nation exactly what it will do for an individual.... We seek a saloonless and drunkenless world.[11]

With the American declaration of war in 1917, prohibition became an impeccably patriotic ambition. Banning alcohol production would save food, create space on freight trains, and keep civilians and servicemen sober. To oppose prohibition, therefore, was to reveal pro-German sympathies. The Wisconsin superintendent of the Anti-Saloon League declared that "Pro-Germanism is ... the froth from the German beer-saloon.... Kaiser Kultur was raised on beer."[12] The main targets of such attacks were the German-American brewers, who had funded the anti-temperance political campaigns before 1917. As one prohibitionist warned, "We have German enemies across the water. We have German enemies in this country too. And the worst of all our German enemies, the most treacherous, the most menacing are Pabst, Schlitz, Blatz, and Miller."[13] Initially, German-Americans regarded insults

11. Andrew Sinclair, *Prohibition: The Era of Excess* (Boston, 1962), 117.

12. Ibid., 122.

13. James H. Timberlake, *Prohibition and the Progressive Movement, 1900-1920* (Cambridge, MA, 1966), 179.

of this kind as simply absurd, and in Kansas, where pro- and anti-prohibitionists were well organized, German-Americans dismissed the temperance movement as *Vassernarren* (water fools). Nevertheless, the war decisively admitted prohibitionism to the national political mainstream; hence the adoption of prohibition as a wartime measure and the eventual ratification of the Constitutional amendment passed by Congress in 1917. Thus, the temperance triumph was aided by the spurious linking of alcohol and the enemy during the war, using the convenient image of the German-American drinker, just as the movement for immigration restriction was given added impetus by the superpatriotism of wartime nativism.[14]

Espionage, real or imagined, became a central element in the growing myth of German treachery in America, and popular belief in it grew partly out of the manner in which the German government attempted to get its message across during American neutrality. German diplomats and their agents created their own propaganda office on Broadway in New York in August 1914, to produce newspaper articles and pamphlets. Funded by the embassy and private donations, its first objective was to convince the American people that Germany was not responsible for the outbreak of war. Reinhard Doerries's study of the workings of this energetic outfit suggests that it was incompetent, even though it succeeded in placing its articles in the early months of the war. One of its difficulties was a lack of direct and frequent contact with Berlin; another was the problem of explaining events such as the sinking of the *Lusitania* in May 1915. Moreover, speakers chosen to spread pro-German news about the war frequently misjudged the mood of the American public, tending to alienate by lecturing, rather than persuading.

Berlin gave financial support to selected German-language newspapers, such as the *New-Yorker Staats-Zeitung*, owned by the Ridder family. Vast sums were also secretly spent on acquiring mainstream papers, including the *New York Evening Mail*, although attempts to buy the *Washington Post* failed. Some links were made with Irish-American organizations, but the most concerted efforts of Ambassador Count von Bernstorff's staff were directed at arousing the *Deutschtum* of the German-American population, in the

---

14. Robert Smith Bader, *Prohibition in Kansas: A History* (Lawrence, KA, 1985), 69–70; David M. Kennedy, *Over Here: The First World War and American Society* (New York, 1980), 67–69.

hope that it would be able to influence American policy at the polls.[15] In this respect, the most effective German-American propagandist, a militant supporter of the German cause and strict American neutrality, was George Sylvester Viereck, who had been born in Munich in 1884 and arrived in the United States in 1896. A poet and journalist, Viereck published a weekly newspaper in English, the *Fatherland,* which received financial assistance from the German government.[16]

In 1915–16, the combination of blatant pro-German propaganda and persistent nativism led American politicians and the press to believe growing rumors about the infiltration of the United States by German spies and saboteurs, assisted by their German-American sympathizers. Although the image of the German traitor in America became firmly embedded in the public consciousness, uncertainty persists over the real extent and effectiveness of the German spy network. Rhodri Jeffreys-Jones refers to "the massive German penetration of 1915–18" and regards the activities of American domestic intelligence agents as "a rational response to a real threat.... German spies displayed ability and constituted a potentially effective force." Roy Talbert Jr. on the other hand, suggests that "the Central Powers had a sloppy propaganda campaign and a poorly developed intelligence operation in the United States."[17] Talbert's view is probably nearer the truth. Several bridges and munitions factories in the United States were bombed in 1916 and 1917, and the rudders were blown off a number of ships leaving American ports carrying munitions, but these incidents did little to halt the flow of materials to the Allies. Agents attempted to acquire loans and war materials for Germany, but with little success. Other activities suggest that covert German operations were sometimes imaginative, but lacked coherence. For example, operations were begun to provide false documents to German reservists in the United States and a harebrained scheme was devised to invade Canada with reservists from Chicago and Detroit armed with cudgels; active discussions were held with Asian Indian and Irish nationalists in the United

15. Reinhard R. Doerries, *Imperial Challenge: Ambassador Count Bernstorff and German-American Relations, 1908–1917* (Chapel Hill, NC, 1989), 39–76.

16. On George Sylvester Viereck and Word War I, see Keller, *States of Belonging,* 141–62.

17. Rhodri Jeffreys-Jones, *American Espionage: From Secret Service to C.I.A.* (New York, 1977), 56; Roy Talbert Jr., *Negative Intelligence: The Army and the American Left, 1917–1941* (Jackson, MS, 1991), 12.

States, in the hope that they would spark rebellions at home to overthrow British rule; attempts were made to cause a war between the United States and Mexico in 1915–16, in order to minimize the chances of American intervention in Europe and to divert American attention from the sea war. But German embassy staff and their agents were extraordinarily careless with their secret documents, several bundles of which were obtained by United States government officials in 1915 and 1916, with the result that much of the German intrigue in the United States became well known. Despite the fact that few of these schemes involved German-Americans directly, and despite the U.S. government's discovery of very few genuine spies and its failure to convict any German agents under the Espionage Act of June 1917, the entire ethnic group was implicated by association in subversion and intrigue.[18] British propagandists, who found a readiness on the part of the American press to carry pro-Allied accounts of events in Europe, made the most of the stories of German espionage, so as to heighten further anti-German feeling in the United States.[19] Especially effective in swinging American opinion behind the Allies were the contributions of former British ambassador Lord Bryce, whose accounts of German "outrages" in Belgium were published in the United States less than a week after the sinking of the *Lusitania,* and Arnold Toynbee, whose volumes on the "German terror" in Belgium and France appeared in 1917.[20] The British also launched specific propaganda attacks on German-Americans, in the form of sensational accounts of espionage and

18. Doerries, *Imperial Challenge,* 141–90; Jeffreys-Jones, *American Espionage,* 57–63; Luebke, *Bonds of Loyalty,* 138–40, 145; Peterson, *Propaganda for War,* 146–51; Christopher N. May, *In the Name of War: Judicial Review and the War Powers since 1918* (Cambridge, MA, 1989), 134. See also French Strother, *Fighting Germany's Spies: A Revelation of German Intrigue in America* (New York, 1918). Secretary of State Robert Lansing later recalled that German spy stories had been considerably exaggerated from 1914 to 1917. Robert Lansing, *War Memoirs* (Indianapolis, IN, 1935), 83–84.

19. Child, *German-Americans in Politics,* 98–101; Peterson, *Propaganda,* 173; Robert Henry Billigmeier, *Americans from Germany: A Study in Cultural Diversity* (Belmont, CA, 1974), 137–39. Since the British were not an ethnic bloc within American society, it was not easy to connect British propaganda and war aims to any particular section of the population. Nevertheless, see J. McCarthy, "The British," in *The Immigrant's Influence on Wilson's Peace Policies,* ed. Joseph P. O'Grady (Lexington, KY, 1967).

20. See James Bryce, *Evidence and Documents Laid Before the Committee on Alleged German Outrages* (New York, 1915); also James Bryce, *Neutral Nations and the War* (New York, 1914); Arnold J. Toynbee, *The German Terror in France; An Historical Record* (New York, 1917); Arnold J. Toynbee, *The German Terror in Belgium; An Historical Record* (New York, 1917).

disloyalty. These persisted after the United States entered the war. In March 1918, on a patriotic tour, the Scottish singer Harry Lauder charged that German propaganda was being pumped out during German-American Lutheran church services in St. Louis.[21]

Woodrow Wilson had made a series of speeches between 1915 and 1917, denouncing the paid lobbyists of the German government and, by implication, the German-American population. The language he used contributed to the atmosphere of suspicion, repression, and collective stereotype. In his State of the Union message of 7 December 1915, he said,

> There are citizens of the United States, I blush to admit, born under other flags, but welcomed under our generous naturalization laws to the full freedom and opportunity of America, who have poured the poison of disloyalty into the very arteries of our national life; who have sought to bring the authority and good name of our Government into contempt, to destroy our industries wherever they thought it effective for their vindictive purposes to strike at them, and to debase our politics to the uses of foreign intrigue.

He told Congress that disloyal elements "must be crushed out."[22] In a Flag Day address in June 1916, Wilson warned the American people:

> There is disloyalty in the United States, and it must be absolutely crushed. It proceeds from a minority, a very small minority, but a very active and subtle minority. It works underground, but it also shows its ugly head where we can see it; and there are those at this moment who are trying to levy a species of blackmail, saying, "Do what we wish in the interest of a foreign sentiment or we will wreak our vengeance at the polls."... Are you going yourselves, individually and collectively, to see to it that no man is tolerated who does not do honor to [the American] flag?[23]

Again, when accepting the Democratic renomination in September 1916, he spoke of the "passions and intrigues of certain active groups and combinations of men amongst us who were born under foreign flags [which have] injected the poison of disloyalty

21. See Frederick W. Wile, *The German-American Plot* (London, 1915); and William H. Skaggs, *German Conspiracies in America* (London, 1915).

22. Luebke, *Bonds of Loyalty*, 146. Insulted, the *New-Yorker Staats-Zeitung* said of Wilson's speech, "Ein Dokument würdeloser als dieses, steht in den Annalen der amerikanischen Geschichte nicht verzeichnet." ("The annals of American History record no document more unworthy than this.") Child, *German-Americans in Politics*, 90.

23. Luebke, *Bonds of Loyalty*, 169–71.

into our most critical affairs."[24] As Frederick Luebke has observed, "Wilson implied that political opposition to his administration by immigrant citizens was tantamount to disloyalty"—an equation that was to be made repeatedly by federal officials and civilian vigilance groups alike once the United States was at war.[25]

In making such speeches, Wilson was exploiting, and contributing to, the increasingly fierce and irrational campaign against "hyphenism"—the persistent desire of immigrant groups such as Irish-Americans and German-Americans to identify with their countries of origin. The leading campaigner on this issue was former president Theodore Roosevelt, who called openly for American intervention in the war in 1915 and claimed that "hyphenated" opponents of American belligerency were obstructing the adoption of a prudent policy of war preparedness because they were more fond of their homelands than of the United States.[26] The German-American Alliance made clumsy attempts to respond to nativist taunts and strengthen its members' resolve. In August 1915, Charles Hexamer, president of the Alliance, defended the German cultural contribution to America: "No one will ever find us prepared to step down to a lesser Kultur; no, we have made it our aim to draw the other up to us."[27] In December, he made the same point even more forcefully: "Whoever casts aside his Germanism from him like an old glove is not worthy to be spat on.... We have long suffered the preachment that 'you Germans must allow yourselves to be assimilated, you must merge into the American people': but no one will ever find us prepared to descend to an inferior culture."[28]

In 1916, German-American leaders and anti-British Irish groups tried to influence the outcome of the presidential election, but, while they may have swung votes in some areas, they did not

24. Child, *German-Americans in Politics*, 148.

25. Luebke, *Bonds of Loyalty*, 71.

26. Ibid., 140-42, 144, 174-75; Child, *German-Americans in Politics*, 129-30. Theodore Roosevelt had been complaining about "hyphenates" since 1894. See Theodore Roosevelt, *The Foes of Our Own Household* (New York, 1917).

27. Allan Kent Powell, "Our Cradles Were in Germany: Utah's German American Community and World War I," *Utah Historical Quarterly* 58 (1990): 378.

28. Keller, *States of Belonging*, 2. The philosopher Reinhold Niebuhr deplored Hexamer's brand of chauvinism and warned that, through their "aloofness," German-Americans had provoked much of the hostility which they were beginning to experience. See Reinhold Niebuhr, "The Failure of German-Americanism," *Atlantic Monthly* 118 (1916): 13–18; Paul Merkley, *Reinhold Niebuhr, A Political Account* (Montreal, 1975), 17–21; Richard W. Fox, *Reinhold Niebuhr: A Biography* (New York, 1985), 43–61.

affect the result. In fact, they probably embarrassed their preferred candidate, the Republican nominee Charles Evans Hughes, more than they assisted him. During the campaign, Wilson hit back at those who reproached him over the pro-British nature of American neutrality, stating that he would "neither seek the favor nor fear the displeasure of that small alien element which puts loyalty to any foreign power before loyalty to the United States."[29]

In January 1917, British naval intelligence intercepted and deciphered German Foreign Secretary Alfred Zimmermann's message to Mexico, offering a military alliance should resumption of unrestricted submarine warfare draw the United States into the war. This note was passed to the American government in late February and released to the press by Wilson during a contest with Congress over the principle of armed neutrality and the nature of presidential war powers.[30] At first, the telegram was dismissed as an American trick by neutrality advocates such as the newspaper magnate, William Randolph Hearst, and as a British trick by German-American publicists such as George Sylvester Viereck. Viereck called it "a preposterous document," an "impudent hoax," and "unquestionably a brazen forgery planted by British agents." When its authenticity was confirmed by Zimmermann, Viereck conceded that Germany had dealt "a cruel blow to Americans of German descent."[31] Like the *Lusitania* crisis, the Zimmermann telegram added to the legend of innate German wickedness, so that the character of German-Americans was further tainted.

In April 1917, convinced of the need to preserve freedom of the seas, break the deadlock in the trenches, and influence the postwar settlement, Woodrow Wilson secured a declaration of war from Congress. Wilson included in his justifications for war the claim that after 1914 Germany had "filled our unsuspecting communities and even offices of our government with spies and set criminal intrigues everywhere afoot against our national unity of counsel, our peace within and without, our industries and our

29. Arthur S. Link, *Woodrow Wilson and the Progressive Era, 1910-1917* (New York, 1963), 230-31, 245-94; Child, *German-Americans in Politics*, 131-37; Luebke, *Bonds of Loyalty*, 169-94; Rippley, *German-Americans*, 183-84; Higham, *Strangers in the Land*, 199-200; see also F. P. Olds, "'Kultur' in American Politics," *Atlantic Monthly* 118 (1916): 382-91.

30. Link, *Woodrow Wilson*, 271-72; Jeffreys-Jones, *American Espionage*, 62; see also Arthur S. Link, *Wilson*, vol. 5: *Campaigns for Progressivism and Peace, 1916–1917* (Princeton, NJ, 1965), 342-59.

31. Keller, *States of Belonging*, 154-55; Luebke, *Bonds of Loyalty*, 203; Link, *Woodrow Wilson*, 272.

commerce." He acknowledged that most German-Americans were loyal to the United States, but warned that "If there should be disloyalty, it will be dealt with with a firm hand of stern repression."[32] Wilson did not mean that lynch law should be applied, but liberal journalist Frederick Lewis Allen feared that "[h]atred will spring up quickly when American blood has been shed in war. Sensationalism will spread the German spy scare. Every suburban gossip will have her story of such-and-such a German-American's concrete tennis court and three-inch gun. Reprisals against loyal Americans of German birth will be advocated, and, one fears, frequently effected."[33]

Much has been written about the infringement of civil liberties during World War I.[34] Definitions of radicalism, disloyalty, and un-Americanism were so broad that any form of social protest or nonconformity could be proscribed. In the Immigration Act of February 1917, aliens had been implicitly linked with "anarchy,... the overthrow by force or violence of the Government of the United States or of all forms of law [and] ... the assassination of public officials."[35] It is not surprising, therefore, that non-naturalized Germans should have been especially suspected after the United States entered the war. In 1917, 4.6 million people living in the United States had been born in what were now the Central Powers and many worked in crucial industries, such as munitions, steel, and coal production. From mid-1916 onwards, the Justice Department had been compiling an index of aliens suspected

32. U.S. Congress, *Congressional Record*, 65th Cong., special sess., 2 April 1917, 102–4; see also Link, *Woodrow Wilson*, 278–81; Robert H. Ferrell, *Woodrow Wilson and World War I* (New York, 1985), 1–12.

33. Frederick Lewis Allen, "The American Tradition and the War," *Nation* 104, 26 April 1917, 485.

34. See, for example, Preston, *Aliens and Dissenters*, 88–180; May, *In the Name of War*, 133–90; Donald Johnson, *Challenge to American Freedoms: World War I and the Rise of the American Civil Liberties Bureau* (Lexington, KY, 1963); Harry N. Scheiber, *The Wilson Administration and Civil Liberties, 1917–1921* (Ithaca, NY, 1960); Horace C. Peterson and Gilbert C. Fite, *Opponents of War 1917–1918* (Seattle, WA, 1963); John Sayer, "Art and Politics, Dissent and Repression: The *Masses* Magazine Versus the Government, 1917–1918,"*American Journal of Legal History* 32 (January 1988): 42–78. Robert Ferrell states: "Considering that the American people never had taken part in a first-class foreign war prior to 1917, the nation's actions during and after World War I demonstrated remarkable maturity, and only in a single respect, attacks upon civil liberties and civil rights, was there an egregious and irreparable failure." Ferrell, *Woodrow Wilson*, 200.

35. Preston, *Aliens and Dissenters*, 83–85; Higham, *Strangers in the Land*, 202–4; *United States Statutes*, XXXIX, 889.

of having broken the neutrality laws, which by 31 March 1917 contained 11,770 names. That day, Attorney General Thomas W. Gregory warned the solicitor general, "There are a very large number
of German citizens in this country who are dangerous and are
plotting trouble, men from whom we must necessarily expect
trouble promptly of a sinister sort." The administration prepared
to apply the Alien Enemies Act of 1798, giving federal agents the
power to intern aliens if they were suspected of posing dangers to
public safety or were about to break the law. Sixty-three aliens
were arrested as soon as Congress declared war. In all, 6,300 Germans were arrested in wartime under presidential warrant, of
whom 2,300 were interned by the military authorities, a few released, and the rest paroled. Internments were reported prominently in local newspapers as a warning to other aliens. Many
aliens were also arrested by local police forces and state officials
and held for extended periods, supposedly on behalf of the federal authorities.[36] Waterfront passes were used to ban alien enemies from the vicinity of naval bases, natural harbors like Puget
Sound, and munitions factories—a device that allowed the government to exclude union organizers of the Industrial Workers of
the World (IWW).[37]

The war saw a massive growth of the domestic intelligence-gath-
ering capacity of the federal government. The Departments of State,
Treasury, Justice, War, Labor, the Navy, and the Post Office were
engaged in various kinds of surveillance, which were out of all proportion to the actual threat. The two most vigorous agencies were
the Bureau of Investigation (BI) of the Justice Department and the
Military Intelligence Branch (MIB) of the War Department's General
Staff.[38] Ostensibly, it was the task of the BI to provide evidence for

36. Preston, *Aliens and Dissenters*, 106; Joan M. Jensen, *The Price of Vigilance*
(Chicago, 1968), 29; Homer S. Cummings and Carl McFarland, *Federal Justice: Chap-
ters in the History of Justice and the Federal Executive* (New York, 1937), 418, 427;
Higham, *Strangers in the Land*, 210-17; Herbert Pankratz, "The Suppression of
Alleged Disloyalty in Kansas During World War I," *Kansas Historical Quarterly* 42
(1976): 277–307. The United States declared war separately on Austro-Hungary in
December 1917. On the internments, see Jörg Nagler, "Enemy Aliens in the USA,
1914–1918," in *Minorities in Wartime: National and Racial Groups in Europe, North
America and Australia During the Two World Wars*, ed. Panikos Panayi (Providence,
RI, 1993), 191–215.
37. Preston, *Aliens and Dissenters*, 161–62.
38. On the origins of the Bureau of Investigation, see Cummings and McFarland,
Federal Justice, 378–82; "Bielaski of the Secret Service," *Delineator* 92 (May 1918): 13;
"German Plotters Fear Him," *Literary Digest* 55 (29 September 1917): 60-64; on the
Military Intelligence Branch see: Talbert, *Negative Intelligence*, 3–19.

criminal prosecutions and that of the MIB to counteract enemy subversion, but by the summer of 1917 both agencies, separately and in cooperation, were gathering information about any individual or organization suspected of "disloyalty." Since a disloyal act could include the utterance of any kind of complaint about government policy, political leaders, or American society, federal officials began to embellish their evidence with "the word as well as the deed, and ... the underlying thought as well."[39] German-Americans were recurrent subjects of investigation in the vast files amassed by the BI and the MIB. In addition, Americans who had been open publicists for the German cause during the period of neutrality, such as the Hearst journalist William Bayard Hale, were subjected to repeated harassment by domestic intelligence agents.[40]

The IWW, a syndicalist union with a large alien membership, especially in western states, had been in conflict with employers and government officials since its formation in 1905. During the war, it was effectively destroyed by a combination of hostile propaganda and wholesale arrests and prosecutions under the Espionage and Sedition Acts.[41] Federal investigators and patriotic newspapers repeatedly made connections between pro-Germanism and left-wing union activity, thereby linking German-Americans with anarchism and the IWW with foreign sedition. The IWW were dubbed "Imperial Wilhelm's Warriors" and an antiradical writer claimed that if they "were not all Huns, they had the foul Hun imagination, and also the methods of the Hun."[42] Similarly, the German element within the Socialist Party, which opposed the war, was often remarked upon.[43]

In the South, American entry into the war was accompanied by widespread fear that German agents and sympathizers had undermined the loyalty of the black population, a refinement which compounded the twin fears of black uprisings and enemy plots. Lutheran clergymen and German saloon-keepers were especially suspected of spreading propaganda among blacks.[44] By the end of

39. Preston, *Aliens and Dissenters*, 6–7, 84.

40. Woodrow Wilson to Thomas W. Gregory, with enclosures, 1 Nov. 1917; Wilson to Rudolph Forster, 7 Nov. 1917, in Arthur S. Link, ed., *Papers of Woodrow Wilson*, 69 vols. (Princeton, 1966ff.), 44: 480-82, 526–63.

41. Preston, *Aliens and Dissenters*, 34–207, passim.

42. Michael P. Malone and Richard W. Etulain, *The West: A Twentieth Century History* (Lincoln, NE, 1989), 77; Emerson Hough, *The Web* (Chicago, 1919), 140.

43. Ibid., 93, 194; Talbert, *Negative Intelligence*, 13, 19, 111, 146; Luebke, *Bonds of Loyalty*, 293–94.

44. *New York Times*, 7, 8, 9 April 1917; *New York Tribune*, 4, 5 April 1917.

the war, this claim had helped to produce a massive investigation of black American organizations, publications, and spokesmen, which became less an attempt to prevent "pro-Germanism among the Negroes" than a hostile surveillance of increasingly radical and confident black campaigns for equal rights.[45]

The Committee on Public Information (CPI), established by executive order on 14 April 1917, was the U.S. government's chief propaganda organization. It was chaired by a western muckraking journalist, George Creel, who developed a close working relationship with Woodrow Wilson and key cabinet officials, including Secretary of War Newton D. Baker. Creel's stated intention was to guide public opinion with open information and truth, but, pressured by superpatriots within and without the government, he increasingly allowed CPI writers and speakers to use extreme language in their attacks on Germany and critics of the war effort.[46] This led to a portrayal of all things German as evil and barbaric, creating an intimidating atmosphere for those who wished to retain and express the dual consciousness of being both German and American. Professional historians, released for war work by their universities, played a major part in conjuring up the image of German *Schrecklichkeit* (frightfulness). The CPI produced almost 7 million copies of Wilson's 1917 Flag Day address, annotated by Wallace Notestein of the University of Minnesota, in which the president dwelled on the amorality of German treachery and militarism. German intrigue in America was described in a CPI pamphlet by Earl E. Sperry of Syracuse University. In addition, Americans clearly needed their own versions of Bryce's atrocity stories, which the CPI tried to satisfy. Writing from Lincoln, Nebraska, a postmaster told the CPI he *wanted* to read "that Germans have bombed hospitals, killed Red Cross workers, raped Belgian women and girls."[47]

45. See *Federal Surveillance of Afro-Americans (1917–1925): The First World War, the Red Scare, and the Garvey Movement*, ed. Theodore Kornweibel Jr. (Frederick, MD, 1986); *Correspondence of the Military Intelligence Division Relating to "Negro-Subversion," 1917–1941* (Washington, DC, 1986).

46. Ferrell, *Woodrow Wilson*, 201–3; Luebke, *Bonds of Loyalty*, 212–14; see for greater depth on the C.P.I., Stephen Vaughn, *Holding Fast the Inner Lines: Democracy, Nationalism, and the Committee on Public Information* (Chapel Hill, NC, 1980); also, James R. Mock and Cedric Larson, *Words That Won the War: The Story of the Committee on Public Information, 1917–1919* (Princeton, 1939).

47. George T. Blakey, "Historians on the Homefront: Propagandists for the Great War"(Ph.D. diss., Indiana University, 1970), 32–45, 64–69, 71–72; for example, see Earl E. Sperry and William M. West, *German Plots and Intrigues in the Unites States During the Period of Our Neutrality* (Washington, DC, 1918); Peter Novick, *That*

The CPI's conduct was mild, however, compared to that of several nongovernmental organizations. A vast range of patriotic bodies was created during the war to spread information, encourage Liberty Loan subscriptions, and root out disloyalty. German-Americans probably experienced more intimidation and actual harassment at the hands of these groups than from the federal authorities. The National Security League (NSL), formed by big business during neutrality as an anti-alien, pro-war body, pilloried all things German.[48] Robert McNutt McElroy, the chairman of both the NSL's Committee on Patriotism Through Education and the history department at Princeton University, damned the German soul as "a soul perverted, and black as hell." In one of his "real poems of the German soul," he wrote:

> I have slaughtered the old and the sorrowful;
> I have struck off the breasts of women;
> And I have run through the bodies of children
> who gazed up at me with the eyes of a
> wounded lion.[49]

Other NSL publications included *Ten Fundamental War Principles*, by Thomas Moran of Purdue University, which conjured up images of a German invasion of America, and Earl Sperry's *The Tentacles of the German Octopus in America*, in which German-American newspapers, clubs, schools, and churches were revealed to be agents of Berlin. Some Germans, Sperry wrote, were simply unassimilable and, whether or not they were actively assisting Germany, they were "a detriment to America. Our national life will be stronger, sounder, and healthier without them."[50]

The long list of civilian vigilance groups which kept watch on German-Americans and enemy aliens included the All-American Anti-German League, the American Anti-Anarchy Association, the Boy Spies of America, and local variants such as the Kansas Anti-Horse Thief Association.[51] The most important was the American Protective League (APL), which claimed 250,000 members in 1918. Its agents, only a tenth of whom were active, wore badges issued by the Justice Department. They assisted in BI inquiries and joined

---

Noble Dream: The "Objectivity Question" and the American Historical Profession (New York, 1988), 111–32.

48. Blakey, "Historians," 39–41; Kennedy, *Over Here*, 35, 53–54, 67.

49. Blakey, "Historians," 63, 88.

50. Ibid., 69, 70, 75.

51. Peterson and Fite, *Opponents of War*, 18; Pankratz, "Suppression," 279, 302.

in raids, and also carried out overzealous operations of their own, watching people who were suspected of disloyalty.[52] Patriotic citizens who were not members of such organizations could report suspicious neighbors direct to the Justice Department, after Attorney General Gregory declared that "complaints of even the most informal or confidential nature are always welcome."[53]

One of the most obvious casualties of anti-German feeling in the United States was the German-language press. In 1910, there were 554 German newspapers and periodicals; by 1920, there were only 234 and the national circulation of German-language dailies had fallen by two-thirds to 240,000.[54] Although a clause providing for national newspaper censorship was defeated in the Senate debates on the Espionage Act (by one vote), the government still found it could act against publications which it disliked in ways which closed them down or forced them to change their tone. Title XII of the act allowed Postmaster General Albert Sidney Burleson to deny second-class mailing privileges to any paper which seemed to him or his officials to have criticized the war effort. The Trading-with-the-Enemy Act of October 1917 outlawed transportation by other means of any such material and required foreign-language journals to submit English translations of all material relating to the government, the belligerent powers, or the war. Finally, in order to cut off funds from radical organizations, the Sedition Act of May 1918 allowed the Post Office to stop mail deliveries to anyone who had tried to mail nonmailable material.[55] (Several states enacted their own versions of this legislation.)

52. Jensen, *Price of Vigilance,* is a detailed account of the American Protective League. For an uncritical contemporary account, see Hough, *The Web.*

53. Cummings and McFarland, *Federal Justice,* 420.

54. *Harvard Encyclopedia,* 423; Luebke, *Bonds of Loyalty,* 271.

55. May, *In the Name of War,* 137, 323; Kennedy, *Over Here,* 67–77; Preston, *Aliens and Dissenters,* 145, 148; Peterson and Fite, *Opponents of War,* 95–100. Title I, section 3, of the Espionage Act outlawed making "false statements with the intent to interfere with the operation or success of the military or naval forces" and attempts to impede the draft or to encourage military insubordination. Title I, section 4, outlawed conspiracy to violate section 3. Title XII barred materials considered treasonable from the mails. See Act of June 15, 1917, *United States Statutes at Large,* XL, 219–20, 209–31. The Sedition Act, which was an amendment to Title I, section 3, of the Espionage Act, forbade obstruction of war bond sales and the use of "disloyal, profane, scurrilous, or abusive" language about the American form of government, the Constitution, the flag or the armed forces. See Act of May 16, 1918, ibid., 553–54. During September–November 1917, Woodrow Wilson voiced repeated concern to Postmaster General Albert Sidney Burleson about the censorship power of the Post

The Post Office set up a network of readers to monitor the foreign press, which provided the Post Office solicitor with a constant flow of material on which to rule.[56] Several public figures spoke out strongly against the German-language press, ensuring that it would be closely scrutinized for illegal statements. Theodore Roosevelt declared, "We are convinced that today our most dangerous foe is the foreign-language press," while Robert McElroy claimed that just by *using* the German language such papers were "oiling the wheels for the German war chariot."[57] The result was that most German papers were careful to publish only pro-Allied statements on the war, effectively censoring themselves and denying many of their readers the kind of discussion they undoubtedly wanted. There were exceptions, however. Jacob Frohwerk, president of the Kansas chapter of the German-American Alliance was indicted under the Espionage Act for his editorial comments in the *Neue Kansas Staats Zeitung*.[58] The most significant German paper to be prosecuted was the *Philadelphia Tageblatt*, which was held to have criticized Wilson, the British, and the Allied war effort and to have published material that was "depressing or detrimental to patriotic ardor." After two years of legal proceedings, three of the paper's managers were sentenced to terms of between two and five years imprisonment.[59]

Anti-German feeling was also demonstrated in several states by assaults on the use of the German language in education. This was not a new phenomenon; state legislatures had been attempting to limit the use and teaching of German and other non-English languages in schools since the 1870s, with occasional success. Indeed, in Pennsylvania, post–Civil War German leaders such as Carl Schurz had concluded that the replacement of German by

Office Department, while assuring protesters that the government was taking great care to be fair. In the end, he let Burleson have his own way. See the series of letters to and from Wilson in Link, ed., *Papers of Woodrow Wilson*, 44: 245, 358, 366–67, 389–90, 396–97, 405, 408–10, 420, 453, 467–72, 491, 493. For Burleson's account of Wilson's final decision, see Peterson and Fite, *Opponents of War*, 97.

56. James R. Mock, *Censorship, 1917* (Princeton, 1941), 62–65.

57. Luebke, *Bonds of Loyalty*, 235–37, 267–68; Peterson and Fite, *Opponents of War*, 97; Blakey, "Historians," 128. The National Security League tried to organize an advertising boycott of the German-language press.

58. Pankratz, "Suppression," 281.

59. Peterson and Fite, *Opponents of War*, 98–99. For a detailed study, see Carl Wittke, *The German-Language Press in America* (Lexington, KY, 1957), Chs. 11–14; see also F. P. Olds, "Disloyalty of the German-American Press," *Atlantic Monthly* 120 (1917): 136–40.

English was an irresistible and acceptable process. However, it was not until during and immediately after World War I that significant steps were taken against the German language.[60] Twenty-one states enacted laws banning teaching in all foreign languages or, specifically, in German, urged on by groups such as the NSL and the American Defense Society. The latter declared that "any language which produces a people of ruthless conquestadors [*sic*] such as now exists in Germany, is not a fit language to teach clean and pure American boys and girls."[61] An educational writer, groping for academic credibility, found the German language "lacking in euphony ...; [it] savors of the animalistic and does not induce a certain polish and refinement essential to civilized people." It was part of a culture that "prides itself in its inhumanity [that] murders children, rapes women, and mutilates the bodies of innocent men." Laws passed to restrict the teaching of foreign languages were not ruled unconstitutional by the Supreme Court until 1923 and again in 1925.[62] College professors and school teachers, many of German birth or ancestry, were summarily dismissed for pacifism, disloyalty, or failing to paint sufficiently hideous images of German society. German music was shunned, there were burnings of German books, and the historians of the NSL assisted in censoring school textbooks.[63]

Violence was almost inevitable in such circumstances. Across the United States, German-Americans and alien enemies were tarred and feathered, or painted yellow, and forced to kneel and kiss the Stars and Stripes. Their houses were wrecked and other property stolen.[64] After several near-lynchings had taken place, one man was

60. Jürgen Eichhoff, "The German Language in America," and Marion L. Huffines, "Language-Maintenance Efforts Among German Immigrants," in *America and the Germans*, ed. Trommler and McVeigh, 223–40; 241–50.

61. Luebke, *Bonds of Loyalty*, 216; *New York Times*, 22 July 1918.

62. Frederick C. Luebke, *Germans in the New World: Essays on the History of Immigration* (Urbana, IL, 1990), 32, 35–36, 45.

63. Peterson and Fite, *Opponents of War*, 196, 102–12; Ferrell, *Woodrow Wilson*, 205; Merle Curti, *The Growth of American Thought*, 2d ed. (New York, 1951), 684–85; Blakey, "Historians," 132–133. In some states, telephone conversations in German were banned. Rippley, *German-Americans*, 186–87. Anti-German feeling in education persisted after the war. In February 1919, the National Education Association and the U.S. Bureau of Education concurred that American Sunday schools should "get away from the German method of specialization." *New York Times*, 2 February 1919. See also Gustavus Ohlinger, *The German Conspiracy in Education* (New York, 1919).

64. Pankratz, "Suppression," 302–306; Peterson and Fite, *Opponents of War*, 196–200; Ferrell, *Woodrow Wilson*, 204; Luebke, *Bonds of Loyalty*, 279–81. According to Luebke, "Washington bureaucrats, of course, had not intended for terror to be

murdered by a mob. Almost exactly a year after Congress declared war, thirty-two-year-old Robert Prager, a Dresden-born immigrant who had been in the United States since 1904, was dragged to the outskirts of Collinsville, Illinois, and hanged from a tree, for no discernible reason other than his nationality and stubbornness. His murder provoked a flurry of denunciation from public figures and major journals, but, after a local jury found all those charged with the killing not guilty, the affair was largely forgotten. No federal action was taken, except for a presidential statement condemning mob violence almost four months later, and this was primarily a response to the much more frequent lynching of black people.[65]

Members of Mennonite, Amish, and Hutterite churches were persecuted more frequently than any other group of German-Americans. Their nonviolent beliefs ruled out any activity that might further the waging of war. Rather than comply with the draft and other war measures, 1,500 Mennonites and Hutterites emigrated to Canada, where religious objectors enjoyed full exemption.[66] Of those men who remained, some were drafted and duly reported to army camps. Mennonites who accepted noncombatant status in the army were usually treated fairly by camp commanders, but those who refused might be knocked about and insulted, and, in some cases, prosecuted. Of the 360 religious objectors sentenced to imprisonment for up to twenty-five years by court-martial, 138 were Mennonites, at least two of whom died in prison.[67] The MIB

used, yet they seriously underestimated the ease with which subtle social pressure could give way to raw violence." Ibid., 273. On the range of experiences of groups of German-Americans in different parts of the U.S., see Malone and Etulain, *The West*, 75–77; Powell, "Our Cradles Were in Germany," passim.; Richard Salet, *Russian-German Settlement in the United States* (Fargo, ND, 1974), 100–109; Klaus Wust, *The Virginia Germans* (Charlottesville, VA, 1975), 231–50; David W. Detjen, *The Germans in Missouri, 1900-1918: Prohibition, Neutrality, and Assimilation* (Columbia, MO, 1985). For a short international comparison, see Mark Ellis and Panikos Panayi, "German Minorities in World War I: A Comparative Study of Britain and the USA," *Ethnic and Racial Studies* 17 (1994): 238–59.

65. Luebke, *Bonds of Loyalty*, 3–24; Peterson and Fite, *Opponents of War*, 202–207. Luebke has compared the treatment of Germans in Brazil and the United States during World War I. In Brazil, which also declared war on Germany in 1917, mob violence was much more frequent, since the German population was proportionately smaller and richer and was more cohesive and culturally distinct. Frederick C. Luebke, "Images of German Immigrants in the United States and Brazil, 1890-1918: Some Comparisons," in *America and the Germans*, ed. Trommler and McVeigh, 207–21.

66. Allan Teichroew, "World War I and the Mennonite Migration to Canada to Avoid the Draft," *Mennonite Quarterly Review* 45 (1971): 219–49.

67. A total of 64,693 bids were made for noncombatant status in the United States in World War I; local draft boards accepted 56,830 claims as genuine. Of the 29,679

and other domestic intelligence agencies regarded Mennonites and other pacifists as subversive, pro-German and possibly in league with the Bolsheviks.[68] Secretary of War Newton D. Baker, however, regarded the religious objectors as more odd than disloyal. In September 1917, Baker visited two dozen objectors at Camp Meade, Maryland, half of whom were Amish and the rest mostly members of other religious sects. He afterward told Woodrow Wilson: "For the most part they seem well-disposed, simple-minded young people who have been imprisoned in a narrow environment and really have no comprehension of the world outside their own rural and peculiar community. Only two of those with whom I talked seemed quite normal mentally."[69]

Civilian treatment of Mennonites could be, if anything, even harsher and less forgiving than that of the military authorities. They were the victims of many tarring-and-feathering and flag-kissing humiliations.[70] In South Dakota, Hutterite livestock was confiscated, sold off, and the proceeds appropriated by the district Liberty Loan fund.[71] In other words, those German-Americans whose expressions of *Deutschtum* were confined to religion and language, and who were not interested in the war or in political power—those who posed no conceivable threat to national security—were among the most abused and injured. Local studies have also suggested that, under the guise of reckless patriotism, old scores were being settled by non-Germans in the

---

claimants who passed the physical examination, 20,873 were inducted into the army as certified religious objectors. In the end, only 3,989 stuck rigidly to their principles and refused military duty in the camps. Most of these men then accepted noncombatant status or were released for agricultural work. Peterson and Fite, *Opponents of War*, 123–38, 261; Pankratz, "Suppression," 283–86; Ferrell, *Woodrow Wilson*, 206; Rippley, *German-Americans*, 188–89. See also Jacob C. Meyer, "Reflections of a Conscientious Objector in World War I," *Mennonite Quarterly Review* 41 (1967): 79–96; Theron Schlabach, ed., "*An Account*, By Jacob Waldner: Diary of a Conscientious Objector in World War I," *Mennonite Quarterly Review* 48 (1974): 73–111; Gerlof D. Homan, "Post-Armistice Courts-Martial of Conscientious Objectors," *Mennonite Life* 44 (1989): 4–9.

68. These ideas were encouraged by British Intelligence. Allan Teichroew, "Military Surveillance of Mennonites in World War I," *Mennonite Quarterly Review*, 53 (1979): 95–127.

69. Newton D. Baker to Woodrow Wilson, 1 October 1917, in Link, ed., *Papers of Woodrow Wilson*, 44: 288–89. Baker ordered the release of the last conscientious objector in November 1920. Ferrell, *Woodrow Wilson*, 207.

70. Luebke, *Bonds of Loyalty*, 274–77, 279, 309–10.

71. Ibid., 275–77; Billigmeier, *Americans from Germany*, 144.

knowledge that little action would be taken against anyone engaging in mob violence. [72]

German-American religious practice did not escape attention. The Lutheran synods had generally taken a neutral view of the war prior to American entry and were careful not to provoke criticism afterwards, but individual churches and clergymen were nevertheless attacked.[73] Their response was often to abandon services in German in favor of English. In 1914, 70 percent of Lutheran church services in St. Louis were held in German; by 1929, 75 percent were held in English. A transition to English was likely to have happened in any case, but the war undoubtedly made it more rapid.[74] German Catholics were less harassed than Protestants, but they, too, made assimilationist adjustments which continued after the war.[75]

Many German-American organizations, businesses, and individuals responded to the pressures of wartime hysteria by demonstrating overt loyalty to the United States and playing down their German origins. At the very least, they sought to minimize their chances of being identified with Germany's war aims. Names were changed. The Germania Sangerverein of Chicago became the Lincoln Club, Kaiser-Kuhn wholesale grocers of St. Louis became the Pioneer Grocery Company, and numerous Schmidt families became Smiths.[76] New names were also imposed by others: German Street in Cincinnati became English Street, sauerkraut became liberty cabbage and East Germantown, Indiana, was renamed Pershing (despite General John. J. Pershing's family name having originally been Pförschin).[77] Many German-Americans ostentatiously

---

72. Gerlof D. Homan, "The Burning of the Mennonite Church, Fairview, Michigan, in 1918," *Mennonite Quarterly Review* 64 (1990): 99–112.

73. Luebke, *Bonds of Loyalty*, 102–5, 180. See also Carol K. Coburn, *Life at Four Corners: Religion, Gender and Education in a German-Lutheran Community, 1868–1945* (Lawrence, KA, 1992), 136–51.

74. Hawgood, *Tragedy*, 300. See also Luebke, *Bonds of Loyalty*, 286–88, 315–16; Pankratz, "Suppression," 282.

75. Luebke, *Bonds of Loyalty*, 292, 317–18. See also Philip Gleason, *The Conservative Reformers: German-American Catholics and the Social Order* (Notre Dame, IN, 1968), 145–203.

76. Luebke, *Bonds of Loyalty*, 270–1, 282.

77. Ibid., 427–48; Billigmeier, *Americans from Germany*, 144; Peterson and Fite, *Opponents of War*, 195–96; Rippley, *German-Americans*, 186. On the alteration of place names, see also *New York Times*, 22 July 1918. In Columbus, Ohio, the city's Schiller Park was renamed Washington Park in 1917 in a ceremony during which German dogs were killed and German books were burned. Klaus Wust, "German-Americans: Eight Million Individual Transplants," in *Germans in America: Retrospect and Prospect*, ed. Randall M. Miller (Philadelphia, 1984), 125.

invested in the government's four Liberty Loans and the postwar Victory Loan. The most prominent German-born supporter of the Allied cause was poet and playwright Hermann Hagedorn. He and his brother had stayed in the United States when the rest of the family returned to Germany at the outbreak of war. While he did not fully accept German war guilt, Hagedorn saw German behavior during the war as morally base. As a pro-Allied propagandist, he had links with Theodore Roosevelt and shared the latter's distaste for the hyphen. Hagedorn advocated the rapid assimilation of the German immigrant population and accused those who supported Germany of being sentimental and disloyal.[78]

Nevertheless, a minority of German-Americans steadfastly refused to apologize for their origins or their constant admiration of Germany. Viereck, although he changed the name of his paper, the *Fatherland*, to the *American Weekly* in 1917 (it became *Viereck's American Monthly* in August 1918), continued to celebrate German culture. He escaped serious censorship by avoiding direct attacks on the American government, but he did criticize the Allies, especially Britain, charging them with having caused the war.[79] As the war ended, other writers began to defend the German-American record, charging the superpatriots with "Prussianism" and slander.[80] The Baltimore journalist, H. L. Mencken, was appalled at the atmosphere of vigilantism and witch-hunting. He refused to report fellow German-Americans to the authorities simply to prove his own loyalty and he despised those who, as he put it, "snitched." Mencken especially loathed what he called "Dr. Creel's herd of 2,000 American historians. They constituted themselves, not a restraining influence upon the mob run wild, but the loudest spokesmen of its worst imbecility. They fed it with bogus history, bogus philosophy, bogus heroics."[81]

This kind of defense came too late to help the German-American Alliance. Under the weight of anti-German propaganda, local chapters of the Alliance began to fold in 1917. By February 1918, when the Senate Judiciary Committee began two months of investigations

78. Keller, *States of Belonging*, 222–24; see also Charles Frederick Heartman, *The Liberty Loan: Why Americans of German and Austrian Origin Should Buy Bonds* (New York, 1918); Otto H. Kahn, "The Duty and Opportunity of German-Americans," *Economic World* 15 (1918): 76–78.

79. Keller, *States of Belonging*.

80. Luebke, *Bonds of Loyalty*, 284–86.

81. H. L. Mencken, *Prejudices: Second Series* (New York, 1920), 83–84, 105–106; H. L. Mencken, *Prejudices: Third Series* (New York, 1922), 141.

into the Alliance, it was already defunct as a national organization. After the hearings, in which the Alliance was charged with illegally acting in the interests of the German government and interfering in American electoral politics, Congress repealed the charter granted to it in 1907.[82]

In electoral politics, a degree of German-American disillusionment with both the Democrats and Republicans is suggested by local voting patterns in the 1918 mid-term elections. Many voted for the candidate with the least pro-war or anti-German record. In many cases, this meant voting for socialists or Senator Robert La Follette's Progressives. In Milwaukee, the anti-war socialist, Victor Berger, was elected to the House of Representatives, but was denied his seat by fellow congressmen. Reelected on two further occasions, he was not allowed to enter Congress until 1923, when the Supreme Court acquitted him on charges of conspiracy and sedition.[83]

The support of some German-Americans for the Socialist Party and the prominence within the party of men like the Austrian-born Berger, may have made the mental shift from anti-Germanism to anti-Bolshevism easier for the American public, the press, and the domestic intelligence agencies. Certainly, the "Red Scare" of 1919 to 1921 would have been much less rapidly generated had the German spy scare and loyalty fury not occurred from 1915 to 1918, and perhaps it would not have happened at all. The war produced a popular willingness to hunt for seditious groups and individuals and saw the creation of federal and local police forces whose continued existence depended on the discovery of a continuing alien threat. Nativism was given a new lease on life, as repressive energies were directed at radicals, especially members of the IWW. On 4 February 1919, the day after plans were announced for a general strike in Seattle, Washington, the U.S. Senate voted to allow a judiciary subcommittee to extend its investigations of German propaganda and brewing interests to include Bolshevik propaganda.[84] As Higham has remarked, "so interlocked and continuous were the anti-German and anti-radical

82. Child, *German-Americans in Politics*, 169–73; Rippley, *German-Americans*, 90-91.

83. Ibid., 190-94; Luebke, *Bonds of Loyalty*, 295–302; Peterson and Fite, *Opponents of War*, 162–66.

84. U.S. Congress, Senate Committee on the Judiciary, *Brewing and Liquor Interests, and German and Bolshevik Propaganda: Reports and Hearings of the Subcommittee on the Judiciary*, 66th Cong., 1st sess., Senate Doc. 62, 3 vols. (1919). On German language teaching and propaganda spread by the Lutheran clergy, see ibid., 2: 1787. On German propaganda among black Americans, see ibid., 2: 1574, 1784–86.

excitements that no date marks the end of one and the beginning of the other."[85] This transition was completed when the Alien Property Custodian during World War I, A. Mitchell Palmer, who liquidated assets of German-owned businesses worth millions of dollars, became the attorney general in March 1919 and presided over the Red Scare.[86]

One effect of wartime intolerance and the chastening of German-Americans was to hasten the repudiation of the "melting pot" ideas put forward by the British playwright Israel Zangwill and the American anthropologist Franz Boas.[87] The attempt to fuse the immigrant communities into a homogeneous nation was pronounced a failed experiment by nativists. During the war, Robert McElroy of the NSL had declared, "In the bottom of the melting pot there lie heaps of unfused metal." In the early 1920s, as pressure mounted for peacetime immigration restriction, there were echoes of this imagery in George Creel's reference to immigrants as "so much slag in the melting pot, [who were] opposed at every point to the American or Nordic stock," and in Maryland Senator William C. Bruce's description of immigrants as "indigestible lumps [in the] nation's stomach."[88]

A few diehards, like Viereck, never ceased to love Germany above all others, and made it plain, but they were a small minority. Other German-Americans, of genuinely divided loyalties, made considerable postwar efforts to gather and send relief aid—*Heimathilfe*—to Germany and Austria, including the transportation of whole dairy herds.[89] However, by 1920, most German-Americans saw little point in overt expressions of *Deutschtum*. Politically, socially, and economically, it was not worth it. Once, as Phyllis Keller notes, their self-esteem had been bound up with being Germans in America; now, to be a German in America did not command respect. If it had been possible to preserve both their Germanness and their place in American society, they would have

85. Higham, *Strangers in the Land*, 218–23; Billigmeier, *Americans from Germany*, 145–46.

86. Kennedy, *Over Here*, 288–91, 311–13.

87. On the origins of the "melting-pot" idea: Higham, *Strangers in the Land*, 124–25.

88. Kennedy, *Over Here*, 67; Higham, *Strangers in the Land*, 277. According to Higham, "The Germans fell subject, not to any of the specific nativist traditions, but rather to the plain and simple accusation in which every type of xenophobia culminated: the charge of disloyalty, the gravest sin in the morality of nationalism." Ibid., 196.

89. Austin J. App, "The Germans," in *Immigrant's Influence on Wilson's Peace Policies*, ed. O'Grady, 48–51.

done so, but the pressure to allow the American self to subordinate the German self became, for most, overwhelming.[90] The German-American Alliance was not reestablished after the war. Not until the smaller German-American Bund was formed in the 1930s would another organization engage in aggressive celebration of the Fatherland. Significantly, the closest immediate postwar parallel to the German-American Alliance, the Steuben Society, created in New York in 1919 and named after a Prussian general who fought on the American side in the War of Independence, chose to concentrate on uncontroversial activities, such as the promotion of good citizenship and the study of early German-American history.[91]

In 1917–18, the U.S. government, the press, and members of the educational establishment initiated, or at least enabled, an outpouring of irrational, yet powerful, negative images about a once highly visible, cohesive, and generally well-regarded ethnic group. This assault hastened the partial destruction of the identity of some eight million Americans and inevitably caused psychological suffering and loss of status at a period in American history when the dignity of the individual was inextricably bound up with the social and economic rank of one's ethnic group. The fact that the demonization of German-Americans was part of a general preparation for total warfare does not alter the fact that the group's reputation was sacrificed to heighten a sense of domestic emergency and fuel an international crusade against *Kultur*. Paradoxically, the presence of a vast German-American population, onto whom ghastly images of America's enemy could be projected and thereby brought to life, far from hindering the abandonment of neutrality, actually bolstered the American mobilization for war.

90. Keller, *States of Belonging*, 117–18; see also Luebke, *Bonds of Loyalty*, xv–xvi and 329. In the 1920 election, the switch of German-Americans away from the Democrats continued, as they rejected Wilsonism, along with most of the electorate. James M. Cox, the Democratic candidate, ritually repudiated the German vote, as Wilson had done in 1916, but German-Americans had already formed an opinion about Cox when he led the Ohio campaign to ban the teaching of German. Luebke, *Bonds of Loyalty*, 322–27; R. A. Burchell, "Did the Irish and German Voters Desert the Democrats in 1920? A Tentative Statistical Answer," *Journal of American Studies* 6 (August 1972): 153–64.

91. Billigmeier, *Americans from Germany*, 147; Luebke, *Germans in the New World*, 58–59, 63–67.

Chapter Eight

"OUR ENEMIES WITHIN"

Nazism, National Unity, and America's
Wartime Discourse on Tolerance

Wendy L. Wall

In September 1944, a war bond advertisement in the labor news-paper *ITU News* pictured the mother of two American service-men. The woman knitted sweaters for her soldier sons, sent them chocolate cakes, and urged her husband to purchase more war bonds. But despite such patriotic acts, the ad charged, this woman was an enemy agent. Through her "thoughtless remarks" about neighbors of different religions, skin colors, and ethnicities, she spread "hatred and distrust" among groups of Americans. "As surely as though you landed on these shores in the dark of night from a submarine, bent on blowing up factories and burning bridges," the ad warned the woman, "in spite of your charming manner and your all-out war record, lady, you are a *saboteur*."[1]

I would like to thank the Stanford Humanities Center, the Social Welfare History Archives at the University of Minnesota, and the National Endowment for the Humanities for their financial support of this project. Thanks also to David M. Kennedy, George Fredrickson, Steven Zipperstein, Daniel Kevles, Andrew Robertson, and the participants in the 1994 Tutzing meeting of the Deutsche Gesellschaft für Amerika-Studien for their comments on this chapter.

1. *ITU News*, 30 September 1944, in Gary Gerstle, *Working-Class Americanism: The Politics of Labor in a Textile City, 1914–1960* (New York, 1989), 296. Gerstle suggests that this ad was produced by officials at the War Advertising Council and the U.S. Treasury Department.

This ad may have been unusual for the superheated rhetoric it used to warn Americans of the dangers of casual bigotry, but the basic message it delivered was broadcast widely in the U.S. during World War II. Historians have written extensively about the racist acts committed by the U.S. and its citizens during the war—the internment of West Coast Japanese-Americans and the race riots of 1943, to give but two examples. Much less attention has been devoted to an alternative strain in America's wartime political dialogue, which contested, and to some degree curbed, such intolerance. From the late 1930s on, many Americans both within and outside of the Roosevelt administration used the contrast with Nazism to portray "Americanism" as tolerance. They defined bigots as internal enemies—Nazi agents who were working to undermine America's pluralistic unity.

This strain in America's wartime discourse on difference has received less attention from historians in part because, as William M. Tuttle Jr. has noted, "tolerance is more difficult to document than hateful behavior."[2] Still, it is possible to show how both public and private agencies used the war to preach—or as they would have said at the time, to *propagandize* for—religious, ethnic, and racial tolerance. Exploring the assumptions that underlay this wartime campaign—its strengths and its limitations—sheds light on the way Americans dealt with key divisions in their nation both during the war and throughout much of the postwar era.[3]

To sketch my argument briefly, in the months following the start of World War II, American liberals and assimilated ethnic

2. William M. Tuttle Jr., *"Daddy's Gone to War": The Second World War in the Lives of America's Children* (New York, 1993), 186. Tuttle makes this comment in the course of explaining why he devotes far more attention to "the persistence of prejudice during the war" than to the "host of educational, religious, entertainment, business, labor and political leaders" who denounced home front hatred. In recent years, a few historians have begun to explore the wartime discourse on tolerance, national unity, and cultural pluralism. This essay benefited in particular from Gary Gerstle, *Working-Class Americanism*, 289–302; Richard W. Steele, "The War on Intolerance: The Reformulation of American Nationalism, 1939–1941," *Journal of American Ethnic History* (Fall 1989): 9–35; Philip Gleason, *Speaking of Diversity: Language and Ethnicity in Twentieth-Century America* (Baltimore, 1992), 153–87.

3. The term "tolerance" can suggest mere civility *or* actual fraternity. I have used the term here to encompass both meanings. While some groups preaching tolerance during the war merely condemned bigotry and advocated social harmony, others hoped to foster a genuine sense of brotherhood among America's religious, ethnic, and racial groups. The former tended to favor the status quo, while the latter pushed for greater social and legal equality in American society. This philosophical fissure, present during the war, widened into a gaping crevasse in the postwar era.

leaders—among whom Jews were particularly prominent—used the call for national unity in America to tie their pleas for "tolerance" to the imperative of national defense. They argued that only by embracing "tolerance" and "brotherhood" could Americans create a sound and democratic national unity, and protect themselves from the Nazi tactic of "divide and conquer." But this message of "tolerance" for the sake of national unity rested on a basic assumption: that Americans were united by a civic consensus, and that key social differences could be relegated to the private realm. In other words, Americans could "tolerate" or even value each others' religious, ethnic, or racial differences as long as they were united by certain civic beliefs. This assumption had very different implications in the arenas of religion, ethnicity, and race.

The story begins with the rise of Nazism and the outbreak of war in Europe in September 1939. During the Depression, many Americans had tuned out news of military buildup in Germany, Italy, and Japan. But if Americans had been slow to awaken to developments overseas, the Nazi blitzkrieg in the spring of 1940—and particularly the fall of France that June—shocked them into rapt attention. Many commentators saw in the contrasting fates of Britain and France a lesson not in military tactics, but in the need for national morale. "If this war teaches anything, it is the power of spiritual unity," declared a radio commentator in Schenectady, New York. While high morale helped the British produce "the miracle of Dunkirk," he continued, "the fortresses of the Maginot line, shot through with dissension, were of no avail." André Maurois, the French refugee writer, echoed this warning in the pages of *Harper's*: "A united country can stand a retreat to the Marne and later make a successful attack; a disunited country is demoralized by retreat and cannot reassemble its forces."[4]

Such assessments triggered an outpouring of appeals for national unity. In June, more than one hundred prominent anthropologists, psychologists, historians, and sociologists formed a Committee for National Morale to apply social science techniques to the building of American unity. The Foreign Language Information Service, for two decades a liaison to the nation's immigrant press, renamed itself the Common Council for American Unity and hosted a "Unity Dinner" attended by Americans of diverse ethnic strains and the First Lady herself. The day after the

---

4. Robert Rienow, "Lost: Labor's Love," *Vital Speeches* (15 May 1941), 471; André Maurois, "A House Divided Against Itself ...," *Harper's* (February 1941), 327.

November presidential elections, the Council for Democracy staged a huge "unity" rally in New York's Madison Square Garden. Declared the historian Henry Steele Commager, "The shadow of war, falling athwart the campaign, dramatized for us the fact that the American people is a nation."[5]

But such bold proclamations of unity generally reflected a widespread fear: on what grounds could Americans unite? Unlike Britain, with its relatively homogeneous population, the United States's 130 million citizens included millions of religious and racial minorities. Moreover, as *Fortune* alarmingly reminded its readers, "There is dynamite on our shores....": nearly one-third of all Americans were immigrants or had an immigrant parent, and many of these traced their roots to the Axis powers. In November 1940 the famed historian James Truslow Adams asked the question on the minds of many Americans: "Are we, as some have said, merely a hodgepodge of minorities? Or are we a nation with a common background and, despite our political battles, a continuing national ideal?"[6]

During and after World War I, Americans had answered this question largely in ethnocentric terms. President Woodrow Wilson paved the way for this nativist hysteria when he warned in 1916 that some naturalized citizens had "poured the poison of disloyalty into the very arteries of our national life." During the war, dozens of school districts and many states banned the teaching of German, and the Iowa governor forbade its use over the telephone and in all public places. Across America, "God bless you" replaced "Gesundheit" and sauerkraut was renamed "Liberty cabbage." In towns from Illinois to Wyoming, German-Americans were assaulted or even lynched.[7]

5. For the formation and makeup of the Committee for National Morale, see *German Psychological Warfare* (New York, 1941), 297–302. On the Common Council for American Unity, see William Charles Beyer, "Searching for *Common Ground*, 1940–1949: An American Literary Magazine and its Related Movements in Education and Politics" (Ph.D. diss., University of Minnesota, 1988), 46, 107; Freda Kirchwey, "Unity for What?" *The Nation* (16 November 1940), 465–66; Henry Steele Commager, "Keystones of Our National Unity," *New York Times Magazine* (10 November 1940), 3.

6. "The Nation of Nations," *Fortune*, September 1942: 137; James Truslow Adams, "The Ideas That Make Us a Nation," *New York Times Magazine* (24 November 1940), 3.

7. David Kennedy, *Over Here: The First World War and American Society* (Oxford, 1980), Ch. 1; Frederick C. Luebke, *Bonds of Loyalty: German Americans and World War I* (DeKalb, IL, 1974); cf. Mark Ellis's contribution in this volume, "German-Americans in World War I." This tendency to define "Americanism" in ethnocentric terms was countered to some degree by the more liberal wing of the "Americanization" movement.

When World War I ended, much of this seething animosity was turned on southern and eastern European immigrants, who were pictured as fomenters of labor unrest, threats to American jobs, and catalysts of "race suicide" among old stock Americans. The immediate postwar years saw a viciously nativist "Red Scare" and the rise of an anti-Catholic, anti-Jewish, anti-black Ku Klux Klan. Even Progressives like the economist John R. Commons argued that southern and eastern European immigrants were "an inferior race that favor despotism and oligarchy rather than democracy." To protect Americans from "race suicide" and despotism, Congress in the 1920s imposed immigration restrictions that slowed non-Nordic immigration to a trickle.[8]

American liberals were painfully aware of this inglorious history when the call for national unity went up again in 1940 and 1941. And if America's history was not a sufficient reminder of the dangers of a coerced and homogeneous unity, they also had the example of Nazi Germany. The Nazi threat seemed to heighten the *need* for unity in America, but it also underscored the dangers of an exclusionary society and made acceptance of diversity and individual freedom almost a definition of democracy. "There can be a national unity that will betoken a democracy gathering new strength," editorialized *The Christian Century.* "And there can be a national unity that will doom a democracy to totalitarian extinction." Added a columnist in *Life* magazine, "We are not in search of the kind of uniformity of opinion that Stalin and Hitler have achieved."[9]

This need to distinguish a totalitarian from a democratic national unity posed a tremendous challenge to American intellectuals, propagandists, and policymakers during both World War II and the Cold War. A 1941 article by James Truslow Adams captures the tension well: pessimists, Adams wrote, "make the big mistake of confusing unity with uniformity. That is where we differ from dictatorship powers.... Our unity comes from the free choice of a free people." The distinction made by Adams between

---

However, those liberal Americanizers who tried to unite ethnics and the foreign-born behind a civic creed were overwhelmed by the resurgent nativism that followed World War I. Only in the years preceding World War II did their vision begin to gain widespread acceptance. For more on this branch of the Americanization movement, see Daniel E. Weinberg, "The Ethnic Technician and the Foreign-Born: Another Look at Americanization Ideology and Goals," *Societas* 7 (1977): 209–27.

8. John R. Commons, *Races and Immigrants in America,* 2d ed. (1907, New York, 1920), 11.

9. "Vigilance and National Unity," *Christian Century* (20 November 1940), 1441; Raymond Clapper, "What About Unity?" *Life* (18 November 1940), 29.

democratic unity and totalitarian uniformity popped up again and
again in the rhetoric of both liberals and conservatives during the
1940s and 1950s. Although different people used the phrase with
slightly different intent, the slogan "unity not uniformity" generally
suggested that Americans shared an ideological or spiritual bond—
a belief in an "American Creed" or "American way of life"—that
was capable of overcoming political, religious, ethnic, class, or
even racial differences. Americans disputed the content of that elu-
sive way of life, but few Americans questioned that it existed.[10]

In the early months of World War II, some liberals and leftists,
notably those with close ties to the labor movement, warned
against a unity defined primarily in national terms. "What we
must unite upon is a bold program of democratic advance," cautioned Freda Kirchwey, editor of *The Nation*. "This struggle is not
only or even primarily an international war. It is a revolutionary
conflict which is being fought simultaneously across national lines
and inside each nation." But many liberals, particularly those concerned primarily with religious or ethnic intolerance, saw in the
call for national unity a chance to promote intergroup harmony
and social cohesion. In the late 1930s, no Americans were more
concerned about these issues than the relatively assimilated Jews
who made up the American Jewish Committee (AJC).[11]

The AJC had been founded by prominent German-American
Jews in 1906 in the wake of a series of Russian pogroms. Charged
with protecting "the civil and religious rights of Jews and [allevi-
ating] the consequences of persecution," the AJC had fought U.S.
immigration restrictions during the 1920s and worked to expose
the anti-Semitism of Henry Ford and the Ku Klux Klan. But for
most of its first three decades, the AJC had focused on aiding Jews
abroad. This changed in the early 1930s, when Hitler sympathizers started distributing Nazi propaganda in the U.S. and the
Depression triggered a surge in indigenous anti-Semitism.[12]

10. James Truslow Adams, "Forces that Make Us the *United* States," *New York
Times Magazine* (13 July 1941), 25.
11. Freda Kirchwey, "Unity for What?", *The Nation*, 16 November 1940: 466.
12. For a useful history of the AJC, including the period dealt with here, see
Naomi W. Cohen, *Not Free to Desist: The American Jewish Committee, 1906–1966*
(Philadelphia, 1972), Chs. 1–9; Morris Waldman to Sol M. Stroock, 12 June 1939,
"Survey Committee, 1936–41, 43 MDW" folder; and "Memorandum on Relationship of Survey Committee and Other Subcommittees to the American Jewish Committee," February 1940, "Survey Committee, Scope and Function, 1940–41" folder,
both in box 39, Morris Waldman Papers, RG 347, American Jewish Committee
Records, YIVO Institute, New York (hereafter cited as Waldman Papers).

In 1933, the AJC formed a special unit to investigate anti-Semitic agitators in the U.S. and to "immunize the American people against the virus of anti-Semitism." AJC staffers initially envisioned a short-term educational program designed to expose the "un-American" bigotry of groups like the Silver Shirts and the German-American Bund. But developments in Europe and the rising popularity of anti-Semites like Father Charles Coughlin in the U.S. soon convinced the AJC's executive committee that a larger effort was called for. In 1935, investment banker Lewis L. Strauss spearheaded an effort to raise funds and recruit prominent Jewish laymen into the defense effort. In 1936, with an initial war chest of $600,000, the Survey Committee was launched. This group, which never had more than thirty members, guided the AJC's defense effort until shortly before the U.S. entry into World War II.[13]

Members of the Survey Committee and AJC staffers believed that the fate of Jews was tied to the fate of liberalism and democracy. "To the extent that we can help promote attachment to the democratic ideal, we must do so," wrote Morris Waldman, the AJC's executive secretary. "We must make plain our opposition to extremism of both right and left varieties." The Survey Committee's program for 1937 reiterated the link between Jews and democracy, and added that "the specific actions relative to educating the public on the truth about Jews must be integrated with the major task of maintaining peaceful relations between the various groups composing our population."[14]

Some AJC members recognized that support for democracy does not necessarily produce a peaceful, pluralistic society. Democracies can also produce majority tyrannies. But members of the Survey Committee believed that a liberal democracy based on a Bill of Rights like the U.S. represented the best hope for minorities in a world increasingly divided between fascists and communists.

13. Like the AJC as a whole, the Survey Committee was made up of successful, assimilated Jews, most of whom were male. As one Survey Committee member later put it, these were men who were "looked upon by the masses [of Jews] as representing the economic royalists, social snobs and religious renegades in American Jewry." In addition to the sources cited in note 12, see "Report of Information & Service Associates," in "Survey Committee, Educational Department Survey, 1933–1942" folder, box 39, Waldman Papers. For comment on the makeup of the Survey Committee, see Alfred L. Bernheim to Richard Rothschild and Sidney Wallach, n.d., "Survey Committee, 1936–1941, 43 MDW" folder, box 39, Waldman Papers.

14. Morris Waldman to James N. Rosenberg, 5 November 1936, "Survey Committee, 1936–41, 43 MDW" folder; and "Program for 1937," "Survey Committee, Educational Department Survey, 1933–1942" folder; both in box 39, Waldman Papers.

As the AJC board member Cyrus Adler put it, "If the liberals in the world fail and everybody becomes a Fascist or a Communist, then, of course, the Jews will fail also."[15]

Working through the Survey Committee, the AJC tried to discredit Nazism and shore up Americans' belief in religious freedom and tolerance. In doing so, it relied heavily on what it referred to as "nerve center work"—influencing those individuals and groups who in turn molded public opinion. Throughout the 1930s, the AJC funded the work of anthropologist Franz Boas and called media attention to his anti-racist findings. It also produced and distributed pamphlets and books; maintained an active speakers' bureau; secured time for, wrote or contributed to hundreds of radio programs; and arranged for dozens of newspapers and national magazines to "carry and/or reprint material of interest to us." To work the "pro-democracy" message into films, and to screen out potentially inflammatory material, the AJC established a committee of sympathetic Hollywood writers and directors headed by the famous producer and Survey Committee member David Selznick. Finally, through direct subsidies or by tapping the pockets and expertise of its members, the AJC quietly channeled advice and financial support to dozens of organizations with similar goals.[16]

One of the groups which benefited most from the AJC's interest was the National Conference of Christians and Jews (NCCJ). The NCCJ had been founded in 1928, after Protestant efforts to convert Jews provoked an angry Jewish reaction. Liberal Protestants had helped found the organization—and it eventually enrolled some Catholics as well—but much of its early support came from American Jews. Roger W. Straus, a Jewish industrialist, contributed the $5,000 needed to launch the NCCJ and served for decades as one of its three cochairmen. (He also served on the AJC's Survey Committee.) Nine of the ten initial affiliating organizations were Jewish, and B'nai B'rith was the NCCJ's largest financial sponsor in its first few years. This heavy Jewish involvement was reflected in the Conference's original name: the National Conference of Jews and Christians. (The name was changed in late

15. Cyrus Adler to Morris Waldman, 7 April 1938, "Survey Committee, 1936–41, 43 MDW" folder, box 39, Waldman Papers.

16. For more on the relationship between Franz Boas and the American Jewish Committee, see "Boas, Franz, 1933–35, 38–40, 42–43" folder, box 5, Waldman Papers. For an example of Survey Committee activities during one five-month period, see "Survey Committee, Report of Activities, January to May, 1938," "Survey Committee Reports, 1938–1939, 41" folder, box 39, Waldman Papers.

1938, coinciding with an effort by American Jews to downplay their role in the anti-Nazi effort.)[17]

Under the direction of Everett Clinchy, the Presbyterian minister who was recruited to head the organization, the NCCJ promoted religious pluralism within a civic consensus—a notion it called the "American Way." In essence, the NCCJ argued that American Protestants, Catholics, and Jews might disagree on things religious, but could still respect one another and work together in the civic arena. The most dramatic example of such cooperation was the "trio tour," a technique the NCCJ pioneered in 1933. A minister, a priest, and a rabbi (or prominent laymen from each religion) would tour the country together, preaching religious tolerance and civic consensus. Members of such "tolerance trios" often borrowed and recast Booker T. Washington's famous defense of racial segregation: "In all things religious, we Catholics, Jews and Protestants can be as separate as the fingers of a man's outstretched hand; in all things civic and American, we can be as united as a man's clenched fist."[18]

The fact that an analogy used to defend racial segregation could be marshaled on behalf of religious pluralism reveals some of the premises underlying the NCCJ's argument. The AJC and the NCCJ both saw a liberal society as one in which there was a sharp distinction between the public and private spheres. They saw religion as essentially a private matter, and thus as one clearly outside the interests of the state. The use of this analogy also suggests some of the problems that would later develop with applying this notion of "tolerance" to blacks.

Not surprisingly, the AJC saw the NCCJ as an important ally in the effort to mobilize American Christians against both Nazism

17. For a useful discussion of the founding of the NCCJ, see Benny Kraut, "Towards the Establishment of the National Conference of Christians and Jews: The Tenuous Road to Religious Goodwill in the 1920s," *American Jewish History* 77 (1988): 388–412; Lance J. Sussman, "'Toward Better Understanding': The Rise of the Interfaith Movement in America and the Role of Rabbi Isaac Landman," *American Jewish Archives* 34 (1982): 35–51.

18. "Dialogue of a Protestant, a Catholic, and a Jew," typescript dated 1933, "The Trio Program" folder, box 1, National Conference of Christians and Jews Papers, Social Welfare History Archives, Minneapolis (hereafter cited as NCCJ Papers). See also Newton Baker, Carlton J. H. Hayes, and Roger W. Straus, eds., *The American Way* (Chicago, 1936). The NCCJ's vision preceded by several decades the "triple melting pot" described by Will Herberg in his 1955 classic *Protestant-Catholic-Jew*. While this notion of tolerant, religious pluralism was embraced by many lay leaders and liberal clergy of all three major faiths, more conservative religious leaders generally opposed it. The Catholic hierarchy proved particularly resistant to this definition of the "American Way."

and domestic anti-Semitism. In 1933, the AJC reported that it was "making an effort to have the National Conference assume the position of importance in the U.S. that it merits." The AJC arranged newsreel coverage of the NCCJ's first trio tour and invented Brotherhood Day, the nationwide celebration used for decades by the NCCJ to spread its themes. The AJC also quietly funded a study of Protestant textbook references to Jews, which was formally sponsored by the NCCJ. Finally, the AJC provided startup funds for the NCCJ's Religious News Service, then used the wire service to feed its messages to the nation's Christian and daily press.[19]

Both the American Jewish Committee and the National Conference of Christians and Jews steered clear of defending Jews directly, fearing that this would only precipitate a "Jewish debate" in the U.S. NCCJ director Clinchy warned in 1939 that an "open approach" to combating anti-Semitism and anti-Catholicism might actually fuel religious intolerance. Members of the AJC's Survey Committee clearly agreed: "Arguments that the Jews are *not* communists, that they are *not* war mongers, that they are *not* dishonest in business—these, though based on fact, only fan the flame of the anti-Semitic issue itself," they declared.[20]

Instead, the Survey Committee called on the AJC and allied groups to shift the debate from "Jews vs. Nazis" to "Nazis vs. civilization/democracy [and] Americanism":

> It must be made perfectly clear that it is the *Nazis* who are the warmongers; the *Nazis* who are demoralizing foreign trade and thus creating unsettlement in the business world and unrest in the ranks of the unemployed; the *Nazis* who are fertilizing the soil for communism and who, in fact, have developed a "Brown Bolshevism" of their own; the *Nazis* who are attacking the bases of religion in all its forms; the *Nazis* who are undermining the home, abolishing liberal education, and destroying everything which modern men have come to respect.
>
> If the issue is stressed of "Nazis vs. Civilization," the Jews will find themselves fighting shoulder to shoulder with all other right-thinking men.

19. "General Educational Program Against Anti-Semitism in the United States" and "Report of Information and Service Associates, 1 May 1935," both in "Survey Committee, Educational Department Survey, 1933–1942" folder, box 39, Waldman Papers. See also Benny Kraut, "Towards the Establishment of the National Conference of Christians and Jews," 410; and Nicholas V. Montalto, *A History of the Intercultural Education Movement, 1924–1941* (New York, 1982), 188–204.

20. "Report of the [NCCJ] Director," 15 May 1939, "Annual Reports, 1928–1939" folder, box 1, NCCJ Papers. The AJC memo quoted in this and the following

As this statement suggests, Survey Committee members believed that Jews could best defend themselves by presenting Nazism as a threat to the self-interest of other Americans.

The fall of France and the resulting surge of concern about American unity gave the AJC and the NCCJ what they saw as "a unique opportunity to discredit anti-Semitism not merely in terms of Americanism, decency and fair play, as in the past, but also in terms of American defense and national survival." Many Americans believed that only a fifth column could have triggered France's speedy collapse. Playing off of Nazi racialism, the AJC and the NCCJ argued that bigots formed just such a fifth column. Anti-Semitism, Clinchy argued, was a "Nazi trick" that Hitler had used to divide and undermine Western democracies. "Anti-Semitism," echoed the AJC, "is the opening wedge for the destruction of all rights." It "has become a political factor of the first magnitude—the emotional spearhead of a world-wide revolutionary program."[21]

In making this argument, the AJC and the NCCJ were building on and inverting the long-standing proposition that the fate of Jews was intimately tied to the fate of liberalism and democracy. If the fate of democracy determined the fate of Jews, they argued in effect, then the fate of Jews foreshadowed the fate of democracy. The implications of this argument stretched far beyond Jews, for Jews were simply the canaries in the mineshaft. In a nation of minorities such as the U.S., other groups would be next. Only by embracing "tolerance" and "brotherhood," the AJC and the NCCJ argued, could Americans create a sound and democratic national unity. Only by condemning bigotry and judging each person as an individual could Americans protect themselves against the Nazi tactic of "divide and conquer."

In the months leading up to the U.S. entry into World War II, a host of liberal organizations joined the AJC and the NCCJ in preaching tolerance in the name of national unity. Schools and civic groups across the country showed the NCCJ filmstrip "The World We Want to Live In" and listened to Conference speakers

paragraph is "Memorandum on Basic Strategy," December 1939, "Survey Committee, Educational Department Survey, 1933–1942" folder, box 39, Waldman Papers.

21. "Proposal for a Review of Our Pro-Democratic Policy" by S. Wallach, 16 November 1939; "Memorandum on Basic Strategy," December 1939; "Report by Riesenfeld to AJC's 34th annual meeting," January 1941; and "Plans for Combating Anti-Semitism in Early 1942" by S. W., R. R. and F. T., January 1942; all in "Survey Committee, Educational Department Survey, 1933–42" folder, box 39, Waldman Papers.

decry religious conflict as "a trick to weaken and destroy us." The newly formed Council Against Intolerance spread the theme through Independence Day celebrations in several cities, which were broadcast on national radio. It also distributed materials to schools, including the aptly named magazine *American Unity*. Inspired by the AJC, a group called Citizens for Educational Service Inc. issued a pamphlet entitled *Footprints of the Trojan Horse*, which depicted anti-Semitism as a device being used to destroy democracy one minority at a time. These examples could be multiplied many times over.[22]

Some of this material used rhetoric every bit as hysterical as that used by nativists during World War I. For instance, a brochure issued by the Chicago chapter of the NCCJ warned readers that "No Ocean Separates Us from Our Enemies Within." The document opened to a collage of Nazi storm troopers, bombed-out buildings, and stricken women and children refugees. "Enemies Within Hastened the Fall of Democratic, Liberty Loving Nations Abroad—National Defense Demands National Unity," the brochure intoned. Only then did the brochure make clear that these internal enemies were those who "propagat[ed] lies, suspicion, misunderstanding and intolerance among American citizens of every creed and race."[23]

With the U.S. entry into World War II, the plea for tolerance in the name of national unity became a staple of the Roosevelt administration's domestic propaganda campaign. In his State of the Union message, delivered one month after the Japanese attack on Pearl Harbor, President Roosevelt warned Americans to "guard against divisions among ourselves" and to be "particularly vigilant against racial discrimination in any of its ugly forms." (Like his contemporaries, Roosevelt was here using "race" to encompass what is now generally referred to as "ethnicity.") A few months later, the Office of Facts and Figures issued a pamphlet entitled "Divide and Conquer," which charged that Hitler and his agents were "sow[ing] seeds of hate and disunity" among Americans. The theme also showed up in speeches by Justice Department officials, in government descriptions of the enemy, in an Office of War Information movie, and in information manuals distributed by the OWI

22. National Conference of Christians and Jews, *Bulletin*, July 1941 and March 1942. Contents of "Council Against Intolerance" folder, Blaustein Library, American Jewish Committee, New York; Steele, "War on Intolerance," 28.

23. "No Ocean Separates Us from Our Enemies Within" brochure, "Annual Reports, 1940–49" folder, box 1, NCCJ Papers.

to radio writers and movie producers. One of these manuals declared simply, "Men and women who foster racial prejudices are fighting for the enemy."[24]

Meanwhile, the NCCJ, with federal approval, carried the message of religious tolerance and national unity into hundreds of American army camps. "Tolerance trios"—the rabbi-priest-minister teams mentioned earlier—visited U.S. military installations from Norfolk to Nome, and the Army incorporated NCCJ materials into GI orientation courses. The NCCJ estimated that, in just the first year of the program, more than two million soldiers and sailors attended interfaith meetings or saw the NCCJ film "The World We Want to Live In." The National Conference also distributed millions of trifaith prayer cards, as well as pamphlets with titles like "United in Service" and "American Brotherhood." Beginning in 1943, the NCCJ's Clinchy lectured on interfaith tolerance to every graduating class of both the Army and Navy Chaplains' Schools.[25]

The American Jewish Committee privately took credit for popularizing "the slogan 'divide and conquer,'" making it "a household phrase in American life." Indeed, many of the nonprofit organizations that preached this message in the early months of World War II received AJC funding. Moreover, federal propaganda officials contacted both the AJC and the NCCJ shortly after the bombing of Pearl Harbor for help in crafting an anti-Nazi message. In any case, whether or not the AJC helped inspire the federal tolerance campaign, the "divide and conquer" message took on new dimensions in federal hands. Liberals within the Roosevelt administration certainly hoped to use the war to promote religious and racial tolerance both at home and abroad. But they also

24. Office of War Information, *The War Messages of Franklin D. Roosevelt: December 8, 1941, to April 13, 1945* (Washington, D.C., 1945), 29; "Divide and Conquer," *CIO News* (20 April 1942), 6, excerpts the OWI pamphlet by that name. "Divide and Conquer," *Victory* (20 January 1943), 89; Office of War Information, Bureau of Motion Pictures, *A List of U.S. War Information Films* (Washington, D.C., 1943), 8; Office of War Information, Domestic Branch, "Information Guide: The Enemy" (Washington, D.C., April 1943); "Washington's Information Manual for Hollywood, 1942," reprinted in *Historical Journal of Film, Radio and Television*, 1983, 3(2). The final quote comes from Office of War Information, Domestic Radio Bureau, *When Radio Writes for War* (Washington, D.C., 1943).

25. The NCCJ's military camp program is described in the January and May 1943 issues of the National Conference of Christians and Jews' *Bulletin*. Also see three pamphlets contained in "World War II Publications" folder, box 11, NCCJ Papers: "Is the Army and Navy Program of the National Conference of Christians and Jews Really Effective? The Answer is Yes!" "Thirty Years Work in One," and "The Message As Given at Camp Wallace...."

worried about other forms of domestic unrest that could under-mine the war effort. If discrimination against blacks and white ethnics could lead to an underutilization of manpower, strikes and lockouts could also hamper the war machine. Prejudice against aliens might turn American ethnics into a dangerous fifth column, federal officials feared; but too much ethnic loyalty—the tradi-tional Irish hatred of the British, for instance—could hinder Amer-ica's cooperation with her allies.[26]

Thus, during the war, the theme of tolerance was applied to an ever expanding list of targets. When the Office of War Information launched a "Stop that Rumor!" campaign in 1943, it noted that "hate rumors" were the most common and dangerous type. The OWI identified Jews, Catholics, and Negroes as common targets of such rumors, but it also listed blood banks, draft boards, business, unions, the Russians, and the British. Hate rumors, the OWI clari-fied, are "the ones that express prejudice, animosity or hostility for religious, racial, social or economic groups other than the enemy."[27]

This definition was telling, for it underscored the fact that toler-ance was simply a corollary of consensus—a consensus defined by a common enemy.[28] This notion put strict limits on the kinds of plu-ralism that "tolerance" could support. Religious pluralism—such as that promoted by both the AJC and the NCCJ—could comfortably coexist with loyalty to the American nation as long as religious affil-iation was considered a private affair. In fact, since American prop-agandists repeatedly portrayed all three Axis powers as hostile to

26. "Memorandum to Nathan Ohrbach from Henry W. Levy," 28 September 1944, "Program and Policy, 1943–49" folder, box 34, Waldman Papers.

27. Office of War Information Radio Background Material, "Subject: Rumors," 10 December 1942; Office of War Information, Domestic Branch, "Information Guide: Rumors," May 1943. According to an official with the War Advertising Council, the federal government eventually called off the "Stop That Rumor!" campaign "be-cause it was found that the rumors that we were endeavoring to stop gained more publicity through the campaign and more people felt that 'if there was smoke there must be fire.'" Douglas Meldrum to Lee H. Bristol, 31 July 1946, "Christians and Jews, 1946" folder, box 1, Washington Office Subject Files, 1942–1981, Advertising Council Papers, Series 13/2/305, University of Illinois Archives, Urbana, Illinois.

28. This observation benefits from Philip Gleason's insightful discussion in *Speak-ing of Diversity*, 166–67. Gleason argues that during World War II "cultural plural-ism [in the U.S.] was predicated upon, and made possible by, a high degree of consensus" about certain civic beliefs, among them "respect for the principle of equality before the law" and "recognition of … the rights of minorities." Although many who preached tolerance advocated such principles, this paper suggests that America's wartime consensus was ultimately defined, not by the "rights of minori-ties," but by a common enemy.

religion, belief in *any* of the nation's three major faiths could actually provide a basis for American unity.[29] But the implications of tolerance and pluralism proved more complex when ethnicity rather than religion was at stake.

By casting intolerance as an alien rather than a homegrown philosophy, both the AJC and the NCCJ defined bigotry as an Old World disease. Thus, they saw recent immigrants—those who had not yet been fully Americanized—as particularly susceptible to prejudice. NCCJ staffers, for instance, argued in 1942 that the Conference should work more closely with organized labor because "this group includes a large percentage of foreign-born who have brought false beliefs into this nation." Similar reasoning may have prompted the AJC to launch a National Labor Service, which provided cartoons, editorials, advertisements, posters, and other materials (see Fig. 8.1) preaching tolerance to labor newspapers and unions.[30]

Federal officials, though less concerned about anti-Semitism per se, also worried about recent immigrants' Old World loyalties and prejudices. Their fears were not limited to those ethnic groups with ties to the Axis powers. Federal officials worried that divisions within and among immigrant groups—the tension between various Slavic nationalities, for instance—might erupt, hindering the war effort. Similarly, they feared that Old World hatreds—such as the Polish hatred of the Russians—would hurt America's ability to cooperate with her allies. During World War I, such concerns prompted President Wilson and other prominent officials to denounce "hyphenated Americans." During World War II, federal officials preached tolerance as Americanism.

Not surprisingly, federal officials worried particularly about both aliens and citizens with ties to Germany, Italy, and Japan. Alan Cranston, chief of the OWI's foreign-language division (and later a U.S. senator from California) explained these concerns in a 1942 speech to editors of foreign-language newspapers. Cranston noted that many German-language newspapers in the U.S. ran

29. For federal depictions of the Axis powers, see three pamphlets put out by the Office of War Information during the war: *Radio Background Material, Subject: The Enemy* (1 July 1942); *Radio Background Material, Subject: Our Enemies: The Nazis* (12 January 1943); and *Enemy Japan* (1945).

30. "Minutes of the NCCJ Board of Trustees, Wednesday, October 7, 1942," "Board of Trustees, 1941–45" folder, box 2, NCCJ Records. For more on the National Labor Service, see "Educational Materials—Labor" folder, box 216, RG 347, American Jewish Committee Records, GEN-10, YIVO Institute.

FIGURE 8.1   American Jewish Committee's National Labor Service
Cartoon Advocating Tolerance

LET HIM BEAT HIS BRAINS OUT!

Source: Reprinted with the permission of the American Jewish Committee
located in New York City at 165 East 56th Street, NY 10022.

articles on war bonds, rationing, and civilian defense, but refused to publish "a single word" condemning Nazism. "If they fail to separate themselves and their people from the Nazis," he asked rhetorically, "how can they possibly expect the rest of the world to make any distinction between the Germans who worship Hitlerism and the Germans who hate Hitlerism? How can they expect Americans in the midst of a death struggle with the Nazis to continue to treat German immigrants as loyal, full-fledged Americans?"[31]

Cranston's quote points up a critical distinction on which the federal call for ethnic tolerance depended. The OWI argued repeatedly during the war that America's enemies were ideologies and leaders—the Nazis, the fascists and the warlords—rather than the German, Italian, or Japanese people. The vast majority of people living in the Axis countries, the OWI contended, were simply "dupes"—dupes who had to be "liberated" from their "despotic rulers" and eventually welcomed into the postwar" brotherhood of man." Thus, in theory at least, a German or Italian immigrant who retained his customs and language could still be considered a loyal American if he forswore the ideology of his native land. Liberals both within and outside of the Roosevelt administration hoped that by making this argument they could derail nativist hysteria and prevent the kind of punitive peace that followed World War I.[32]

But this distinction proved too subtle for many Americans, including some within the administration. Many sided with Bob Maxwell, the director of the children's radio show "Superman." When an OWI official encouraged Mr. Maxwell to tone down the virulence of his program, the director responded:

> I control the destinies of three juvenile radio programs with audiences running into the millions. I can, in some small way, formulate ideologies for these youngsters.... I am, at the moment, teaching this vast audience to hate. If not to hate individuals, to hate that for which they stand. And, unfortunately, there is no cleavage between the individual and the state whose ideology he defends. A German is a Nazi and a Jap is the little yellow man who "knifed us in the back at Pearl Harbor."

31. "MacLeish Attacks Divisionists and Defeatists," FLIS Press Releases, 23 March 1942; and "Address by Alan Cranston, Chief, Foreign Language Division, Office of War Information, Before the Editors and Publishers of Foreign Language Newspapers in New York City, August 25, 1942," both in the microfilm edition of the American Council for Nationalities Service Papers, reel 19.

32. See for example: Office of War Information, Domestic Branch, "Information Guide: The Enemy," (Washington, D.C., April 1943); and Office of War Information, "'I Am Not Crazy Enough to Want War'... Hitler," (Washington, D.C., 1943).

To argue otherwise, Mr. Maxwell concluded, was simply to "make for confusion."[33]

The OWI had neither the means nor the will to enforce its approach. Thus, during the war, appeals for "tolerance" appeared side by side with cartoons that portrayed the Germans and particularly the Japanese as animalistic or demonic. Such messages of hate—even if aimed at Germans and Japanese abroad—often ricocheted and hit their American kin. The best example of this is undoubtedly the internment of thousands of West Coast Japanese-Americans, including many who had never set foot in Japan.

The internment of Pacific Coast Japanese-Americans also provides a striking example of the potentially conservative implications of linking tolerance to national unity. In late 1945, the National Conference of Christians and Jews sponsored an essay contest for high school students on the subject "The Best Example of Teamwork I Know…" Essays were supposed to illustrate "how Americans of diverse backgrounds work together for the good of their school or community, or the nation." The winning composition, dramatized by Hollywood film stars, was to be featured on a national radio program during American Brotherhood Week in February 1946.[34]

Noble Oyanagi, a Japanese-American student then living in St. Paul, Minnesota, won the contest. Noble wrote about the day he and his family were taken from their unidentified West Coast home to a relocation camp. "As we worked in our home until the train time preparing to leave, in popped one of our dearest friends—Callahan by name, an Irishman if there ever was one," wrote Noble. Callahan took time off from work to drive the Oyanagi family to the train station, where Noble found all his "buddies" waiting. Joe Mineth, an Italian, and Gus Martigopolus, a Greek, carried the Oyanagis' luggage to the train concourse. Another friend gave Noble a comic book. As the train started to pull away, Noble saw "chums of every nationality," who had come to see him off—"Eric Liljas, a blond Swede, Bobby Feldman, a Jewish pal, the entire Wing family, who, although their homeland was ravished by the Japanese, had no harsh feelings toward us."

Here was a picture of pluralistic America helping to "ease the burden of evacuation" for the Oyanagi family. As Noble Oyanagi

33. See George Zachary to Allen Ducovny, 3 April 1943, and Bob Maxwell to George Zachary, 12 April 1943, both in folder 240, box 24, Child Study Association of America Papers, Social Welfare History Archives.

34. Press release and essay entitled "The Best Example of Teamwork I Know …," "Frank Trager" folder, box 9, NCCJ Papers.

wrote, "It was truly teamwork in action that I witnessed that day." But teamwork for what? Neither Noble nor his friends challenged the legitimacy of the evacuation, although he did note that for him it was a "gloomy, dismal day." Rather, the winning essay implied that internment was simply the sacrifice Japanese-Americans had to make for their country—just as German-Americans had to denounce Nazism, and the soldiers' mother in the war-bond advertisement had to abandon her thoughtless bigotry. Tolerance in the name of national unity celebrated social harmony and good sportsmanship; as a tool for critiquing national policy, it was severely limited.

As this suggests, the promise of the "tolerance" campaign was sharply limited when it came to America's largest racial minority, African-Americans. Throughout the war, some liberals tried to link the notions of "brotherhood" and "racial equality," of racial discrimination and Nazi "divide and conquer" tactics. Certainly, fears that prejudice and discrimination would undermine blacks' wartime morale contributed to President Roosevelt's historic decision to ban racial discrimination in the defense industry. The Fair Employment Practices Committee, set up as a result of the president's 1941 order, was the first federal agency since Reconstruction to deal exclusively with minority problems and was an important forerunner of the civil rights movement.[35]

At the same time, racial prejudice was embedded far more deeply in American law and social custom than was religious prejudice. Religious differences could be safely relegated to the private realm—and tolerated there. But central issues facing American blacks—legal equality and integration—were unquestionably public concerns. Thus, challenging racial prejudice was far more likely to trigger social upheaval. During the war, many public and private agencies that advocated religious, and even ethnic, "tolerance" took the path of safety when it came to race. The National Conference of Christians and Jews refused to extend its opposition to prejudice beyond religious ecumenicism. And when the Conference's "tolerance trios" visited army camps, they spoke to troops segregated by race.[36]

America's public discourse linking "tolerance" to national unity not only survived the war, but flourished in the postwar period. In

35. Merl E. Reed, *Seedtime for the Modern Civil Rights Movement: The President's Committee on Fair Employment Practice, 1941–1946* (Baton Rouge, LA, 1991).

36. The decision of the NCCJ board to avoid taking on racial intolerance directly can be traced through a series of memos and reports contained in "Board of Trustees, 1941–45" folder, box 2, NCCJ Records.

1946, the newly formed Advertising Council launched a public service campaign dubbed "United America" that portrayed bigots as "Typhoid Marys." The NCCJ's Brotherhood Week—renamed American Brotherhood Week—emerged as a nationwide celebration chaired honorarily by the president himself. Even America's favorite radio superhero joined the campaign. After five years of "pure blood, thunder and atomic energy," the *New York Herald Tribune* reported in 1946, the producers of "Superman" had made tolerance their dominant theme. In the late 1940s, Superman battled the "Guardians of America," the "Hooded Klan," and the "Knights of the White Carnation," while his sidekick Jimmy Olsen joined a nonsectarian boys' club called Unity House.[37]

The specific twists and turns of this postwar discourse on tolerance are beyond the scope of this chapter. However, it is worth noting this discussion's ambivalent legacy. The interfaith movement, represented most prominently by the National Conference of Christians and Jews, became almost synonymous with Americanism during the Cold War. In part, this reflected the assimilation of America's Jewish and Catholic immigrant communities. But it was aided by the fact that communism—like Nazism—was portrayed as hostile to religion. In 1955, when Will Herberg published *Protestant-Catholic-Jew*, he was able to write that "virtually every civic enterprise possessing any moral, cultural or spiritual aspect is today thought of, and where possible organized, along interfaith—that is, tripartite—lines." The tripartite arrangement "is so obviously American and so obviously all-inclusive of the total American community."[38]

The fact that an interfaith America was not necessarily all-inclusive is shown by the fact that the civil rights movement was just gathering steam as Herberg wrote. Martin Luther King Jr. and other black activists also appealed to "tolerance" and "brotherhood," but their path was more difficult for some of the reasons suggested above. Civil rights activists argued that prejudice and segregation hurt the morale of black Americans and damaged the

37. "Addition of Social Conscience Swells Child Serial Popularity," *New York Herald Tribune*, 14 July 1946. For more on the "United America" campaign, see "Advertising Council" folder, box 3, Waldman Papers. The NCCJ Papers include numerous files devoted to postwar Brotherhood Weeks. The transformation of "Superman" can be traced through the contents of folder 240, box 24, Child Study Association of America Papers.

38. Will Herberg, *Protestant-Catholic-Jew: An Essay in American Religious Sociology* (Chicago, 1955, 1960), 243.

nation's image during the Cold War. But racist white Southerners and their allies also used the divide-and-conquer argument. As one woman wrote, in opposing integrated viewing of a major national exhibit in 1948, "To highlight any minority rouses its fighting spirit and focuses the prejudice against it,—and this leads to disunity.... It is important that we do not stir one group of Americans against another."[39]

Finally, the divide-and-conquer argument honed by interfaith advocates before and during World War II was in the late 1940s and 1950s appropriated by "Red-baiters" and redeployed in the name of anti-communism. Yoking tolerance to the need for national unity assumed an ideological consensus—a consensus defined most easily by a common enemy. During World War II that enemy was clearly Nazi Germany. But, as the Cold War deepened, communism replaced Nazism as America's principal ideological threat. Thus, an argument used to discredit religious, ethnic, and racial prejudice helped pave the way for a new form of intolerance: McCarthyism.

39. Margaret Patterson, a trustee of the American Heritage Foundation, opposed the integration of the Freedom Train, which circled the U.S. between 1947 and 1949. Margaret Patterson to Winthrop Aldrich, 12 January 1948, "American Heritage Foundation, January 1948" folder, box 20, Correspondence File II, Winthrop A. Aldrich Papers, Special Collections, Baker Library, Harvard Business School, Boston.

Chapter Nine

"KNOW YOUR ENEMY"

American Wartime Images of
Germany, 1942–1943

Michaela Hönicke

"Know Your Enemy": A Problem

I n late summer of 1942 a prescient opinion analyst, Hadley Cantril,
found that American views of the German enemy were characterized by "a lack of crystallization and a high degree of suggestibility." He warned that "the implications of this for the
postwar world are clear—almost anything can happen."[1] Two
years later, with American troops close to the German border, it
appeared that this disquieting state of public opinion had not significantly changed. Informing his superiors in the British Foreign
Office of the American governmental and public debate on "what
to do with Germany"—recently sparked anew by the leaked

---

1. Office of Public Opinion Research (OPOR), "The Nature of the Enemy," Con-
fidential Report prepared for the Bureau of Intelligence (BOI), Office of War Infor-
mation (OWI), 13 August 1942, box 11, Philleo Nash Papers, Harry S. Truman
Library (hereafter cited as HST-L). Hadley Cantril was the director of the OPOR at
Princeton University. For a similar assessment of public opinion at this time, see
James MacGregor Burns, *Roosevelt: The Soldier of Freedom, 1940–45* (New York,
1970), 272ff. For a brief overview of the early public opinion research institutes, see
Norman M. Bradburn and Seymour Sudman, *Polls and Surveys: Understanding
What They Tell Us* (San Francisco, 1988), Ch. 2.

Morgenthau Plan—Isaiah Berlin wrote: "Out of this brief storm has come at least a lightning flash which has illuminated the public landscape, revealing a state of wide ignorance and perplexity. If the Administration genuinely desires to support a stiff postwar settlement, it still has time, and now also the opportunity, to educate its people accordingly."[2]

Both contemporary observers pointed to the fact that, contrary to commonly held beliefs, even after Americans had entered the war against Nazi Germany, popular views of that country did not coalesce into a well-focused image of the enemy.[3] Instead the United States witnessed a lively, rather well-informed and sophisticated debate, both in governmental and in public circles, on the "nature of the enemy" and on "what to do with Germany."[4] Moreover, Cantril,

2. H. G. Nicholas, ed., *Washington Despatches, 1941–1945: Weekly Political Reports from the British Embassy* (Chicago, 1981), 426, entry for 30 September 1944. Since spring of 1942 Isaiah Berlin had been entrusted with writing the first draft of these despatches "on changing attitudes and movements of opinion in the USA;" see Berlin's introduction to this volume. For his critical reporting on what he saw as "pro-German" sentiment in the American population as well as a remarkable diversity of opinions on the German question, see 222, 229, 235, 286, 299, 325, 340, 356, 394, 412f., 419, 422ff., 436, 441f., 499, 504, 508. See also "The 'German Lobby' in the United States," Report for the Central Department of the Foreign Office by the Political Intelligence Department, 21 January 1943, printed in Anthony J. Nicholls, "American views of Germany's future during World War II," in *Das "Andere Deutschland" im Zweiten Weltkrieg: Emigration und Widerstand in internationaler Perspektive,* ed. Lothar Kettenacker (Stuttgart, 1977), 218–21.

3. See for example John Morton Blum, *V Was for Victory: Politics and American Culture During World War II* (San Diego, 1976), 45–52, who discusses almost exclusively literary products and movies. For a different view, albeit only for the early period, based on Office of War Information documents and unpublished public opinion polls, see Richard W. Steele, "American Popular Opinion and the War Against Germany: The Issue of a Negotiated Peace, 1942," *Journal of American History* 55 (1978): 704–23. Incidentally, this state of confusion worried not only government officials. Journalists, intellectuals, and other public commentators were equally disturbed. Thus Cecil Brown reported "confusion over what we are fighting to eradicate from the world and what we propose to substitute in its place prevails throughout the country.... I asked hundreds of people from coast to coast: 'What is Fascism?'... people could not agree, or had no idea whatever." *Colliers* 112, 11 December 1943, 14.

4. Specific sources are cited in the respective context. For the governmental debate see Günter Moltmann, *Amerikas Deutschlandpolitik im Zweiten Weltkrieg: Kriegs- und Friedensziele 1941–45* (Heidelberg, 1958) and more specifically Ilse Dorothee Pautsch, *Die territoriale Deutschlandplanung des amerikanischen Außenministeriums, 1941–43* (Frankfurt, 1990) as well as Petra Marquardt-Bigman, "Nachdenken über ein demokratisches Deutschland: Der Beitrag der Research and Analysis Branch zur Planung der amerikanischen Deutschlandpolitik" in *Geheimdienstkrieg gegen Deutschland,* eds. Jürgen Heideking and Christof Mauch (Göttingen, 1993),

the pollster, and Berlin, the philosopher-turned-Foreign-Office-employee, referred to the ultimate relevance of American wartime images of Germany, namely, the effect they had on American thinking on postwar issues. In spite of Roosevelt's insistence that the war first had to be won before peace plans could seriously be considered, no one interested in a peaceful Europe assumed that military victory itself would solve the German problem; instead "to eradicate [Germany's] false ideologies ... was considered just as important as curtailing [its] physical ability to make war."[5] Public support for a specific solution to the "German problem," however, could only have been rallied with the help of a preceding, well-orchestrated propaganda campaign promoting the appropriate messages concerning the nature of the Nazi threat.

Why then did Americans hold competing and conflicting views on Germany? In search of an answer, I will first recapitulate what public opinion analysts found when they studied popular views of the enemy during the first year of the American war effort. Next we will need to turn our attention to the challenges and constraints that official wartime propaganda faced in the American context.

122–41. My assessment regarding the corollary effect of this official ambiguity on the public debate is primarily based on my own analysis of the periodical *In Re Germany*, selected periodical articles, scripts of radio talk shows, newsreels, propaganda films, commercial movies, public opinion polls, the papers of Dorothy Thompson, of the Society for the Prevention of World War III, and of the Non-Sectarian Anti-Nazi League, governmental and military publications on Nazi Germany as well as contemporary books on Germany. See also Donald F. Lach, "What They Would Do About Germany," *Journal of Modern History* 17 (1945): 227–43; cf. the articles by Sigrid Schneider, Wulf Koepke, Claus-Dieter Krohn, Alfons Soellner, and Guy Stern in *Deutschland nach Hitler: Zukunftspläne im Exil und aus der Besatzungszeit, 1939–1949*, ed. Thomas Koebner (Opladen, 1987); with the same emphasis on emigrants in the context of the American debate on Germany: Joachim Radkau, *Die deutsche Emigration in den USA: Ihr Einfluß auf die amerikanische Europapolitik, 1933–1945* (Düsseldorf, 1971); Robert D. Schulzinger, *The Wise Men of Foreign Affairs: The History of the Council on Foreign Relations* (New York, 1984), and Michael Wala, *Winning the Peace: Amerikanische Außenpolitik und der Council on Foreign Relations, 1945–50* (Stuttgart, 1990), 48–66, are two studies covering just one of the think tanks which contributed to both the governmental and the public debate as did the Brookings Institution, primarily with studies to the German war economy, its societal effects, and Nazi exploitation of occupied Europe. Very insightful on press coverage of the Third Reich are Deborah E. Lipstadt, *Beyond Belief: The American Press and the Coming of the Holocaust, 1933–1945* (New York, 1986), and Michael Zalampas, *Adolf Hitler and the Third Reich in American Magazines, 1923–1939* (Bowling Green, 1989).

5. William Reitzel, Morton A. Kaplan, and Constance G. Coblenz, *U.S. Foreign Policy, 1945–55* (Washington, 1956), 59, and Albert Norman, *Our German Policy: Propaganda and Culture* (New York, 1951), 9.

Against this background I will briefly outline the president's own views of Germany and contrast them with the official information policy which the Office of War Information, the governmental propaganda agency, devised in response to the pollsters findings in 1942/43. In conclusion I will briefly present an alternative view of the enemy, namely that propagated by the U.S. Army.[6]

Public Opinion Analysts at Work

Several times over the course of 1942 public opinion analysts working for the government sounded the alarm. "The superficial unity following Pearl Harbor is not only gone but the sentiment favoring acceptance or consideration of a peace offer from Germany, even by Hitler is by no means insignificant," a pollster warned in March of 1942.[7] Opinion surveys registered insufficient emotional and intellectual commitment to the war against Nazi Germany and a number of misconceptions regarding the "nature of the enemy." They noted that to a people remote from its actual battle lines, the issues of this war had remained cast in platitudes and the image of the enemy had not developed beyond simple stereotypes.[8] More than half of the people surveyed in June 1942 admitted they did not have a clear idea of what the war was about. Only about half of the adult males surveyed in June of 1942 were ready "to go to Europe in person and kill some German soldiers, if this were possible." And most importantly, more than 30 percent favored a peace with Germany if the German Army overthrew Hitler.[9] This

6. The ambiguous yet important role that authors of periodical articles, books, radio speeches, and movie scripts played in the debate on Germany—partly opinion makers, partly opinion gauge—transcends the framework of this chapter. Thus, observations about reactions to or reflections of official directives on how to portray Nazi Germany are for the most part relegated to the footnotes of my exposition. For literature see note 4.

7. Survey of Intelligence Material No. 12, 2 March 1942, President's Secretary's File (PSF) OWI, box 155, Franklin D. Roosevelt Papers, Franklin D. Roosevelt Library (hereafter: FDR-P, FDR-L).

8. "American Estimates of the Enemy," Intelligence Report of the Office of War Information, p. 3, 2 September 1942, PSF OWI, box 155, FDR-P, FDR-L. This report summarized the findings of earlier public opinion studies.

9. "The Nature of the Enemy," 13 August 1942, box 11, Nash-P, HST-L; around 10 percent of Americans surveyed were disposed to accept a peace offer by Hitler himself, "What People Think About Peace and the Role of the U.S. in the Post-War World," Confidential Report by Office of Public Opinion Research (OPOR), 14 February 1942, Official File (OF) 788, FDR-P and "Pre-Pearl Harbor Interventionists and

discrepancy among Americans between the psychological requirements for total war and the lack of resolve to fight worried government officials and military leaders. "A grasp of the issues, an understanding of the enemy, are essential implements for victory; men need to know what they fight for—and what they fight against," presidential advisers admonished.[10]

Pollsters had early on recognized the correlation between the confusion in the definition of the enemy and the inadequate popular understanding of the issues in this war: "[T]he lack of a sharp and correct focus which characterizes the image of the enemy in the U.S. might also be partly responsible for the fact that some strata among the American population do not yet identify themselves fully with the fight against Fascism."[11] And, indeed, the surveys recorded a number of misconceptions regarding the nature of the Nazi enemy. The president and most of his advisers regarded Germany as the nation's chief enemy, both for military and ideological reasons. Accordingly, they portrayed the Nazis as the brains behind the Axis assault, relegating the Japanese and Italians to the rank of Nazi followers and Hitler's "chessmen."[12] Contrary to this official view, however, Americans were much more enthusiastic about fighting the Japanese, feared and hated the Japanese people more than the Germans, and found the "treacherous, sly and cruel" nature of Japanese soldiers more despicable than their "efficient and obedient" German counterparts.[13]

Non-Interventionists, " OPOR, 3 August 1942, Democratic National Committee Records, box 1172, FDR-L; *The Gallup Poll: Public Opinion, 1935–71*, vol. I *1935–1948* (New York, 1972), 954; Richard W. Steele, "American Popular Opinion and the War Against Germany: The Issue of Negotiated Peace, 1942," *Journal of American History* 55 (1978): 704–23.

10. "American Estimates of the Enemy," 2 September 1942, PSF OWI, box 155, FDR-P, FDR-L. "High public morale is a crucial factor in any war effort, and of inestimable military value," concluded another report, "Intelligence Report: Trends in American Public Opinion Since Pearl Harbor," 11 September 1942, PSF OWI, box 155, FDR-P, FDR-L.

11. "The Nature of the Enemy," 2, box 11, Nash-P, HST-L; "Personal Identification with War," 28 October 1942, box 156, PSF OWI and "An analysis ...," 10 September 1942, President's Personal File (hereafter: PPF) 4721, FDR-P, FDR-L.

12. See "State of the Union Address, 6 January 1942," in Samuel I. Rosenman, ed. *The Public Papers and Addresses of Franklin D. Roosevelt* (hereafter FDR-PPA), vol. 1942 (New York, 1950), 32–42, here: 35. See also Mark A. Stoler, *George C. Marshall: Soldier-Statesman of the American Century* (Boston, 1989), 94.

13. "An Analysis of American Public Opinion Regarding the War: A Confidential Report by George Gallup," 10 September 1942, American Institute of Public Opinion (AIPO), PPF 4721, FDR-P, FDR-L. "Report from the Nation," p. 27, 7 December 1942, PSF OWI, box 156, FDR-P, FDR-L. "Special Intelligence Report No. 77: The Enemy in the Movies," 25 November 1942, p. 3. Cantril, "The Nature of the Enemy," 13 August

Moreover, some pollsters were concerned about considerable evidence of wishful thinking on the part of Americans distinguishing between a few evil Nazis and the majority of innocent Germans. About a third of Americans surveyed in the summer and fall of 1942 thought that the German generals and their army were not loyal to Hitler. Forty percent were convinced that the German people were not behind their Führer and almost as many, namely 37 percent, saw a good chance that the Germans would revolt against Hitler. The slight majority of those who realized that there was little domestic opposition in Nazi Germany credited the fact to the Nazi use of force and terror, not to the fascist convictions of ordinary Germans.[14]

Yet those same reports that expressed the urgency of the mission to educate Americans about "why we fight" as well as the nature of the enemy also pointed to the problematic, even dangerous aspects of such an undertaking. In the fall of 1942, an opinion analyst concluded that there were still "millions of people with spiritual reserves that have not been touched ... [because] they are uninformed and misinformed about some of the most basic ideological issues involved in the struggle against tyranny."[15] But a look at the specific misinformed opinions of those millions, according to the surveys of early 1942, suggested that a consensus might not easily be reached on the "ideological issues." The polls detected a sizable minority, up to 30 percent of Americans, forming an infamous "divisionist," "peace," or "turtle" bloc. All of these titles described behavior or mindsets that made this group suspect in the eyes of officials, because its members were seen as fomenting disunity

---

1942, p. 21ff. The numbers of Americans who identified either Germany or Japan as "Enemy No. 1" fluctuated considerably: in April 1942, 46 percent considered Germany the main adversary. In the same poll, however, the number of 35 percent who saw Japan as the main enemy rose to 62 percent when the question was reformulated to inquire about which Axis power should be eliminated first. See Intelligence Survey No. 21, 29 April 1942 and also Intelligence Report No. 39, 4 September 1942, both in PSF OWI, box 155, FDR-P, FDR-L. The numbers continued to shift; thus, in February 1943 a Gallup poll recorded 53 percent of Americans identifying Japan as the country's chief enemy, as opposed to 34 percent who held that view of Germany, *Gallup Poll*, vol. l, 370. For some anecdotal evidence that to "the ordinary American" the war in the Pacific made much more sense then the war in Europe, see "An Analysis ...," Gallup, 10 September 1942, p. 5, PPF 4721, FDR-P, and F. R. von Windegger to FDR, 12 February 1943, PPF 7213, FDR-P, FDR-L.

14. "Intelligence Report No. 39," 4 September 1942, p. 10, PSF OWI, box 155 and "Report from the Nation," p. 28, 7 December 42, PSF OWI, box 156, FDR-P, FDR-L.

15. Jerome S. Bruner, "OWI and the American Public," *Public Opinion Quarterly* (Spring 1943), 133

among a people involved in a life-and-death struggle, willing to accept a negotiated peace with Nazi Germany, and propagating a purely defensive approach limited to the Western Hemisphere. Continuities in sociological and ideological makeup between these dissenters and the isolationist, noninterventionist core before Pearl Harbor were quickly established.[16]

Particularly ominous for any campaign to clarify the ideological differences in this war was the "divisionists'" desire to "convert the war into a crusade against Communism," leaving Germany as a counterweight against Russia. Equally disturbing were the more than 45 percent of Americans who felt that "Jews have too much power and influence" in the United States and a hardcore of 16 percent who expressed outright sympathy with Hitler's "taking away the power of the Jews in Germany."[17] Anti-Semitism, anti-communism and general distrust of the Allies, but in particular of the Soviet Union, as well as readiness to "do business with Hitler," or at least to find some arrangement with "agreeable" elements in Nazi Germany, characterized the political credo of this group. The aims of their activists, according to the official view, included, in addition to seeking a negotiated peace with Nazi Germany, to elect isolationists to Congress, to prevent U.S. postwar participation in any kind of international league, to remove the present administration from office, to discontinue aid to the United Nations, to bring about a breakup of the alliance, and to promote anti-Semitic attitudes and policies.[18]

Internal governmental studies had tried to gauge the scope and composition of this group before and after Pearl Harbor. Inasmuch as

16. "Survey of Intelligence Materials No 19," 15 April 1942, PSF OWI, box 155, FDR-P, FDR-L; "Isolationist Aims, Arguments and Organizations," 7 April 1942, box 1842, Entry 171, RG 44, Federal Record Center (hereafter cited as FRC). For a chronology that traces noninterventionist, anti-war and anti-Allied sentiments since 1936, see "What People Think about Peace and the Role of the U.S. in the Post-War World," OPOR, 14 February 1942, OFF 788; updated information on the divisionist bloc was made available in "Survey of Intelligence Materials No 12," 2 March 1942 PSF OWI, box 155; "Intelligence Report: Trends in American Public Opinion Since Pearl Harbor," 1 September 1942, PSF OWI, box 155, FDR-P; "Pre-Pearl Harbor Interventionists and Non-Interventionists," OPOR, 3 August 1942, Democratic National Committee Records, box 1172, FDR-L.

17. "Intelligence Survey No 19," 15 April 1942, p. 7, PSF OWI, box 155, FDR-P, FDR-L; "The Nature of the Enemy," p. 9, 13 August 1942, box 11, Nash-P, HST-L;" Isolationist Aims, Arguments and Organizations," 7 April 1942, box 1842, Entry 171, RG 44, FRC.

18. "Isolationist Aims, Arguments and Organizations," 7 April 1942, p. 1, box 1842, Entry 171, RG 44, FRC.

its members represented a constant object of greatest concern to the administration, a considerable amount of research and analysis as to their aims, tactics, and activities was also focused on them. It is clear from these analyses that officials differentiated between the lunatic fringe of native fascists such as Father Coughlin and Gerald L. K. Smith, the radical fraction in the American First Committee, anti-administration publishers and editors, and certain formerly isolationist congressmen.[19] While these groups and individuals varied in their ideological makeup, they all turned into one coherent source of concern for the administration as far as their influence on a much larger group of Americans was concerned. The latter, usually estimated to be around 30 percent, was seen as susceptible in various degrees to the different anti-democratic, anti-administrative, anti-Allied and anti-Semitic arguments these activists had to offer: the Germans are only doing what the British and U.S. did earlier, the American people were forced into the war by F.D.R.'s subservience to warmongering Jews, the Axis had no aggressive intentions toward the U.S., this war was being fought to save the British Empire, labor used this opportunity to improve its position at the expense of the nation, and so on. The pollsters detailing these views suggested as remedy "immunization by propaganda"—"it has to begin immediately with the ISSUE and the NATURE OF THE ENEMY as the central themes."[20]

Mobilization: "Men Need to Know What They Fight Against"

But what the public opinion analysts and information officials working for the president had in mind went further than the president

19. Among printed mass media Colonel Robert McCormick of the *Chicago Tribune*, Joseph Patterson of the *New York Daily News*, his sister Eleanor "Cissy" Patterson (*Washington Times-Herald*), and the William R. Hearst chain formed a small but powerful group of isolationist newspapers. On congressional isolationist leaders and Roosevelt's assessment and handling of them, see Wayne S. Cole, *Roosevelt and the Isolationists, 1932–45* (Lincoln, 1983) and Richard W. Steele, "Franklin D. Roosevelt and His Foreign Policy Critics," *Political Science Quarterly* 94 (1979): 15–35. On right-wing extremists see Geoffrey S. Smith, *To Save a Nation: American Countersubversives, the New Deal, and the Coming of World War II* (New York, 1973); Leo P. Ribuffo, *The Old Christian Right: The Protestant Far Right from the Great Depression to the Cold War* (Philadelphia, 1983) and Sander A. Diamond, *The Nazi Movement in the United States, 1924–1941* (Ithaca, NY, 1974).

20. "Isolationist Aims, Arguments and Organizations," 7 April 1942, p. 9 (capitalization in the original), box 1842, Entry 171, RG 44, FRC.

was willing to go at this point.[21] "You cannot kill an idea by killing the man who holds it"—accordingly, the reasoning went among the propaganda advocates that the administration ought to sketch out a vision as to what this country was fighting for and fighting against in the current war.[22] For months the pollsters had recorded and deplored that American popular thinking on issues, i.e., war aims and causes, "lacked definiteness and consistency."[23] They were in fact so alarmed by those fellow citizens who could not even recall the points of the Atlantic Charter as well as by that sizable minority who openly doubted the good cause that they could barely conceal their criticism of the administration for allowing this state of affairs where "as things stand now, Americans have no positive goals to fight for." With a more distinctly cynical overtone another commentator observed that "our war aims as stated in the Atlantic Charter and the Four Freedoms were undoubtedly intended for world consumption—they have not registered a very deep imprint at home." At the same time, though, the analysts themselves recorded the views of such opponents as the Hearst and McCormick-Patterson newspapers as well as of conservative and formerly noninterventionist columnists, who warned that any formulation of war aims "must be necessarily visionary, impractical and may endanger the system of private enterprise"—an echo of exactly those ideological conflicts the president wanted to avoid. [24]

As much as Roosevelt was troubled by these attitudes, he did not heed another of his liberal supporters' warning "that domestic

21. For an example of their preference for an ideological offensive against the domestic divisionists, see "An Ideological Offensive," 17 April 1942, box 1853, Entry 171, RG 44, FRC.

22. Letter by Basil O'Connor to FDR, with attached memo by Stanley P. Lovell, 31 May 1941, box 5, PPF 1820, FDR-P, FDR-L.

23. Intelligence Report No. 39, 4 September 1942, PSF OWI, box 155, FDR-P, FDR-L.

24. The Atlantic Charter and the Four Freedoms were the two most prominent official statements of U.S. war aims, see "War Aims and Postwar Policies," 17 April 1942, box 1849, Entry 171, RG 44, FRC; "What People Think About Peace and the Role of the U.S. in the Post-War World," 14 February 1942, OF 788; "An analysis of American Public Opinion ..." (Gallup), 10 September 1942, PPF 4721, which recorded that nearly 40 percent expressed their confusion in such statements as "We don't know whether it is for money, power, or so-called freedom;" "I don't know what we are fighting for and I don't think those in charge of the government are sure about it;" "I can't tell exactly what we are fighting for from our president. He talks one way and does some other;" "I can see why we are fighting the Japanese but I can't see why we are fighting the Germans;" "We have no reason to be involved in this war. It is just another war to protect the English Empire." Intelligence Report No. 45, 16 October 1945, box 156, PSF OWI, FDR-P, FDR-L.

political unity is today utterly impossible and any attempt to sacrifice the democratic cause for its fiction disastrous."[25] The president was in the end equally concerned with political unity as with overcoming the more dangerous aspects of the "divisionists'" arguments and thus found himself in a circular dilemma. In order to build public morale for this war, explicit statements outlining the political credo with which the United States was fighting the fascist enemy, openly condemning racial stereotypes and undemocratic attitudes at home, would be necessary. Those, in turn, however, would help alienate the divisionists and their sympathizers even further and thus undermine domestic unity, a prerequisite for high public morale in any war.

Certain limits to any attempt to overcome this dilemma by emotionally loaded campaigns had already been set by the preceding "great debate" as to whether the United States had to involve itself formally in this war. Before the United States's declaration of war, Roosevelt had opted against establishing a national morale building institution or any other means to conduct an all-out propaganda effort as his supporters in- and outside the administration had urged him to do.[26] Primarily relying on his own considerable skills in handling the nation's press and public opinion, he had instead chosen to educate his compatriots to the formidable fascist threat building up around them through an informal as well as informational strategy. Opinion leaders and private activists had added their voices to those politicians who shared the president's anti-fascist, interventionist outlook and had been further assisted by the largely voluntary cooperation of the mass media in disseminating information prepared by and reflecting administrative defense concerns and efforts.[27] The reason for this indirect approach was

25. George P. West, "Mr. Roosevelt's Supreme Test," in *The New Republic*, 8 February 1943, clipping enclosed in letter from F. R. Windegger to FDR, 12 February 1943, PPF 7213, FDR-P, FDR-L.

26. Richard W. Steele, "Preparing the Public for War: Efforts to Establish a National Propaganda Agency, 1940–41," *American Historical Review* 75 (1970): 1640–53. Illustrating Steele's argument regarding reliance on voluntary cooperation with nongovernmental institutions for a specific media category: Claudia Schreiner-Seip, *Film- und Informationspolitik als Mittel der Nationalen Verteidigung in den USA, 1939–41: Eine Studie über die Umsetzung außenpolitischer Programme in Filminhalte* (Frankfurt, 1985).

27. Evidence of nongovernmental public figures participating in the mobilization effort can be found in the Roosevelt Papers: article on James W. Gerard and his views on Germany in *Daily Times*, Chicago, 16 June 1942, PPF 977; Roger Scaife of Little, Brown and Co. to FDR, 9 June 1941 on Douglas Miller, *You Can't Do Business with Hitler*, PPF 373; Newspaper clipping from the *Chicago Herald*, 19 May 1941 on

twofold. Before Pearl Harbor, American public and congressional opinion as perceived and documented by the administration seemed to put severe limits on Roosevelt's initiatives for a bolder foreign and military policy. On the other hand, as one presidential adviser remarked, there could be no successful governmental propaganda operation educating public opinion with respect to national policy until there was an accepted national policy.[28] But, here too, Roosevelt was reluctant to formulate that national policy since he himself appeared to be undecided as to which course to follow—and "he wanted a public that was confident in him not one that was fully informed," including about his own uncertainties and conflicts.[29] Moreover, he had chosen to engage his most severe foreign policy critics, the isolationists, not in an open national debate but by discrediting them by publicly questioning their ethics, patriotism, and loyalty, as well as by portraying them as conscious or duped Nazi stooges.[30] Thus he had helped stifle

speeches by local politicians in celebration of "I am an American" Day, PPF 1820, box 5, 1941; DT's column "On the Record" of 31 May 1941, PPF 1820, box 5; Russell W. Davenport, CBS broadcast, 28 April 1941, which he gave right after Charles Lindbergh, PPF 1820; Clipping from *The Evening Star*, 19 May 1941, PPF 1820, 1941; Alfred Bergman to Colonel M. H. McIntyre, 3 September 1940, PPF 5237, feeding into FDR's attempt to discredit political opponents by insinuating pro-Nazi leanings: "Both Willkie (Wendell Willkie, Republican presidential candidate in 1940 election) and Buell (Raymond Buell, Willkie's foreign policy advisor) are of direct German extraction and blood is often thicker than water … (Willkie's) whole propaganda is similar to Hitler's rise to power. Even his lock of hair on his front forehead looks a bit like Hitler." In FDR's defense one needs to point out that the president, in spite of some rather questionable, and at times outright devious tactics, never stooped to the use of these kinds of insinuations. For Willkie's strategy on the war issue during the 1940 election campaign, see Robert Dallek, *Franklin D. Roosevelt and American Foreign Policy, 1932–45* (Oxford, 1979), 249f.; Richard Steele, "The Great Debate: Roosevelt, the Media, and the Coming of the War, 1940–41," *Journal of American History* 71 (1984): 69–92, here: 70; William M. Tuttle Jr., "Aid-to-the-Allies-Short-of-War versus American Intervention, 1940: A Reappraisal of William Allen White's Leadership," *Journal of American History* 56 (1970): 840–58; Mark L. Chadwin, *The War Hawks of World War II* (Chapel Hill, 1968).

28. This objection came from Lowell Mellett, former Scripps-Howard newspaperman, and director of the Office of Government Reports, a kind of official information agency, 1939–42. Subsequently, he served as the director of the Office of War Information's Bureau of Motion Picture. He is quoted in Steele, "Preparing," 1647, who comments, "While propaganda efforts would gain from a clear statement of administration policy, the adoption of a firm policy depended on a change of public attitude—the very object of the proposed agency."

29. Steele, "Great Debate," 88.

30. See Cole, *Roosevelt*, whose account, however, ignores completely critical breaches of national security by the opposition that resulted in FDR's ordering a

national debate rather than take his opponents and their arguments head on, with the consequence, as one historian formulated,
that when war did come, "a great many Americans remained
uncertain of the circumstances (beyond the Japanese attack on
Pearl Harbor) that led them into global conflict."[31]

In the eyes of contemporary impatient advisers and latter-day
omniscient historians, Roosevelt had made several mistakes, first
in dealing with the isolationist sentiment before the American
entry into war and then in trying to combat flagging fighting spirits resulting from confusion and doubts regarding the reasons for
American participation. According to the former, the president
should have silenced his critics by articulating the vision of a
brighter, namely more liberal, more democratic, no longer discriminating, and fairer future, not only for Americans, but also
one extending eventually as a kind of global New Deal to the rest
of the world—thus offering Americans something worth fighting
for.[32] Some voices in this group also deplored his reluctance to

more careful supervision of isolationists by the FBI. By not discussing such epi-
sodes as Tyler Kent's making the U.S. diplomatic codes available to an Italian spy
ring that eventually also benefited the Germans and the leaking of the American
victory program, Cole makes the opposition out to look more harmless than it
must have appeared in Roosevelt's eyes. On this matter see Gerhard L. Weinberg,
A World At Arms: A Global History of World War II (New York, 1994), 157. Incidentally, Roosevelt's primary interest in any kind of propaganda agency becomes
apparent in his correspondence with Secretary of the Interior Harold Ickes in early
March 1941 discussing "a proposed agency to combat subversive propaganda"
and its possible director. Correspondence between FDR and Ickes, 3 and 6 March
1941, OF 1661a Fifth Column, 1941–45, FDR-P, FDR-L; see further Richard W.
Steele, "Franklin D. Roosevelt and His Foreign Policy Critics," *Political Science
Quarterly* 94 (1979):15–32. See also Arthur M. Schlesinger Jr.'s subsequent critique
of Steele's article, ibid., 33–35, in which he acknowledges that "there is a sound
and legitimate point buried in this piece" but deplores that "omissions, over-
statements, and the pervading prosecutorial zeal carry it far away from history."
The most valid aspect of Schlesinger's argument from my own point of view and
research is his criticism of Steele's underestimation of the sense of crisis that the
contemporary politician must have felt believing on the one hand that Hitler and
Nazi Germany posed a mortal threat to the very existence of the United States and
watching, on the other hand, the disinterested complacency of a great many of his
fellow citizens. Moreover, it is by no means certain that in an open and democratic society common sense will always assert itself in time to prevent disaster. Thus
,it is certainly the historian's task to record any illegal and devious tactics employed by Roosevelt, but by the same token, the context of clear national danger
in which he acted also has to be documented.

31. Steele, "Great Debate," 69.

32. See for example letter by Edgar A. Mowrer to Archibald MacLeish, 11 April
1942, quoted in Julian G. Hurstfield, *America and the French Nation, 1939–45* (Chapel

arouse publicly hatred and fear of the German people, or at least of Germany as such.[33] According to the less ambitious and less activist historians, he had left the path of righteousness when he consciously blurred the distinction between a few wacky native American fascists and legitimate foreign policy critics and tried to combat both with all means at his disposal.[34] Both arguments deserve serious consideration. In the end, however, one can only conclude that both sides chose to neglect an important facet that Roosevelt apparently found harder to ignore: the overriding need for domestic unity in a total war, whether it carried the name "people's war" or "survival war."[35] While—be it for pragmatic or personal and vindictive reasons—the president lumped together fifth columnists and former isolationists, stigmatizing both as subversives, he clearly separated those activists from the overwhelming majority of Americans with respect to whom he wanted to preserve unity—not at all costs, but at the relatively low cost of putting visionary ideological questions on the back burner. The situation of national crisis did not allow the luxury of differentiating between subversive intentions and unintended subversion— arguments, aims, and tactics were judged by their effects.

Moreover, in Roosevelt's defense it should be added that while the effect of this indirect approach "much to the disappointment of militants, was not to shock or enrage, but to numb the resistance to war [so that] Americans were not compelled by the logic of events or driven by emotion to demand involvement," it also had positive consequences.[36] As one contemporary observer, mindful of how this country had fought its last war, pointed out, both sides, interventionists and noninterventionists, had minimized the use of indignation and had instead appealed to "enlightened self-interest." The acceptance of this "framework of a tough-minded, realistic, self-interested approach to foreign policy" had been pervasive

Hill, 1986), 143. A useful summary of this argument is offered by Richard W. Steele, "American Popular Opinion and the War Against Germany: The Issue of a Negotiated Peace, 1942," *Journal of American History* 55 (1978): 704–23.

33. Cantril, "The Nature of the Enemy," 13 August 1942, p. iii and viii, box 11, Nash-P, HST-L; Gallup, "An Analysis of American Public Opinion Regarding the War," 10 September 1942, p. 4, PPF 4721, FDR-P, FDR-L

34. See Steele, "Foreign Policy Critics," for example.

35. In May 1942 government officials had debated what the best name for the current war might be. See Memorandum by Paul Lyness to J. A. Swords, 2 May 1942, Office of Facts and Figures (hereafter: OFF), box 1849, Entry 171, RG 44, FRC.

36. Richard W. Steele, *Propaganda in an Open Society: The Roosevelt Administration and the Media, 1933–1941* (Westport, CT, 1985), 172.

and precluded stirring up emotions of hatred, outrage, or vengeance. Yet when Roosevelt in early 1942 referred to the nation's "mood of quiet and grim resolution" in entering the fight, his observation also had the ring of an incantation.[37]

Interlude: The President's View of Nazi Germany

Before turning to the educational work carried out by the official propaganda agency that was eventually founded, we need to consider briefly President Roosevelt's own attitudes toward Germany.[38] After World War II, George F. Kennan would profess to have been shocked when he realized that Roosevelt was one of the many people who could not grasp the essential difference between the German menace in World War I and Nazism.[39] But this was less a deficiency on Roosevelt's part than a deliberately

37. "Attachment B—Pros and Cons on Hate and Atrocities," 22 May 1942, box 360, Entry 368, RG 208 OWI, FRC. Roosevelt's quote is from his State of the Union address, 6 January 1942, *FDR-PPA*, vol. 1942, 33.

38. Useful material for FDR's understanding of the "German problem" can be found in Brooks Van Everen, "Franklin D. Roosevelt and the German Problem: 1914–1945" (Ph.D. diss., University of Colorado, 1970). The following is based on my own studies. As is well known, Roosevelt almost never expounded his views on any topic in a systematic or comprehensive manner. Accordingly, his understanding of Nazism can only be gleaned from scattered remarks and from his expression of appreciation regarding other people's more detailed expositions on the "German problem." A good point in case is his relationship to the German-born Swiss emigrant historian Emil Ludwig, whose *The Germans: Double History of a Nation* (1942) one reviewer called a "grade A *Black Record*" referring to the famous book by Lord Vansittart. Their relationship dated back to at least 1935, when the president had asked Ludwig to write him about his impressions of Europe. During 1937 Ludwig was allowed to sit with the president on several occasions, posing as an artist and listening to conversations Roosevelt had with other visitors. During the same period Ludwig finished a biography of the president. In 1942 Sumner Welles suggested that Ludwig could be engaged as a lecturer at the newly established military government school at Charlottesville in courses on German history and recent developments in Germany. The director of the OWI precursor, the Office of Facts and Figures (OFF), Archibald MacLeish, had not obliged the president's secretary's earlier request to employ Ludwig at the OFF. In 1944 Ludwig was working under the direction of the director of civil affairs in the War Department, Major John H. Hilldring, on plans for German occupation. In January 1945 Roosevelt wrote a personal note to Secretary of State Edward Stettinius, introducing Ludwig as "an old friend of mine (who) has been doing valiant work for us" and asking him to find new assignments for Ludwig. For all of the above see PPF 3884, FDR-P, FDR-L.

39. George F. Kennan, *Memoirs, 1925–1950* (Boston, 1967), 123.

employed device to link the terror and aggression of the Third Reich to certain older German traditions. Such a view by implication would not be compatible with a postwar solution that removed a few criminal Nazis and absolved the German people. Roosevelt's belief in what could be termed a *Sonderweg* (peculiar path) interpretation of German history did not prevent him, however, from recognizing the revolutionary and totalitarian character of the Third Reich.[40]

What accounts for the subsequent confusion on the subject of the president's wartime convictions regarding Germany is that they did not always translate into public statements. Thus it is clear from personal communications that Roosevelt did not share the belief that one could or should differentiate between the government and the people of the Third Reich.[41] As early as 1936, he had warned— then still publicly—that "it is idle for us ... to preach that the masses of the people who constitute those nations which are dominated by the twin spirits of autocracy and aggression are out of sympathy with their rulers ... that unfortunately is not so clear."[42] But in characteristic fashion Roosevelt had gone underground with this view

40. See for example a speech that Russell W. Davenport gave on CBS, a copy of which he sent to FDR, 28 April 1941, PPF 1820, box 5, FDR-P, FDR-L. PPF 1820 was the file in which Roosevelt collected material for his upcoming speeches. Davenport had outlined in his speech how Hitler's ambitions encompassed everything that the Kaiser had ever wanted but also went beyond those goals; he explained that the "real secret of Hitler's counter-revolution is that it despises humanity." Together with a number of other themes of the Davenport text, this formulation resurfaced in both of Roosevelt's State of the Union speeches of 1942 and 1943, see *FDR-PPA*, vol. *1942*, 41 and vol. *1943*, 32f. See also William E. Kinsella Jr., "The Prescience of a Statesman: FDR's Assessment of Adolf Hitler before the World War, 1933–1941," in *The Man, the Myth, the Era, 1882–1945*, ed. Herbert D. Rosenbaum and Elizabeth Bartelme (New York, 1987), 73–84. On Roosevelt's view of Nazi Germany most recently, see Robert E. Herzstein, *Roosevelt and Hitler: Prelude to War* (New York, 1989), whose analysis is mainly on target except for his obvious desire to make more of Roosevelt's concern for the Jews than can be documented. Herzstein concludes "to Roosevelt, World War II was a civil war within Western culture. The values dear to him were warring against forces of darkness erupting within a sick, but curable, society" (ibid., 409).

41. In light of my following exposition of Roosevelt's personal view, it is ironic that a number of opinion analysts and propaganda officials could point to presidential speeches to back their assertion that this government followed a policy of distinguishing between government and people of the enemy nations. See for example, OWI Evaluation of Newsreels, p. 16, Spring 1943, box 3, Entry 6A, RG 208, FRC); "Report from the Nation," p. 26, 7 December 1942, PSF OWI, box 156, FDRP, FDR-L and OWI Bureau of Research and Analysis' compilations of FDR quotes on the subject, 4 June 1943, box 294, Entry 367, OWI Records, RG 208, FRC.

42. "Annual Message to Congress," 3 January 1936, *FDR-PPA*, vol. *1936*, 10.

during the war, knowing that his was not a particularly popular view among Americans.[43] Behind the scenes, however, in a letter to William Donovan, recently appointed coordinator of information, Roosevelt suggested in 1941 the use of Lord Vansittart's *Black Record* for psychological warfare purposes, adding that "those paragraphs should be stressed which place the blame on the German people for following utterly destructive leadership."[44]

One of the most comprehensive expositions of Roosevelt's understanding of the German problem can be found in a private letter he wrote to a British friend in March 1940. Again, he reiterated, that he had "little patience with those who seek to draw a clear distinction between the German Government and the German people." He went on to describe the present conflict as a "war to end German militarism ... a Crusade to save ... civilization from a cult of brutal tyranny which would destroy it and all the dignity of human life"—a theme that anticipated some of his most powerful remarks about the "German menace" in his 1942 State of the Union address, highlighting the ideological, civil war nature of this war and ruling out any compromise.[45] Roosevelt then proceeded to lay out "the record of the German people" as he saw it:

43. Thus in his 1942 State of the Union address, which also served Archibald MacLeish, director of the OWI precursor Office of Facts and Figures (OFF) as a blueprint for official information campaigns (see Memorandum by Archibald MacLeish, 8 April 1942, OF 4619, FDR-P, FDR-L), the president referred to the "enslaved people" of the fascist countries, an image that surely allowed for an interpretation of the German people as the "first victims" of Hitler, see *FDR-PPA*, vol. *1942*, 35. His true convictions found more direct expression in the context of the intra-administrative debate on the Morgenthau Plan when he impatiently rejected Hull's and Stimson's views by informing them that "too many people hold the view that only a few Nazi leaders are responsible. That unfortunately is not based on fact. The German people as a whole must have driven home to them that the whole nation has been engaged in a lawless conspiracy against the decencies of modern civilization." Quoted from Cordell Hull, *The Memoirs of Cordell Hull*, 2 vols. (New York, 1948), 2: 1603. For the public's preference see *Public Opinion*, 503; *Gallup Poll*, 356: in a November 1942 survey 6 percent believed that the German people were America's chief enemy, 74 percent stated that it was only the German government.

44. FDR to William J. Donovan, 7 November 1941, *F.D.R.: His Personal Letters*, vol. II *1928–1945*, ed. Elliott Roosevelt (New York, 1950), 1234f. In the same letter Roosevelt distances himself from other interpretations of "Vansittartism" by rejecting "efforts to prove that the Germans have always been barbarians for a thousand years as a nation." For a good overview of "Vansittartism" in the British debate on Germany see Aaron Goldman, "Germans and Nazis," *Journal of Contemporary History* 14 (1979): 155–91.

45. FDR to Arthur Murray, 4 March 1940, PSF Diplomatic, GB: Murray, box 38, FDR-P, FDR-L. He charged those who made that distinction—"some of them with

enthusiastic support for repeated devious and brutal attacks on other nations in 1870, 1914, 1938, and 1939. The threat that Germany posed to European and world peace, he explained "has been and still is anchored in the faith of the German people in the Frederician tradition and in the Bismarck policy of the 'big stick,'" and he continued, "we should do well not to believe … that defeat will cause it to disappear overnight."[46] To enhance the authority of his assertions, Roosevelt referred—as he had done before and would again later in the context of the Morgenthau debate—to his own schooling experience in Imperial Germany.[47]

The president picked up the same theme in his 1942 State of the Union address—a speech which was characterized by a mixture of the inspirational and the pragmatic and which subsequently served as a blueprint for official American propaganda campaigns.[48] In it, Roosevelt drew a powerful contrast between the two worlds at war: the Christian world of freedom and the godless world of slavery—good versus evil. Using mostly religious terms, the president characterized the enemy's "brutal cynicism" and "unholy contempt for the human race," its "world of tyranny and cruelty and serfdom" as the antithesis of what Americans were fighting for, namely, "to uphold the doctrine that all men are equal in the sight of God." Propagating a kind of intentionalist interpretation of Nazi foreign policy, he emphasized that the plans for those "gargantuan aspirations of Hitler and his Nazis" for world conquest had been drawn up even before they had come to power and that the ruthless execution of these plans could not have been averted through appeasement. In a similar fashion he warned "no compromise can

great names and in high places"—with bearing a heavy "responsibility for the final catastrophe" as they had deliberately tried to obscure Hitler's true designs.

46. Ibid., 4. This "German record" was later incorporated in the War Department's propaganda output: see in particular the two Capra movies *Your Job in Germany* and *Here Is Germany*, as well as the *Soldier's Pocket Guide to Germany* (Washington: GP0, 1944).

47. For a more detailed discussion of Roosevelt's blending of actual experience with subsequent false memories, see my M.A. thesis "Franklin D. Roosevelt's View of Germany Before 1933: Formative Experiences of a Future President" (University of North Carolina, 1989), 14–22.

48. For the State of the Union address *FDR-PPA*, vol. *1942*, 32–42. See also Waldemar Besson, *Die politische Terminologie des Präsidenten Franklin D. Roosevelt: Eine Studie über den Zusammenhang von Sprache und Politik* (Tübingen, n.y.). See also the discussion of the War Department's movies by Frank Capra below. Finally, this interpretation was outlined in the OWI's manuals for the motion picture industry; see two documents, one of March 1943, the other one without date, box 3, Entry 6A, RG 208, FRC.

end that conflict. There never has been—there never can be—successful compromise between good and evil."

A final note on the postwar implications of the president's views is required here: Roosevelt's portrayal of the German problem as that of a militaristic attitude combined with a destructive philosophy of "might makes right" appears to point in the direction of radical reeducation. Thus, announcing officially the Allied policy of unconditional surrender, in January 1943, Roosevelt explained that while it did not aim at the destruction of the enemy population, "it does mean the destruction of the philosophies in those countries which are based on conquest and the subjugation of other people."[49] How to destroy a philosophy that had taken such a deep hold of that country's citizens, as he saw it, remained unexplained. But it clearly could not be achieved by military defeat alone. Unconditional surrender, beyond its military purpose, aimed at creating a tabula rasa, an opportunity for complete restructuring and reeducation of the society.[50]

The Office of War Information: Legacies and New Constraints for Propagandists

Two weeks after the president's announcement of a policy of unconditional surrender at the conference at Casablanca in January 1943, the number of Americans who would have accepted a peace offer by the German Army if it overthrew Hitler hovered around 28 percent. This figure, which had been as high as 33 percent three months earlier, not only reflected a continued willingness to compromise in order to obtain peace, but it also showed that a considerable minority did not understand or did not share the president's insistence on total defeat of Germany. What lay behind these two opposing stands on how to deal with the main enemy were fundamentally different attitudes toward the German people and conflicting definitions of the nature of Nazi Germany. There was

49. *The Complete Presidential Press Conferences of Franklin D. Roosevelt*, vols. 21/22: 1943 (New York, 1972), 88f. See also Raymond G. O'Connor, *Diplomacy for Victory: FDR and Unconditional Surrender* (New York, 1971).

50. Brian L. Villa, "The U.S. Army, Unconditional Surrender, and the Potsdam Proclamation," *Journal of American History* 63 (1976): 69ff.; Warren F. Kimball, *Swords or Ploughshares? The Morgenthau Plan for Defeated Nazi Germany, 1943–46* (Philadelphia, 1976), 18; Axel Gietz, *Die Neue Alte Welt: Roosevelt, Churchill und die europaeische Nachkriegsordnung* (Munich, 1986), 75ff.

indeed a considerable gap between the president's strong views on Germany and the public opinion as recorded in official surveys.[51] In order to understand what accounts for this divergence we need to turn to the work of the official propaganda agency, the Office of War Information. In June 1941 the journalist Dorothy Thompson, one of the earliest, most persistent and prominent voices warning of Nazi Germany, had implored the president: "[C]an't you get us the means of setting up a thorough hard-boiled really organized bureau of journalists, artists, listeners, research workers, writers, speakers to drive Herr Hitler into an insane asylum? It is the dream of my life."[52] It would take another twelve months and the formal American entrance into World War II before Thompson's hopes were at least partly realized. The Office of War Information (OWI), which was established by executive order on 13 June 1942, employed a variety of highly motivated and talented people mobilizing the home front and propagandizing abroad on the Allies' behalf, but it might not have been the United States' most effective weapon in its fight against Herr Hitler.[53]

The road to an official information and propaganda agency had been a long and tortuous one. As mentioned above, in view of widespread isolationist thinking in the American public, high-ranking military and civilian officials as well as prominent concerned citizens had urged the president since the outbreak of the war in Europe to meet this problem head on by establishing a national information and propaganda agency.[54] But Roosevelt—though no less concerned about the defensive mindset of many Americans—had been slow in responding to these demands and suggestions.[55]

51. See Jerome S. Bruner, "OWI and the American Public," *Public Opinion Quarterly* (Spring 1943), 133.

52. Dorothy Thompson (DT) to FDR, undated and FDR to DT, 26 June 1941, PPF 6650, FDR-P, FDR-L. On Thompson see Peter Kurth, *American Cassandra: The Life of Dorothy Thompson* (Boston, 1990).

53. Allan M. Winkler, *The Politics of Propaganda: The Office of War Information, 1942–45* (New Haven, 1978) is the most thorough study of the OWI to date. See also "Historical Appraisal on OWI World War II—Remarks by Philleo Nash to Mrs. Sharp, 9 January 1952," OF 5015, FDR-P, FDR-L. Executive Order No. 9182 "Consolidating Certain War Information Functions into an Office of War Information," box 4, Entry 6H, RG 208, FRC.

54. In addition to the literature cited above see David L. Jones, "Measuring and Mobilizing the Media, 1939–1945," *Midwest Quarterly* 26 (1984): 35–43; Harwood Childs, "Public Information and Opinion," part of "The American Government in War-Time," *American Political Science Review* 37 (1943): 56–68 for the OWI's predecessors.

55. Examples of private and official recommendations include "On Handling the Press and Morale Problem," 31 May 1941, PPF 1820, box 5; Early to Archibald

250 | *Michaela Hönicke*

His reluctance to allow for a full-fledged propaganda organization seems to be validated in view of later attacks on the Office of War Information by domestic political opponents who loathed the agency as a partisan vehicle promoting New Deal ideology at home and possibly even abroad.[56]

The OWI was from its very inception restricted by a limited mandate that did not allow for censorship, for example. It was further weakened by a lack of presidential support and guidance, and it was finally handicapped by intense congressional hostility. These obstacles which the OWI officials faced resulted in part from this country's experience of having fought a more overtly ideological "war to end all wars" only a generation earlier.[57] In response to the excesses of George Creel's Committee on Public Information and to the anti-model of Goebbels-style indoctrination in Nazi Germany, mistrust of government-directed information campaigns was widespread among the media, Congress, and the public in general. As late as October 1939, 34 percent of Americans believed that their country had been the victim of propaganda and selfish interests in entering World War I. This number is all the more significant against the background of 68 percent of Americans who at the same time still deemed their country's involvement in World War I a mistake, an opinion to which a third of Americans surveyed clung till September 1942.[58]

This time, however, American propagandists would take a different approach. In their official information guide it was called

MacLeish, 13 October 1941 with reference to "Memorandum on Educating Public Opinion on the Peril from Hitler" by John Franklin Carter, OF 4514; Memorandum to FDR from Basil O'Connor with text by Stanley P. Lovell advocating "a Ministry of Propaganda called, in the American way, a Department of Sales."

56. Dutifully, the OWI recorded even such public opinion that suspected it of serving as "an extravagant, overstaffed (agency) advocating social theories of the New Deal." "Public Opinion on Propaganda and War Information, No. 26," 3 June 1942, PSF OWI, box 155, FDR-P, FDR-L. See also Winkler, *Propaganda*, 65ff.

57. N. Gordon Levin, *Woodrow Wilson and World Politics: America's Response to War and Revolution* (London, 1968).

58. Gallup, Confidential Report, 10 September 1942, p. 3; Hadley Cantril and Mildred Strunk, *Public Opinion , 1935–1946* (Princeton, 1951), 202; James R. Mock and Cedric Larson, *Words That Won the War: The Story of the Committee on Public Information, 1917–1919* (New York, 1939). Although the authors of this book in some measure defended the work of the Creel Committee and certainly aimed at advocating a similar agency for the near future, they admitted that George Creel was one of the most disliked members of government even during World War I; Steele, "Preparing," 1642. On the work of the Creel Committee see Stephen Vaughn, *Holding Fast the Inner Lines: Democracy, Nationalism and the Committee on Public Information* (Chapel Hill, 1980).

"the truth above all." This was on the one hand a promise to the American people, whose mood was expressed in the remarks of New York mayor Fiorello LaGuardia, who briefly headed the Office of Facts and Figures (OFF), precursor to the OWI: "Whatever anybody says ... the Office of Facts and Figures is not a propaganda agency. There are three reasons why it is not. The first is that we don't believe in this country in artificially stimulated high-pressure, doctored nonsense, and since we don't, the other two reasons are unimportant."[59] On the other hand, the strategy of truth corresponded with the preferred professional self-image of the liberal intellectuals who were running the agency. Those included the Librarian of Congress and poet Archibald MacLeish, who headed the OFF as soon as it had become an independent government agency in October 1941 and continued to work as assistant director under the radio journalist Elmer Davis, who was appointed director of the OFF's successor, the Office of War Information.

MacLeish's political activism as a writer in the 1930s deserves brief mention as one example of the deeply felt anti-fascist convictions that characterized the first crew of the OWI, which also included the playwright Robert Sherwood, newspaperman Gardner Cowles Jr., financier and publicist James Warburg, journalist Joseph Barnes, Leo Rosten, and historian Arthur M. Schlesinger Jr., as well as the usual number of emigrants, including German refugees.[60] MacLeish belonged to that group of liberal, occasionally even left-wing intellectuals, who had early on paid close attention to the manifestations of fascism in Mussolini's Italy and the rise of Hitler in Germany and who did not hesitate as to which side to choose in the Spanish Civil War. Although during that latter conflict he had been quite willing to associate

59. Steele, "Preparing," 1652.

60. For more information on the OWI staff, their respective positions in that agency, and their previous activities, see Winkler, *Propaganda*, 10–37, 40f., 74ff.; see also Clayton R. Koppes and Gregory D. Black, "What to Show the World: The Office of War Information and Hollywood, 1942–45," *Journal of American History* 64 (1977): 87–105, here: 88. For the emigrants see "Memo über die Anti-Hagen Kampagne," p. 10 and 15, Paul Hertz Papers, Seite 9, Mappe F, Folder 7, International Institute for Social History (IISH), Amsterdam, Netherlands; critical of them is Elmer Davis in his personal narrative of 1945: "I wished we didn't have to have them ...," p. 17, box 3, Entry 6H, RG 208, FRC; the more prominent wartime institution with emigrants is of course the Office of Strategic Services (OSS); for personnel overlap between OWI and OSS, see Barry Katz, *Foreign Intelligence: Research and Analysis in the Office of Strategic Services, 1942–45* (Cambridge, 1989), 33 and 38f.

himself, at arm's length, with Communists, this mostly pragmatic stance did not affect his basic insight that "the real struggle of our time [is not between communism and fascism] but the
much more fundamental struggle between democratic institutions on the one side and all forms of dictatorship, whatever the
dictator's label, on the other." MacLeish's early advocacy of
American intervention on the European scene and his harsh
criticism of "the irresponsibles" who tried to stay indifferent
and aloof could not but recommend this activist to the president
in the long run.[61]

The director of the OFF, however, was not only representative
of his colleagues in his political convictions but also in the thor-
oughness, idealism, and enthusiasm of a writer accustomed to
working by himself. The complaint about a bunch of brilliant and
zealous individuals who "could not work as part of a team," let
alone subordinate themselves to the orders of politicians or the
requirements of military expediency, runs like a leitmotif through
the brief history of American official wartime propaganda.[62] Predictably, the State and War Departments had a wary eye on the
"starry-eyed" and "long-haired circles" of left-wing liberals in the
OFF and OWI who "are more concerned with the ideological
aspects of the war than the military and who sincerely feel that
unless the struggle against Nazism and Fascism is won in its
entirety, the military defeat of our enemies would be of no value."[63]
Predictably, too, they were not anxious to include these people in
their departmental deliberations. This, however, was exactly what
some OWI officials saw as a prerequisite for the success of their
work. Deputy director Warburg argued that "the influence of a
nation's top propagandists should properly reach into the counsel
chambers where basic public policy is being formulated," and the
chief of OWI German desk, Hans Speier, concluded in retrospect
that "the effectiveness of OWI suffered because high officials of the
agency were not included in high-policy discussions."[64] This question, however, had been decided early on in an internal discussion

61. Scott Donaldson, *Archibald MacLeish: An American Life* (Boston, 1992), 262ff.
and 348–65 on his activities as a propagandist.

62. See Elmer Davis' narrative, p. 16 and passim, box 3, Entry 6H, RG 208 OWI,
FRC, as well as Winkler, *Propaganda*, 42ff., 55, 92ff.

63. Henry L. Stimson's Diary, 17 November 1942 and 22 December 1942, vol.
35–40, Reel 7 (microfilm); State Department memo, 17 February 1943, quoted in
Hurstfield, *French*, 182.

64. William E. Daugherty, ed., *A Psychological Warfare Casebook* (Baltimore, 1958),
276, 299.

between MacLeish and another OWI deputy director, Milton Eisenhower. Still debating the problem of war aims in the education and mobilization of the American public, the poet held the view that the OWI should "excite and encourage discussion" on these issues among the American people as well as provide direction. Eisenhower, recognizing the practical consequences of this strategy, countered with a reference to the scope of their responsibilities: "I must insist that our job is to promote an understanding of policy, not to make policy." In view of the indeed limited mandate of the OWI, quite in contrast to the Creel Committee, and its generally precarious position as a latecomer in the merry yet confused circle of new administrative agencies, Eisenhower's approach won out almost by default.[65]

The picture of dedicated intellectuals who showed a high profile on ideological questions but failed on pragmatic matters, however, deserves further clarification. Not only did the OWI have to operate within a much more limited statute and a more suspicious, and occasionally openly hostile, congressional and public climate than its World War I precursor, but it also was saddled with the additional task of measuring and analyzing public opinion through the newly available polling techniques—an assignment which, as we will see, had a considerable impact on its information policy. But as becomes apparent from the internal quarrels in the agency, the "strategy of truth" itself was open to a variety of interpretations depending on artistic inclinations, ideological orientations, and personal temperament even among the staff.[66] Finally, Roosevelt who, as we have seen, held deeply rooted and definite convictions on the German problem, did not bother to translate those into basic guidelines that would have helped the information officials in their definition of the nature of the enemy, nor did he provide case-by-case instructions as to how to deal with specific aspects of the war policy and postwar planning with respect to Nazi Germany. And he certainly refrained from backing his propagandists in their ongoing conflicts with the heads of the other departments.

65. "Instructions to A. MacLeish to prepare a project on OWI's part in "Post-war Planning," 30 November 1942, Letter from Milton S. Eisenhower to Archibald MacLeish, 1 December 1942, Memorandum to Archibald MacLeish from Tris Coffin, n. d., Letter from M. S. Eisenhower to Elmer Davis, 3 December 1942 and Letter from M. S. Eisenhower to MacLeish, 3 December 1942, box 5, Entry 1, RG 208, FRC.

66. Blum, *Victory*, 21–39. Sydney Weinberg, "What to Tell America: The Writers' Quarrel in the Office of War Information," *Journal of American History* 55 (1968): 73–89.

OWI Analysts Further Probe Popular American Images of Nazi Germany

Thus the OWI was left alone in its important task of focusing the image of the Nazi enemy and illustrating the nature of the threat it presented. Unable to obtain more specific guidance from their superiors, the information officials turned instead to probing the existing attitudes in the American populace. In addition to the general polls that had been conducted by the OFF and OWI as well as private polling institutions for the president, the two information agencies carried out their own, more specific polls concerning how the American public saw and how the media portrayed the Nazi enemy. They found much fault with those homemade images. With respect to the "identity of the enemy" OWI pollsters reported that only five out of one hundred Americans felt that the German people was America's chief enemy, a number that rose to 18 percent when the Nazi government was also included, but still stood in stark contrast to the 74 percent who saw themselves at war only with that government. Some tension in those views, however, became apparent when they were considered in the context of specific characteristics that those being interviewed attributed to the German people. Sixty-eight percent selected the descriptive "warlike," and more than half of them also considered the Germans "cruel." Just as many, however, thought of them as "hardworking," an adjective with slightly more "sympathetic connotations" as the analysts observed. Asked about the Japanese, the overwhelming majority of Americans could agree on the terms "treacherous," "sly," and "cruel."

The pollsters solved the apparent tension in the responses to the two sets of questions with a reference to the portrayal of the enemy people in the media, in particular newspaper cartoons that depicted "Germans, as distinct from their leaders, in the role of stupid, brutish automations." Clearly unhappy with this characterization, they warned that "it is doubtful that such stereotypes indicate any real awareness of the nature and motivations of the enemy peoples."[67] According to "Special Intelligence Report No. 45," the comic strip, which the information officials considered to be "a powerful agent for the inculcation of attitudes and the dissemination of ideas," had so far failed to make its contribution to

---

67. "Intelligence Report: American Estimates of the Enemy," p. 7ff., 2 September 1942, box 155, PSF OWI, FDR-P, FDR-L.

the war effort by ignoring the OWI recommendation of a "realistic portrayal" of the enemy's strength, motives and objectives.[68]

Other media hardly fared any better in OWI's assessment. Thus the newsreels had reportedly "added little to the clarification of the issues [and] there had been little sober appraisal of the enemy and much ridicule." The last point was of great concern to government officials as Americans, of course, would not even see the need for a more intense war effort if they considered the enemy to be a pushover.[69] Similarly, the outlines of the enemy in the press remained "fuzzy" according to an August 1942 report: the Axis's "basic political, economic or social motivations" were unclear and imprecise. The strictness of the OWI's criteria, however, becomes apparent when one follows the details of that same analysis. After all, particularly in the context of reporting on the razing of the Czech town of Lidice, journalists had turned their attention to the fate of Nazi-occupied territories and thus to a discussion of the meaning of a Nazi victory in general.[70] And this aspect, as we will see, lay at the core of the OWI's programs and information guidelines. The deep impact that the murder and abduction of the entire population of that town had made in the United States had also registered in the media's approach to a possible distinction between Nazi leaders and the German people. While the press comments tended to "place full responsibility for the slaughter of the Jews on Nazi leaders alone," no such distinction was made with regard to the razing of Lidice.[71] Apparently such a distinction, however, would have corresponded more closely with OWI guidelines on the enemy. On the other hand, only four out of thirty-two newspapers which had dealt with this event had discussed it as a typical expression of the nature of the enemy.[72]

68. "Special Intelligence Report No. 45: Newspaper Comic Strips," p. 3 and 13, 17 June 1942, box 1844, Entry 171, RG 44, FRC. See also "Report from the Nation," p. 26, 7 December 1942, box 156, PSF OWI, FDR-P, FDR-L.

69. "Newsreels and OWI Campaigns and Programs: February, 1943," Report No 8, 12 March 1943, box 1845, Entry 171, RG 44, FRC. This had also been a sore point in the evaluation of the comic strips.

70. "Nature of the Enemy in American Media," 29 August 1942, box 1846, Entry 171, RG 44, FRC. On 9 June 1942 the Nazis had wiped out the Czech town of Lidice as a reprisal for the murder of Reinhard Heydrich. See also Gordon Wright, *The Ordeal of Total War, 1939–45* (New York, 1968), 155. "Special Intelligence Report No 59," 1 July 1942 was exclusively devoted to American media reaction to this event, box 1845, Entry 171, RG 44, FRC.

71. "Comment on the Enemy in the Media, June–December, 1942," p. 4, 2 February 1943, box 1846, Entry 171, RG 44, FRC.

72. "Special Intelligence Report No 59," 1 July 1942, box 1845, Entry 171, RG 44, FRC.

But it was the regular analysis of Hollywood movies that disappointed OWI officials most. Summarizing their complaints, they found that in the overwhelming number of commercial feature length movies produced between May and November 1942, the enemy had not been portrayed as a philosophy or a way of life, nor as a threat to the American political and social system. But instead the enemy appeared to be "a man with a gun who is attacking us," a threat that could simply be met by force and that "the reasons why we are fighting these men-with-guns is not clear." The German soldier, more specifically, was depicted as "a gentleman whom it would be possible to greet as an equal," quite contrary again to the Japanese soldier who "can only be killed." As in previous reports the analysts deplored the "wide-spread tendency to underestimate the enemy." Here in particular they were referring to incidents of German display of pro-Allied sympathy, disaffection with National Socialism, or plain incompetence. In addition to further points of disapproval that have already been mentioned in the context of the other media surveys, the movie critics were also worried about the lack of realistic depiction of life under Nazi rule and the absence of any explanations as to what the enemy was fighting for, with the consequence that "the enemy often appear admirable and praiseworthy."[73] Quite obviously this list of complaints reflected a negative mirror image of what the OWI had determined should be the characteristics of the enemy as portrayed in the American media.

Not surprisingly, the polls conducted to measure public opinion yielded a correspondingly faulty image of the Nazi threat. Americans underestimated the internal cohesion of Nazi society as well as the military strength and resources of that country. Around 30 percent also misjudged their enemy's intention by denying that the Nazis were committed to subjugating the United States.[74] In the early summer of 1942 the Bureau of Intelligence of

73. "Special Intelligence Report No 77: The Enemy in the Movies," 25 November 1942, box 4, Nash-P, HST-L. Slightly more positive "Short and Documentary Films and OWI Campaigns and Programs," 15 February 1943, box 1845, Entry 171, RG 44, FRC. The Motion Picture and Broadcast Division of the Library of Congress holds the individual evaluations of Hollywood movies done by OWI officials. See also Gregory D. Black and Clayton R. Koppes, "What to Show the World: The Office of War Information and Hollywood, 1942–45," *Journal of American History* 64 (1977): 87–105 and id., "OWI Goes to Hollywood: The Bureau of Intelligence's Criticism of Hollywood, 1942–43," *Prologue* 6 (1974): 44–59.

74. "American Estimates of the Enemy," 9 September 1942, box 155, PSF OWI, FDR-P, FDR-L.

the OWI had commissioned Hadley Cantril of the Office of Public Opinion Research at Princeton to conduct a survey of public opinion with regard to "the nature of the enemy." The OWI as well as representatives of other government branches had contributed to the list of questions being asked.[75] The result, the most comprehensive wartime analysis of the popular attitudes toward Nazi Germany and Japan, was submitted in August of that year. Cantril came to the conclusion cited in my introduction: that there was a "lack of crystallization [and] a high degree of suggestibility" in the American image of the enemy. He recapitulated what earlier studies had found: Americans had not yet grasped that there was a difference between the German Army and the German people, or correspondingly that there was no difference between the Nazi government and the Wehrmacht, and they also indulged in a few other comforting illusions.[76] But the further details of his report, in fact, provided a picture that should have more reassured than alarmed the government as it closely reflected some of the most dearly held articles of faith with respect to the enemy which the government had so far propagated.

To begin with, Cantril's report announced the results of some "quizzes" on Nazi Germany which the pollsters had conducted with their interviewees: Was the German Reichstag, i.e., the German parliament, elected the same way the American Congress was? Fifty-four percent answered no. Had they ever heard of the Gestapo? Seventy-nine percent had. Was Rommel, Göring, or Himmler the head of it? Forty-four percent answered with Himmler. What was Goebbels' job? Sixty-three percent knew him to be the Minister of Propaganda. This was not a bad breakdown compared with 46 percent and 36 percent who in September could not identify Charles de Gaulle and Henry L. Stimson respectively.[77] Similarly, responses to seven questions regarding the domestic situation in Nazi Germany with respect to basic rights and freedoms documented an impressively "high degree of accurate information among the public." A follow-up question inquiring about the

75. The interdepartmental correspondence regarding the questionnaire is in box 1836, Entry 171, RG 44, FRC.

76. "The Nature of the Enemy," 13 August 1942, box 11, Nash-P, HST-L. On pg. 12: 30 percent still thought the German generals as well as the German soldiers not loyal to Hitler. That figure rose to 39 percent when Americans were asked whether the German people were behind their Führer.

77. "An Analysis of American Public Opinion," by George Gallup, 19 September 1942, PPF 4721, FDR-P, FDR-L.

content of Nazi teachings of the young, moreover, clearly reflected what members of the administration themselves would have wished their fellow countrymen to understand: 39 percent believed that the German youth were taught militarism, 28 percent named race superiority and anti-religious ideas respectively, and 26 percent trailed with "disrespect for women and morality."

An overwhelming number of Americans also showed a realistic assessment of Nazi rule in occupied countries and accordingly judged their own future grimly if Germany defeated the United States. Between 88 percent and 95 percent expected the Nazis to keep an army in the U.S. to police Americans, to make them pay for the cost of the war, to kill some of their political and business leaders, and to force them to work for the Nazis instead of for themselves. Those opinions, however, stood in stark contrast to what most Americans felt should be done to the Germans if they were defeated. Ten percent were in favor of annihilating them, as the most extreme measure, 13 percent would have punished their leaders, 16 percent thought it necessary to divide Germany, and the highest percentage, namely, 23, wanted to disarm them, thereby stripping them of power. The military might of Germany was clearly the gravest concern in the popular mind. The tension between American fears regarding a Nazi victory and American preferences as to the postwar treatment of that enemy was further heightened by the surprisingly small number, namely 5 percent of those surveyed, who considered the German people to be their enemy and the even smaller, 29 percent, that is less than 1.5 percent of the entire sample, who justified that attitude with reference to the "always warlike" nature of that people.

Cantril concluded from these incongruities that "repressed fear is plentiful" and that anxieties were piling up, but that Americans had not been officially encouraged to become afraid and hate and therefore continued to voice lenient views on the enemy people. Clearly opposing the government's policy of not arousing hatred of the enemy people, he warned that a "fearful people, if not brought together by a common hatred, are apt to hate each other." He also submitted for consideration the idea that Americans had not yet gone "more than ankle deep" into this war and that those registered opinions might easily change when the ravages of war hit closer home.[78]

One of the most remarkable features in Cantril's as in the other surveys on these matters is the consistently recorded refusal to

78. "The Nature of the Enemy," 13 August 1942, box 11, Nash-P, HST-L.

succumb to hatred.[79] The evaluation of this phenomenon, however, points to an altogether different aspect of these reports of
1942. It has less to do with the recorded opinion and images but
more with the interpretation of the analysts themselves: they varied
in their assessment of what was wrong with the popular attitudes
toward Germany. In particular, there was no consensus as to
whether Americans should regard the Nazi government or the
entire German people as their chief enemy. Some deplored that the
public was differentiating between guilty Nazi leaders and innocent Germans, others were critical that the overwhelming number
of Hollywood movies failed to draw that distinction.[80] Similarly,
one set of analysts was alarmed by the susceptibility to hatred
which, they warned, would degenerate into a spirit of vengefulness
against the enemy peoples if it was not redirected against the evils
of the enemy system of government.[81] As one of the commentators
observed, this confusion in interpretation clearly reflected governmental ambiguity on the aims of propaganda campaigns.[82] While
on the other hand, an exasperated Hadley Cantril remarked in a
confidential report for the government: "It should be unnecessary
to mention that wars involve emotions—especially those of fear
and hate." But, he continued, American officials appeared to have
deliberately sidestepped this elementary principle.[83]

Indeed, in May 1942, 82 percent of Americans surveyed professed not to hate the German people.[84] Cantril joined another pollster, George Gallup, in his appeal to the Roosevelt administration
"to pursue a much stronger and more direct policy of arousing fear
of Germany."[85] Gallup urged the government to acknowledge that

79. "Intelligence Report: American Estimates of the Enemy," 2 September 1942,
box 155, PSF OWI, FDR-P, FDR-L; "Nature of the Enemy in American Media," 29
August 1942, box 1846, Entry 171, RG 44, FRC; "Intelligence Report …," p. 17, 2
September 1942, box 155, PSF OWI, FDR-P, FDR-L.

80. Hadley Cantril to FDR, 14 September 1942, OF 857; "Trends in American
Public Opinion Since Pearl Harbor," p. 18f., 11 September 1942; "Intelligence
Report No. 27," p. 7ff., PSF OWI, box 155, FDR-P, FDR-L; "Special Intelligence
Report No 77: The Enemy in the Movies," p. 3 and passim, 25 November 1942, box
4, Nash-P, HST-L.

81. "Intelligence Report No 39," September 1942, p. 11, box 155, PSF OWI, FDR-
P, FDR-L.

82. "Report from the Nation," 7 December 1942, PSF OWI, box 156, FDR-P, FDR-L.

83. "The Nature of the Enemy," 13 August 1942, p. iii, box 11, Nash Papers, HST-L.

84. *Public Opinion*, 954.

85. "An Analysis of American Public Opinion Regarding the War," (Gallup), 10
September 1942 , p. 4, PPF 4721, FDR-P, FDR-L and "The Nature of the Enemy," 13
August 1942 (Cantril), p. viii, box 11, Nash Papers, HST-L.

every attempt to differentiate between the guilt of German leaders and the guilt of the people who had, in his view, willingly followed these leaders, obscured what he termed the "real menace of the German philosophy of conquest ... and the essential relationship between the present war and the last." For Gallup, National Socialism was only the most recent and most brutal version of an older German disease, called militarism or Prussianism. His views were shared by other prominent Americans, such as the journalists Edgar A. Mowrer and William Shirer, World War I propagandist George Creel, and former ambassador to Germany James Gerard, as well as the emigrant historian Emil Ludwig who testified accordingly in March 1943 on "the German people" before the House Committee on Foreign Affairs.[86] This interpretation, which emphasized the guilt of the German people in tandem with ideological and political roots of Nazism in German history, was most importantly favored by the president himself. But it was not the picture that America's official propagandists chose to sketch of the main enemy.

"Explaining Nazism to the American People Is No Easy Assignment"[87]

The Joint Committee on Information Policy within the OWI struggled throughout the better part of 1942 with the problem of distinguishing between people and government. It started out with a position that reflected the majority view among the liberal propagandists, namely that "the enemy is not the German people." Under the influence of sharp protests from its European allies it

86. Edgar A. Mowrer, *Germany Puts the Clock Back* (1933); William Shirer, *Berlin Diary* (1941). See also Richard M. Brickner, "Is Germany Incurable?" *Atlantic Monthly* 171 (March 1943): 84–92, a summary of the same author's book "diagnosing" the German disease of militarism and aggression in psychological terms as "paranoia." For Creel and Gerard see their contributions to "The Open Forum: What to Do with the Germans" in *The American Mercury* 56 (April 1943), 505ff. U.S. House of Representatives. Committee on Foreign Affairs, *The German People: Testimony of Mr. Emil Ludwig before ...* 78th Congr., 1st Sess., 26 March 1943 (Washington, 1943). See also Henry A. Wallace's 1942 speech "The Price of Free World Victory," printed in Henry A. Wallace, *Democracy Reborn* (New York, 1973), 194: "... because Hitler and the German people stand as the very symbol of war." This speech was dramatized by Paramount Pictures, *The Price of Victory*, released 17 October 1942, script in box N-R, OWI Film Evaluations, Motion Picture Division, Library of Congress, Washington, DC (hereafter LC).

87. "Our Enemies the Nazis," OWI Radio Background Material, 12 January 1943, p. 39, box 14, Nash-P, HST-L.

slowly moved on to a more ambiguous one that included the people in the definition of the enemy, yet asserted that "the German people itself was the first victim of the plot to enslave the world."[88] This formula also appeared to be in congruence with the president's words regarding the "enslaved people" in his 1942 State of the Union address.[89] This consensus, however, had not come about easily and was not uncontested among the officials. A "qualitative and quantitative analysis of U.S. government statements" by the OWI with respect to "who is the enemy? peoples? or regimes?" of August 1942 had come to a similar conclusion: the absence of a consensus in the administration. The problem was not so much the respective officials' own beliefs in this matter as the political relevance of the decision. From the standpoint of psychological warfare, it was recognized, a distinction would be very useful in driving a wedge between the enemy people and their leadership and winning the support of the former to overthrow the latter. From the standpoint of actual combat, no distinction, and hatred toward all, might be more effective. Yet again, from the standpoint of postwar planning "it would probably be easier to keep contention at a minimum and to foster eventual unanimous cooperation in a family of nations."[90] This about summed up the various opinions within the Roosevelt administration.

At the conclusion of this internal clarification process in early 1943, the OWI issued guides and directives advising the motion picture industry, radio producers, and journalists to identify the enemy with respect to Nazi Germany by singling out those who benefited from National Socialism as opposed to those who suffered under it.[91] There is no indication that the information officials were interested in, or even conceived of, a third, more ambiguously defined group of fellow travelers and opportunists. The list of the beneficiaries, i.e., the enemy, represented a compilation of institutions that formed the social, political, and economic elites of Nazi Germany. It included the Nazi

88. The long and tortuous road to that statement is documented in the Minutes of the Committee on War Information Policy, 2 September 1942, box 2, Entry 1; Joint Committee on Information Policy, 10 and 17 September 1942, box 5, Entry l; MacLeish memorandum, 5 October 1942, box l, Entry 6A, OWI Records, RG 208, FRC.

89. State of the Union address, 6 January 1942, *FDR-PPA*, vol. *1942*, 35.

90. "Who Is the Enemy? Peoples? Or Regimes?" 1 August 1942, box 1849, Entry 171, RG 44 and Minutes of the meeting of the Joint Committee on Information Policy, 17 September 1942, p. 2, box 5, Entry 1, RG 208, FRC.

91. Incidentally, the following two lists were identical with those that the U.S. Army of occupation used to sort out the chaff from the wheat in defeated Nazi Germany.

Party, but not in a legal sense since membership was compulsory or semicompulsory, as the authors argued, rather only its officials and leaders, a differentiation which held true also for the other following Nazi institutions: the SS, the Gestapo, the Hitler Youth, the German Labor Front, the Nazi professional and occupational organizations, the Nazi economic overlords, i.e., big business and high finance, the Army, but again, not its rank and file, the political and judicial bureaucracy, and finally the ideologists—that is, every type of collaborating intellectual.[92] The opposing group of "victims," on the other hand, included German business, labor, farming, free professions, religious groups, women, and children.[93] What was the rationale behind depicting the overwhelming majority of Germans as victims? In order fully to understand the motives of the propagandists one needs to recall their overriding concerns.

In January 1943 in an information guide to radio writers and producers on the subject "Our Enemies: The Nazis" the OWI admitted "explaining Nazism [to the American public] is no easy assignment." Yet, the authors continued, "the importance of such a campaign must never be underestimated. This is no simple facet of the war. Instead, it's one of the main themes—the thing we're fighting against, the reason for all our war effort, the menace that can transform our future into horror if not destroyed in time." To explain exactly who the enemy was and to define the nature of the Nazi threat lay for the OWI specialists at the core of the campaign to mobilize their fellow citizens, to "make America conscious of the primal law of survival: If we don't destroy the Nazis, then they'll destroy us." Their most important advice to the radio script writers, journalists, moviemakers, cartoonists, newsreel producers, and other colleagues in the effort to sharpen

92. "The Nature of the Enemy," OWI-BOI, 21 December 1942, and "Radio Background Material. Subject: Our Enemies The Nazis," 12 January 1943, box 14, Nash Papers, HST-L.

93. In addition to documents cited in previous note, see also: "Notes on the Negative Quality of Nazism," prepared by OWI's Bureau of Research and Analysis, 13 July 1943, box 291, Entry 367, OWI Records, RG 208, FRC, listing "groups which Nazism seeks to destroy: the middle class, civil servants, the asocial type, scholars, labor and churches." It is important to note that Nazi victims, as defined by the OWI, of course also and primarily included the peoples of the countries overrun by Nazi Germany; see pamphlets warning of the "divide and conquer" tactic: *The Trojan Horse* (1942) in OF 1661a Fifth Columns, *Unconquered People* (1942), and *Tale of a City* (Warsaw) in OF 5015, FDR-P, FDR-L, as well as the early movies of the "Why We Fight" series: *Prelude to War, The Nazis Strike, Divide and Conquer.*

the image of Nazi Germany was to "tell in unvarnished words just what life would be like for us under Nazi overlords."[94] Apparently, the anti-fascist, liberal intellectuals-turned-propagandists had come to the conclusion that if in almost a decade of reporting on Nazi rule in Germany and increasingly central Europe, too, Americans still had not grasped the consequences that a German victory would have for this country, it needed to be spelled out in specific terms and illustrated in everyday life scenes. Indeed, the urgent call to "explain what [Nazism] would mean in terms of every-day American life" runs like a leitmotif through the propagandists' guides as well as their personal correspondence.[95] A poll of June 1942, in fact, had informed the officials what the American public still regarded at that point to be an information desideratum. And although only 9 percent of Americans expressed a desire to know more about what would happen if the Axis won, the OWI decided to turn this issue into a fulcrum for their larger strategy of bringing this war and its meaning closer home.[96]

The rationale then behind the policy of depicting the overwhelming majority of the German people as victims apparently was to alert Americans more directly to the Nazi threat by inviting them to identify themselves with these victims. Clearly, the purpose was not to evoke sympathy, but to arouse a more urgent sense of the danger and to heighten American resolve to fight back by dramatizing the fate of these victims in whom American businessmen, workers, farmers, and housewives could recognize themselves. Yet, apparently, information officials had taken note of surveys which culminated in a confidential report by Gallup documenting that 41 percent of Americans considered Germans "to be as good as we are in all important respects." While the French people reached the same points on the identification scale, Greeks, Jewish refugees, Poles, and Russians—more obvious candidates qualifying

94. OWI, "Radio Background Material. Subject Our Enemies: The Nazis," 12 January 1943, pp. 39 and 43, box 14, Nash-P, HST-L.

95. See Archibald MacLeish memo, 9 April 1942, OF 4619 OFF; Hadley Cantril to Anna Rosenberg, 3 March 1941, PPF 1820, box 5, FDR-P, FDR-L, expressing his disappointment that the president in his latest speech "did not spell out any more specifically the personal effects of a Nazi victory or the whole Nazi ideology." The analysis of "The Pre-Pearl Harbor Non-Interventionists," box 1172, Democratic National Committee Records, FDR-L, suggests that the "personalized approach" strategy must have been primarily directed at them.

96. Government War Information Policy Report No. 22, cited in "Short Subjects for Motion Pictures" 27 June 1942, box 1846, Entry 171, RG 44. FRC.

264 | *Michaela Hönicke*

as victims of German aggression—found themselves at considerably lower levels of acceptance as equals.[97]

A fairly straightforward example of this mobilization strategy
focusing on the German people itself was the Universal picture
"What Are We Fighting For." In this short, which was released in
May 1943, a grumbling, noncooperative American citizen is taken
by the air-raid warden to the house of his neighbor, a German
refugee. This victim of Nazi terror proceeds to illustrate for the
benefit of her neighbor the grandness of American war aims, the
Four Freedoms, by contrasting them with the fate of her family in
Nazi Germany: her husband had one day been abducted by the
secret police and soon afterwards shot in the back while her daughter had "died asking for bread." Similarly, one had to pay with
one's life for listening to the underground radio and, of course,
there had neither existed such a thing as a liberal education nor
freedom of religion in Nazi Germany.[98] The OWI's policy of excul-
pating the German people, albeit for the purpose of helping Americans to grasp more fully and fear more tangibly the meaning of a
German victory, also had the consequence of downplaying, if not
negating, the roots of Nazism in German history. Instead, National
Socialism appeared to be a totalitarian nightmare that had descended unexpectedly and uninvited on the German people.[99]

The way in which government officials and journalists used
religion illustrates once more how the image of the enemy was
anchored in the American self-image. The persecution of church
members in Nazi Germany became one of the most prominent
themes in American governmental and private anti-Nazi campaigns from 1933 on.[100] The Nazis' hostility toward and indeed

97. "An Analysis of American Public Opinion Regarding the War," p. 10, 19
September 1942, PPF 4721, FDR-P, FDR-L.
98. OWI Evaluation of "What Are We Fighting For," 12 April 1943, box U-Z,
OWI Movie Evaluations, Motion Picture and Broadcast Division, LC.
99. See Radio Background Material, 12 January 1943, Nash Papers and OWI's
critique of a State Department brochure on Nazi ideology, 22 January 1943, box 12,
Nash Papers, HST-L.
100. "Cross or Swastika" pamphlet of the Non-Sectarian Anti-Nazi League
(NSANL), General Office Files, box 1, Folder 1938, Butler Library, Columbia University; religion was also a big theme in the "Tenth Anniversary Campaign" in January 1943; see Memo on "Ten Years of National Socialism," December 1942, box 293,
Entry 367, RG 208 OWI, FRC; Memo on "10th Anniversary," box 8 and *Look* magazine articles as part of this campaign: 29 December 1942 and 12 January 1943, box
9, Nash Papers, HST-L; Memo Harry Hopkins, 3 July 1941, PPF 4096; Harold Ickes
to FDR, 6 January 1942, PSF Interior; FDR to Archbishop Spellman, 25 October
1941, box 31, PSF Diplomatic Correspondence Germany; transcripts of speeches ...,

incompatibility with the Christian faith was used to sharpen the contrast between what the Nazis stood for and what Americans were fighting for. At the same time this presentation reinforced the notion that the Christian people of Germany were indeed victims of its own regime, but otherwise very much like ordinary Americans. Finally, this approach had the unfortunate side effect of subsuming the persecution of Jews under the broader category of Nazi harassment of religious groups. As one propaganda guide explained, "the attack on the Jews is actually an attack on Christianity."[101] Because, as Secretary of the Interior Harold Ickes pointed out, "Judaism is not Hitler's ultimate enemy"—ultimately, National Socialism seeks to destroy Christianity.[102]

Indeed, the OWI's handling of information on the Holocaust —the most dramatic evidence regarding the nature of the enemy—corroborates the argument that at important junctures the agency bowed before rather than shaped public opinion. Even after substantiated information on the Nazi policy of systematically murdering European Jews became available to the American administration and public in the summer and fall of 1942, the OWI decided against using it in a prominent way to define the enemy. Partly, that decision can be explained by their policy against the use of atrocity stories.[103] More specifically, propagandists argued that

---

19 September 1939, PPF 423 Myron C. Taylor; Basil Manly to FDR, 1 May 1941, box 5, PPF 1820, FDR-P, FDR-L.

101. OWI Radio Background Material, p. 224, Nash Papers, HST-L, also ibid., p. 5: "From the outset, an attack on the Jews was employed as a smoke screen behind which Nazism began its real assault on other groups, on labor, business and all opposition."

102. Ickes' speech, "Protestantism answers Hate," 21 February 1941, OF 6 Interior Department, FDR-L.

103. See "Pros and Cons on Hate and Atrocities," 22 May 1942, box 360, Entry 360; Huse to Barnes, 14 July 1942, box 4, Entry 1; MacLeish memo 7 June 1942, box 2, Entry 6A; Policy Directive on Hate Propaganda, 9 April 1943, box 1, Entry 6A, RG 208 OWI, FRC. Certainly the decision against the use of hate propaganda and the extremely cautious approach to atrocity stories has again to be seen against the backdrop of the United States's World War I experience. See Robert Wolfe, ed., *Americans As Proconsuls: United States Military Government in Germany and Japan, 1944–1952* (Carbondale, 1984), xvii, and Lipstadt, *Belief,* 8f. The OWI was not engaged in censorship with regard to the Holocaust; indeed, many booklets and pamphlets put out by other organizations detailing the stages of the Holocaust can be found in the records of the OWI. See for example *Nazi Guide to Nazism,* put out by American Council on Public Affairs, box 292, Entry 367; *Conditions in Occupied Territories,* No. 6 *Persecution of the Jews,* published by the United Nations Information Office, December 1942, box 294, Entry 367; *The Nazis at War,* No. 42 (18 December 1942), published by the Wiener Library, box 290, Entry 367, RG 208 OWI, FRC.

"open atrocities directed against.... the Jews cover up the normal daily terror of National Socialism for an entire strata of the German population"—still the OWI's main emphasis. The officials also feared that the "story of Nazi conquest and ... terrorism of occupied countries will be confused and misleading if it appears to be simply a story affecting the Jewish people."[104] Clearly, propagandists were taking into account polls of the summer of 1942 showing, in the words of one self-critical analyst that "German ideas of racial superiority find their counterpart in our own theories of racial and cultural superiority."[105]

A comparative look at the OWI handling of the Japanese reinforces the notion that a racial bias worked in favor of the German people. In this same survey, the Japanese found themselves at the bottom of the list with 12 percent of Americans accepting them as equals. This difference in attitudes toward the two main enemies is highlighted in an OWI comparison of the enemy's political systems and atrocities. Contrasting "German political astuteness" with "Japanese political stupidity" the document termed "German theory of race an ersatz product which can easily be modified." German atrocities, the text went on, "represent the application of a theory of conquest,... they are applied scientifically, the results are calculated, they can be turned off at will." Japanese atrocities, on the contrary, "arise out of the very nature of Japanese civilization." This interpretation led the authors to the conclusion that "there is little hope of fitting Japan into any kind of world order.... The job of fitting a defeated Germany into a more or less peaceful world, compared with this is simple."[106] This attitude was shared by 67 percent of Americans who in April 1943 expected their country to

104. See OWI Radio Background material and Leo Rosten to Sweetsen, 1 December 1942, box 233, Entry 75, RG 208 OWI, FRC. In general on this topic see David S. Wyman, *Abandonment of the Jews: America and the Holocaust, 1941–1945* (New York, 1985) and Lipstadt, *Belief.*

105. It hardly needs to be emphasized that the American anti-Semitism detected by the pollsters of the following surveys was in nature fundamentally different from the murderous racism propagated by the Nazis. Gallup, An Analysis of American Public Opinion, September 1942, p. 10, PPF 4721; while Canadians, with 76 percent ranked even before the English people of whom 72 percent of Americans thought that they were "as good as we are in all important respects," Germans followed Dutch (62 percent), Scandinavians (60 percent), and Irish (56 percent) with 41 percent (together with the French). Jewish refugees found themselves closer to the bottom with 26 percent. See also several reports of fall 1942 and spring 1943 in PSF, box 155, FDR-P, FDR-L.

106. Minutes of the Joint Committee on Information Policy, 12 January 1943 and 27 February 1943, box 11, Entry 6E, RG 208 OWI, FRC.

get along with Germany after the war, as opposed to 8 percent who held that view with regard to Japan.[107]

The extensive media campaign in the spring of 1943 marking the tenth anniversary of Hitler's coming to power with the slogan "The Dark Decade" documents the OWI's effectiveness in keeping the American public well informed on all the grim and dreary aspects of the Third Reich. It covered a whole array of issues ranging from NS foreign policy and the "Nazi International" through "Changes in Nazi Ideology," and terror in the Third Reich and occupied countries to the "Nazi attack on the intellect," and the fate of business, the middle class, labor, and mothers under Nazi rule.[108] But in this world of horror the German people were, for the most part, not portrayed as perpetrators or even supporters, but as victims. This peculiar strategy had been shaped by the perceived exigencies of the day: to raise the level of popular commitment to this war by dramatizing the consequences of a Nazi victory in a manner that brought it down to a personal level for most Americans. In rejecting the alternative strategy of arousing fear and hatred of the German people, OWI officials appear to have been equally guided by their rejection of World War I style propaganda and by their recognition of existing public sentiment with regard to Allies and enemies. It thus seemed that the very source of information that enabled the administration to learn about public attitudes, the newly available opinion polls, also restrained, almost hamstrung, it in its efforts to direct public opinion.

The Nature of the Enemy Defined Differently: The Army's View

No account of American wartime propaganda would be complete without considering the military's educational effort. It was primarily directed at the newly recruited GIs. But as the general mobilization turned citizens into soldiers, military officials such as

107. *Gallup Poll*, 388.

108. For this campaign Ben Shahn created some of the most powerful government posters depicting Nazism. Shahn became a victim of the institutional purge later in 1943, see Weinberg, "Quarrel." Extensive material on the preparations for the campaign, devised and coordinated by the OWI, but for the most part executed by independent newspapers, magazines, radio broadcast stations, and movie studios, is to be found in box 9, Nash Papers, HST-L as well as in box 233, Entry 75 and box 293, Entry 367 OWI Records, RG 208, FRC.

Army Chief of Staff General George C. Marshall pointed to the close mutual influence that civilian and military morale had on each other. The low fighting spirit and confusion over war aims were a reflection of the attitudes among families, friends, and neighbors "back home."[109] The military propaganda campaign was begun parallel to the OWI's work. But while the civilian officials' labor was continually hampered by the War or State Department's obstructionism and generally made more difficult through presidential neglect, the military's effort benefited from the interest of high-ranking administrative officials as well as from the experimentation with new social scientific techniques, such as regular, long-term polling and psychological training.[110] Moreover, the Army chose to take a different approach to alerting its people to the threat of Nazi Germany and drew a picture of that country that did not always comply with OWI guidelines but, on the other hand, was more in sync with the opinion of leading members of the administration, including the president himself.

Telling departures from the OWI policy are apparent in the War Department's own "Guide to the Use of Information Materials." Following the Manichaean world-view dominating much of the official propaganda outside the OWI, the pamphlet opened with the identification of the enemy with "falsehood" and its own position with "truth." While this line is reminiscent of the OWI's "strategy of truth," the War Department's less scrupulous and unambiguous approach immediately becomes clear in the following delineation of the concept of enemy. Should it include "rulers," "systems," "ideas," or "peoples?" What gave rise to endless discussions at the OWI's Committee of Information was resolved in one clear-cut sentence: all of them, "because ... they are being used in combination against us and are indivisible."[111] The same sensible pragmatism characterized the—for the OWI so difficult—

109. Richard W. Steele, "'The Greatest Gangster Movie Ever Filmed': *Prelude to War*," *Prologue* 11 (Winter 1979): 220–35, here: 224.

110. David Culbert, "'Why We Fight': Social Engineering for a Democratic Society at War" in K. R. M. Short, ed., *Film and Radio Propaganda in World War II* (Knoxville, 1983), 173–91, here: 173. Like the OWI, the War Department commissioned studies to measure the effects of their educational campaigns; see the "What the Soldiers Thinks" report, box 34, Nash Papers, HST-L, of which the Military Branch in the NA also holds a complete copy and the published version; Samuel A. Stouffer et al., eds., *The American Soldier*, vols. 1, 2, Studies in Social Psychology in World War II (Princeton, 1949).

111. War Department Pamphlet No. 20-3: Guide to the Use of Information Materials, 10 December 1943, p. v, 8, box 14, Nash-P, HST-L.

issue of hatred. The army guide simply postulated that hate indoctrination—while not an end in itself—should be regarded as a "practical training question rather than a moral issue" and as an indispensable prerequisite for the determination to fight and, in the end, to kill. Accordingly, the Army approved of the use of "horror stories and pictures" if authenticated and officially vouched for and as far as they are "relevant to any occurring situation." Photographs of emaciated Greek civilians in the summer of 1942 are cited as an appropriate example to document that "Hitler is deliberately employing famine as a military weapon" and as a "striking illustration of the utter ruthlessness of the German military character."[112] As in the official OWI guidelines, no mention is made of the deprivation of rights and jobs, or the systematic starvation, torture, and murder of the European Jews. In conclusion, the guide's special admonition "not to exculpate the Germany Army or to ignore the history of prewar Germany" deserves our attention. This instruction resulted in a depiction of Nazi brutality as only the latest sequel in the long record of German military aggression—outlined early on in the above-mentioned letter by Roosevelt and soon to become a standard feature of the War Department's output in movies and pamphlets.[113]

The Army's most successful educational medium was the film. In the fall of 1942, U.S. recruits saw a movie as part of their mandatory training which provided them with "factual information as to the causes and events leading up to our entry into this war and the principles for which we are fighting."[114] In retrospect, one might have to admit that the film was not only providing facts but also some unambiguous interpretation, powerful images, and emotional appeals. It was, as *Time* magazine found, "the first impressive attempt in a U.S. film to present the theory and practice of Fascism."[115] The film had been commissioned by the War Department. Its actual production was closely supervised by Army Chief

112. Ibid., 10, 11.

113. *The Soldier's Pocket Guide to Germany* (Washington, 1944), 26f. See also scripts of *Here Is Germany* and *Your Job in Germany*, box 9, RG 111, Motion Picture and Sound Recording Division, National Archives, Washington, DC.

114. The quotation is drawn from the trailer of the film *Prelude to War*. My description of this film as well as of its sequels discussed further down in this chapter is based on my viewing of the films, which are available at the Audiovisual Archives Division at the National Archives in Washington, D.C., and the National Audiovisual Center at Capital Heights, MD, as well as in Germany through the Institut für den Wissenschaftlichen Film, Göttingen.

115. Clipping from *Time*, 31 May 1943 in box 3, Entry 1, Record Group 208, FRC.

of Staff General George C. Marshall and Secretary of War Henry L. Stimson, and its final version expressed the administration's official interpretation of the origins of the current war.[116] The movie was called *Prelude to War*. The series of which it formed the first part had been drafted along the lines of the orientation lectures given to new recruits and was executed by a Hollywood team under the direction of Frank Capra. For the German aspects of the series, the assistance of the journalist William L. Shirer, author of the bestseller *Berlin Diary*, had been secured.[117] As its title suggested, the series was meant to provide an answer as to "Why We Fight." The opening sequence of *Prelude to War* questioned the conventional and seemingly obvious reason why Americans were fighting: the Japanese attack on Pearl Harbor. This indeed was the purpose of the movie and its sequels—which half a year after its production for the armed forces was released to a general public—to broaden the view and to deepen the understanding of the average American as to the origins of the current conflict and its ideological nature.[118]

At the heart of the current war, the movie claimed, lay the "fight between a free world and a slave world."[119] The film's presentation merged Nazi Germany, Fascist Italy and militaristic Japan into one monolithic enemy bloc, the slave world. This portrayal was explained with reference to the similarity of the enemy countries' offensive beliefs and brutal methods, which were contrasted with

116. Richard W. Steele, "'The Greatest Gangster Movie Ever Filmed,' *Prelude to War*," *Prologue* vol. 11 (1979): 220–35, here: 227. For the whole series see also David Culbert, "'Why We Fight': Social Engineering for a Democratic Society at War," in Short, *Film and Radio Propaganda in World War II*, 173–91. For an account from the director's perspective see Frank Capra, *The Name Above the Title* (New York, 1971), Chap. 17 "Why We Fight," 325–51; for the military, especially General Marshall, the moving force behind this undertaking, cf. Forrest C. Pogue, *George C. Marshall: Organizer of Victory* (New York, 1973), 91 and Larry I. Bland, ed. *The Papers of George C. Marshall*, vol. 3 *The Right Man for the Job* (Baltimore, 1991), 447–53. For an analysis of the content see Thomas William Bohn, *An Historical and Descriptive Analysis of the "Why We Fight" Series* (New York, 1977). For background on the production see David Culbert, ed., *Film and Propaganda in America: A Documentary History*, vol. 2 (New York, 1990).

117. In addition to his *Berlin Diary* see *20th Century Journey: The Nightmare Years, 1930–40* (Boston, 1984).

118. The date of the public release was 27 May 1943; see Culbert, "Social Engineering," 189.

119. The fact that the closing shot linked the two geographical halves of the world with the two sides of the struggle, the Western Hemisphere as the free world, the Eastern Hemisphere as the slave world, was rightly viewed as an "appalling boner" by reviewers who otherwise generally found this film a useful educational device.

the values and traditions of the Allied countries among which the viewers' own country assumed a paramount position. In view of alternative interpretations that characterized the war against Nazi Germany in particular as a defense of Western civilization, this universal approach deserves special attention. Across national, ethnic, geographical, and religious borders, Moses, Mohammed, Confucius, and Christ were evoked as the founding fathers of the free world. The principles of the free world found expression in such documents as the Declaration of Independence—"all men are created equal"—and—again across national borders but with a certain centrality accorded to the American Revolution—were the ones for which men like Washington, Jefferson, Garibaldi, LaFayette, Kocziuski, Bolivar, and Lincoln had fought: individual and national freedom.[120] From these lofty principles the conflict was brought back again to the level of those who would have to fight it and who at the same time gave this struggle, in the eyes of the American propagandists, its universal and democratic meaning: this was "the common man's life and death struggle against those who want to put him back into slavery."[121]

To which specific events and ideological characteristics did the film point in its explanation as to why Americans had to fight the Axis? In the case of National Socialist Germany the rise of the dictator Adolf Hitler was to a small extent attributed to World War I "postwar confusion," in particular the social consequences of high inflation. More importantly, though, the viewer was informed that Hitler had "certain distinctive German characteristics" to play off, namely, "an inborn love of regimentation and harsh discipline," a burning desire for revenge for the unacknowledged defeat in the last war, and, finally, the scheming industrialists willing to back anyone who could guarantee the preservation of their wealth and

120. This list of names should have appealed to the allegiance of different ethnic groups in the United States, African-Americans, Poles, Italians, as well as to citizens of Latin American countries that were threatened by Nazi Germany. The selection of freedom fighters moreover, reflects some preference for the right kind of revolution. After all the Nazis claimed, too, that they had produced a revolution. For American preferences as to different kinds of revolutions see Michael Hunt, *Ideology and U.S. Foreign Policy* (New Haven, 1987), 92–124.

121. This closing statement of the movie was a direct reference to Vice President Henry Wallace's speech of May 1942, on "The Century of the Common Man," obviously an alternative vision to Henry Luce's "The American Century." The image of the fight between the free world and the slave world is also drawn from this speech, which is printed in Richard Polenberg, ed., *America at War: The Home Front, 1941–1945* (Englewood Cliffs, NJ, 1968), 158–63.

power. According to this view, a fundamental share of the blame for subsequent events then lay with the German people, who like their counterparts in the other Axis countries had given up their rights as individual human beings and citizens. To Hitler's call to "stop thinking and follow me, I will make you masters of the world," the people had responded with enthusiastic cheers of "Sieg Heil." Their unquestioning support for Hitler had enabled the Nazis to eliminate one by one political and personal freedoms and democratic institutions. Without encountering organized resistance, the Nazis turned the German parliament, the Reichstag, into a rubber stamp institution and abrogated freedom of speech, press, and assembly. The independent judiciary, labor unions, and collective bargaining were abolished. In their place a ministry of propaganda exerted complete control and unabashedly broadcast lies while a secret police ruled with ruthless force. In the former country of "poets and philosophers," a cult of "might over right" and brute force had replaced the appreciation of works of art and culture seeking and celebrating political and personal freedom. A Nazi official was quoted as saying: "Whenever I hear the word culture I reach for my gun."

In passing, the film referred to the Roehm putsch during which Hitler in the so-called Night of Long Knives had eliminated a potential internal Nazi opposition to his dictatorship. This event of June 1934 marked the consolidation of Hitler's total and uncontested rule. The film reminded its audience that at this point only one obstacle was left, the church, on which the Nazis' "theoretician" Alfred Rosenberg had consequently declared war.[122] But this embattled stronghold of opposition appeared doomed in the face of another aspect of Nazi reality that was dramatized next in the movie: the indoctrination and regimentation of children at all ages, born and brought up to die for their Führer. Children were shown repeating lines expressing fanatical submission in the classroom, marching in military formations, feeding canons with ammunition. The scenes culminated in the shot of a pile of newborn, naked, pitifully whimpering babies evoking the image of an assembly-line production of new human material. The surrender of the German people and their transformation into automatons or slaves ruled by one single militaristic mind was finally visualized in seemingly endless minutes of footage showing marching

---

122. Pastor Martin Niemöller of Berlin-Dahlem was briefly mentioned as one of those who led the resistance in the church struggle.

and "heiling" soldiers, presumably taken straight from Leni Riefenstahl's celebrated oeuvres.[123]

The Army's first official propaganda movie again offers a lesson in how the image of the enemy is invariably rooted in one's self-image. Contrary to the OWI's emphasis on identification with the victims of Nazi ideology and practice, which, as we have seen, included the German people, the War Department authors emphasized the contrast, the incompatibility of the two worlds. The aspects of Nazi life and ideology which had been selected and highlighted for this presentation reflected much of American priorities—albeit in a mirror-image reversal. The loss of political and personal freedom was contrasted with scenes of American life showing free elections, shop windows displaying books including those by Hitler and Stalin—indeed, a stark contrast to a country burning its own authors' books—churchgoing families, and children growing up freely. For the most part this orientation to American values and standards pointed the authors of the film straight to the central features in Hitler's totalitarian regime. Occasionally, however, it led to a misjudgment. The story of the persecution of Jews did not figure prominently either visually or verbally in this presentation. It was touched upon in the context of Nazi anti-religious stance and harassment of Catholics and Protestants. While the movie explicitly discussed Nazi racism, it did not relate it to the Jewish experience in Germany but rather dealt with the Jews solely as a religious group. Instead, Nazi racism in this movie, like Japanese beliefs of superiority, was presented solely in its foreign policy, i.e., military consequences. The master race or *Herrenvolk* was bent on a military drive to conquer the world: "[T]oday we rule Germany, tomorrow the world." To link the drive for world domination more directly to the fate of the American people, the latter were reminded of Germany's advance through Europe to the Middle East and North Africa and told about their foes' plans to use these bases as a launching pad for an attack on the Western Hemisphere.

Hitler's diplomatic actions and military exploits, as well as his future projects, were presented in this propaganda series as a step-by-step execution of a program that had been drawn up even before the Nazis had come to power, laid out in the Nazi bible, *My Struggle*. This interpretation of Nazi foreign policy, which in subsequent

123. Capra made extensive use of original Nazi newsreels and movie footage as part of a propaganda strategy also adopted by other governmental agencies as well as journalists to let the Nazis speak for themselves. See also Thomas Doherty, *Projections of War: Hollywood, American Culture, and World War II* (New York, 1993), 16ff.

historiographical debates became known as the "intentionalist" view, served the purpose of convincing Americans of the futility of appeasement as well as isolationist approaches in dealing with their adversary.[124] The future "lesson of Munich" first appears in these propaganda movies: you cannot seek deals and compromises with totalitarian dictators who will not be appeased by partial surrenders and you cannot hide behind oceans and turn inward, insisting on your pacifist state of mind, if your adversary is bent on world conquest. Thus, the film's answer to the question of what the free world had done while the slave world had prepared for its attack implicitly indicted isolationism and criticized the neutrality laws of the 1930s.

The second and third part of the series, *Divide and Conquer* and *The Nazis Strike*, which focus more exclusively on Nazi Germany, continued to emphasize the relation that these events in foreign countries bore to the fate of the American way of life. The films impressed on their audience how Germany had defeated its European neighbors through a dazzling military effort, carefully planned and prepared, in which early and massive rearmament had played an important role, as well as the regimentation of the German people itself. While this was the main message of *The Nazis Strike*, stunning its viewers with images of the Nazis' blitzkrieg in the Low Countries and Poland, *Divide and Conquer* told the lesson of the French defeat, which the film attributed to Germany's strategies of undermining the morale of its victims before vanquishing them militarily. The film picked up the topic of infiltration, of fifth columnist activities sowing the seeds of distrust and internal strife. It argued that France had not been beaten by weapons but by the "gospel of defeatism." Germans were characterized as "Huns," evoking images of brutality and aggression of the past Great War, as "gangsters," emphasizing their lawlessness, and as "treacherous," pointing to those strategies that lay at the heart of the ominous, warning message of this film. The French people unfortunately had been an easy prey to the poison that Hitler's agents had spread across Europe: propaganda insinuating the hopelessness of armed resistance.[125] After the French had succumbed to this propaganda of defeat and surrender, terror carried out by the Nazi secret police,

124. For the debate see Ian Kershaw, *The Nazi Dictatorship: Problems and Perspectives of Interpretation* (London, 1991), 107–30.

125. The "gangster" metaphor is a typical one in the American official characterization in particular of the Nazi leaders: in this film Adolf Hitler is likened to John Dillinger. The most typical example of this iconography is the movie *The Hitler Gang*.

the Gestapo, and a complete press censorship finished the job of rendering the French immobile. Images of agitated, panicky French men and women crying out accusations against the government, the church, labor unions, and democracy itself were contrasted with shots of president Franklin D. Roosevelt and American citizens calmly refuting the argument that free political and religious institutions were to blame for social and economic hardship. The narrator's assurance, however, that "our government tells the truth" and "unlike the people of Europe, we are not frightened and hysterical" has a ring of incantation rather than simple observation. The topic of vigilantism in the face of fifth columnist activities and the fight against the "gospel of defeatism" was of utmost importance to the official American propaganda material.[126] It was taken up in the final installment of the series, *War Comes to America*, which referred to the popular film *Confessions of a Nazi Spy* as not just a movie but a reality, showing pictures of the Nazi organization in the United States, the German-American Bundists.[127]

The Nazis Strike, finally, completed the picture of Nazi Germany with the important detail of historical perspective. It put Germany's current militaristic conduct in an older tradition of power and conquest symbolized by a depiction of earlier leaders such as Bismarck and Emperor Wilhelm—a sort of early visualization of the future historiographical continuity thesis of German history. The film also picked up the topic of the fate of the German people. The viewers had learned in the first sequel, *Prelude*, that the Germans bore a certain amount of responsibility for the Third Reich, as they themselves had chosen to give up their political rights and freedom in order to follow the promises of their leader. Now we see them being forced to work, forced to produce, or else threatened with concentration camps and death. Hitler and his cohorts, such as Heinrich Himmler, head of the secret police, had turned Germans into "unthinking, insensible weapons."[128] The metaphor of the "automaton" was indeed an important variation of the theme of slavery to which the Germans had submitted.[129] Fascism

126. See OFF and OWI pamphlets on the "Trojan Horse," "Divide and Conquer."
127. Eric J. Sandeen, "'Confessions of a Nazi Spy' and the German-American Bund" *American Studies* 20 (Fall 1979): 69–78, and on the Bund in general Diamond, *Nazi Movement* and Bruce F. Ashkenas, "A Legacy of Hatred: The Records of a Nazi Organization in America," *Prologue* 17 (Summer 1985): 93–106.
128. Bohn, *Analysis*, 145f.
129. The American journalist Howard K. Smith, *Last Train from Berlin* (New York, 1943), 11–16, uses this metaphor of the automaton extensively.

was slavery and the people who did not fight it were turned into a mechanized, dehumanized force serving the militaristic, evil purposes of the fascist leaders. In *The Nazis Strike* the slave theme and its relevance for the American people is intoned in Hitler's own words: "There will be a class of subject alien races. We need not hesitate to call them slaves."

In summing up the aspects of this official cinematic portrayal of the Third Reich by the Army, it becomes apparent that the primary purpose was not just to demonstrate how evil the Nazis were but also to dramatize the threat they posed to the Western world and to the United States itself. The slavery theme suggested the totalitarian nature of Hitler's regime in which the people had been reduced to mindless, obedient automatons. Pointing to Germany's history and the collective character of its people, a certain propensity for militarism and aggression was detected. Germans were not portrayed as the first victims of the National Socialist assault but rather as the ones who overwhelmingly welcomed it. The leaders of Nazi Germany were in various ways likened to gangsters, a simile highlighting their contempt for and violation of—in this context international—laws and rules. Apart from the references to history and national character, shots of the current regimentation of the German people through compulsion, force, and indoctrination yielded a picture of a country completely oriented to military conquest and world domination. The indoctrination aspect, in particular, deserves special mention as it involved the very young—a threat that Americans continued to take very seriously up to the eventual defeat and occupation of their enemy's country. The content of the gospel of fanaticism instilled in the children and appealed to in the grownups was shaped by Nazi notions of race superiority and contempt for the lessons of religion. Finally, the link to the United States was provided in a twofold manner: first, a number of characteristics of the Third Reich derive their negative quality from the contrast with American values and rules that the movies evoke. But secondly, Nazi Germany not only presented a challenge to the American way of life in an ideological way; it also presented a military threat which the authors of the series documented by using the Nazis' own newsreels and film footage that celebrated German military prowess and exploits, emphasizing the early recorded determination for world conquest and the impressive military buildup. The sense of danger was finally heightened by constant reminders of the poisonous effects of Nazi propaganda, subversion and fifth columnist activities.

Conclusion

The OWI was not happy with the Army product: it clearly failed
to meet the standards that the civilian agency had set for domestic propaganda—balance and objectivity. Moreover, it could not
tolerate the implicit wholesale condemnation of the peoples in the
Axis nations.[130] As the war continued, though, not surprisingly
the military's portrayal of the enemy won increasing popular and
official support. Yet, this tougher stance did not lead to the high-
pitched tone of hatred and condemnation that characterized Nazi
attitudes toward their real and imagined enemies. The conceptual
difficulty of distinguishing between Nazi ideology and German
culture runs like a leitmotif through all American deliberations of
the German problem. In probing the roots of certain Third Reich
phenomena, Americans were called upon to render an early judgment on the *Sonderweg*, the peculiar path, debate. Noteworthy, in
any case, is the ubiquity of the metaphor of "disease" in the official, and also public, characterization of what was wrong with
Germany. An ambiguous concept, it cut both ways: Secretary of
State Cordell Hull and Roosevelt repeatedly referred to the "dis-
eased mentality" of Nazi Germany, which sounded both hopeless
and certainly repulsive. Yet, this was the most severe image used
to describe the German problem—it still implied a degree of cur-
ability. Even in the worst case scenario, working from the assumption that the fascist and militarist mentality was indeed a birth
defect of the German nation, it was also clear from the responses
in the national debate on this issue that American ingenuity could
not and would not rest until it had devised a cure. Accordingly,
the State Department Committee on Postwar Planning had sponsored a conference of seven mental health organizations and a
number of prominent psychiatrists and psychologists in the spring
and early summer of 1944 in order to discuss the nature of and
possible solutions to the German problem.[131] This was indeed a
very different concept from the German definition of the enemy
based on race—immutable, incurable.

In the period covered in this presentation, 1942/43, official propaganda activity was dominated by the OWI. As the war continued and transformed American attitudes, the image of Germany

130. Steele, "Gangster movie," 232f. and Motion Picture Guidance for Commercial Films …, 21 April 1944, box 2, Entry 6B, RG 208, FRC.
131. Copies of the comprehensive report of this conference are to be found in OF
198a Germany, FDR-P, FDR-L and box 294, Entry 367, RG 208, FRC.

also underwent considerable change. In mid-1943 the domestic branch of the OWI, which was responsible for the home front, was effectively voted out of business through congressional budget cuts.[132] Other government branches became more influential—in particular the War Department, whose orientation programs, especially Frank Capra's "Why We Fight" series, were more in harmony with Roosevelt's preferences. But the War Department could not achieve what the OWI had already failed to do: a wholehearted, all-out effort to shape the public image of Germany. After all, the United States was still a democratic and free society; thus, the debate on the nature of the enemy continued in radio shows, magazines, and roundtables across the country. At the end of 1944 there still was no conclusive answer in the American public's mind to the question asked by the survivors in Hitchcock's movie *Lifeboat* after they finally overcome the German: "What do you do with people like that?"[133]

---

132. Winkler, *Propaganda*, 65ff.

133. See the intriguing account of the multiple endings to this movie, together with the conflicting reactions in Clayton R. Koppes and Gregory D. Black, *Hollywood Goes to War: How Politics, Profits and Propaganda Shaped World War II Movies* (London, 1987), 309ff. For public attitudes toward postwar treatment of Germany see Public Attitudes on Foreign Policy, Special Report, No 33: Treatment of Germany, 9 September 1944, box 1; American Public Opinion on Postwar Treatment of Germany, October 1944, box 34, Report of 29 December 1944, box 34; fluctuations in public opinion from February 1942 to May 1945 are traced in *Latest Opinion Trends in U.S.A.*, 2 June 1945, box 34, Office of Public Opinion Studies, State Department Records, RG 59, NA.

Part V

The Cold War

Chapter Ten

FRIENDS, FOES, OR REEDUCATORS?

Feindbilder and Anti-Communism in the
U.S. Military Government in Germany, 1946–1953

Jessica C. E. Gienow-Hecht

The German word *Feindbild* (literally "enemy image") stems from the Germanic terms *fijoend*, hated, and *bilde*, sample.[1] Thus, *Feindbild*, no common word in the English language, connotes the personification of an object or a trend despised by a group or a person.[2] The present chapter deals with an object of American national resentment, communism, and one of the target groups identified with this trend, German-Jewish émigrés serving in the American military government in Germany after VE Day.

In the years following World War II, the specter of communism grew into the most forceful enemy image in the United States. Scholars such as Melvyn Leffler, David Oshinsky, and many others

I wish to thank members of the Graduiertenkolleg-Arbeitsgruppe in the history department of the Universität Bielefeld as well as Heiko Hecht, Olaf Blaschke, Till van Rahden, Bill Waltz, and Mike Groen for reading drafts of this chapter and offering many helpful editorial and analytical suggestions.

1. Friedrich Kluge, *Etymologisches Wörterbuch der deutschen Sprache*, 22d ed. (Berlin, 1989), 84, 208.

2. See also: Michael Jeismann, *Das Vaterland der Feinde: Studien zum nationalen Feindbegriff und Selbstverständnis in Deutschland und Frankreich 1792–1918* (Stuttgart, 1992); *Feindbilder: Die Darstellung der Gegner in der politischen Publizistik des Mittelalters und der Neuzeit*, ed. Franz Bosbach (Cologne, 1992).

have shown how the containment of the Soviets abroad and the anti-communist crusade at home fused internal social and geopolitical threats confronting U.S. postwar society.[3] Anti-communism, scholars agree, was not only reflected in the geopolitical desire to contain the Soviets and their ideology abroad but also in a fundamental national postwar identity crisis at home. At the heart of the anti-communist craze lay a deep confusion over the nature and values of American society.[4] The word "American," while remaining an unclear and rather amorphous notion, embodied all those core values and principles which presumably defined U.S. society and tradition. It constituted a source of purity and energy fostering immunity to communist influences. Personae, tendencies, and writings of different origins evinced un-American influences and, by virtue of being "other," posed a potential social, political, and cultural threat.

This chapter examines a selected, highly visible group of German-Jewish émigrés operating in the American military government in Germany (OMGUS) between 1945 and 1949. Originally, their binational identity did not put them at a disadvantage. Only the mounting tension between the Soviets and the Anglo-American forces led many U.S. observers to doubt the émigrés' loyalty to American society and political principles. For a short time, these German-born soldiers supplied a target vital to the development of America's number one postwar enemy image: communism.

Due to their intricate lingual and cultural knowledge, German-Jewish émigrés played a distinct role in the American war effort at the Western front. The Psychological Warfare Division (PWD) of the War Department hired hundreds of German-born refugees who produced broadcasts and leaflets designed to destroy the German Army's morale. By 1944 the division had attracted hundreds of German-born professors, teachers, artists, poets, psychologists, lawyers, journalists, authors, and craftsmen. Occasionally, these men evoked suspicion. They did not fight with weapons but with ideas, and developed a close group spirit isolated from the combat troops. While they were intellectually talented, they tended to sneer at professional soldiers, military orders, bureaucracy, and hierarchy. Moreover, their often liberal or leftist backgrounds did not comport well with the political outlook of many

3. Melvyn P. Leffler, *The Specter of Communism* (New York, 1994); David M. Oshinsky, *A Conspiracy So Immense: The World of Joe McCarthy* (New York, 1983).

4. Stephen J. Whitfield, *The Culture of the Cold War*, 2d ed. (Baltimore, MD, 1996), Leffler, *The Specter of Communism*.

American-born soldiers, whose parochial upbringing chafed at utopianism or socialism.[5]

Once the war was over, the PWD, now renamed Information Control Division (ICD), employed the same émigrés in its effort to reconstruct the German media system and to reeducate the Germans along democratic principles. On 18 October 1945, the ICD created a newspaper, *Die Neue Zeitung*, in Munich's famous bohemian quarter, Schwabing. The paper had two purposes: it would present German readers with news on U.S. diplomacy, culture and ideas, and it would provide German editors with a model democratic, American newspaper. Some two dozen German-Jewish émigrés who had originally worked in the PWD led *Die Neue Zeitung*, which quickly turned into one of the most frequently read newspapers in postwar Germany.[6]

While their passports identified these men as U.S. citizens, many of them, particularly the older ones, remained German at heart. They had been born and baptized in German culture. They had gone to school and worked in Europe before fleeing Hitler's discriminatory laws. Their first love had been an Austrian or a German girl. Many would always retain their thick German accent. Hans Wallenberg, for example, held the position of editor-in-chief of *Die Neue Zeitung* from 1946 to 1947 and 1949 to 1953. He continuously strove to prove "that he was not an American."[7] The son of a Jewish family from Berlin, Wallenberg had received his editorial training in the famous Ullstein publishing house. Under the worst financial strains, he emigrated to the United States in 1938, where he eventually founded a printing shop in downtown New York and received U.S. citizenship.[8] Nonetheless, with his heavy Berlin

5. William E. Daugherty, *A Psychological Warfare Casebook*, 4th ed. (Baltimore, MD, 1968, orig. 1958), 126, 131, 157ff.; David Lerner, *Propaganda in War and Crisis*. (New York, 1951), 278ff.; David Lerner, *Psychological Warfare Against Nazi-Germany: The Sykewar Campaign, D-Day to VE-Day* (Cambridge, MA, 2d ed., 1971), 350–64; Peter Wyden, "Die bunte Truppe von Camp Shapiro," *Rheinischer Merkur* 18 (5 May 1995): 37; Hans Habe, *Im Jahre Null. Ein Beitrag zur Geschichte der deutschen Presse* (Munich, 1966), 10–13; Harold Hurwitz, *Die Stunde Null der deutschen Presse: Die amerikanische Pressepolitik in Deutschland 1945–1949* (Cologne, 1972), 24.

6. Jessica C. E. Gienow, "Cultural Transmission and the U.S. Occupation in Germany: The *Neue Zeitung*, 1945–55," (Ph.D. diss., Charlottesville, VA, 1995), 155–164.

7. Interviews with Hans-Joachim Netzer, Munich, 13 December 1991, and Carl Hermann Ebbinghaus.

8. "Profilierter Publizist und rühriger Organisator: Gespräch mit Hans Wallenberg," *Allgemeine unabhängige Wochenzeitung*, Düsseldorf, 24 December 1971, 11;" Herbert A. Strauss and Werner Röder, *International Biographical Dictionary of Central European Émigrés 1933–1945*, 3 vols. (Munich, 1980–1983), 1: 790–91; questionnaire

slang, his love for German *Kultur*, and his journalistic bent in the Weimar tradition he did not impersonate a typical U.S. editor.[9]

In the same vein, none of the leading staff at the Munich press was of American descent. Sergeant Ernest Wynder from West-phalia, an aspiring medical student, had come to the United States in 1938 when he was sixteen years old. In Munich, he directed the monitoring services. Sergeant Erich Winters, a former business student, led the world news section. Karl Löwenstein from New York, born in Rietberg, Westphalia, attended to technical matters. Sergeant Jules Bond and Arthur Steiner from Vienna joined the editorial board.[10]

An analysis of the contents of *Die Neue Zeitung* between 1945 and 1947 attests to the editors' cognition and approval of German culture and American democracy. They familiarized German readers with American political ideas, while at the same time catering to German cultural needs as well. Articles on German music and poetry complemented essays on U.S. elections and portrayals of American middle-class life.[11]

The German-Jewish editors of *Die Neue Zeitung* understood that Germans would never accept American culture as *Kultur* simply because it was not their own culture or their own history. While American culture represented a way of life open to anybody, the German notion of *Kultur* embodied a sacred fetish with clearly identifiable historical and Germanic roots. It exclusively embraced high culture, representing a distinct part of a country's national heritage.[12] To obtain the interest of German readers, it was therefore vital to appeal to their admiration of high culture. Such reasoning represented a natural conclusion for the Jewish émigrés. After all, German education and *Kultur* had formed their own intellectual and educational experience.

---

filled out by Hans Wallenberg, MA 1500/62, Institut für Zeitgeschichte, Munich (hereafter cited as IfZ).

9. W. P. Davison, "Building a Democratic Press," address delivered before the Nassau Club, Princeton, NJ, 8 January 1947, manuscript, RG 260, OMGUS/ISD 5/238-3/11, IfZ; interview with Peter Bönisch, Munich, 22 September 1992.

10. Gienow, "Cultural Transmission," 59–69.

11. Ibid., 108–20, 129–36.

12. For further study on the correlation between *Bildung* and *Kultur* see Georg Bollenbeck, *Bildung und Kultur: Glanz und Elend eines deutschen Deutungsmusters* (Frankfurt, 1994); Franz Rauhut, "Die Herkunft der Worte und Begriffe 'Kultur', 'Civilisation' und 'Bildung,'" *Germanisch-Romanische Monatsschrift* III (April 1953): 81–91; Todd Curtis Kontje, *The German Bildungsroman: A History of a National Genre* (Columbia, SC, 1993), 110.

The German response to *Die Neue Zeitung* proved the success of the émigrés' formula.[13] By January 1946, circulation had jumped from initially 500,000 to 1.6 million copies per issue.[14] Readers also liked to communicate with *Die Neue Zeitung*: at the end of the paper's first year, an official report counted a total of 140,000 letters to the editors.[15]

U.S. officials approved the paper's success and interfered only sporadically with the émigrés' editorial practices. Until early 1947, the War Department took very little interest in the United States' foremost mouthpiece in Germany. To U.S. officials, meeting material needs, such as food, housing, clothing, resettlement, and other issues, seemed more urgent than the dissemination of culture and information.[16] Even within the ICD, the Jewish editors' single-handed editorial course sometimes provoked harsh criticism but never any personnel change. ICD officials complained about the absence of more laudatory features on U.S. culture and history. Press officers as well as visitors from the United States noted that the paper did not look at all like an *Amerikanische Zeitung*.[17] In the end, however, other pressing concerns as well as the overwhelming appeal of the paper among German readers, dismissed any call for counteraction.

In the developing conflict, between the Western and Soviet occupation powers, during the years 1946–47, *Die Neue Zeitung* underwent a dramatic transformation. Within a few months, it changed from an almost accidental by-product of U.S. press policy to a viable instrument for information policy in all occupied zones.

13. "Public Relations," Historical Report Eastern Military District and Headquarters of the Third United States Army, 15 October to 14 November 1945, RG 260, OMGBY (Office of Military Government in Bavaria) 13/147-2/15, Bayerisches Hauptstaatsarchiv, Munich (hereafter cited as BHStA).

14. OMGBY Weekly Government Report No. 38 for week ending 31 January 1946, RG 260, OMGBY 13/142-2/4, BHStA.

15. Interview with Olaf Meitzner; Hans Wallenberg, "Dank an die Mitarbeiter. Tausend im Haus, Hunderttausende draußen," *Die Neue Zeitung*, 21 October 1946, 11; interview Alfred Fischer with Hans Wallenberg; Hurwitz, *Stunde Null*, 262.

16. Lucius D. Clay, *Decision in Germany* (Garden City, NY, 1950), 281–305f.; Wolfgang Krieger, *General Lucius D. Clay und die amerikanische Deutschlandpolitik 1945–1949* (Stuttgart, 1987), 86.

17. J. H. Hill, USFET/ICD (United States Forces in the European Theater/Information Control Division), "Control of the German Press: A Study of Nazi Methods in Relation to Democratic Objectives," 22 September 1993, RG 260, OMGBY 10/116-3/5, BHStA; letter from W. P. Davison to this author, 2 December 1993; W. P. Davison to Arthur Eggleston, *Die Neue Zeitung*, 19 November 1945, RG 260, OMGBY 10/116-3/5, BHStA.

Once U.S. officials became aware of the potential publicity power of *Die Neue Zeitung* in the unfolding Cold War, they began to wonder if the political and ethnic background of the émigrés would not interfere with the paper's job of reeducating German readers. Could an ex-German Jew convey American values to the country where he or she had been born?

Starting in January 1946, Soviet officials repeatedly confiscated cartloads of copies of *Die Neue Zeitung* designed for distribution in the eastern zone. Moreover, the Soviet Information Control Division suggested limiting the exchange of newspapers, much to the fury of the U.S. political adviser, Robert Murphy. In both cases, Soviet officials argued that the importing of newspapers from zones other than their own violated their administrative jurisdiction in Berlin and East Germany.[18]

U.S. officials interpreted such action as a breach of the principle of freedom of speech. "The Russians want to prevent the circulation in their Zone of those papers which present a political, economic, or social point of view out of line with basic tenets of Marxian [*sic*] communism, or that have been most critical of Soviet policies," Murphy's assistant, T. B. Wenner, stated furiously.[19] Criticism of the United States and headlines such as "Inconsistencies of the U.S. Occupation Authorities," "Street Battles Between Danes and Americans," or "Ten Million Americans Have No Right to Vote" in East German newspapers further stirred U.S. officials' scorn.[20]

As tensions worsened over reparations, dismantlement, Berlin, and the exchange of information material, individual U.S. officials began to consider using *Die Neue Zeitung* for propaganda purposes against the Soviet Union.[21] ICD chief Robert McClure and H. Freeman Matthews, chief of the division for West European

18. Telegram from Robert D. Murphy to Secretary of State, 2 February 1946, RG 84, Records of the Foreign Posts of the State Department, Office of the Political Advisor for Germany, Berlin, Classified Cables Sent to the State Department, 1945–1949, box 4, Washington National Research Center, Suitland, MD (hereafter cited as WNRC).

19. T. B. Wenner, "Free Speech and Press in Germany, under Potsdam. Interzonal Transmission of Newspapers in Germany," 22 July 1946, RG 84, POLAD (Political Adviser) Berlin, classified general correspondence, 1946, dec. file 891, box 122, WNRC.

20. W. P. Davison, Chief Plans and Directives Branch, to the Director of Information Control, "Increase in Frequency of *Die Neue Zeitung*," 19 September 1946, RG 260, OMGUS/ISD 5/241-1/7, Bundesarchiv Koblenz (hereafter cited as BArch).

21. Anthony F. Kleitz (OMGBY/ICD), to Chief of ICD, OMGUS, 8 April 1947, RG 260, OMGUS 5/241-1/11, BArch.

affairs in the State Department, agreed that the official press was vital for the United States' influence on German public opinion.[22] Starting December 1946, *Die Neue Zeitung* as well as selected German radio stations and the newswire service DENA (*Deutsche Nachrichtenagentur*), received special, secret instructions detailing the kind of topics and material they should publish.[23] Such memos typically pressed for the reprint or rewrite of articles on subjects ranging from denazification to atomic energy. Officials displayed particular concern about editorials on Soviet occupation policy and the union of the SPD and the KPD.[24] Finally, McClure ordered Hans Wallenberg to establish an editorial page according to the U.S. model.[25]

The leaders of *Die Neue Zeitung*, above all Wallenberg, supported the shift to anti-communism. Still, they were not ready to follow orders. The editor in particular became increasingly exasperated with his task in Munich. Editorial control as well as material shortages, such as lack of paper supply and gas, curtailed his journalistic freedom. What right did the State or the

22. H. Freeman Matthews to Secretary of State, 6 November 1946, courtesy of Harold Hurwitz, Berlin.

23. Cables from Robert Murphy to James Byrnes, 28 December 1946, RG 165, Entry 463, 014, Sec. XVII, box 236, National Archives, Washington, D.C. (hereafter cited as NA); James Byrnes to Robert Murphy, 30 December 1946, ibid.; Lucius Clay to the War Department, 28 February 1947, RG 165, War Department, CAD (Civil Affairs Division), 0007, Sec. IX, box 226, NA.

24. Douglas Waples (Lt. Col., Chief, Publications Control Branch) to Col. Kind for General McClure, "Mr. Tombs' Memoranda re Klostermann," 7 July 1946, OMGUS/ISD 5/269-1/7, IfZ; Edward T. Peeples to Hans Wallenberg, 10 July 1946, RG 260, OMGUS 5/241-1/7, IfZ; "*Die Neue Zeitung* Editorializes on the Venedey Case," 20 August 1946, ibid.; hand-scribbled note from Arthur Eggleston to Robert McClure, 22 August 1945; scribbling added by McClure, n.d., ibid.; "Notes on Trip to Berlin," 16 and 17 July 1946; Press Control Directives, August 1946, RG 260, OMGBY 10/117-2/5, BHStA; Historical Report, September 1946, OMGBY, Land Director, RG 260, OMGBY 13/147-3/2, BHStA.

25. OMGB/ID, "Reaction on the change in the editorship of *Neue Zeitung* (interrogation, reports)," "Brief from Berlin, 28 August–3 September: Reactions to New Editorial Page of *Neue Zeitung*," RG 260, OMGBY 10/71-1/8; Col. B. B. McMahon, Infantry Div., to Robert Schmid, OMGUS/ICD, Intelligence Division, 25 September 1946, RG 260, OMGBY 10/109-2/12, BHStA; "Hiroshima," *Die Neue Zeitung*, 9 August 1946, 3; John Hersey, "Hiroshima—Tatsachenbericht vom Untergang einer Stadt," repr. from *The New Yorker* in *Die Neue Zeitung*, 16 September 1946, Feuilleton; cable from Lucius Clay to the War Department, Civil Affairs Division, 14 September 1946; cable from J. G. Nyland (Maj. GSC, Administrative Officer), to OMGUS, Berlin, 25 September 1946; cable from USFA Vienna to War Department, CAD; cable from J. G. Nyland to Robert McClure, 9 October 1946, RG 165, Documents of the War Department, Civil Affairs Division, Entry 463, 0007, Sec. IV, box 225, NA.

War Department or the ICD have to censor news and editorials if they could not even provide the paper or the gasoline necessary for the venture? Such fundamental dissatisfaction turned every petty dispute between ICD officials and the editor into a major debate.[26]

While Hans Wallenberg and his staff became increasingly infuriated with their ICD superiors, ICD researchers turned increasingly critical of *Die Neue Zeitung*'s staff. Around the New Year 1947, analysts noted an augmentation of "un-American" features in the paper. The division accused the paper of disregarding American news services in favor of other obscure sources of information.[27] *Die Neue Zeitung*, one researcher found, ignored the hundreds of magazines and several thousand books available in the U.S. Information Center in Munich as well as articles offered by the Reorientation Branch of the War Department. Only six out of two hundred "reeducational" contributions submitted to the émigrés between July 1946 and June 1947 had appeared in *Die Neue Zeitung*. Cultural affairs and the rise of Hitler covered more space in the paper than news from the United States.[28]

These disputes between the editors of *Die Neue Zeitung* and their American colleagues reflected U.S. officials' mounting skepticism. Some officials such as Bernard McMahon, commanding officer of the 6870 District Information Services Control Command in Bavaria, outwardly called for a "leaven" of American personnel at *Die Neue Zeitung* to prevent World War III.[29] Even the military governor, Lucius Clay, was hesitant to continue employing émigrés in the military government because he doubted their ability to represent the United States.[30] In April 1947, Clay issued a secret

26. Gienow, "Cultural Transmission," 180–85.

27. *Die Neue Zeitung*, 30 November 1945, 4. "Functional Program for Period January 1 to June 30, 1947 (revised 1 April)," Information Control, Annex A, RG 260, OMGBY 10/112-3/1, BHStA; interviews with: Hans-Joachim Netzer, Munich, 13 December 1991; Dr. Ernst Wynder, New York City, see above; letter to this author from Andreas Gregoriades, Geneva, 6 December 1992; Habe, *Im Jahre Null*, 111.

28. Edward T. Peeples to Editors, *Die Neue Zeitung*, "Employment of Research Personnel," 13 May 1947, RG 260, OMGUS 5/315-3/12; Minutes of Stuttgart Meeting of the Exhibitions and Information Centers Branch, 11–13 August 1947, RG 260, OMGUS 5/315-3/15, IfZ; "Cumulative Annual History Report of Publications Control Branch, ICD, 1 July 1946–30 June 1947, RG 260, OMGBY 10/66-1/39, BHStA; Hurwitz, *Stunde Null*, 122.

29. Colonel B. B. McMahon (Infantry, Chief of Division) to Major General John Hilldring (Assistant Secretary of State), 21 June 1946, RG 185, Entry 463, Box 233, dec. file 014, Sec. X, NA.

30. Interview with Henry Kellermann, Chevy Chase, MD, 16 March 1994.

order urging the removal of non-American-born soldiers from military government. Earlier that year, rumors had spread in the American press that OMGUS would drop German-born employees who had been U.S. citizens for less than ten years. In May 1947, the *New York Times* reported that some officials suspected the émigrés of "using their official positions for personal ends." Clay flatly denied any rumors according to which the dismissals were "grounded in anti-Semitism." Yet he admitted that the records of the émigrés were getting "close scrutiny," and that OMGUS had already discharged four such cases.[31] Finally, in 1948, the State Department itself launched an initiative to eliminate all foreign-born Americans from the military government.[32]

Why, after two years of cooperation, did U.S. officials all of a sudden doubt and even fear the émigrés' loyalty and autonomy? In 1947, the election of a Republican congress swung American public opinion into a decisively anti-communist direction. Conservative politicians attempted to obliterate the legacy of the New Deal. Under the umbrella of anti-communism, these politicians formed an exotic coalition with religious right-wingers, Southern segregationists, and patriotic businessmen. Republicans identified anti-communism with values and customs lying at the heart of their identity. Business leaders denounced members of the labor movement as cohorts of Joseph Stalin. Southern whites applied the same charge to civil rights leaders, while conservatives of all social strata perceived working women as communist conspirators. Orthodox clergymen, finally, likened the ideological conflict to the last battle between Satan and Christ. Most importantly, both conservatives and liberals truly feared Soviet political and ideological power in the international arena and its influences at home. They believed that the successful containment of Joseph Stalin abroad required the destruction of communism at home.[33]

31. Frank A. Keating (Deputy Military Governor), to Director, OMG Hesse, "Employment and Renewal of Contracts of Naturalized American Civilian Employees," 7 April 1947, RG 260, OMGUS, U.S. Occupation HQ, box 581, file AG 49, B43, WNRC. The same directive went to the Directors, OMG Bavaria, Württemberg-Baden, Bremen. I am indebted to Guy Stern for this reference. "Geburtsland: Deutschland. Amerikaner deutscher Herkunft in der Militärregierung," *Die Neue Zeitung*, 26 May 1947, 1; Delbert Clark, "Clay Will Retain German-Born Help," *New York Times*, 5 May 1947, 5.

32. Ulrich M. Bausch, *Die Kulturpolitik der US-amerikanischen Information Control Division in Württemberg-Baden von 1945 bis 1949. Zwischen militärischen Funktionalismus und schwäbischem Obrigkeitsdenken* (Stuttgart, 1992), 79f.

33. Leffler, *The Specter of Communism*, 59–63.

In 1947, the House Un-American Activities Committee (HUAC), originally founded a decade earlier to investigate a fifth column invasion from Nazi Germany, started to uncover domestic communist influences in a series of hearings. HUAC's exposures led to the dismissal of thousands of government employees. All over the country, colleges and universities excluded lecturers. In Hollywood, popular movie stars became the most visible target group of anti-communist investigation. Public officials across the United States had to sign loyalty oaths if they did not want to lose their jobs. Anti-communist crusaders encouraged the American people to spy on their families, neighbors, and colleagues to contain Bolshevist influences at home.[34]

Back in Germany, remnants of wartime anti-Semitism may also have played into U.S. officials' perception since practically all of the émigrés at *Die Neue Zeitung* were of Jewish descent. Although there is next to no direct evidence for this, parallel developments in the United States hint at this possibility.[35] Anti-Semitism had been prevalent in the country at least since the latter part of the nineteenth century when a wave of East European Jews immigrated to the United States. Resentment ran high among Northeastern Protestants, Catholic émigrés, Southern and Midwestern populists. Racist theories fashionable around the turn of the century further stirred American prejudices against Jews. Anti-Semitism intensified markedly during the interwar period as movements and leaders such as the German-American Bund and Father Coughlin built on an ideology that vaguely linked the New Deal, the Depression, international crises, and fears of war to a Jewish conspiracy, be it capitalist or communist.[36]

34. For more on the Cold War at home, see Mary Sperlin McAuliffe, *Crisis on the Left: Cold War Politics and American Liberals, 1947–1954* (Amherst, MA, 1978); Robert Griffith, *The Politics of Fear: Joseph R. McCarthy and the Senate* (Lexington, KY, 1970); Elaine Tyler May, *Homeward Bound: American Families in the Cold War* (New York, 1988).

35. Anti-Semitism circumscribes a system of beliefs and actions "designed to distance, displace, or destroy Jews as Jews." Helen Fein, "Dimensions of Antisemitism: Attitudes, Collective Accusations, and Actions," in *The Persisting Question: Sociological Perspectives and Social Contexts of Modern Anti-Semitism*, ed. Helen Fein (Berlin, 1987), 67. I am indebted to Till van Rahden for this hint.

36. For a bibliographical summary of interpretations of anti-Semitism in the United States, see David A. Gerber, "Anti-Semitism and Jewish-Gentile Relations in American Historiography and the American Past," in *Anti-Semitism in American History*, ed. Gerber (Urbana, IL, 1986); Jonathan D. Sarna, "Anti-Semitism and American History," *Commentary* 71(March 1981): 42–47; for a survey on American Jews in the interwar period, see Leonard Dinnerstein, *Anti-Semitism in America* (New York, 1994), 78–129; Henry L. Feingold, *A Time for Searching: Entering the Mainstream, 1920–1945* (Baltimore, MD, 1992), 189–224.

Above all, immigration legislation reflected a broad consensus among Americans to restrict Jewish immigration into the United States. The U.S. Immigration Act of 1924 had already made it very hard for Jewish refugees to enter the United States. During the Third Reich, the U.S. government had never granted a specific quota to German Jews fleeing from Hitler. Instead, Jews had to immigrate under the allotment assigned to Germany. Even the Displaced Persons Act, drafted in 1948, designed to help victims who did not want to return to their home countries, favored ethnic Germans over Jewish immigrants.[37] "The word 'refugee' is synonymous with *Jew*," a New Yorker wrote to Congress in 1947, "and the *latter* is synonymous with Red!"[38]

Jews living in postwar America remained a target in an overwhelmingly Protestant and Anglo-Saxon culture.[39] Silent job discrimination continued to bar Jewish applicants from individual positions in law and business. Social acceptance in professional clubs and networks continued to be difficult for Jewish aspirants. Many Americans loathed Jews due to what they perceived as a threatening mixture of conspiratorial kinship and occult premodern customs. Others, in contrast, feared Jews precisely because they seemed to control everything related to modernity, including capitalism, big corporations, the media, and a consumer society. The war had intensified anti-Semitic feelings in the United States because isolationists increasingly viewed Jews as warmongers or at least outsiders dragging the country into an unwanted global conflict. In 1945, the psychologist Gordon Allport found that up to

37. Robert S. Wistrich, *Antisemitism: The Longest Hatred* (New York, 1991), 114–125; Richard Breitman and Alan M. Kraut, *American Refugee Policy and European Jewry, 1933–1945* (Bloomington, IN, 1987); Leonard Dinnerstein, *Uneasy at Home: Anti-Semitism and the American Jewish Experience* (New York, 1987), 197–217; Alan M. Kraut and Richard D. Breitman, "Anti-Semitism in the State Department, 1933–44: Four Case Studies," in *Anti-Semitism in American History*, ed. Gerber, 167–97.

38. Quoted in Dinnerstein, *Anti-Semitism in America*, 161.

39. David Gerber and Leonard Dinnerstein have noted a decline of anti-Semitism in the postwar period. They argue that after 1945, the horror of the Holocaust inspired Jews and non-Jews to join in a global fight against anti-Semitism. While anti-communism may have targeted individual Jews, Joseph McCarthy directed his crusade primarily against "boys born with a silver spoon in their mouth," including the Northeastern establishment and elite schools. Jews joined the fight against communism even if this required an impeachment of their religious cohorts. Yet anti-Semitism played a vital role during the "Red Scare" in the United States. Since the end of World War I, many Americans had identified Jews as silent import agents of Bolshevism. David A. Gerber, "Anti-Semitism," 34; Dinnerstein, *Anti-Semitism*, 150–174; Edward S. Shapiro, *A Time For Healing: American Jewry Since World War II* (Baltimore, MD, 1992), 28–59.

one-tenth of all Americans professed to be extremely anti-Semitic. According to his research, almost half of the American people showed at least traces of anti-Semitism and believed that Jews held too much power and influence in the country.[40]

In this situation, Jews—like communists—often became identified with everything that seemed to go wrong in American society. Already in the interwar period, various anti-Semitic groups had jumped on the bandwagon of Franklin D. Roosevelt's most fervent critics. They interpreted the New Deal—often called the "Jew Deal" —as a communist conspiracy.[41] The common Jewish intellectual bent as well as their preeminence in politics, education, and the media business caused many Americans to believe that Jews were delegates of the Kremlin.[42] Some scholars even claim that charges voiced by HUAC often involved "a trace of anti-Semitism,"[43] which culminated in the showcase trial of Julius and Ethel Rosenberg in 1950.

In 1947, the anti-communist surge stirred fundamental doubts about the existence of German-Jewish émigrés serving abroad in the name of the U.S. government. Notwithstanding their pledge of allegiance, could they be loyal to America? Could a European-born Jew who had once adhered to or perhaps still sympathized with leftist ideas, be an appropriate promoter of American life and American principles in Germany?

U.S. proconsuls working in Europe seemed to be particularly susceptible to communist infiltration. In occupied Germany the internal criticism sparked a wave of anti-communist paranoia throughout the military government. According to T. B. Wenner, an assistant in Robert Murphy's office, the entire ICD, which had become a haven for many German-Jewish émigrés, was not above suspicion due to "extreme liberalism if not 'pinkism' in responsible places" and "a wishy-washy attitude" in the implementation of

40. Frederic Cople Jaher, *A Scapegoat in the New Wilderness: The Origins of Anti-Semitism in America* (Cambridge, MA, 1994), 177–241, 246, 247; Dinnerstein, *Uneasy at Home*, 128–49, 154ff.; Shapiro, *Time for Healing*, 6f.

41. M. J. Heale, *American Anticommunism: Combatting the Enemy Within, 1830–1970* (Baltimore, MD, 1990), 105–21. For more on Jews and the New Deal, see Benjamin Ginsberg, *The Fatal Embrace: Jews and the State* (Chicago, IL, 1993), 104–19; Myron T. Scholnick, *The New Deal and Anti-Semitism in America* (New York, 1990).

42. Michael N. Dobkowski, *The Tarnished Dream: The Basis of American Anti-Semitism* (Westport, CT, 1979), 171–208; Dinnerstein, *Anti-Semitism*, 161.

43. Ginsberg, *The Fatal Embrace*, 120. This argument, however, should be considered with caution. Recent studies have rejected Ginsberg's concept of a clear link between anti-communism and anti-Semitism. David A. Hollinger, *Science, Jews, and Secular Culture: Studies in Mid-Twentieth Century American Intellectual History* (Princeton, NJ, 1996).

the U.S. information program in Germany. "ICD had not tackled the job of political reorientation and the campaign to combat anti-American propaganda as aggressively as some of us had hoped," Wenner claimed. Despite the political tensions with the Soviets, "I often hear statements to the effect that we must not proceed too aggressively lest we be accused of non-objectivity.... It is often hard to determine whether this is due to outright sympathy with the other side, or to a lack of realism." To disseminate successfully pro-American information in Germany, the division had to "clean house," Wenner suggested.[44] The scapegoat of this "housecleaning" campaign, it turned out, would be *Die Neue Zeitung*.

Meaanwhile, the editors of *Die Neue Zeitung* had come to perceive inter-Allied conflicts between the Anglo-American and the Soviet forces from quite a peculiar standpoint. While their tone represented an anti-communist stance from the beginning, it never offended the Soviets. Instead, *Die Neue Zeitung* openly criticized East German Communists, particularly the Socialist Unity Party (SED), for pouring oil on the fire and deepening the rift between the East and the West.[45] This editorial line comported well with U.S. foreign policy as long as officials such as Clay and Byrnes refused to let inter-Allied tensions break into the open.[46]

Yet as the Cold War intensified, and as U.S. officials began to consider their official media in Germany as tools against Soviet propaganda, intelligence officers questioned the loyalty of individual contributors to the newspaper. In the spring of 1946, a study initiated by the State Department stated that three men, namely Hans Wallenberg, Egon Jameson, and Arthur Steiner, ran the U.S. paper in Germany with a readership of ten million people. "None of these is a U.S. national," the report complained, notwithstanding the fact that Steiner and Wallenberg had received U.S. citizenship upon entry into the U.S. Army.[47]

A few months later, the Hearst Press denounced the famous Jewish writer Alfred Kantorowicz, an émigré from New York, as "one of Russia's top espionage agents" in the United States. Like Wallenberg,

44. T. B. Wenner, Secret Estimation, no date, RG 84, Foreign Service Posts, POLAD Berlin, Top Secret Correspondence of Robert Murphy, 1948, box 1, WNRC.

45. Gienow, "Cultural Transmission," 189–99.

46. Harold Hurwitz, *Die Eintracht der Siegermächte und die Orientierungsnot der Deutschen 1945–1946* (Cologne, 1984), 15–21, 130, 142, 161.

47. "Jim," OMGUS/ICD, to Henry P. Leverich, Chief Area V, OIC, Department of State, "Trip to U.S. Zone," 15–17 April 1946, courtesy of Harold Hurwitz; Colonel B. B. McMahon to Major General John Hilldring, 21 June 1946, RG 165, Entry 463, box 233, dec. file 014, Sec. X, NA.

Alfred Kantorowicz had been an editor for the renowned *Vossische Zeitung*. In 1931, the thirty-two-year-old had joined the German Communist Party, KPD. Two years later, he went underground and eventually into exile. After the war, Kantorowicz became a frequent contributor to the *Feuilleton* section of *Die Neue Zeitung*. Upon Kantorowicz's arrival in Berlin in early 1947, Clay himself made sure that security thoroughly checked the writer before he got any position in the postwar press.[48]

During the same year, the Jewish émigré and writer Curt Riess applied for a job at *Die Neue Zeitung*. A student in Berlin and Heidelberg, Riess had emigrated in 1933. During the war, he had been working for Naval Intelligence in Washington, D.C., and the Office of Strategic Services.[49] The Counter Intelligence Corps, however, declared him "not eligible for entry into occupied Zones" because he had befriended "leading communists."[50] Hans Mayer, a literary scholar born in Cologne, had spent much of the war in Switzerland writing for national newspapers such as *Die Tat*. After the war, he became editor-in-chief of the Hessian Radio in Frankfurt,[51] and occasionally wrote book reviews for *Die Neue Zeitung*. The Intelligence Branch of the ICD identified him as "a member of a Communist organization in Switzerland ... though he allegedly

48. *International Biographical Dictionary*, 2, 1: 593; file "Alfred Kantorowicz," MA 1500/29, IfZ; Alfred Kantorowicz, *Meine Kleider* (Hamburg, 1968), 39ff.; Alfred Kantorowicz, autobiographical summary, manuscript, John Lehmann collection, Harry Ransom Humanities Research Center, University of Texas, Austin; A. F. Hennings (Capt. Ass. Executive, USFET) to Director of Intelligence, OMGUS, "Investigation of Alfred Kantorowicz," 13 February 1947, RG 260, OMGUS 5/246-3/29, IfZ; curriculum vitae and statement by Alfred Kantorowicz, Berlin, 4 March 1947, RG 260, OMGUS 5/246-3/29, IfZ; and letter from Kantorowicz to Arthur Eggleston, 6 March 1947, ibid.; cable from Lucius D. Clay to War Department, 21 January 1947, RG 260, OMGUS 5/246-2/12a, IfZ; Jens Wehner, *Kulturpolitik und Volksfront. Ein Beitrag zur Geschichte der Sojwetischen Besatzungszone Deutschlands 1945–1949* (Frankfurt, 1992), 405–420.

49. *International Biographical Dictionary* 2, 2: 970.

50. Memorandum from Robert Murphy to Colonel Gordon E. Textor, Berlin, 3 November 1947; letter from Curt Riess, New York, to Robert Murphy, Berlin, 23 November 1947; Robert Murphy, London, to Curt Riess, New York, 5 December 1947; Gordon E. Textor, Berlin, to Robert Murphy, 5 December 1947; Huebner, EUCOM, to Chief, Public Information Division, Department of the Army, 23 January 1948; Curt Riess, New York, to Robert Murphy, 30 January 1948; Curt Riess, New York, to Major King, 30 January 1948; Memorandum from Curt Riess, Berlin, to Robert Murphy, 24 May 1948; Curt Riess, Berlin, to Lucius D. Clay, Berlin, 31 May 1948, all of the above in RG 84, Office POLAD Berlin, classified general correspondence of POLAD, 1948, box 8, WNRC.

51. *International Biographical Dictionary* 2, 2: 791.

denies any connection with the KPD of Germany."[52] Franz Roh, cultural editor for *Die Neue Zeitung* evoked similar suspicion. Roh had spent his vacation near the a scenic lake in Bavaria. Intelligence researchers quickly detected that the resort belonged to "a string of Communist-infiltrated head points" in the U.S. zone. Simultaneously, under the pretext of investigating trends in German public opinion, members of the ICD interviewed various staff members about their expectations of the impending Moscow Peace Conference in March and April 1947.[53]

American public opinion echoed these suspicions. In May 1947, numerous newspapers demanded the discharge of all U.S. soldiers of German origins from OMGUS. The *New York Times* reported that many military officials felt that the exiles "themselves were not yet sufficiently used to life in a democracy in order to give an example to the Germans." Their exposure to special "emotional influences" in German affairs impeded their actions, while the Army did not need them anymore.[54] "Only persons of American schooling and education who thoroughly believe in our American form of democracy, its Constitutional background and practices, should be our United States representatives in Germany," a group of U.S. entrepreneurs advised the secretary of war. "If we hope to bring the principles of democracy to the Germans we must send persons who will be living examples of our thinking upon government at its best."[55]

In the United States, one of the staunchest opponents of *Die Neue Zeitung* was Joseph McCarthy, the notorious senator from Wisconsin. At least three times, in 1948, 1952, and 1953, Hans Wallenberg found himself accused of communist sympathies. The charges led to a prolonged investigation of the editor-in-chief's record. Appearing before McCarthy's committee on 5 May 1953, Julius Epstein, a New York writer, accused Hans Wallenberg of

52. James O'Sheen, Lt. Colonel, Chief of Intelligence, OMG Hesse, to Chief of Intelligence, OMGBY, 6 March 1947; note by Anthony F. Kleitz, Lt. Col., Chief of Intelligence Branch, ICD, 19 March 1947, RG 260, OMGBY 15/101-3/26, BHStA.

53. "Berlin Brief on the Peace Conference," OMGBY/ICD, 17 March 1947, RG 260, OMGBY 10/69-2/11, BHStA.

54. "Geburtsland: Deutschland. Amerikaner deutscher Herkunft in der Militär-regierung," *Die Neue Zeitung*, 26 May 1947, 1; Clark, "Clay Will Retain German-Born Help," 5; Edward N. Peterson, *The American Occupation of Germany: Retreat to Victory* (Detroit, MI, 1977), 164.

55. L. M. Mac Donald, T. W. Smith Jr., Henry E. Luhrs, "Report of Representatives from the Toy Manufacturers of the U.S.A. Inc. on their trip to Germany sent to the War and the State Dept.," June 1947, RG 107, Correspondence Howard Peterson, dec. file 091 (Germany), box 7, Office of the Secretary of War, Assistant Secretary of War, NA.

membership in a Communist organization while working for *Die Neue Zeitung*. Epstein also claimed that Wallenberg had hired Communist agitators for *Die Neue Zeitung*, all of whom were of German-Jewish descent: Stephan Heym, Johannes R. Becher, F. C. Weiskopf, and Anna Seghers. Of the four writers mentioned, only one, Heym, was ever a staff member of *Die Neue Zeitung*. However, he left the paper about three months before Wallenberg received his assignment as editor-in-chief. Moreover, except for one poem by Becher, none of the four writers in question appeared in the columns of the paper after 1947. Eventually, the Wallenberg case was dismissed thanks to the intervention of Shepard Stone, Chief of the State Department's Division for Public Affairs.[56]

Nonetheless, McCarthy continued to assail the paper after the main edition closed down in mid-1953. In a hearing before Congress on 15 June 1953, the senator confronted the civilian successor of Clay, High Commissioner James Conant, with the statement that "one of the most heavily subsidized papers is run as of today by a Communist editor." When McCarthy announced a trip to Germany in 1953, he threatened to take a close look at the paper. In a letter to John Foster Dulles, he fiercely opposed the funding for the German press, arguing that German editors continued to denounce U.S. foreign policy while abusing their funds, roughly three million dollars per annum, for communist purposes. Officials from the State Department refuted these charges.[57]

56. *New York Times*, 7 May 1953, 16; Max W. Kraus, Silver Spring, MD, to the editor of the *New York Times*, 7 May 1953, Max Kraus collection, 92/09/105-5-14, SHGB; "Statement by Hans Wallenberg," 7 May 1953, ibid.; "Statement by Ernest J. Cramer," 7 May 1953, ibid.; Hans Wallenberg to Max Kraus, Wheaton Hills, MD, 17 July 1953, ibid.; "Kaghan verteidigt Wallenberg vor dem McCarthy-Ausschuß," *Die Neue Zeitung*, 6 May 1953; "HICOG zu den Vorwürfen gegen Wallenberg. Volle amtliche Billigung seiner Tätigkeit," *Chronik der Arbeit*, 8 May 1953; "Epstein zu seinen Äußerungen über Hans Wallenberg," *Die Neue Zeitung*, 11 May 1953; "Shepard Stone weist Angriffe gegen Kaghan und Wallenberg zurück: Brief des ehemaligen HICOG-Beamten an die 'New York Times,'" *Die Neue Zeitung*, 12 May 1953; "Bitterer Lorbeer," *Der Spiegel* 40 (30 September 1953): 14.

57. Nonetheless, shortly thereafter the State Department closed down the venture altogether, albeit for financial rather than ideological reasons. *Supplemental Appropriation Bill 1954: Hearing before the Committee on Appropriations, United States Senate, 83rd Congress, 1st Session on H.R. 6200* (Washington, D.C., 1953), 26–32, 35–36, 65–68, 73, 122; "Bitterer Lorbeer," *Der Spiegel* 40 (30 September 1953):14; "'New York Times' zu den Krediten für die deutsche Presse," *Amerika Dienst*, 29 April 1953, MF 1424 (*Die Neue Zeitung*), Bundespresse- und Informationsamt, Bonn; *Frankfurter Allgemeine Zeitung* clip, 27 April 1954, Zeitungen und Zeitschriften, dtsch. *Die Neue Zeitung* – Finanzierung, UAAB.

Ironically, German leaders also expressed concern over the suitability of the émigrés for their job, although for different reasons. German journalists accused them of being too resentful of the Germans. "We do not want to have anything to do with them [émigrés] as politicians," one W. H. Hebsacker exclaimed shortly after *Die Neue Zeitung's* inauguration. Later he added: "[I]t was obvious that during the years 1945 and 1946 the evil influence of those émigrés who had stayed abroad was still alive. They totally condemned those who had stayed in Germany in order to present their own merits in the liberation of Europe to their best advantage."[58] The émigrés displayed ignorance regarding the circumstances within Germany, CDU member Maria Sevenich charged in June 1946. "They are full of hatred and resentment. The Jewish emigration in particular has forced its views upon the foreign world.... Most of the difficulties come from those who now run around in Allied uniforms."[59]

In a way, this development underlines the most tragic aspect of the German-Jewish émigrés existence: their split identity. While they were assigned to talk of bringing together both American institutions and German philosophy and creating the necessary popular consensus, neither the German audience nor their American hosts trusted them.[60] In the eyes of their former compatriots, they had betrayed their German heritage by emigrating. They were, in fact, more American than any GI. The U.S. public, in contrast, questioned the exiles' loyalty because of their pre-exile and often socialist past—they were not "American" enough.

This no-win situation dealt a blow to many émigrés. They believed they were in a unique position to have absorbed the American spirit while still possessing a bond with their homeland. The German intelligentsia had failed repeatedly, *Die Neue Zeitung* emphasized, and new democratic ideas had to come from emigrated intellectuals. The editors pointed to the "moral and political" benefits that every returned exile brought home. They underlined their extensive experience with Anglo-Saxon democracy and their acquaintance with different cultures. "[O]ne cannot separate the émigrés from us [the Germans]," said Leopold Goldschmidt, a colorful Austrian-Jewish journalist with years of work on leading Viennese and Sudeten newspapers.[61] "In reality, we all pulled

58. Leopold Goldschmidt, "Über die Emigranten," *Die Neue Zeitung*, 22 August 1947, 5.
59. "Paraphrase zu den Wahlen," *Die Neue Zeitung*, 3 July 1946, 2.
60. Peterson, *Retreat to Victory*, 164.
61. Leopold Goldschmidt had spent the war in London, from where he returned in 1946. Until 1947, he worked for *Die Neue Zeitung* before he was licensed

together, and any artificial separation is destructive."[62] Unlike
Thomas Mann, who refused to resettle in postwar Germany, *Die
Neue Zeitung* tirelessly pointed out, "[m]ost of us DO WANT to go
home! But do you want the home comers?"[63]

After 1946 anti-communism played a significant role in OMGUS's
personnel politics in postwar Germany, creating a perplexing
friend-enemy image. As in the United States, the confrontation of
the evil within figured prominently at the top of OMGUS officials' agenda, discriminating against all things un-American.
After two years of tolerance, the occupation army could not afford
anymore to employ men and women who, like Wallenberg,
wanted to show "that he was not an American." Non-Americans
incarnated communism. It was imperative that the promoters of
the U.S. reorientation and anti-communist crusade were not only
loyal to but direct hereditary descendants of the United States.

A subtle anti-Semitism may have played into this perception
since many Americans tended to descry Jews as an incarnation of
socialism. Traditionally, Jews had represented one of many "others," the different, the potentially troublesome in American society. The war forced Americans to integrate these "strangers" into
a homogeneous, governable community, the U.S. Army. Yet the

---

as copublisher for the *Frankfurter Neue Presse*. "History of the Press Control Branch,
ICD, through June 30, 1946," RG 260, OMGBY 10/66-1/5, BHStA; *International Biographical Dictionary*, 1:234.

62. Manfred George, "Der große Ausverkauf: Ein europäisches Reise-Tagbuch,"
Die Neue Zeitung, 6 January 1947, 3; F. C. Weiskopf, "Die Schule des Exils," 29 June
1946, Feuilleton; Weiskopf, "Das deutsche Buch im Exil," 9 August 1946, Feuil-
leton; Weiskopf, "Deutsche Zeitschriften im Exil," 23 September 1946, Feuilleton;
W. Sternfeld, "Die Arbeit des P.E.N.-Clubs," 4 October 1946, Feuilleton; Weiskopf,
"Der Sprung in die fremde Sprache: Abenteuer der deutschen Exilsliteratur," 8
November 1946, 3; Weiskopf, "Getarnte Exilliteratur," 22 December 1946, 8; Weis-
kopf, "'Denk ich an Deutschland in der Nacht ... Die Themenkreise der deutschen
Literatur im Exil," 7 February 1947, 4; Karl O. Paetel, "Heimkehr," 4 January 1947,
3; Alfred Kantorowicz, "Mein Platz ist in Deutschland," 14 February 1947, 3;
Weiskopf, "'Die Heimat ist weit ...': Die Themenkreise der deutschen Literatur im
Exil (II)," 3 March 1947, 4; Weiskopf, "Haß, Ironie und philosophische Betrachtung:
Die Themenkreise der deutschen Literatur im Exil (IV)," 16 June 1947, 4; "Weiskopf, "Märchen der dunklen Zeit," 7 July 1947, 4; Leopold Goldschmidt, "Welt-
politische Rundschau: Über die Emigranten," 22 August 1947, 5. "History of the
Press Control Branch, ICD, through June 30, 1946," RG 260, OMGBY 10/66-1/5,
BHStA; *Biographical Dictionary of Émigrés*, 1: 234. For more on exile literature in
postwar Germany, see Gerhard Roloff, *Exil und Exilliteratur in der deutschen Presse
1945–1949: Ein Beitrag zur Rezeptionsgeschichte* (Worms, 1976).

63. Karl O. Paetel, "Heimkehr," *Die Neue Zeitung*, 4 January 1947, 3; Alfred Kantorowicz, "Mein Platz ist in Deutschland," 14 February 1947, 3.

German-Jewish émigrés, while contributing significantly to Hitler's defeat, never quite fit in. As long as the necessities of combat and reeducation dictated their employment, their ethnic,
historical, and political background did not affect their image
among the ranks of OMGUS. However, when inter-Allied conflicts intensified and the Soviets banned *Die Neue Zeitung* from
their zone, the State Department came to recognize the newspaper as a viable tool for inter-Allied policy and the promotion of
American ideology in the eastern zone. Simultaneously, U.S. observers began to dispute the émigrés' aptitude for their job. They
perceived the émigrés as too leftist and emotional, and therefore
inappropriate for service in the anti-communist information program. An émigré identity, many believed, implied a communist
leaning that might endanger America's self-image and mission
in Germany.

Émigrés operating in information control represented a formidable target for anti-communists. While it was hard to distinguish
a communist from an anti-communist in 1947, their actions and
their accents rendered the émigrés highly visible. In other words,
to U.S. observers the binationals' non-American origins betrayed
their leftist bent.

If anti-Semitism played a role in this context, it bore a political
meaning and defined itself mostly as a brand of anti-liberalism
coupled with nativism.[64] This complex mélange renders the historical analysis of isolated anti-Semitic elements extremely difficult. For example, after World War II there did not exist a clearly
anti-Semitic lingo. The case of the 1940s should therefore not be
confused with the many vicious, racial, and religious types of anti-
Semitism witnessed by other generations and countries. Still, it
cannot be overlooked that so many of the targets of the anti-communist purge in OMGUS were Jews.

Surprisingly, in the long run these suspicions bore few consequences; émigrés worked in the military government and, after its
dismissal, within the American High Commission in Germany
(HICOG) well into the 1950s.[65] Moreover, Jewish émigrés continued to operate in leading positions within OMGUS. Fritz E.
Oppenheimer, a Jewish lawyer from Berlin who had emigrated to

64. For the concept of nativism: John Higham, *Strangers in the Land: Patterns of
American Nativism, 1860–1925,* 13th ed. (New York, 1971).

65. Interview with Henry Kellermann and Max W. Kraus, 16 May 1994; Jack M.
Stuart, 20 March 1994; letters to this author from Ernst Cramer, 9 March 1994, and
W. Phillips Davison, 15 March 1994.

the United States in 1938, served as Clay's legal adviser in 1945–46. Felix Gilbert, a historian born in Baden Baden, enrolled as research analyst in the Office of Strategic Services and the State Department in Washington, London, Paris, and Germany. Heinz Kissinger, a student from Fürth who had emigrated in 1938, worked for the U.S. news service in Europe before he became resident officer for the district of Krefeld.[66]

Feindbilder materialize and intensify in times of crises. They serve as antidotes to self-doubts and signify the search for spiritual reorientation, political loyalty, and/or cultural redefinition. In the surge of anti-communism in postwar Germany, the increasing suspicions vis-à-vis German-Jewish émigrés fulfilled all three of these needs. Most importantly, they served as discernible if short-lived targets facilitating the distinction between "us" and "them." At a time when it was hard but imperative to define who was a Communist among the U.S. military government's own ranks, the émigrés provided an answer to the most difficult but also most momentous question of the "Red Scare": who and what was an American?

---

66. *International Biographical Dictionary*, 1: 365f, 542; ibid., 2, 1:376f. For more on "rémigrés," see Claus-Dieter Krohn, Erwin Rotermund, Lutz Winckler, and Wulf Koepke, eds., *Exil und Remigration* (Munich, 1991).

Chapter Eleven

THE GREEK LOBBY AND THE REEMERGENCE OF ANTI-COMMUNISM IN THE UNITED STATES AFTER WORLD WAR II

Peter A. Zervakis

Introduction

S cholars of American immigration have emphasized the stunning fact that many first-generation Americans have somewhat
paradoxically been able "to become assimilated into U.S. culture
yet still retain enough ethnic identification to pursue foreign policy
objectives affecting [their] old countries."[1] Immediately after World
War II and shortly before the onset of the Cold War the political
activities of organized Greek-Americans regarding their home
country seemed especially promising; after all, they had loyally
fought alongside their fellow Americans during the war, and thus
achieved a status as freedom-loving allies. Moreover, after
Franklin Delano Roosevelt's death, American foreign policy found
itself in a state of instability. Roosevelt's successor, Harry S. Truman, lacked foreign policy experience; after the demobilization of
American troops in Europe there seemed to be no guidelines to

---

I wish to thank Mr. Mathias Eberenz, M.A., for his assistance in translating this
chapter and for his helpful criticism.

1. Mohammed E. Ahrari, ed., *Ethnic Groups and U.S. Foreign Policy* (New York,
1987), xvi.

determine the future role of the United States in foreign policy. A U.S. Congress more concerned with budget cuts than with foreign affairs, as well as a public opinion more engaged with domestic affairs than with overseas events, influenced foreign policy making at the top level in a way that led to sometimes contradictory decisions when it came to counteracting the obstructive Soviet course of action in the European peacemaking process.

It was only after Truman's "Special Message to the Congress"[2] of 12 March 1947, better known as the Truman Doctrine, that the "postwar confusion" (Patricia D. Ward) ended. Truman, citing communist subversion that threatened to decide the outcome of the Greek civil war, announced a $400 million, mainly military, aid package to Greece, thus for the first time effectively engaging the U.S in the eastern Mediterranean. This was followed shortly thereafter (in June 1947) by the Marshall Plan, which was designed to aid in the economic recovery of non-communist Europe, and by the North Atlantic Treaty Organization (NATO), a military and political anti-Russian defense alliance that was founded on 4 April 1949 and in which Greece and Turkey were included on 18 February 1952. The new concept of standing firm against the perceived communist aggressor was labeled "containment" by George F. Kennan, whose historical analyses on the expanding nature of the Soviet Union were eagerly translated into action by the Truman administration. To justify the reckless use of the instruments of a "Preponderance of Power" (Melvyn P. Leffler), Truman employed a strategy of ideological polarization that contrasted pluralistic European democracies with communist totalitarianism (for the moment, however, without pointing his finger at the Soviet Union). The Greek civil war, a minor political conflict at that time, was taken as an opportunity to manifest U.S. partisanship for the "legally elected" Greek government. The Truman administration was thus able to successfully reawaken prewar anti-communist sentiments ("Red menace") in the American public because it could rely on the existence of widespread, subliminal fears of a communist conspiracy within American society that was believed to threaten America's very social and economic system. This enemy image, then, led to the demise of the liberal forces of the Roosevelt coalition and, ultimately, to the infamous McCarthyism that helped the American as well as the Greek anti-communist

2. "Special Message to the Congress on Greece and Turkey: The Truman Doctrine. March 12, 1947," *Public Papers of the Presidents of the United States: Harry S. Truman, January 1 to December 31, 1947* (Washington, 1963): 176–180.

regimes to pursue any kind of internal opposition with the help of legal measures.[3]

It is against this background that the relevance of the Greek lobby for the resurgence of anti-communism in the United States after World War II will be discussed. Whereas historians of the genesis of the Cold War have thoroughly studied diplomatic, economic, and social events in Greece during and after Axis occupation,[4] the role of Greek-Americans during that time has long been neglected, although World War II marked a significant transformation in the political nature of the Greek Diaspora.[5] In fact, the emergence in 1945 of the Justice for Greece Committee—a political action committee—can be described as an early, self-styled attempt by the vast majority of the only temporarily united ethnic Greeks in the United States to support their old homeland, effectively ending uncertainties about Greece's postwar geopolitical disposition between East and West.[6]

This chapter is composed of four sections: (1) In order to fully understand the motives of the Hellenic Diaspora acting on issues relating to Greece it is necessary to first consider the ambiguous feelings of Greek-Americans toward their native land and how these old ties led to the formation of the Greek lobby in the U.S. (2) It is then useful to take a close look at the extent to which World War II, consequently, changed American public opinion toward organized Greek-Americans. It was only with the help of receptive American public opinion, it will be argued, that it was possible to launch the Justice for Greece Committee in 1945. (3) The ways and means with which the Justice for Greece Committee managed to influence public perception of the Greek postwar situation will be explained. (4) Finally, the extent to which the Greek lobby actually succeeded in contributing to a revival of anti-communist sentiments in the immediate postwar era will be discussed.

3. Minas Samatas, "Greek McCarthyism: A Comparative Assessment of Greek Post-Civil War Repressive Anticommunism and the U.S. Truman-McCarthy Era," *Journal of the Hellenic Diaspora* 13, 1 and 2 (1986): 5–75.

4. For a recent annotated bibliography see Howard Jones and Randall B. Woods, "Origins of the Cold War in Europe and the Near East: Recent Historiography and the National Security Imperative," *Diplomatic History* 17, 2 (Spring 1993): 251–76.

5. See Alexandros K. Kyrou, *Greek Nationalism and Diaspora Politics in America, 1940–1945: Background and Analysis of Ethnic Responses to Wartime Crisis* (Ann Arbor, 1993).

6. For further reference see Peter A. Zervakis, *Justice for Greece. Der Einfluß einer gräkoamerikanischen Interessengruppe auf die Außenpolitik der USA gegenüber Griechenland, 1945–1947.* Studien zur modernen Geschichte; 47 (Stuttgart, 1994).

The Formation of the Greek Lobby

The entire number of Greek immigrants up to the outbreak of World War II amounted to approximately half a million. Still, compared to figures from countries like Italy, Ireland, or Germany, Greek immigration represented only 1.3 percent of the entire European immigration to the U.S. The great majority of these Greek immigrants consisted of economically underprivileged males from rural Greece.[7] Most Greeks settled in the urban centers all across the U.S., mainly in the so-called mill towns of New England. Others went to major cities like Chicago or New York, where they found employment as unskilled workers. In the urban centers, Greek ethnic neighborhoods were soon formed that came to be known as "Greektowns." Within these neighborhoods Greeks also organized their various regional societies and their Orthodox Church communities, of which there were some four hundred (with about three hundred thousand paying members) all over the country around 1945. Organizing these *topiká somateía* appears to have been a Greek-American mania. The groups' membership figures were usually closely tied to the local strength of Greek immigrants from a particular region in Greece. As was the case with other immigrant groups, a tight community centered around churches helped to retain the group's cultural identity. Not surprisingly, the Greek Orthodox Church, a close family, and the clubs became the institutions most likely to resist Americanization. At the same time, however, this kind of community life promoted social isolation of the group as a whole, and thus led to certain anti-Greek resentments among those Americans who showed little understanding for the "oriental" way of life.

Although Greek-American newspapers, reporting on anti-Greek riots, advised their readers to familiarize themselves with the American way of life, many Greek immigrants still felt a close affinity toward their own version of an expansive nationalism as a collective identity, the *Megáli Idéa* (Great Idea). By 1907 they had already founded more than one hundred organizations of Greek expellees. That same year, the first nationwide Greek-American society (the Panhellenic Union) was organized by the Greek ambassador to Washington, whose intent it was to link

7. Roger Daniels, *Coming to America: A History of Immigration and Ethnicity in American Life* (New York, 1990), 201–6. Of the major European ethnic groups Greeks had the highest proportional amount of male immigrants (87.8 percent), and they were also most likely to return to their home country (53.7 percent).

the Greek Diaspora closely to the government of Greece. At the time, Athens regarded the Greek colony in the U.S. as an integral part of its own Greek population; Greek immigrants, therefore, had all the rights and duties of ordinary Greek citizens. Little was done by the Panhellenic Union, however, to aid Greek immigrants in practical matters. With the onset of World War I and the political turmoil in Greece, the Union disintegrated.

During the war Greece was deeply split between two political camps and their respective leaders: whereas King Constantine I wanted Greece to maintain a friendly neutrality toward Imperial Germany, his antagonistic prime minister, the stoutly liberal Eleftheros Venizelos, favored a Greece more actively involved with its Western allies. He also fought for a modern constitutional republic. This schism between conservative "royalists" (supporters of the monarchy) and liberal "Venizelists" (supporters of the republic) was well reflected among the Greeks in America and in their organizations and newspapers for more than half a century. As time went by, however, more and more Greek immigrants began to appreciate the advantages of U.S. citizenship. As fellow citizens they were more easily accepted by Americans, and their journeys to Greece were facilitated, as they could then return to the States, avoiding the strict immigration quotas (they could even take their Greek spouses with them). While around 1910 only 6.8 percent of all Greek immigrants had acquired U.S. citizenship, by 1920 the figure had gone up to 16.6 percent. By 1930 as much as 49.9 percent of all Greek immigrants had become U.S. citizens.[8] In spite of this formal integration, however, newly naturalized Greek immigrants developed a dual identity which was pitted against an ever increasing pressure to Americanize. Greek immigrants respected American democratic traditions and values and supported the U.S. during World War I financially and by serving in the U.S. Army. Yet they still retained much of their traditional way of living. Moreover, they often followed Greek representatives and politicians unquestioningly and lobbied vehemently for their country of birth.

Americans resented these political activities of organized immigrant groups, especially if these immigrants came from European countries which had opposed the Western Allies during World War I. During the second decade of the twentieth century, America, leaning heavily toward isolationism, was swept by a wave of

8. Theodore Saloutos, *The Greeks in the United States* (Cambridge, MA, 1964), 239 (hereafter cited as Saloutos, *Greeks*).

Americanism.[9] While there was an official avoidance of the metaphor of the melting pot because it was feared that immigrants
might easily link this concept to the destruction of their ethnic cultures, it was, however, widely held that immigrants were to "blend"
into a superior Anglo-Saxon culture. Nativists tried to lock out of
the political system immigrants who, it was felt, had not become
"true" Americans. As a result of this form of xenophobia, American immigration laws increasingly stiffened between 1917 and
1924, the year in which legislation was passed to drastically reduce the further influx of Asians and eastern as well as southern
Europeans. Newly arrived immigrants and those suspected of
being subversive or disloyal to America were confronted with
nativism ("hyphenated Americanism").[10]

In the meantime a new supra regional Greek-American organization tried to overcome both Greek particularism and American
nativism. This organization, called the American Hellenic Educational and Progressive Association (AHEPA), was founded in July
1922 by Greek businessmen in Atlanta, Georgia. Its articles of
incorporation and certain of its rites were meant to show white
Anglo-Saxon Americans that the members of this association were
"modern" in the sense that they respected the separation of church
and state and were loyal to the United States. "Any white male"
person could become a member, but only U.S. citizens could reach
a position of leadership within the Supreme Lodge, the highest
level of command within AHEPA. Beginning in 1924 all members
of AHEPA were required to be U.S. citizens; or at least they had to
be "willing to become such." In 1928, practically all of the 17,000
members of AHEPA's 192 local chapters were Greek immigrants;
many were also well-to-do. They had become members because
they hoped to benefit from insurance plans, but they also believed
that membership in that voluntary organization could lead to a
higher degree of acceptance among America's white middle class.
Moreover, they were keen on keeping their "Greekness" alive.
Prominent non-Greek-Americans were welcome to join the association as long as they were willing to advertise the organization
and praise the continuity of ancient Greek culture and the successes of their descendants, the Greek-Americans. They were not,

9. See Russell A. Kazal, "Revisiting Assimilation: The Rise, Fall, and Reappraisal
of a Concept," *The American Historical Review* 100/2 (April 1995): 437–71.

10. By the time of World War I the American use of the Greek "yphén" (together)
emphasized both the aspect of separation and the issue of distrusting the loyalty of
the newly naturalized citizens ("dual loyalty").

however, granted any real rights to shape the organization. AHEPA's main objective, according to article II/33 of its charter, was "to promote in the U.S. a better understanding of the Greek Nation and its People and of the ideals of Hellenism." Therefore, English was designated as the official language at the association's public events.

In the late 1920s, AHEPA leaders organized a number of social activities: they initiated classes that taught immigration and naturalization issues and rights; they conferred upon the then governor of New York, Franklin Delano Roosevelt, an honorary membership, they organized charity balls that attracted the presence of senators and other government notables, and they issued numerous calls for donations. All of these social and charitable activities certainly contributed to the growing reputation of Greek-Americans. Symbolically, in 1924 the organization had already located its headquarters in Washington, D.C., where contacts with government agencies could be more easily established. Political differences within the organization's leadership—leading to two permanent rival groups, the Venizelists and the royalists—as well as conflicts in the Greek-American community over the best way to preserve traditional Hellenic culture, ultimately resulted in the organization's inner-directness until World War II. The association's main political activity up till then seems to have been to remind its members of their patriotic duty to vote.

In terms of domestic politics, most Greek-American voters turned to Roosevelt and the Democratic Party. Also, the fact that Roosevelt talked softly about immigrants from southern Europe helped the Democrats to gain the majority of these immigrant votes, although the Democrats' immigration policy differed only marginally from that of the Republicans. Because of their small numbers, Greek-American voters (unlike the Germans or the Italians) never had a decisive influence upon elections; however, politicians of all parties sought the Greek-American vote. While radical socialist or communist ideas and movements found supporters among some Jews, Italians, and Russians, very few Greek-Americans showed sympathy for these ideas. This can be partly explained by the Greek-Americans' main preoccupation with Greece and the schism over the Greek monarchy, which cost them a lot of energy and had little to do with class conflict.

The situation changed, however, when the first Greek dictatorship (1936–1941) under Ioannis Metaxas began to use immigrants and their organizations in the U.S. for its propaganda activities.

Representatives of the authoritarian right-wing Greek regime, which constantly prosecuted all suspected communist activities within the trade unions, sought close contacts with the representatives of the major Greek-American organizations, especially with the conservative part of the leadership of AHEPA, to win the support of Greek-Americans. But the homeland Greeks failed to establish a popular base for the Greek dictator in the U.S. As a consequence, in 1939 the relationship between Athens and the Greek-American community deteriorated dramatically when AHEPA dissociated itself from the dictatorship in Greece. It was feared among Greek-Americans that Metaxas, because of his fascist sympathies, would lead his country into an alliance with Nazi Germany.

World War II and the Emergence of the Justice for Greece Committee

Until World War II began to affect southeastern Europe, the American public cared little for the peculiarities of its "national minorities." This attitude, however, changed strikingly when the media pitted democracy against fascism at the onset of the war. With the unexpected, successful resistance of the Greek Army to the Italian invaders in the Epirus Mountains, Greeks were used ideologically. The "Greek miracle in Albania," which began with the famous "*óchi* (no)" of Metaxas against the ultimatum set by the Italian ambassador to Athens on 28 October 1940—a date since turned into a national holiday in Greece—led overnight to a more positive image of Greeks in the U.S. media and among the general public. The dictator, Metaxas, became a Greek national hero. *Life* magazine, for example, on 16 December 1940, presented on its front page a Greek infantryman (*eúzonos*) of the elite corps of the Greek Army in his traditional costume, and declared: "The Amazing Greeks Win Freedom's First Victory."

Greek-Americans were able to take an active interest in their native country's affairs with full public consent. Within Greek communities at the time people said: "I'm proud to be an American and I'm proud today that I'm a Greek."[11] All Greek-American organizations were united in their effort to alleviate hunger in occupied Greece. Also, many Americans of non-Greek back-

---

11. Saloutos, *Greeks*, 257. See Charles C. Moskos, *Greek Americans, Struggle and Success* (New Brunswick and London, 2d ed., 1989).

ground participated enthusiastically in the calls for donations. The Greek-American community, in close cooperation with the American Red Cross, thus not only saved one-third of the population in Greece from starvation but also gave a blueprint for the massive American relief of Europe after 1945.

But after the U.S. entered the war on 7 December 1941, the Roosevelt government decided to treat most ethnic groups and political migrants from occupied Europe as a political security risk. They were handled by a special secret service division subordinated to the Office of Strategic Services (OSS), the predecessor of the CIA. The Foreign Nationalities Branch (FNB) was formed on 22 December 1941 and operated from 1943 until its dissolution on 24 September 1945. This organization, which proved to be so reliable that its expertise was in high demand among all government agencies, was to report regularly on the activities of thirty-five immigrant groups within the United States, including the Greek-Americans.[12] This happened despite the fact that the Roosevelt government regularly and publicly showed confidence in the loyalty of America's nationalities and their offspring (which amounted to more than one-quarter of all Americans). Thus Greek-Americans, who found themselves being spied on by their American neighbors, colleagues, and close friends, tried passionately to demonstrate that they were able to combine a commitment to America with their Greek ethnic pride. With Greece and the U.S. having become allies in the war effort, it was only natural that both countries managed to reconcile their interests. Thousands of Greek-Americans joined the U.S. Army; AHEPA got out the word that "America comes first" and was allowed to sell war bonds valued at half a billion dollars for the U.S. government (no other ethnic organization had been granted this privilege), and Orthodox rogation services were held for President Roosevelt in all Greek-American churches.

But no consensus could be reached among Greek-Americans regarding Greece's future political order. Conservative royalists, liberal Venizelists, and a small number of Greek Communists fought over the future role of the Greek monarch, George II, who, by collaborating with dictator Metaxas, had disavowed himself. Venizelists opted for a decision by plebiscite, while the royalists,

---

12. U.S. Office of Strategic Services (OSS), *Foreign Nationalities Branch, Files, 1942–1945*, 2 vols. (Washington, D.C., 1988). See Elias Vlanton, ed., "The O.S.S. and Greek Americans," in *Journal of the Hellenic Diaspora* 9 (1982): 1–4 (hereafter cited as Vlanton, OSS).

obviously, wanted to reinstate the monarch. To their delight, the British had the same intentions, and Roosevelt usually followed Winston Churchill's advice in issues concerning Greece. Although well-informed observers reporting for the FNB were convinced that "a substantial majority" of the Greek-American community identified themselves with the "liberal Venizelists," Greek-Americans were equally guided by a new wave of deep Greek nationalism. When the occupation of Greece by the Axis threatened that country's territorial integrity, they busily made sure that Greece's postwar territorial goals were taken care of and were especially encouraged in their activities by the royalist Greek government-in-exile in London: "The purpose of this propaganda ... differs from the propaganda of previous governments in that it seeks primarily to use Greek-Americans to create public opinion favorable to Greek postwar claims. Greek-Americans are expected to spearhead the general American public's demand that Greece receive adequate relief, territorial compensation, and aid for reconstruction."[13] Many Greeks in Greece and the U.S., however, demanded not only the full restitution of Greek territorial integrity but also the irredentist expansion of Greece's frontiers; in fact, these claims contradicted the national interests of Greece's immediate neighbors—a reality often denied by ethnic Greeks. As long as the war was being waged, the question of Greek territorial claims was more or less agreed upon by all sides because Greek-Americans wanted to win the war alongside the Western Allies. Liberals and conservatives alike agreed also that U.S. support in liberating and rebuilding Greece was most welcome.

After the "liberation" of Greece by the Western Allies in October 1944, the U.S. media and government had begun to seriously consider the situation in that country. Attention was especially paid to the impending famine which needed to be relieved by food shipments. Also of interest were Greece's economic recovery and the politics of Greece's future form of government, as well as the role the British were to play in all of this. Roosevelt, although publicly declaring that the U.S. was willing to help financially, also indicated his administration's intent not to intervene in Greece's internal affairs—in spite of a memorandum by the State Department dated 23 October 1944 which recommended that Roosevelt "take a sympathetic attitude toward Greece's claims to

13. Constantine Yavis, *Propaganda in the Greek American Community: Foreign Agents Registration. War Division. Department of Justice* (Washington, 21 April 1944), Manuscript Collection, Tamiment Library, New York University: 16.

contiguous territories and islands to which she has valid ethnic and historical claims."[14] Both the Department of State and the media, however, took a critical, even hostile stance toward British imperial designs on postwar Greece. This British-American controversy lasted until mid-January of 1945 and was spurred in part by the U.S. press and its correspondents in Athens, who had been critically documenting the British intervention. Popular sentiments in the U.S., as expressed by its media, strongly opposed any American support of British foreign policy that tried to retain the British sphere of influence in the Near East.

When the British successfully intervened in Athens and finally crushed the Communist-led revolt in December 1944 (*Dekemvrianá*), traditional liberalism among Greek-Americans faded and the stout anti-communist royalists began to have their hand strengthened within their ethnic group. Like the leading figures in the OSS, Greek-Americans perceived the revolt in Athens as a first sign of the growing Soviet threat in the Balkans. While Vournas, AHEPA's archliberal president (well known within the OSS for both his anti-British and anti-communist views), tried in vain to mobilize public opinion in the U.S. against "British imperialism," the Greek-American conservative royalists gathered at that time around Victor Chebithes, Harris J. Booras, and George E. Phillies in order to form an opposition in AHEPA against the ruling "Republican" faction. In a sensational pamphlet entitled "The Order of AHEPA Under Dictatorship," Chebithes warned that AHEPA was on its way to becoming a "one-man organization" and that the organization's democratic structure was endangered since no elections had taken place since 1942. Vournas was also attacked for his unconstitutional interventions in Greek affairs in the name of the "non-political fraternity." This opposition was seconded propagandistically by Kimon Diamantopoulos, Greece's ambassador to Washington (and, according to OSS assessments "a relic of the Metaxas regime").[15]

In the early summer of 1945 Greeks in America were surprised by news of Russian designs to secure ports in the islands of the Dodecanese and by Slavo-American as well as Slavo-Macedonians claims concerning an "autonomous Macedonia." Despite the fact that Belgrade had signaled repeatedly that it was "at the moment" not interested in the Greek part of Macedonia, Greek-American

---

14. Memorandum for the Political Committee, 23 October 1944, *Foreign Relations of the United States (FRUS)*, 1945 (Washington, 1969), 8:301.

15. Vlanton, OSS, 2: 90.

royalists used this propaganda by Macedonian nationalists within the U.S. as a pretext to launch Greek territorial claims publicly. Closely following these political events in the Balkan region, the members of AHEPA planned their annual meeting for 20 August 1945 in Washington. A new president was to be elected because Vournas was heavily criticized by the conservatives for having involved the U.S. in internal Greek affairs through his political statements in the U.S. media. The newly elected president of AHEPA, Harris J. Booras, a royalist, immediately announced an aid program for Greece. He succeeded in getting the majority of the votes because he struck the right chord with AHEPA members when he lamented that Greek demands at international postwar conferences had not been met and had also not found much sympathy among U.S. government officials, who were "leftist" anyway and played into the hands of a Soviet ally, Communist Bulgaria. On 15 September the new president of AHEPA sent a first telegram to the foreign ministers of the five permanent members of the Security Council of the newly founded United Nations as well as to the Greek government. The message was formulated by Phillies and signed by AHEPA President Booras in the name of "about a million Americans of Greek descent." Referring to the principles of the Atlantic Charter, AHEPA asked those addressed to take into consideration the "just claims of Greece." With the help of the U.S. government, Greek interests were to be appropriately recognized at the decisive Allied conferences.

After exploratory talks at a meeting of all major Greek-American organizations in Chicago on 14 October 1945, Booras decided to also invite representatives of a number of regional Greek-American societies such as the Panepirots, the Panarkadians and the Panmacedonians to Washington on 30 October. The objective was to found the Justice for Greece Committee. To many nationalist Greek-Americans the failure of the London Conference of Foreign Ministers seemed to signify a partition of Europe; Greece was in danger of becoming a border country between two ideologically estranged systems. Since George E. Phillies, a lawyer in Buffalo, NY, and a personal friend of Booras, had pursued coordinated activities to convince Western powers to aid Greece in its territorial ambitions ever since August 1945, and since he had gained considerable administrative experience as former president of AHEPA, he was put in charge of the newly established committee by the convention of Greek-American dignitaries. Phillies was elected chairman and asked to take care of the organization's public relations; his Justice for Greece Committee was to begin work under the patronage of AHEPA almost immediately.

Organization and Program of the Justice for Greece Committee

Organization As a Means to Disseminate Enemy Images

The Justice for Greece Committee was formed by the then Greek conservative leadership of AHEPA and a majority of the smaller, decentralized, and extremely nationalistic Greek-American groups with strong anti-communist sentiments. The organization's ultimate purpose of existence could be inferred from its name: to fulfill the historically legitimate Greek territorial claims, to have its northern boundaries "consolidated," and to create a stronger Greece as a buffer zone between the communist East and the liberal-democratic West which would keep peace in the Balkans. Because Communist Russia seemed to be the only power opposing this concept—Russia protected an "aggressive" Bulgaria—it was absolutely necessary to win over American foreign policy makers at the postwar conferences. George Phillies' election as coordinator and managing director of the committee was not only a mark of confidence, but was also intended to secure the legality of the organization's public actions. Phillies had made his election (on 31 October 1945) subject to two conditions: during the organizing phase no statement of accounts was to be made public (so that the project was not endangered by public debate), and as coordinator he was to have the final word about the recruiting of members and the formulation of the organization's program.

Phillies, who was the only member of the committee to need a replacement in his lawyer's office during the time of its existence, created a so-called "General Committee." This committee he divided into two sub-units ("Greek-Americans" and American "Philhellenes") into which he placed two kinds of members (who were to serve different functions). The first unit consisted of AHEPA's entire Greek-American membership and all other Greek-American organizations. Phillies, AHEPA, and the Greek Orthodox Church claimed that the combined numbers of "Americans of Greek heritage" potentially backing the Justice for Greece Committee would exceed one million. This number, however, appears to be exaggerated. In 1943

U.S. Secret Service figures had estimated that between 400,000 and half a million "Greeks" resided in the United States. As the largest Greek-American organization AHEPA, in 1945, had a membership of only 21,345, which by 1946 had risen to 24,782.[16] The actual figures for membership of the other "sectional derivative societies," as these grassroots groups of Greeks originating from different regions in Greece were officially classified, are far more difficult to calculate. According to estimates by the Justice Department in 1944, there may have been some one thousand local, autonomously led voluntary associations with close personal ties to the Greek-American community and its institutions (multiple membership). To gain a nationwide popularity and to carry out the financial campaigns necessary for the realization of its activities, the Justice for Greece Committee had to rely on the infrastructure of the hierarchically organized, local AHEPA groups. The then anti-communist presidency of AHEPA, as well as all the presidents of its locally organized groups, were appointed officers. For reasons of efficiency and to save costs, the first unit was subsequently merged with a division that was to collect donations for an "AHEPA Hospital in Greece" and placed under the auspices of AHEPA's Educational and Welfare Section, which was controlled by the conservative Booras. AHEPA carried the greater part of the financial burden and coordinated the local divisions' activities. The few political activists were integrated into the General Executive Committee; individual Greek-American donors were recognized by name in AHEPA's monthly magazine.

To facilitate the organization's access to the East Coast establishment, it intended to engage prominent Anglo-Saxon Americans in a second organizational unit ("Philhellenes"). University faculties, church officials, journalists, and politicians were sought after, as their respective social position would help to articulate AHEPA's special interest within the process of policy making. Another reason to engage prominent Americans for the organization was to avoid a reputation as an ordinary pressure group. Also, it was unlikely that an ethnic organization such as AHEPA would ever accumulate enough political power to really influence the American public and the Truman government. In order to realize his ambitious goals, Phillies organized the core of the advisory committee around people like Sumner Welles, James Mead, and Robert Taft; people who were close to the Greek-American community and

16. *AHEPA Yearbook* (Washington, 1946), Order of AHEPA, 9 and Vlanton, OSS, 1: 76–77.

were willing to cooperate without pay. The public relations managers recruited from the *New York Times,* however, were royally paid for their services.

Following the advice of both bodies, Phillies, beginning 15 December 1945, sent more than 250 letters to the "honorary members" of the Justice for Greece Committee. One hundred thirty-four of those addressed were ultimately willing to cooperate with the committee, among them thirty-eight active senators, twelve members of the House, and six governors. There were also representatives of the judiciary system, the Protestant denominations, the business sector, and those of the media who could be secured to work for the committee. All of these "honorary members," including the widow of former President Calvin Coolidge, were among those citizens well acquainted with Greek classicism and therefore harbored philhellenic sentiments. They all unconditionally accepted Phillies' mode of operation, either because they liked him or because they appreciated the fact that he was apparently distancing himself from traditional ethnic interest—and left-wing pressure—groups. The mutual esteem expressed by both Greeks and Americans concerning common cultural and democratic values even found its way into the official "Briefing Book Paper" of the State Department to President Truman on the eve of the Potsdam Conference: "Classical education derived through Rome from Greece ... helped to shape the republican ideas of the emergent United States."[17] Therefore, Truman regularly invited members of AHEPA and the Greek-Orthodox Archbishop Athenagoras to official receptions at the White House because he sincerely believed "all Greeks are Democrats."[18]

The everyday operations of the committee were organized around opportunistic principles. The majority of non-Greek members were hardly ever consulted; however, their names appeared on the committee's letterhead, petitions, and resolutions, thus signalling their consent to the committee's activities. They were not even asked for financial contributions. The small number of activists moved into their offices in Washington, Boston, and New York and began to work. Advised by professional public relations experts and directed by Phillies, they developed strategies that were to influence the general public and government officials. Editors of

17. FRUS, *The Conference of Berlin (The Potsdam Conference),* 2 vols., 1945 (Washington, 1960), 1: 651.

18. Ronald H. Ferrell, *Off the Record: The Private Papers of Harry S. Truman* (New York, 1980), 25.

the *New York Times* were employed to devise information material, and the then well-known radio commentator Cedric Foster (who was quite sympathetic toward Greek-Americans) was used to spread the messages via this relatively new medium. Aside from the committee for public relations, a private agency was employed to distribute brochures and pamphlets efficiently. AHEPA head-quarters in Washington, and its regional and local offices became clearing centers for the committee's correspondence. The local offices of AHEPA also served as organizers of social events and advised the main office regarding local publicity campaigns. Between 1946 and 1947 a total of 61,200 copies of the information brochures were distributed within the U.S. and the English-speaking world. In his search for facts in favor of Greek demands, Phillies was aided by the Greek Information Bureau in New York, which was in fact a subdivision of the Greek embassy —a fact which reveals the political proximity of the Justice for Greece Committee to the Greek government.

Enemy Images Within the Program of the Justice for Greece Committee

In its programmatic publications the founders of the Justice for Greece Committee appealed to what they believed to be a philhel-lenic sentiment among better-educated Americans. They asked Americans to stand by a former brave ally in a time of need. Greece was, they argued, the only Balkan state that did not stand in contrast to the U.S. in ideological or social terms. They insisted that domes-tic problems in Greece were due merely to the usual difficulties a nation undergoes after years of occupation by a "barbaric" op-pressor. Americans did not have to meddle in these "internal differ-ences of ideology" which the Greek government would take care of in democratic elections, the fair and exemplary process of which Americans were invited to watch. These Greek-Americans strongly denied that the Greek civil war had already developed into an inter-national problem because of foreign involvement. The fact that at that time Greek royalists—stout anti-communists ready to wipe out the Greek left—were almost certain to win in the impending elec-tions was duly concealed from their American audience in order not to provoke distrust of the Greek monarchy, with its sympathies to the extreme Greek right. The true extent of the instability result-ing from the ongoing Greek civil war was not disclosed. The founders of the Justice for Greece Committee pretended to be impartial but they spoke only for the old Greek establishment. Not the "white terror" of the right extremists in Greece, but the lack of American support at international conferences was portrayed as the real cause of the "Greek problem." The legitimacy of Greek territorial claims was set forth by referring to the Greek people's early and decisive resistance to fascist aggression and their truly important role as wartime allies for the Americans. Therefore, it was only appropriate to ask for "justice." Greece deserved adequate compensation for damages deriving from the time of occupation; it deserved massive financial aid for the recovery of its economy, and it deserved assistance in boundary disputes with its neighbors, so that it could reintegrate "productive areas" "illegally" in the hands of some of its neighbors and thus eliminate its strategic vulnerability. The authors had in mind the "return" of the Dodecanese Islands, which were held by the Italians, and of "Northern Epirus," which was an integral part of southern Albania. In the case of Bulgaria, "slight modifications" along the common border were demanded.

According to the initiators of the committee (who referred to a Senate resolution of 17 May 1920), the general public as well as the U.S. government, ever since the establishment of the new Greek nation-state, had stated their support for Greece's wish to have the Dodecanese and "Northern Epirus" territories returned. They also claimed that, following historical, geographical, and ethnic criteria, an "absolute" majority of the inhabitants of these territories were Greek. Even if much mingling had been going on between Greeks and Muslims in "Northern Epirus," there was at most some bilingualism in this area. However, since all Greeks in "Northern Epirus" allegedly advocated annexation, the committee did not go into more detail as to an exact definition of the disputed territory. That region had been an issue since the Balkan Wars of 1912–13, and all Greek governments had used the unsettled "Albanian Question" ever since—even against the will of the major powers. It was hoped by the committee that the forthcoming peace conference in Paris (1946) would approve of both the "natural" right for self-determination of the "ethnic" Greeks in Albania and an agreement concerning "strategically secure" borders between Albania and Greece. To Phillies, the insecurity of the existing Greek-Bulgarian border was also an established fact because of three Bulgarian invasions into the Greek plains in Macedonia and Thrace that had occurred since 1912, causing major losses among the Greek civilian population. In order to prevent further Bulgarian aggressions, Greece, according to the authors, needed to gain control of the mountain ranges along the Greek-Bulgarian border. This, they claimed, would not result in any "serious territorial losses" for the Bulgarian state. Moreover, the inhabitants of the Rhodope Mountains were not really of Bulgarian ethnic background, but mostly Muslim Pomaks who could be easily integrated into Greece with its tiny Turkish-Muslim minority. In this way, the "organized terrorism" along the northern borders of Greece (which was known as the "Macedonian Question" at international conferences) and the Bulgarian attempts to expand into the Greek parts of Macedonia and Thrace could be stopped once and for all.

It appears that what was in fact accomplished was to lay out in English the traditional foreign policy concepts of the Greek right, who were ready to take control of the Greek government in the first months of 1946. The conformity in territorial and economic issues is all too obvious. The fact that Cyprus was not even mentioned is also of importance, especially since this issue had continually been brought to the attention of Greece's allies since 1942 by all Greek governments.[19] With the help of a democratic ideology and its anti-communist rhetoric (Albania and Bulgaria were in the process of being transformed into communist countries) the leadership of the Justice for Greece Committee hoped to convince its American audience that only a massive U.S. diplomatic intervention would lead to a greater Greece. As a Western-oriented buffer state, they argued, Greece could then oppose its communist neighbors more effectively.

The Addressees

The Indoctrination of the American Public

Phillies and his public relations specialists knew they had to reach editors and radio commentators and convince them to report on the committee's activities if they wanted to gain access to the corridors of power in Washington. They also were well aware that the targeted key figures in the media would not be taken in by simple propaganda. A fact-oriented presentation of the Greek issue, however, could do the job, leaving to the journalists the commentary

19. See Klaus-D. Grothusen, Winfried Steffani, and Peter Zervakis, eds., *Handbook on Southeastern Europe, Vol. 8, Cyprus* (Göttingen, 1997).

and assessments. Still, the Justice for Greece Committee worked like any other interest group at the time, effectively employing all available techniques of public relations. The committee published full-page ads with a list of its members on the occasion of the forthcoming conference of foreign ministers in Paris; 450 papers nationwide received portfolios full of information regarding the committee and its activities. With the help of Democrat Senator Claude Pepper, who supported the committee because of his Greek-American constituency in Florida, several press conferences were held in Washington. On the occasion of Greek Independence Day on 25 March 1946 Truman—like Roosevelt before him—was presented with AHEPA's highest order. AHEPA's president, Booras, was aided in this affair by House majority leader John McCormack (D) who came from the same state as Booras and was a member of the Justice for Greece Committee. This event was followed by other festivities organized by AHEPA in May and June that same year, as well as by the intensive lobbying activities of its active members which led to the passage of a Senate resolution calling upon the Truman administration to aid Greece at the Paris conference in getting control over "Northern Epirus" and the Dodecanese.

In February 1946 Booras learned that General Alexandros Papagos, the Greek war hero of the 1940 "miracle of Albania" (where the Greeks succeeded in halting the Italian invasion temporarily), had accepted an invitation by AHEPA to come to the U.S. Papagos, it was known, was not only popular among Greek royalists because he supported the return of the Greek king, but could also count on a friendly welcome from Greek-Americans. Booras planned to have Papagos as a guest of both AHEPA and Truman around 10 July, after which he would tour the U.S. and direct the public's attention toward the glorification of the Greek contribution to the Allied victory against the former common enemy, fascist Italy. Representative McCormack (D) and Senator McCarran (D) spoke on behalf of AHEPA at the end of June at the White House. The President, however, denied an official invitation to Papagos because such formal gestures were exclusively reserved for heads of states. Still, it was agreed that "every courtesy" was to be extended to this "distinguished foreign visitor." At the White House reception, Papagos met President Truman and received a medal of bravery from the hands of the popular Commander-in-Chief of U.S. troops in Europe, General Dwight D. Eisenhower. He was also received by both houses of Congress, where he was introduced by Booras.

According to an internal note sent to Truman's advisers by the State Department, American diplomats had voiced "no real objection" regarding Papagos's and AHEPA's visit to the White House. However, they did point out that there existed several other Greek-American organizations besides AHEPA and asked "does the White House wish to favor this particular one?" "No," was the answer from the White House, written in pencil and dated 8 July.[20]

During the first six months of the Greek-American Committee's campaign, U.S. media reaction was rather sparse. The *New York Times* featured two brief stories in March–February of 1946 on the program of the Justice for Greece Committee (fully in accordance with Phillies' wish not to disclose the Greek-Americans operating behind the scenes). Sumner Welles proved to be an active member of this ethnic interest group, asking for American intervention in his regular and detailed commentaries in the *New York Herald Tribune* on the occasion of the meetings of foreign ministers and the forthcoming peace conference. He, too, wanted "to make sure that … Justice [sic] is done to Greece" (6 March 1946; 10 April 1946). Of the local or regional papers, the *Buffalo Courier Express* was first (23 February 1946) to carry the "Justice for Greece" appeal on its editorial page. The Greek-American press, of course, euphorically celebrated in its editorials even the scantiest mention of the Justice for Greece Committee in the general press. Toward the end of August, Phillies intensified the campaign, regularly contacting by mail or phone the editors of the leading national papers and urging them to comment on the issue as defined by the committee. AHEPA members were asked by Booras to write letters to the editors of their respective local papers.

The editors of the major papers, although generally willing to "seriously consider" the committee's requests, could not be convinced by the "information" presented to them to fight the committee's cause and support Greek territorial claims. Even if the number of reports on the committee and the Greek question increased over the second half of 1946, American journalists preferred to discuss ideological rather than territorial issues. It was as the one remaining democracy in the Balkans (and surrounded by hostile communist neighbors) that Greece was of interest to them. Regional and local papers, however, were much more sympathetic toward Greece's territorial ambitions. In these papers, editors lauded the committee for being a factor in the successful cultural

20. Handwritten notice from 8 July 1946, Truman Official File, Harry S. Truman Library.

approximation between Greek-Americans and more established Americans, thereby overlooking the relevance of some of the real issues the committee was trying to advocate.

In contrast to the optimistic reports released by the Justice for Greece Committee itself, in which the impression was given that since 1946 the U.S. media was clearly supportive of the Greek point of view, the efforts by Greek-Americans and their Anglo-American supporters were of little consequence. At no time did they really succeed in gaining front page coverage in the nation's leading papers. One of the reasons why the organization was unable to reach a broader U.S. audience had to do with the nation's general unwillingness to react toward foreign policy issues at the time. Another factor was the difference in evaluating the situation in Greece between members of AHEPA and U.S. opinion leaders. American politicians and opinion makers usually set up moral guidelines for the nation's foreign policy whenever U.S. interests were not directly involved—as was the case with Greece. Therefore, it was possible at times to describe Britain's policy in the Balkans as "imperialistic power politics" and temporarily deny the British any further credit funds. It was left to Winston Churchill, then a private citizen, to direct the attention of the American public opinion to Soviet expansionist ambitions and the growing polarization between Soviet Russia and the Western democracies in his momentous "iron curtain" speech, delivered on 5 March 1946 in Truman's home state of Missouri. The term "Red menace" became socially acceptable again, and the "Greek problem" would now be seen in a different light. In the U.S. media, the Greek civil war turned into an arena of ideological dispute where communist and democratic interests clashed. After the Paris peace talks, the demands by the Justice for Greece Committee for a territorial compensation of postwar Greece appeared out of question to the U.S. media; they did not fit the image of a "freedom-loving" Greece "with its immortal glories" that was being taken over by the communists. "Justice for Greece" acquired a different meaning to many in the U.S. media. The *New York Times*, for example, on 27 August 1946 called Greece "the only citadel of freedom east of Russia's iron curtain." Truman accepted Churchill's rhetoric because he intended to shift his administration's course of action toward a more assertive foreign policy. The enemy image of an aggressive Soviet Union came in quite handy. Nor was it surprising that George Phillies and his committee, during the second half of 1946, tried to utilize this new anti-communist trend to fulfill their mission of Greek territorial expansion.

The Anti-Communist Congress

Although the Justice for Greece Committee officially intended to exert only "indirect" pressure on Congress and the Truman administration, they did, however, secure early on the cooperation of twelve House members and thirty-six Senators, all of whom agreed to become a member of this Greek-American interest group. Since the majority of the cooperating members of Congress were on the Democratic side in the election year of 1946 (21 Democrats vs. 13 Republicans), and since it was expected that the number of Republicans in Congress would rise after the election, AHEPA feared that it would lose some of its influence.

One of the most active supporters of Greek territorial ambitions in the U.S. Congress was Democratic Senator Claude Pepper from Florida. Ever since August 1944 Pepper had unsuccessfully attempted to introduce a resolution in support of a Greek annexation of the Italian occupied Dodecanese (which were inhabited mainly by Greeks). In February of 1945 he added "Northern Epirus (including Korytsa)" to his Resolution No. 82, but he was again unable to officially introduce it in the Senate. Senate Resolution 82 had its historical roots in a similar Senate resolution (No. 324) introduced by Senator Henry Cabot Lodge and passed without objection on 17 May 1920. At that time, a number of Greek immigrants based in New York had initiated the resolution. Senator Pepper's sympathy for Greece can be explained primarily by the fact that his electorate consisted to a considerable degree of immigrants from the Dodecanese who had settled in Tarpon Springs and who vehemently argued for the annexation of their islands by Greece. Also, in 1945 Pepper had seen firsthand the destruction in Europe and had spent a few days in Athens. On his return to the U.S., Pepper asked President Truman for U.S. economic aid to Greece and support for its territorial claims. Moreover, when visiting the Nuremberg war crimes trials, Pepper had listened closely to General von Brauchitsch's historically doubtful claim that it had been due to the Greek and Yugoslav resistance that Germany's attack on Soviet Russia had to be postponed for at least six weeks, which meant that the resistance had proved invaluable to the Allied cause, as the German campaign subsequently ran into the Russian winter. Pepper therefore considered Greek territorial claims as just compensation for its soldiers' "brave" war efforts. A member of the eroding left wing of the Democratic party and ironically referred to as "Red Pepper" by political opponents, Pepper decidedly opposed Churchill's confrontational policy. He got himself into trouble with the State Department when after having personally met Stalin he became a believer in the dictator's "peaceful" ambitions and had later teamed up with Truman's former Secretary of Trade Henry Wallace to oppose the military part of Truman's aid package to Greece. In close cooperation with the Greek ambassador to Washington Kimon Diamantopoulos, the Justice for Greece Committee decided in February 1946 to support Pepper's resolution—despite the fact that the border changes between Greece and Bulgaria fought for by the Greek-American interest group were not even mentioned in the resolution.

Every week between November 1945 and April 1946 Phillies spent three to four days in Washington to present his point of view before more than fifty senators. The senators were mainly interested in ideological and strategic issues. To them, Greece was an "outpost in the outer defenses of democracy."[21] Of considerable help to Phillies were two Greek-American aides to Democratic senators, Jerry Dragonas and Michael Manatos, the second of whom was to work his way up in the Kennedy and Johnson administrations. Together with Pepper, Robert A. Taft ("glad to do honor to good soldiers"), and other senators, they officially introduced the resolution to the Senate and were able to pass it on 27 March 1946, two days after AHEPA had honored Truman at its banquet. But because of the forthcoming conference of foreign ministers in Paris, House Resolution No. 136 was not immediately made public. Phillies contacted important senators between 23 and 25 July and found out that Senator Barkley had voiced certain objections regarding the resolution (he was referring to statements by Secretary of State James F. Byrnes). Phillies then asked Pepper to talk this issue over with Byrnes. Finally, on 29 July, two days before another meeting at the Paris Peace Conference took place and four days before the Senate's summer recess, Phillies was able to have the so-called "Pepper Resolution" (Senate Resolution 82) passed without any adverse vote.[22] Exaggeratingly hailed by both Greek diplomats and Greek-Americans alike as "the most potent force from America at the Peace Conference,"[23] Phillies had

21. *AHEPA National Conferences, Proceedings* (Washington, 1946), 277 (hereafter cited as *AHEPA, Proceedings*).

22. U.S. Congress, Congressional Record (CR), 92nd Cong., 2d sess., 1946, 2644.

23. Report of George E. Phillies, "The Justice for Greece Committee" to the 22d Annual Convention of the Order of AHEPA (August 1948), George E. Phillies

pushed the resolution through the Senate systematically, employing every classic means of lobbying: festivities (organized by AHEPA), letters, telegrams, and personal interventions. And by his introducing the resolution very shortly before the Senate's summer recess, Bulgarian-Americans and Albanian-Americans were given virtually no chance to respond or intervene in time.

The Greek-American action committee was again successful when both houses of Congress passed a common resolution in favor of Greece and the Greek-Americans. Much rhetoric accompanied these declarations, especially in the House, where Representatives Chester E. Merrow (D) and William H. King (D)—both having already shown their sympathies toward AHEPA in the previous years—argued outspokenly for more "justice for Greece," relying heavily on the publications by the Justice for Greece Committee. Their speeches were included in the Congressional Record, as was a petition to both Truman and the Senate initiated by Phillies and introduced by Senator Mead (D). In it, the U.S. government was urged to support Greece's territorial claims at the Paris Peace Conference.

Phillies' most influential addressee in the Senate was undoubtedly Republican Senator Arthur H. Vandenberg, then a member of the important Committee on Foreign Relations. Vandenberg, having turned into an outspoken internationalist after the war (he had been an equally outspoken isolationist before) with deep anti-Soviet feelings, influenced by the eastern European ethnic mixture of his home state, had made himself known as the architect of a so-called "bipartisan foreign policy" (David R. Kepley). This consensual approach in foreign policy issues between Republicans and Democrats was maintained for the time being because of his close cooperation with Senator Tom Connally (D), the Secretary of State, Byrnes, and the president. Consensus was thus often reached before an issue arrived at the legislative level. Vandenberg felt strongly that the U.S. would be able to convincingly demonstrate its role as a superpower opposed to Moscow and to avoid another world war only if the president was backed by Congress in foreign policy issues. Since his speech on 27 February 1946 on the Senate floor, Vandenberg had been in accord with Truman and Byrnes—but ahead of public opinion—with his demand "for a new policy of firmness toward the Soviet Union." As the Republican's foreign policy spokesman, he took part in the constituting session of the United Nations. Both he and Connally had represented the U.S. at the Paris Peace Conference of 1946. The Truman administration regularly consulted him; the State Department played up to him, trying to evade his potential criticism and seeking his cooperation (since Vandenberg had become chairman of the Senate Committee on Foreign Relations in November 1946 Republicans, many of them anti-communists, had become the majority in Congress).

Even if most Greek-Americans traditionally leaned toward the Democrats, the Greek royalists Booras and Phillies knew full well that their cooperation with Vandenberg was of great significance, for Vandenberg, as of 1947, was not only the Republican majority leader in the Senate but also stood a fair chance of winning against Truman in the 1948 elections. What better ally to have? Vandenberg, however, thought it politically "unwise" to formally join the Justice for Greece Committee because he did not want to appear politically biased. Early in March 1946 Phillies and Vandenberg had begun an intensive exchange of letters in which the senator proved to be a skilled tactician. Vandenberg managed to fit the interest group's program into his world-view while at the same time adjusting the organization's program to his needs. He promised to work for the solution of the Greek issue as long as this did not interfere with U.S. security interests vis-à-vis an ever expanding Soviet-type world communism. In his correspondence with Phillies, Vandenberg slowly but surely managed to push the issue of Greek territorial ambitions into the background, instead putting the emphasis on Greece's political integrity. To him, "Justice for Greece" could best be achieved by a well-meant rhetoric: "Since I met those two Greeks [Phillies and Booras], I have become a Greek myself."[24] Phillies for his part recognized Vandenberg's intentions and at the end of May 1946 used them opportunely for his own discussion of the issue, attributing to the territorial claims an ideological meaning. His warning of what would happen if these claims were not taken seriously was, however, in vain:

> In pleading it [the cause of Greece] as an American who has *primarily America's future and her best interest in mind, I sincerely believe:* 1) That henceforth America and not Great Britain will be the Master

24. *AHEPA, Proceedings, 1946,* 308.

of, and responsible for, the "Seven Seas"... 2) It behooves American ... economy and security to have these routes kept open for trade and safe ... 7) Everybody knows that Greece is the border line state, and, as such, the proving ground of the two ideologies which vie for predominance. 8) The Greek people are fundamentally democratic. They love America. They want to be America's proud friends. But the little nation is seething with infiltration of Soviet propaganda and influence.... 10) It is a historic fact that Greece has been wronged in the last war. The Communists will use the argument as their clarion call if Greece be wronged again. 11) ... there are bound to be political dislocations and economic upheavals in Greece if her Delegates return to Athens empty-handed or simply with the rocky Dodecanese as a token satisfaction. 12) In that event the brave ally of America and Great Britain ... will go Communistic. 13) Please keep the "swinging door" of Eastern Mediterranean open for our American boys and our American way of life.[25]

At the Paris Peace Conference, Vandenberg consequently argued for Greece's wish to annex the Dodecanese Islands—against strong Russian opposition. As for the tiresome issue of "Northern Epirus," he and Secretary of State Byrnes pleaded for an adjournment in order not to challenge unnecessarily Albania, which was not treated as an enemy state, although representatives of the Greek government furiously opposed this decision. Vandenberg also had a hand in efforts to make Italy and Bulgaria pay reparations to war-torn Greece. Yet on 29 November 1946, after the official closing of the conference (the New York Conference of Foreign Ministers was still under way) and after he had clearly won election to the Senate, Vandenberg suddenly halted his support for Greece's territorial claims. A subdued Phillies wrote to Vandenberg: "Your personal advice and guidance will be appreciated."[26] Still, as Phillies was to learn only later, Vandenberg remained a significant player on this issue even on the eve of the Truman Doctrine. When President Truman met secretly with congressional leaders on 27 February 1947 to ask for their support for a massive aid program to benefit Greece and Turkey, Vandenberg demanded that the president personally speak before both houses of Congress and publicly link the program to the Soviet-style communist expansion threatening the free Western world.

25. Phillies to Vandenberg, 28 May 1946, in *George E. Phillies Papers*, box 4, Manuscript Collection, Harry S. Truman Library (hereafter cited as *Phillies Papers*). Emphasis in original.

26. Phillies to Vandenberg, 14 December 1946, *Phillies Papers*.

Greek-American Anti-Communism and the Truman Doctrine

Around February 1946 members of the Justice for Greece Committee began to mail "information" about their organization to the White House and the different government departments. The recipients regularly forwarded these messages to the Near Eastern Division of the State Department, as this administrative unit was in charge of the peace negotiations. Early in February 1946 Phillies and Chauncey J. Hamlin, the Anglo-American "chairman" of the Greek-American Committee, who also happened to be Phillies' close friend from Buffalo, personally visited officials of this division at the old State Department office building to discuss informally their programmatic ideas. At this occasion they also met with Under Secretary of State Dean Acheson and Secretary of State James F. Byrnes, as well as some of their staff. Their talks were rather informal. Later, however, while formally seeking advice on how to proceed in the Greek territorial question at the State Department, Phillies gave them to understand the position of his committee, which was "… that the State Department will not act correctly with respect to the interests of Greece unless public pressure is brought on the Department."[27] The bureau chief of the Near Eastern division at the time, William Baxter, assuring Phillies that he too preferred a "strong, independent [and] democratic Greece,"[28] acknowledged the receipt of the informational material while otherwise avoiding any further comment.

This reaction did not prevent Phillies from telegraphing the State Department on 22 March 1946, listing the reasons why Greek-Americans would insist on carrying out their territorial ambitions: the Allied victory would not have been possible without the assistance of Greece and a number of smaller states; rejecting the territorial claims would shake Greek-American confidence in the great powers' fairness; a pragmatic Russia wanted to see friendly and strong states at its periphery—a factor of insecurity for Greece in relation to its northern neighbors; the impending passing of Resolution 82 stood in direct relationship to the new "policy of firmness," as proclaimed by Byrnes at American-Russian negotiations over Greek territorial claims. Moreover, Greece's strategic location, its ideological reliability, its traditional economic ties to the Balkans

27. Phillies to Baxter, 12 February 1946, RG 59, 868.00/2-946, National Archives (hereafter cited as NA)
28. Baxter to Phillies, 14 February 1946, RG 59, 811.001 Truman (MISC), NA.

and the Near East, as well as its natural resources, should provide
enough motives for the U.S. to take an active interest in a "strong
and secure Greece" that would "guarantee" peace in the Balkan
region.[29] Charles Merriam, Baxter's successor, in his answer to the
Justice for Greece Committee on 15 April 1946, promised: "It is the
firm intention of this government that Greece's claims be given
thorough consideration at the final peace settlement."[30] At its own
expense and without identifying the source, the committee immediately published this answer in the Congressional Record, treat-
ing it as an official statement by the State Department.[31] Merriam
contacted the legal branch of the State Department to explore
whether the publication could be legally challenged. The lawyers,
however, were unable to find any violation of the law by the
Greek-American interest group. More letters and telegrams to
Byrnes and Truman followed, in which it was pointed out that the
Greek people were worse off than others in postwar Europe.

Both the Justice for Greece Committee and the newly elected
Greek royalist government in Greece under Konstantinos Tsal-
daris hoped that the Anglo-American delegates to the second
meeting of the foreign ministers on 25 April (which was to prepare
the peace treaties with the former German allies) would put
Greece's territorial claims on the agenda.[32] At the beginning of the
conference, Secretary of State Byrnes, having shown his sympathy
for the Greek position in Paris, was reluctant to take on this issue,
as he needed more time for consultations with Vyacheslav M.
Molotov, his Russian counterpart. But the correspondent for the
New York Times, Cyrus L. Sulzberger, reported on 17 April that the
U.S. delegation was prepared to talk tough with the Soviets in
order to secure at least the Dodecanese Islands for Greece. As the
Greek delegation in Paris was not allowed to participate at the
Foreign Ministers Conference and the newly elected royalists in
Greece had committed their foreign policy to gaining control over
what the Greeks traditionally call "Northern Epirus" (southern
Albania) and the islands of the Dodecanese, Phillies and Hamlin
were approached at the end of April 1946 (probably by the Greek
foreign ministry) and asked to travel to Paris to facilitate contacts

29. Telegram, Phillies to Rockwell, 22 March 1946, RG 59, 868.00/3-2246, NA.
30. Merriam to Hamlin, 15 April 1946, RG 59, 740.00119EW 4-1546, NA.
31. *CR 1946*, 92/2: 689, 785.
32. *FRUS 1946* (Washington, 1970), 2: 80 See Basilis Kontis, *I Angloamerikaniki Politiki kai to Elliniko Provlima: 1945–1949* [Anglo-American Politics and the Greek Problem] (Thessaloniki, 2d ed., 1984).

between the Greek and U.S. delegations. Hamlin then contacted the only American newspaper in Paris, the *New York Herald Tribune*, and on 11 May the paper featured a long article (actually an interview) which effectively familiarized western Europeans with the Justice for Greece Committee. A large reception for the Greek delegation was organized by the American Cathedral Church on 17 May, the main purpose of which was to discuss how effectively to present the Greek problem on the agenda of the Paris Peace Conference. As a result, a number of American businessmen, supported by the traditional Greek community of small businessmen in Paris, formed the American Delegation for the Justice for Greece Committee in Paris. In an ad placed in the *Tribune*, two hundred "prominent Anglo-Americans" were named as members of this interest group. Additionally, 25,000 promotional brochures were printed and distributed (in both English and French).

In the meantime, Phillies contacted the Greek and American delegations. On 9 May he met with Byrnes's advisers. They informed him of the Americans' official position that Greece could well survive economically without "Northern Epirus." Still, Phillies was assured that the U.S. would support Greece. On 13 May the Greek ambassador to Washington, Kimon Diamantopoulos, lodged a complaint with Phillies: neither Vandenberg nor "the others" had shown any willingness to talk to the Greeks. He asked "his last hope," Phillies, to act as mediator. This worked out, and Phillies met Vandenberg privately for an hour, as both resided at the same hotel. The senator, his re-election in Michigan in mind, confidentially promised Phillies: "We will fight to get for Greece substantial reparations.... We will support Greece in her Bulgarian boundary claim but that is a matter for the Peace Conference. Greece will have a better chance there." But Russia, according to Vandenberg, was not interested in a peace conference: "I have in mind that Russia seeks to force Greece into Communism." Therefore, he continued, the question of "Northern Epirus" had to be shifted to the peace conference (which was to follow the conference of foreign ministers).[33] On 16 May, shortly before his departure to the U.S., Vandenberg apologized for not having conferred with the Greeks, but stressed that his position should have been clear to Phillies: "I am for Greece. I will help Greece to get, what she asks for deserving to have."[34] He pointed out that he had, at one of the secret meetings, sternly

---

33. *Phillies Diary*, 13 May 1946, *Phillies Papers*.
34. Phillies, *Report*, 84.

defended Greece's position when a Russian delegate had put Bulgaria's territorial claims regarding the Greek part of Thrace on the table. According to Vandenberg, his intervention had been the first favorable action on Greece.[35]

Phillies then had several other meetings with members of the U.S. press, such as those with Sulzberger on 17 and 19 May, where he talked about the meetings he had organized between U.S. and Greek advisers. Sulzberger told Phillies of the poor impression the Greek delegation had made on him. Their territorial claims lacked a clear definition. They needed to be better prepared if they wanted to convince the Americans. To Sulzberger, Vandenberg was the one person whose support Greece needed: "Greece will have a chance if he supports her case," because Greece was not to be lost to the Communists.[36] On 21 May the Greek ambassador to France, Raphael, told Phillies and Hamlin that he had received two telegrams from Moscow, from which it could be inferred that the Russian news agency Tass and the Russian print media had been reporting unfavorably on the Justice for Greece Committee. The American delegation had been also accused of territorial expansionism in favor of the Greek government.

At the end of May 1946, Phillies left Paris and traveled to Athens, where he was enthusiastically welcomed by the Greek nationalist press and members of the ruling parties. Many Greeks, in fact, had great hopes for AHEPA and its Greek-American representative. However, it is likely that neither Phillies nor the Greek people were aware of certain information already available to the Greek government at the end of May (presented by the U.S. Department of State to the Greeks after a Greek diplomatic initiative on 6 April 1946). In judging the real strategic value of "Northern Epirus" and the Greek's border dispute with Bulgaria, U.S. military experts had concluded that redrawing the borderlines between Greece, Albania, and Bulgaria would not result in any strategic, economic, or political advantages for Greece, but would instead endanger the peace in the entire Balkan region.[37] Already on 7 May, at the conference of the Allied foreign ministers, it had been agreed upon that with the implementation of a Bulgarian peace settlement the borders set in 1941 were to retain their validity. Nevertheless, Anglo-American delegates wished to enable Greek delegates and delegates of other countries in the Balkan

---

35. *Phillies Diary*, 16 May 1946, *Phillies Papers*.
36. *Phillies Diary*, 19 May 1946, *Phillies Papers*.
37. *FRUS 1946* (Washington, 1969) 7: 145 and 161.

region to present their respective cases at the public part of the Paris Peace Conference. But the U.S. government, as of May 1946, clearly felt that its own security interests were incompatible with Greece's territorial claims on Bulgaria and Albania. Only the issue of the Dodecanese remained a bone of contention between Byrnes, Vandenberg, and Molotov. In February 1946, the Russian ambassador to Greece had offered the Greek government urgently needed supplies in exchange for a naval base on one of the Dodecanese Islands. This was rejected completely by the Greek government. Finally, on 27 June (at the second session of the meeting of foreign ministers), Molotov surprisingly gave in: "Very well; we agree that the Islands shall go to Greece."[38] For the Soviet foreign minister there was apparently not much to be gained if the issue remained on the table. Molotov's new position, however, confused Vandenberg, who remarked that "Everybody is speculating tonight as to what it means."[39]

Greeks living in Greece and Greek-Americans alike were delighted on hearing that the Dodecanese Islands were finally to be united with Greece. Nevertheless, as of June the Justice for Greece Committee kept sending countless memoranda to the State Department, reiterating its remaining demands: "Northern Epirus," changes along the border with Bulgaria, and adequate reparations. Referring to Resolution 82, the committee warned on 26 July: "Without more American support ... the Western Powers will virtually throw Greece in the lap of Russia who thus will form a solid and impenetrable block in the Balkans."[40] Also, the committee vainly protested efforts to formally include Albania in the United Nations. Like the government in Athens, the Greek-American Committee regarded Communist Albania as an enemy, since that country, together with Italy, had attacked Greece in 1941. Albania therefore was to be excluded from any international organization. At the peace conference American Philhellenes took the same stubborn position as the Greek delegation. The Greek government, grossly misjudging the international situation, simply did not want to accept that an annexation of "Northern Epirus" was clearly not in the interest of either the British or the Americans. Doggedly they sought to talk the Americans into changing. But for U.S. diplomats, the Albania question

38. *FRUS 1946*, 2: 661.

39. *Vandenberg Diary*, 27 June 1946, Sen. Arthur S. Vandenberg Papers, Michigan Historical Collection, University of Michigan.

40. Phillies to Baxter, 26 July 1946, *Phillies Papers*, box 3.

was "to be settled on political grounds, possibly as a matter of Conference tactics."[41] All that Byrnes was willing to do was to allow Greece to present its arguments. At the end of the Paris Peace Conference, on 11 October 1946, the Western Allies agreed on a compromise regarding Greece: Greece was assured reparations (to be paid by Italy and Bulgaria), though at a far lower level than previously demanded. Despite a Soviet veto, Greece's border with Bulgaria was to be demilitarized. The open question of "Northern Epirus" was passed on to the Council of Foreign Ministers, as the issue could not be debated at the Paris Peace Conference because Albania was not treated as an enemy state by the four Allies.[42] This, however, was meant by Anglo-American delegates only as a rhetorical concession to the Greek government. Greece was formally asked to abandon her position on Albania. In sum, the U.S. ambassador to Greece, Lincoln Mac-Veagh, commented on the outcome of the peace conference that the U.S. had treated Greece fairly, and this in full accord with U.S. interests.[43]

Because of continuing unrest along Greece's borders with Albania, Yugoslavia and Bulgaria, the Justice for Greece Committee and the Greek government, as of 12 November 1946 (eleven days prior to the conference of foreign ministers in New York), renewed their demands for a revision of Washington's position toward the question of "Northern Epirus" and asked to have the issue put on the agenda in New York. *"A weak Greece will not survive long the intensive aggression of Pan-Slavism and Communism."*[44] The State Department, however, refused to treat Albania as an enemy state and continued to regard the question of "Northern Epirus" as settled. Phillies, aided by Representative John McCormack, managed to get an appointment with Under Secretary of State Dean Acheson, which took place on 20 November 1946 and included the Director of the Near Eastern Division, Loy W. Henderson, and three delegates from the Justice for Greece Committee. The basis for their talks was an express letter from the committee to Byrnes

41. General Norstad to Bonesteel, 1 September 1946, RG 319, P&0 092, Section IV, Case 44/2, NA.

42. *FRUS*, 1946, 3 (Washington, 1970): 616. Neither Italy nor Bulgaria ever compensated Greece fully. Athens was formally in a state of war with Tirana until 28 August 1987!

43. John O. Iatrides, ed., *Ambassador Mac Veagh Reports. Greece, 1933–1947* (New Jersey, 1980), 706.

44. Phillies to State Department, 12 November 1946, RG 59, 740.00119 EW/11-1246, NA. Emphasis in original.

from 12 November, in which the U.S. government was urged to rethink its position regarding Greece's territorial claims.[45] When Acheson asked the members of the committee to specify their demands, William Dinsmoor, an American Philhellene, admitted that what was meant was the annexation of "Northern Epirus" and of certain mountainous regions in southern Bulgaria. Without these territories, he added, Greece would not be able to recover economically. Phillies noted that Greece might very well fall to Communists should her territorial demands not be heeded. Again, Acheson referred to the upcoming conference of foreign ministers where the Greek government would be able to have its demands discussed. But then, according to notes taken on 20 September 1946, Acheson gave a first, serious hint that in the near future the U.S. might support Greece's claims more substantially:

> ... in the opinion of the Department it would be advantageous to Greece if that nation would devote its energies towards achieving Greek unity and to promoting economic reconstruction. He [Acheson] assured the delegation of the deep and sincere interest of the United States in the future of Greece and of the determination of the United States to do everything proper and possible to aid Greece in this time of need. He described the various measures which already had been taken by the U.S. to assist Greece financially and economically, mentioning among them our plans to send an economic mission to Greece in the near future. Mr. Acheson added that we were contemplating additional measures for assisting Greece economically and financially.[46]

Members of the Justice for Greece Committee were therefore probably the first outsiders to learn from Acheson that a wide-ranging aid package for Greece was already being laid out at the State Department. Further letters from Henderson and Francis H. Russell in December 1946 and January 1947 confirmed Acheson's statement (Acheson was decisively involved in the conception of the Truman Doctrine). When President Truman, on 12 March 1946, declared before both houses of Congress that "the United States has formally committed itself to whatever assistance, economic and military, is necessary to preserve Greek freedom," an overwhelming majority of organized Greek-Americans unequivocally supported Truman's program. After all their efforts since

45. Justice for Greece Committee to Byrnes, 12 November 1946, 868.014/11-1246, NA.
46. Memorandum, 20 November 1946, RG 59, 868.014/11-2046, NA.

1944, organized Greek-Americans had finally reached their goal: the U.S. was on its way to entangling itself in Greek affairs for good. AHEPA and its Justice for Greece Committee were proud that they had again successfully managed to help out their old home country independently: "Even if it is a voice in the wilderness ... this organization, which is American first, last and always, has a letter "H" in it. It is American-Hellenic. And in that letter "H" which has given us the ... crown of preserving the land where democracy was born AHEPA has a responsibility ... to pay tribute to that little country."[47]

With the Truman Doctrine on their side, the majority of Greek-Americans were in a position to declare their loyalty to Greece without any longer having to fear social repression. Greece had officially been linked to U.S. interests. After Truman's message, former Greek immigrants ceased to be hyphenated Americans. They were united with all Americans in their enemy image of anti-communism. But "AHEPA Blends Americanism with Hellenism"[48] not only meant that the leading Greek-American organization would follow Truman's foreign policy, but it would also introduce so-called McCarthyism into its own ranks: the new "liberal" leadership, aside from immediately disbanding the Justice for Greece Committee, decided to check all new applicants for membership in their organization for any possible subversive activities.[49] Future members of AHEPA were to be free of any communist background. The transformation process of the Greek-American community that had started in World War II was thus accomplished: by assuming voluntarily the prestigious role of national protector and advocate of the Greek cause, organized Greek-Americans responded to the traumatic experience of the Greek civil war with its apparent threat of communism and fear of territorial dismemberment. As a consequence, they shifted their Weltanschauung from its traditional prewar liberalism to political conservatism, supporting the Greek king and lobbying for Greek national interests as loyal anti-communist Americans in the emerging East-West confrontation. Thus, the historically divided community overcame its own antagonistic particularism and reached a degree of internal unity rarely experienced before.

47. *AHEPA National Conferences, Proceedings*: 1947 (Washington, 1947), 256, 305.
48. *The AHEPAN*, March/April 1948: 12.
49. *AHEPA National Conferences, Proceedings*: 1947, 549.

Conclusion

The relevance of the Greek lobby, however, does not lie so much in the field of foreign policy. While the organizers of the Justice for Greece Committee were involved in the process of transforming traditional U.S. foreign policy in southeastern Europe from its "non-policy" (Geir Lundestad) toward a gradual acceptance of responsibility from 1946 on (culminating in the Truman Doctrine), acting as mediators between the Greek position in the open territorial questions and supporting massive economic, financial, and political aid, Greek-American attempts to seriously influence U.S. foreign policy against American national interests did not prove successful, even if their publications and internal communications claim otherwise. American security interests in the eastern Mediterranean were clearly superior and were at best rhetorically compatible with the territorial ambitions of Athens (these territorial claims were not even undisputed within Greece; as a result they could not really be presented convincingly at the Paris Peace Conference). Thus, the Greek lobby achieved relatively little in terms of its ambitious territorial program, even if after 1947 the Dodecanese Islands were handed over to Greece and the question of an annexation of "Northern Epirus" was kept open at the United Nations (against Albania's interests).

But the public activities of the Greek community had a lasting effect on American domestic politics. After the disappointing results of the Paris Peace Conference in May 1946 and at a time when the traumatic Greek civil war was in its second phase (the Greek monarchists fought alongside with Great Britain—still regarded as a colonial power by the American public—against leftist/communist opposition forces supported by all Greece's communist neighbors), the founders of the Justice for Greece Committee, strengthened by off-the-record remarks by Senator Vandenberg and the Truman government, turned to anti-communist rhetoric as a last resort. Phillies and his committee, along with the official rhetoric of the Truman administration (which was then positively reflected by the media), openly accused the Soviet Union and its Balkan satellites of full responsibility for the constant internal and external threat to the only (formally) democratic regime in southeastern Europe, Greece. While the royalist Greek-American free riders hoped in vain to be rewarded for their political opportunism with new territories for their old *Heimat*, they helped to publicly identify the adversary of American internationalism—

Soviet-style communism. The U.S., their new home, was supposed to help the ruling Greek royalists successfully terminate the civil war and at the same time get rid of their left wing and Communist foes. Anti-communism smoothed the way for American public support of the Truman Doctrine for Greece and, less enthusiastically, for Turkey. In fact, from 1947 to 1949 the Truman administration heavily supported the legal Greek government with dollars and advisers—and especially with military equipment to contain and destroy the falsely perceived communist revolt. American foreign interference, with its stubborn anti-communism, thus helped to cement a semidictatorial regime with its anachronistic social establishment and secured the dependence of all Greek governments on the U.S. until 1974.

PART VI

THE PROBLEM OF SYNTHESIS

Chapter Twelve

CULTURE WARS

The Sources and Uses of Enmity
in American History

David M. Kennedy

I t is a melancholy reflection on human nature that the subject of
enmity has spawned such a large library of literature. Though I
don't pretend to have mastered the entire corpus of that literature, I
would like to begin by invoking two authors who can provide us
with a useful framework for thinking about the sources and the uses
of enmity in American history. The two authors are, respectively,
European and American: Sigmund Freud and George Kennan.

In the depressingly lengthy bibliography dealing with hatred
and aggression, few voices speak more mordantly than Freud's.
Writing in *Civilization and Its Discontents* (the somewhat sanitized
English translation of *Das Unbehagen in der Kultur*) in 1930, he said:

> It is clearly not easy for men to give up the satisfaction of this incli-
> nation to aggression. They do not feel comfortable without it. The
> advantage which a comparatively small cultural group offers of
> allowing this instinct an outlet in the form of hostility against
> intruders is not to be despised. It is always possible to bind together
> a considerable number of people in love, so long as there are other
> people left over to receive the manifestations of their aggressive-
> ness.... In this respect the Jewish people, scattered everywhere,
> have rendered most useful services to the civilizations of the coun-
> tries that have been their hosts.... [A]nd it is intelligible that the

attempt to establish a new, communist civilization in Russia should find its psychological support in the persecution of the bourgeois. One only wonders, with concern, what the Soviets will do after they have wiped out their bourgeois.[1]

To Freud's specific question about whom the Bolsheviks would hate after they had fully triumphed over the Russian bourgeoisie, the American author and diplomat George Kennan provided an answer some seventeen years later. In so doing he elaborated some refinements of Freud's theory of enmity. In one of the most famous documents of the Cold War, the notorious "Mr. X" article in *Foreign Affairs* of July 1947, Kennan argued that for the Soviet Communists, the internal bourgeois enemy had been replaced by the external enemy of world capitalism. He went on to make a useful, if somewhat cynical, observation about what might be called the practical political utility of enmity:

> [T]remendous emphasis has been placed, on the original Communist thesis of a basic antagonism between the capitalist and Socialist worlds. It is clear, from many indications, that this emphasis is not founded in reality.... But there is ample evidence that the stress laid in Moscow on the menace confronting Soviet society from the world outside its borders is founded not on realities of foreign antagonism but in the necessity of explaining away the maintenance of dictatorial authority at home.[2]

Between them, Freud and Kennan in these passages define a fairly familiar set of assumptions about the sources and uses of enmity. I wish to dwell upon two of those assumptions. First, the image of an "enemy," Freud suggests, originates in the most fundamental, even primitive, need of a group to have a sense of its own identity. A group can only achieve and sustain that identity, so his argument runs, by measuring itself against an "other." What's more, as the specific cases of anti-Semitism and Soviet communism are meant to illustrate, for Freud the requisite "other" must be endowed with certain attributes. It is not enough merely to be *alien;* to do the cultural work of an enemy, in Freud's definition, the "other" must be seen to embody some deeply menacing threat to the integrity and survival of the group that bestows upon it the status of "enemy." Second, Kennan adds the suggestion that in the case of Soviet communism, at least, "enmity" has little or nothing to do with objective reality, or the actual record of

---

1. Sigmund Freud, *Civilization and Its Discontents* (New York, 1961), 72–73.
2. George F. Kennan, *American Diplomacy*, expanded ed. (Chicago, 1984), 113.

transactions between two groups. Rather, it has everything to do with the internal political requirements of the group that, in effect, "invents" its enemy.

My task is to explore the application of these two analytical constructs to American history—the need for an enemy, perceived as possessing deeply menacing characteristics, to crystallize a sense of national identity; and the origins of enmity in the realm of subjective psychological or political need rather than in objective reality.

The general thesis of this chapter contains four propositions: first, that the American experience does not conform precisely to Freud's analysis of the psychological sources and functions of enmity; second, that the effort to apply Freud's diagnostic to American society highlights an important distinction between "enmity" and simple "otherness"; third, that the record of American history confirms Kennan's suggestion that enmity is a politically and historically conditioned construction, one that does owe its existence to certain kinds of "objective realities"; fourth, and finally, that the particular "objective realities" of the twentieth century have generated some especially appalling transformations in the uses—and abuses—of enmity.

Let me take up Freud first. In *Civilization and Its Discontents*, Freud goes on to speculate that all groups, as groups, may be afflicted by an inherent psychopathology. A version of that idea, after all, is the central informing premise of *Civilization and Its Discontents*. In this particular passage he calls that pathology "the psychological poverty of groups." He sees this condition as inevitably dangerous. And he sees certain historical populations, the American population in particular, as especially susceptible to it.

> This danger is most threatening where the bonds of a society are chiefly constituted by the identification of its members with one another, while individuals of the leader type do not acquire the importance that should fall to them in the formation of a group. The present cultural state of America would give us a good opportunity for studying the damage to civilization which is thus to be feared. But I shall avoid the temptation of entering upon a critique of American civilization; I do not wish to give an impression of wanting myself to employ American methods.[3]

Freud here presents us with a special challenge—to examine whether there is a peculiarly American version of the apparently universal experience of designating and defining the enemy. Freud

3. Freud, *Civilization and Its Discontents*, 74.

summons distinguished company into his presence to support his suggestion that American culture is an especially fertile breeding ground for the particular psychopathology he conjures. That brief reference to the unstable, dangerously susceptible situation where "the bonds of a society are chiefly constituted by the identification of its members with one another," echoes Alexis de Tocqueville's classic description of Americans as a rootless, anomic people, whom "equality places … side by side, unconnected by any common tie," living in a society where "the woof of time is every instant broken, and the track of generations effaced," a society where "each class approximates to other classes, and intermingles with them, [and] its members become indifferent, and as strangers to one another."[4] If we accept the Freudian notion that the concept of enmity serves to shape a required sense of group identity and cohesion, then the remarkably inchoate, fragmented character of American society would seem to generate an extraordinarily strong need for defining an enemy image to offset that society's otherwise chaotic disarticulation.

But will the historical record support that theoretical prediction? Let's begin at the beginning of the history of the United States, by revisiting the subject matter of Jürgen Heideking's chapter[5] on images of England and America in the Revolutionary era.

Figure 12.1 dates from 1776, at the outset of hostilities between the colonies and Britain. It depicts Britain as a lady of fashion, and her rebellious daughter, America, as an Indian. The British lady is saying "I'll force you to obedience, you rebellious slut," while the Indian maiden replies: "Liberty, liberty forever, mother, while I exist." There are many remarkable features of this representation: the relative civility of its imagery, despite its rendering of women in pugilistic poses; its stark juxtaposition of "obedience" and "liberty;" and its salty language. But in addition to these, the artist has done two further things that bear upon our discussion of enmity: first, he has drawn upon the by-then rich iconographic tradition of letting an Indian serve metonymically for America; second, and no less interestingly, he has cast the Revolutionary conflict in terms of a family dispute, in this case a clash between mother and daughter.

Figure 12.2 dates from approximately 1783, at war's end. Here a different artist has employed almost identical iconography, not least of all the imagery of family, in order to present a visual portrayal of

4. Alexis de Tocqueville, *Democracy in America* (New York, 1956), 194, 195.
5. Cf. Jürgen Heideking, "The Image of an English Enemy During the American Revolution," in this volume.

FIGURE 12.1 The Female Combatants, 1776

FIGURE 12.2 The Reconciliation Between Britannia and
Her Daughter America

the reconciliation between Britain and America. Dame Britain is now attired not in eighteenth-century fashion, but in classical garb. But with that slight alteration, it is evident that this cartoonist drew upon the same cultural stock of imagery as our cartoonist of 1776. America is again represented by an Indian maiden, and the scene once again invokes the idea of family, as America says "Dear Mama, say no more about it," and Britannia replies, "Be a good girl and give me a buss [kiss]."[6]

Freud can be helpful to us in assessing the significance of these Revolutionary era images. Once again in *Civilization and Its Discontents*, he referred to what he called "the narcissism of minor differences." As he explained, "it is precisely communities with adjoining territories, and related to each other in other ways as well, who are engaged in constant feuds and in ridiculing each other—like the Spaniards and the Portuguese, for instance, the North Germans and South Germans, the English and the Scotch, and so on."[7] From that perspective, these cartoons quite logically play upon the genuine cultural intimacy of Britain and America by relying upon the motif of the family—a notorious locus of both conflict and reconciliation, affection as well as aggression. Their employment of that motif calls to mind a telling observation of William James, one that could as easily have come from Freud's ruminations on the vexed relation of Eros and Thanatos. "The closest human love," said James, "incloses a potential germ of estrangement or hatred."[8] (The conciliatory motif of the second cartoon, incidentally, also provides a kind of eighteenth-century preface for the remark attributed to Bismarck a century or so later: that the greatest diplomatic fact of the modern era was that the Americans spoke English—a simple cultural datum whose weighty political implications were twice demonstrated in the world wars of this century.)

In short, a brief glance at the Revolutionary era and at the two subsequent centuries of British-American relations reminds us that cultural proximity can serve as a precondition not only for cultural cooperation and even military alliance, but can also, and by the very nature of its proximity, furnish the basis for ferocious cultural antagonisms. That bivalent potential of cultural *proximity* has two implications for situations where a large cultural or geographical

6. Cartoons are from Thomas A. Bailey and David M. Kennedy, *The American Pageant*, 10th ed. (Lexington, MA, 1994), 121 and 155.

7. Freud, *Civilization and Its Discontents*, 72.

8. James, quoted in Peter Gay, *The Cultivation of Hatred* (New York, 1993), 7.

distance separates two groups. In those circumstances, *both* cooperation *and* sustained enmity may be impossible. The first of those implications is, I suppose, self-evident; the second at first seems paradoxical, but it might be best understood as the reciprocal of the old saying that "familiarity breeds contempt"—and, by simple inversion, lack of familiarity removes the grounds for contempt.

Thus it is important, and I hope not simply belaboring the obvious, to emphasize that these Revolutionary era cartoons both draw on an already well-established inventory of cultural images to convey their message. To the extent that both the cartoonists we have seen relied naturally on visual conventions and metaphorical protocols familiar to eighteenth-century readers—America as Indian maid, family quarrel, and reconciliation—we might wonder how enmity, or any other emotionally invested relationship, could be sustained when the cupboard of available imagery was substantially bare.

I emphasize this point because I would like to suggest that the United States entered this century without a well-stocked cupboard of cultural images of *foreign* peoples who might perform the functions of enmity as Freud defined them. To be sure, nineteenth-century Americans had their prejudices and harbored their stereotypes about other national cultures. Indeed, it is commonly and correctly said that nineteenth-century Americans habitually defined their sense of national identity against their imagined view of what Europe was all about—as the novels of Henry James so eloquently testify. The virtual obsession of nineteenth-century Americans with distinguishing their national culture from European forms—Ralph Waldo Emerson's 1837 essay "The American Scholar" can be taken as a summary example—and their simultaneous obsession with remaining isolated from European diplomatic and military entanglements, powerfully suggests that *otherness,* or "alterity," may be essential to the definition of identity, but that, Freud to the contrary, it need not take the form of outright, hostile, aggressive *enmity* in order to do its cultural work. If Europe constituted a defining other, it was scarcely an *enemy* in the sense that Freud intended—defined as a menacing threat, and made into an object of bellicose hatred.

In short, I believe that those nineteenth-century American biases and images about other peoples did indeed perform the function of helping to define American national identity, but I don't believe that those images carried strong psychic valences. Tocqueville reminds us why this might be so in a little-noticed passage in *Democracy in America* in which he tried to explain what he regarded as the remarkably tiny size of the American military establishment in the 1830s (some six thousand men, at a time when France could field an army of more than two hundred thousand): "Fortune, which has conferred so many peculiar benefits upon the inhabitants of the United States, has placed them in the midst of a wilderness, where they have, so to speak, no neighbors; a few thousand soldiers are sufficient for their wants; but this is peculiar to America, not to democracy."[9]

Now, substituting "enemies" for "neighbors" in that passage illuminates what I mean by the thinness of the cultural inventory of materials that might satisfy a Freudian definition of an enemy image. Just as nineteenth-century Americans could make do with only a handful of soldiers, so could they get by with weakly defined notions of foreign enmity—and for the same reason: namely, that they shared an isolated continent with virtually no other people who could plausibly be construed as a deeply menacing threat to the integrity of American society.

Surely Americans had foreign adversaries, from colonial times right down to the present century, but I'm skeptical that many of them, at least before the opening of this century, very powerfully performed the first of the psychological functions of enmity which Freud described—the shaping of group identity against the contrasting image of a menacing "other." At various times and places and with varying degrees of intensity, British North American settlers in the colonial era hated and feared the French, the Spanish, and the Indians. Yet even before the eighteenth century ended, the French dropped out of this picture. The Spanish were largely forgotten until the exhilaratingly brief episode of the Spanish-American war at century's end. In the Revolutionary era, to be sure, Britain was a real enemy—an opponent in a shooting war, and a distinct other against which the very idea of America was newly defined. But, as we have seen, the remarkable thing about British enmity in the Revolutionary era was the speed and ease with which it disappeared. As the nineteenth century wore on, the former colonial masters in Britain appeared once again as real enemies in the War of 1812, but then devolved to a much less emotionally freighted status as merely rhetorical enemies for some time thereafter, when "twisting the lion's tail" was a relatively harmless staple of American diplomatic and political discourse.

9. Tocqueville, *Democracy in America*, 274.

Mexico was a formal enemy in the war of the 1840s, and an object of cultural contempt in the United States both before and after that war, but scarcely formed the whetstone on which a sense of North American national identity was sharpened. The Indians, too, especially after Andrew Jackson's removal of the southern "civilized tribes" in the 1830s, faded as genuine enemies in Freud's sense of constituting a deep menace to the very existence of white society. By the 1890s they had certainly lost whatever identity-forming psychological value their enmity might have conferred upon non-Native Americans.

Now the case of the Indians, often legally treated as foreign nations but also regarded as an alien presence *within* American society, serves as a reminder that enmity can just as easily define and divide national subgroups as it can differentiate sovereign nations from one another. Indeed, Freud's first example in the passage quoted above dealt with the role of the Jews in binding together the peoples of "the countries that have been their hosts." This description of the function of minorities in shaping the identity of majorities is a familiar one, and is repeatedly exemplified in the American case. Racial and ethnic differences in the United States, class and regional distinctions, political partisanship, religious rivalries, even gender relations can imaginably be understood by the Freudian model that makes group cohesion dependent upon the perception of a threatening other. Surely, for example, the earliest Puritan settlements in New England derived some of their sense of solidarity from the unsettling presence in their midst of nonbelievers, or even of Quakers and Baptists. In the Civil War era, the crystallizing notion of the slave power helped to generate a sense of northern solidarity, just as the specter of black Republicanism united the south and fanned the flames of rebellion. All of these examples of internal enmity appear, in fact, to conform to Freud's description of the "narcissism of minor differences."

Most notoriously of all, in the late nineteenth century the new immigrants, mostly Jews and Catholics from eastern and southern Europe, provoked waves of virulently strong nativism, and nativism satisfies much of Freud's definition of enmity. As John Higham argues in his landmark study *Strangers in the Land*, nativism both invokes and reinforces "the connecting, energizing force of modern nationalism. While drawing on much broader cultural antipathies and ethnocentric judgments, nativism translates them into a zeal to destroy the enemies of a distinctively American way of life."

Higham rightly insists that mere antipathy, ethnocentrism, big-otry, or scorn may be necessary ingredients of nativism, but they are not sufficient. For the full manifestation of nativism, another ingredient must also be present—what Higham describes as the sense of a threat to the very life of the nation, to the integrity of the national cultural fabric—and such a sense, he argues, arose inde-pendently of the nature of the immigrant group under attack. As Higham demonstrates at length, nativist imagery, including visual conventions and verbal tropes, changed little from the eighteenth century to the twentieth; what *did* change was the psychic charge invested in those images under changing historical circumstances, particularly economic and political crises.

Higham focuses his attention on two egregiously nasty epi-sodes, the economically depressed decade of the 1890s, and the politically turbulent years of World War I. Two points about his conclusions deserve emphasis: first, his sharp distinction between distaste or prejudice or condescension on the one hand and full-blown *enmity* (or nativism) on the other; second, his finding that the nativism (or enmity) that afflicted American culture around the turn of the century was in fact *episodic*. It was not a systemic, constant element in American society, proceeding from some chronic yearning for national identity. Rather, it waxed and waned according to a rhythm determined by events originating in realms that often had little directly to do with the designated enemy—especially changes in the economic and psychic health of American society as it negotiated the painful transition from a pre-dominantly rural, agricultural, disarticulated society to a pre-dominantly urban, industrial, corporatized society. "The big changes," Higham writes, "were not so much intellectual as emo-tional. The same idea might be mildly innocuous at one time and charged with potent feelings at another. For the history of na-tivism, therefore, emotional intensity provided the significant measurement of change. If nativism was an ideological disease, perhaps one might best diagnose it by observing when the fever raged and when it slackened."[10] In sum, as Higham makes clear, the fever chart of nativism did in fact rise and fall in response to undeniably objective realities—but the realities had to do with the character of the economy, unsettling changes in social organiza-tion, and the requirements of modern warfare, much more than they had to do with the nature of the immigrants themselves.

10. John Higham, *Strangers in the Land* (New York, 1963), xiii, 4.

What I have tried to suggest thus far is the difficulty of applying a literal version of Freud's argument to the circumstances of nineteenth-century American life. Whatever sense of national cohesion Americans then possessed did not seem to owe heavily to the shaping force of an external enemy image. Nor did what some might see as the weak sense of national identity in that era spontaneously generate a need to invent such an image, out of whole cloth if necessary. If I might summarize the argument I have been trying to make to this point, America seemed to have no "natural" foreign enemies in the nineteenth century, seemed equally to have little felt need to create them, and had in consequence a thin inventory of images with which to define enmity itself. And yet the nativist episodes to which I have referred remind us that under certain circumstances—or under the pressure of certain objective realities—American culture did indeed conform to the Freudian typology, suddenly charging old images with new meaning and defining itself in relation to a purportedly menacing other whose redefined image reflected internal cultural needs as much as it did the intrinsic character of the purported "enemy."

We might therefore modify Freud's analysis, at least as applied to the nineteenth-century American case, to allow for the possibility that alterity, in a relatively benign form well short of enmity, may in fact be sufficient for the purposes of identity formation in a group. But Higham's data also suggest that alterity is susceptible of transmutation into outright enmity under certain conditions. Alterity may be necessary to enmity, in short, but it is not sufficient. Put another way, we might say that all enemies are others, but not all others are enemies. To this it might be added that the degree of otherness does not in and of itself determine the degree of enmity—indeed, as the family motif in those Revolutionary cartoons reminds us, the ferocity of enmity may correlate inversely with the extent of otherness: the closer the cultural relation with the other, the more savage the hatred under a regime of enmity. Again, Higham reminds us that, in the nineteenth-century American case at least, *internal* aliens, in the very bosom of the host society, could provoke more passionate feelings than any foreign adversary.

In this complicated nexus of alterity and enmity, internality and externality, we might be led to speculate about what cultural forces would be unleashed if an internal other, long branded as alien, with an ample stock of cultural imagery to sustain that branding, were somehow associated with an external foe under conditions of genuine threat. To anticipate a bit, those conditions all obtained in the case of the Japanese-U.S. war in the Pacific from 1941 to 1945, to which I shall turn below.

This then is the legacy of "enemy imagery" that the United States carried into the twentieth century. This century early on began to furnish repeated circumstances of the sort that excited the nativistic reactions of the 1890s. Three episodes are of particular interest in this regard: World Wars I and II and the Cold War.

The imagery from these conflicts is familiar, and I offer just two specimens—an anti-German cartoon from World War I (Fig. 12.3), and an anti-Japanese cartoon from World War II (Fig. 12.4). What strikes the viewer immediately about these images is how much more savage and ferocious they are than the relatively tame cartoons of the Revolutionary War era. Here the enemy is not simply an adversary in a combative pose, but is demonized and animalized, accused of sexual atrocities and mass butcheries.[11] If these cartoons are indicative, and I believe they are, then clearly the matter of enmity has become a much more serious and emotionally freighted affair in the twentieth century. Why should this be so?

It is too easy, I believe, to explain this emotional intensification of enemy imagery as just another instance of the ineluctable vulgarization and coarsening of everything in the modern world. Other things, besides aesthetic standards and notions of civility, have also changed in the last two centuries. Among the observers who first sensed the newness of what might be called the circumstances of enmity in this century was the British economist John A. Hobson, famous for his views on imperialism, but no less deserving of our attention for a little book he wrote as the century opened: *The Psychology of Jingoism*, published in 1901 as a tract against British prosecution of the Boer War. He defined jingoism in terms that will be familiar to us as students of enmity: "[T]hat inverted patriotism whereby the love of one's own nation is transformed into the hatred of another nation, and the fierce craving to destroy the individual members of that other nation."[12] That sentiment, he wrote, anticipating Freud, grew from "primitive passions"; but, also anticipating Kennan, Hobson argued that jingoism in addition owed much of its character to the peculiar social and political circumstances of modernity. "Jingoism," he insisted, "is essentially a product of 'civilized' communities, though deriving its necessary food from the survival of savage

11. The anti-German cartoon is from Bailey and Kennedy, *The American Pageant*, 676, the anti-Japanese cartoon from John W. Dower, *War Without Mercy* (New York, 1986), 187.
12. John A. Hobson, *The Psychology of Jingoism* (London, 1901), 1.

FIGURE 12.3   Anti-German Propaganda, World War I

FIGURE 12.4   How Tough Are the Japanese? A British Commentary
on the Japanese Soldier, World War II

nature; it presents therefore a number of more complex moral and intellectual problems for consideration."[13]

Hobson went on in his impassioned little book to indict those aspects of the modern social condition most strongly conducive to jingoism: the concentration of large masses of people in cities; the progressive weakening, in those populations, of the bonds of community (here Hobson spoke in the accents of the German social theorist Ferdinand Tönnies, who in 1887 made the famous distinction between *Gemeinschaft* and *Gesellschaft*); and the cynical exploitation of what he called "the neurotic temperament of town life" by political elites acting through the principal organs of mass communication in his day, the newspapers. Jingoism, he shrewdly observed, was the "passion of the spectator ... not of the fighter," and reflected the essential passivity, ignorance, and manipulability of people who inhabited an emerging culture of consumerism, saturated with media images that played shamelessly on their basest emotions.[14] (One wonders what Hobson would have to say about late twentieth-century Western culture, which has amplified these spectatorial, consumerist phenomena to levels that he could scarcely have imagined.)

To Hobson's indictment we might further add items that contribute to an explanation of the nature of enmity in this century. Conspicuous are the emergence of mass democratic polities, and the enormous escalation of the physical and human requirements of modern warfare. In contrast to the Revolutionary War, in this century's wars whole populations must be imbued with the martial spirit. They must be sufficiently imbued that they will not only give their political consent to the military enterprise; they have also been required to furnish their sons, and in some cases their daughters, to the huge conscript armies that have replaced small professional forces. And even those who never leave the home front—itself an expression of modern origin that speaks volumes about the character of warfare in the industrial age—must also be induced to undertake and sustain for long periods of time prodigious efforts of economic production and personal sacrifice.

This, then, is in rough outline the condition in which the United States entered the first great international crisis of this century, World War I. America in 1917 was a country with a scant inventory of images of foreign peoples, suddenly called upon to mobilize its economy and fight a war in a distant locale for reasons that

13. Ibid., 2, 12.
14. Ibid., 8.

the political leadership had great difficulty making clear. Small wonder, then, that images of a savage enemy were manufactured out of whatever materials were at hand.[15] The point I wish to stress here is that the need for an enemy image grew out of a specific historical and political circumstance; it would be exceedingly difficult to argue, in the case of American relations with Germany in 1917, that an antecedent conception of Germans as "the enemy" was a factor in precipitating American involvement in World War I. To put the point differently: this is one case where there the old question of which came first, the chicken or the egg, is easy to answer. War did not grow from some preexisting germ of hatred; rather, if I may put it this way, the chicken of warfare surely laid the egg of enmity.

And yet, once that egg was laid, it displayed some characteristics that are distinctively American, and which begin to suggest a pattern that is also observable in the American construction of enmity in our two later conflicts, World War II and the Cold War. The American image of Germany in World War I was, first of all, not so much summoned into active duty from a warehouse of previous imagery, but *manufactured* anew by the political and cultural elite, and purveyed by organs of mass communication, including not only newspapers but also the infant medium of film. Largely because of its occasional, instrumental origins, that image was easily erasable as soon as the occasion passed and its instrumental utility vanished. This transient nature of such imagery may be an oddly beneficial product of the lack of extended prior contact between the two peoples, and of the volatile, ill-informed mass social conditions in which it was formed, and which Hobson so lamented. "Easy come, easy go," to use an American idiom: if the masses are susceptible to being emotionally manipulated into a frenzy of hatred, they are no less susceptible of lapsing easily from that state of mind. Surely the speed with which American images of Russia were revised from friend to enemy as World War II passed into the Cold War, or the even more remarkable speed with which Japan and Germany were transformed from enemies to allies after 1945, testify to the shallow roots and easy reversibility of American notions of enmity.

To this generalization, the case of Japan provides an instructive exception. As John Dower points out in his fascinating book, *War Without Mercy*, American images of Japan in World War II "have a

15. Cf. also Mark Ellis's contribution in this volume, "German-Americans in World War I."

pedigree in Western thought that can be traced back to Aristotle, and were conspicuous in the earliest encounters of Europeans with the black peoples of Africa and the Indians of the Western Hemisphere. The Japanese ... were actually saddled with racial stereotypes that Europeans and Americans had applied to non-whites for centuries ... [including] the core imagery of apes, lesser men, primitives, children, madmen."[16]

In contrast to most of the other cases I have discussed, in other words, American conceptions of the Japanese enemy did in fact draw upon a well-stocked inventory of preexisting cultural images, and the ability to utilize that malignant inventory may have measurably increased the ferocity of American enmity toward Japan. Moreover, at least on the West Coast of the United States, Japanese immigrants by 1941 had constituted for more than half a century a strange, contemned alien presence. Thus we have here that most fearsome of combinations: the association of internal aliens with external threat, in a context that provided genuine menace and was well furnished with a usable inventory of pejorative images.

It is by now a truism that American sentiment, nurtured by that inventory and fed by resentment over the assault on Pearl Harbor, was far more hotly anti-Japanese than anti-German. Indeed, Franklin Roosevelt on more than one occasion invoked that cultural fact to threaten the British with shifting American resources to the Pacific War if they did not agree with his strategic preferences. And the kind of sentiment expressed by a Marine to war correspondent John Hersey on Guadalcanal in 1942 was repeated all over the Pacific theater: "I wish we were fighting against Germans. They are human beings, like us.... But the Japanese are like animals."[17]

The contrasting Japanese and German cases confirm the general argument I have been making: that the absence of a substantial, preexisting cultural inventory of emotionally charged imagery about other peoples by and large served to impede the formation of deep, lasting enmities even in situations of warfare.

There is another aspect of American imagery about Japan in World War II that Dower mentions and on which I wish to dwell just for a moment. It is the image that formed the principal motif of Frank Capra's wartime propaganda film in the "Why We Fight" series[18], entitled *Know Your Enemy—Japan*. As Dower describes it:

16. Dower, *War Without Mercy*, 10.

17. John Hersey, *Into the Valley: A Skirmish of the Marines* (New York, 1943), 56.

18. For further information on the "Why We Fight" series see Michaela Hönicke's chapter "'Know Your Enemy': American Wartime Images of Germany, 1942–1943,"

[T]he message was simple, conveyed in a stark metaphor and a striking visual image. The audience was told that the Japanese resembled "photographic prints off the same negative." Visually, this was reinforced by repeated scenes of a steel bar being hammered in a forge.... Capra ... provided ample scenes of group activity and regimentation to reinforce the impression of a people devoid of individual identity.[19]

That description takes us back to Freud's notion that there is a relationship between self-imagery, or identity, and enemy imagery. Thus while it may not be true that Americans *needed* an enemy image in order to define themselves, when they were compelled to construct the portrait of an enemy they did in fact reveal their sense of themselves. The theme of individualism versus collectivism inheres not only in World War II images of Japan, but in all three of the twentieth-century conflicts under discussion: whether the enemy was German "Kaiserism" in World War I, Japanese regimentation in World War II, or Russian collectivist communism in the Cold War, a central component of the American definition of the adversary had to do with the enemy's embodiment of anti-individualist values. Indeed, even those Revolutionary era cartoons with which we began contained a not-unrelated reference to the opposition of "obedience" and "liberty." Here, I think, is a telling clue to Americans' definition of their own identity.

What happens to a nation's sense of identity when its enemies are utterly vanquished, and no longer provide the energizing force of a threat to that nation's very existence? That is the situation that faces the entire Western world, of course, but especially the United States, now that the Cold War is ended. (Here again it might be noted that the very concept of the "West" is another of those peculiar neologisms, like "the home front," that mirror the sometimes awful realities of our century.) Are there any clues in this brief historical overview of American uses of enmity that might shed light on the future?

It is always dangerous to extrapolate from the past to the future. The utility of historical study, it has been rightly said, is not to make us smart for the next time, but wise forever. Though properly cautioned by those considerations, I will nevertheless venture a thought about this matter.

---

in this volume; for further information on the image of the Japanese enemy see Wendy L. Wall's chapter "'Our Enemies Within': Nazism, National Unity, and America's Wartime Discourse on Tolerance," in this volume.

19. Dower, *War Without Mercy*, 19.

It could be argued that the period that we call "the Cold War" constituted the *only* period in American history when the United States played a consistent, reliable international role, forsaking its heritage of isolationism and entering into all kinds of political, economic, and military relations with other countries. Among the factors that sustained that forty-five year international engagement was the vitality of the image of the Soviet Union as an implacable enemy, godless, communist, and assuredly anti-individualist. Americans may not have needed an enemy image in order to define themselves, but they apparently needed one in times of crisis to mobilize themselves for collective effort, as they did in World War I and World War II, as well as during the Cold War. From President Truman's deliberate demonization of Soviet communism in the Truman Doctrine address of 1947 to President Reagan's invocation of the idea of an "evil empire," American leaders for more than two generations rallied their fellow citizens to unprecedentedly durable commitments to military service, high taxation, foreign aid, and free trade. With the collapse of that image, will the discipline and focus and commitment to internationalism that have been part of the American landscape for two generations disappear, as the United States reverts to some version of its nineteenth-century indifference to the rest of the world? Will an unmenaced America be an isolationist America? Or will the internal stresses that sometimes were only barely contained in the so-called Cold War consensus—stresses involving race, religion, class, and, not least of all, immigration—now generate their own energizing enmities, as in the cases of the Civil War and late-nineteenth-century nativism? The intensification of those stresses is everywhere evident in the former "enemy" lands of the East, so why should the West, America included, be exempt?

LIST OF CONTRIBUTORS

Ulrich Beck, Institute of Sociology, University of Munich

Volker Depkat, Member of the Graduiertenkolleg, "Sozial-geschichte von Gruppen, Schichten, Klassen und Eliten," University of Bielefeld

Mark Ellis, Department of History, Strathclyde University, Glasglow

Ragnhild Fiebig-von Hase, Institute of Anglo-American History, University of Cologne

Jessica C. E. Gienow-Hecht, Center for U.S. Studies, Stiftung Leucorea, Martin Luther University, Halle-Wittenberg

Jürgen Heideking, Institute of Anglo-American History, University of Cologne

Michaela Hönicke, John F. Kennedy Institute for North American Studies, Free University, Berlin

Hartmut Keil, Institute for American Studies, University of Leipzig

David M. Kennedy, Department of History, Stanford University

Ursula Lehmkuhl, Social Science Department, Ruhr-University at Bochum

Berndt Ostendorf, Amerika Institut, University of Munich

Kati Spillmann, Dipl.Psych.SPV Psychoanalyst in private practice, Zurich

Kurt R. Spillmann, Director, Center for Security Studies and Conflict Research, ETH Zurich/University of Zurich

Wendy L. Wall, History Department, Duke University, Durham, N.C.

Peter A. Zervakis, History Department, University of Hamburg

BIBLIOGRAPHY

Acheson, D.G. *Present at the Creation: My Years at the State Department.*
    New York, 1969.
Adams, W.-P. "Ethnic Leadership and the German-Americans." In *America
    and the Germans: An Assessment of a Three-Hundred-Year History,* vol. 1:
    Immigration, Language, Ethnicity, ed. F. Trommler and J. McVeigh.
    Philadelphia, 1985, 148–175.
———. "Ethnic Politicians and American Nationalism During the First
    World War: Four German-Born Members of the U.S. House of Represen-
    tatives." *American Studies International* 29 (April 1991): 20–34.
———. *Republikanische Verfassung und bürgerliche Freiheit: Die Verfassungen und
    politischen Ideen der amerikanischen Revolution.* Darmstadt, Neuwied, 1973.
Adler, L.K., and T.G. Paterson. "Red Fascism: The Merger of Nazi Germany
    and Soviet Russia in the American Image of Totalitarianism, 1930's-
    1950's." *American Historical Review* 75 (1969/1970): 1046–64.
Adorno, Th.W., E. Frenkel-Brunswick, D.J. Levinson and R.N. Sanford. *The
    Authoritarian Personality.* New York, 1950.
Ahrari, M.E., ed. *Ethnic Groups and U.S. Foreign Policy.* New York, 1987.
Alba, R. *Ethnic Identity: The Transformation of White America.* New Haven,
    CT, 1990.
Alexander, R.D. *Darwinism and Human Affairs.* Seattle, London, 1979.
Allen, F.L. "The American Tradition and the War." *Nation* 104, (26 April
    1917): 485.
Allport, G.W. *The Nature of Prejudice.* Cambridge, MA, 1954.
Almond, G.A., and S. Verba, eds. *The Civic Culture Revisited.* Newbury Park,
    London, New Delhi, 1989.
———. *The Civic Culture.* Boston, 1965.
Anderson, B. *Imagined Communities. Reflections on the Origin and Spread of
    Nationalism.* London, 1983.

Armstrong, J.A. *Nations before Nationalism.* Chapel Hill, 1982.

Ashkenas, B.F. "A Legacy of Hatred: The Records of a Nazi Organization in America." *Prologue* 17 (1985): 93–106.

Axelrod, R. *Die Evolution der Kooperation.* Munich, 1991.

Azmeh, Aziz Al. *Islamisierung des Islam: Imaginäre Welten einer politischen Theologie.* Frankfurt a.M., 1996.

Bader, R.S. *Prohibition in Kansas: A History.* Lawrence, KA, 1985.

Baerentzen, L., J.O. Iatrides and O.L. Smith, eds. *Studies in the History of the Greek Civil War 1945–1949.* Copenhagen, 1987.

Bailey, Th.A., and D.M. Kennedy. *The American Pageant.* 10th ed. Lexington, MA, 1990.

Bailyn, B., et al. *The Great Republic: A History of the American People.* Boston, Toronto, 1977.

―――. "Common Sense." In *Fundamental Testaments of the American Revolution.* Library of Congress Symposia on the American Revolution. Washington, D.C., 1973.

―――. *The Ideological Origins of the American Revolution.* 13th ed. Cambridge, MA, 1976.

Baker, N., C.J.H. Hayes and R.W. Straus, eds. *The American Way.* Chicago, 1936.

Bausch, U.M. *Die Kulturpolitik der US-amerikanischen Information Control Division in Württemberg-Baden von 1945 bis 1949: Zwischen militärischen Funktionalismus und schwäbischem Obrigkeitsdenken.* Stuttgart, 1992.

Bean, L.H., F. Mosteller and F. Williams. "Nationalities and 1944." *Public Opinion Quarterly* 8 (1944): 368–75.

Beck, U., and E. Beck-Gernsheim, eds. *Riskante Freiheiten.* Frankfurt a.M., 1994.

Beck, U., A. Giddens and S. Lash. *Reflexive Modernization—Politics, Tradition and Aesthetics in the Modern Social Order.* Cambridge, 1994.

Beck, U. *Risk Society: Towards a New Modernity.* London, 1992.

―――. *The Renaissance of Politic.* Cambridge, 1996.

Beeman, R., S. Botein and E.C. Carter II., eds. *Beyond Confederation: Origins of the Constitution and American National Identity.* Chapel Hill, NC, London, 1987.

Benn, G. *Essays und Reden.* Frankfurt a.M., 1989.

Bercovich, S. *The American Jeremiad.* Madison, WI, 1978.

Berding, H., ed. *Nationales Bewußtsein und kollektive Identität: Studien zur Entwicklung des kollektiven Bewußtseins in der Neuzeit.* vol. 2. Frankfurt a.M, 1994.

Berger, P.L., and Th. Luckmann. *The Social Construction of Reality: A Treatise in the Sociology of Knowledge.* New York, 1966, German translation: *Die gesellschaftliche Konstruktion der Wirklichkeit: Eine Theorie der Wissenssoziologie.* Frankfurt a.M., 1980.

Berghahn, V.R. *Militarism: The History of an International Debate, 1861–1979.* Cambridge, 1981.

―――, ed. *Militarismus.* Cologne, 1975

Berlin, E.A. "The Ragtime Debate." In *Ragtime: A Musical and Cultural History.* Berkeley, CA, 1980.

Besson, W. *Die Politische Terminologie des Präsidenten Franklin D. Roosevelt: Eine Studie über den Zusammenhang von Sprache und Politik* Tübingen, n.y.

Beyer, W.C. "Searching for *Common Ground*, 1940–1949: An American Literary Magazine and its Related Movements in Education and Politics." Ph.D. diss., University of Minnesota, 1988.

Billigmeier, R.H. *Americans from Germany: A Study in Cultural Diversity.* Belmont, CA, 1974.

Black, G.D., and C.R. Koppes. "OWI Goes to Hollywood: The Bureau of Intelligence's Criticism of Hollywood, 1942–43." *Prologue* 6 (1974): 44–59.

Black, G.D., and C.R. Koppes. "What to Show the World: The Office of War Information and Hollywood, 1942–45." *Journal of American History* 64 (1977): 87–105.

———. *Hollywood Goes To War: How Politics, Profits and Propaganda Shaped World War II Movies.* London, 1987.

Blakey, G.T. "*Historians on the Homefront*: Propagandists for the Great War." Ph.D. diss., Indiana University, 1970.

Bloch, R. *Visionary Republic: Millennial Themes in American Thought, 1756–1800.* Cambridge, MA, London, New York, 1985.

Blum, J.M. *V Was For Victory: Politics and American Culture During World War II.* San Diego, 1976.

Bohn, T.W. *An Historical and Descriptive Analysis of the "Why We Fight" Series.* New York, 1977.

Bollenbeck, G. *Bildung und Kultur: Glanz und Elend eines deutschen Deutungsmusters.* Frankfurt a.M., 1994.

Bönker, D. "Maritime Aufrüstung zwischen Partei- und Weltpolitik: Schlachtflottenbau in Deutschland und den USA um die Jahrhundertwende." In *Zwei Wege in die Moderne: Aspekte der deutsch-amerikanischen Beziehungen, 1900–1918*, ed. R. Fiebig-von Hase and J. Heideking. Trier, 1997.

Boulding, K.E. *The Image.* Ann Arbor, 1956.

Boyer, P. *When Time Shall Be No More: Prophecy Belief in Modern American Culture.* Cambridge, MA, 1992.

Braisted, W.R. *The United States Navy in the Pacific.* 2 vols. Austin, TX, 1958 and 1971.

Breen, T. H. "Ideology and Nationalism on the Eve of the American Revolution: Revisions Once More in Need of Revising." *Journal of American History* 83 (1997): 13–39.

Breitman, R., and A.M. Kraut. *American Refugee Policy and European Jewry, 1933–1945.* Bloomington, IN, 1987.

Brickner, R.M. *Is Germany Incurable?* Philadelphia, 1943.

Briggs, J., and F.D. Peat. *Die Entdeckung des Chaos.* Translated from English by C. Carius. Munich, Vienna, 1990.

Bruce, S. *The Rise and Fall of the New Christian Right.* Oxford, 1990.

Bryce, J. *Evidence and Documents Laid before the Committee on Alleged German Outrages.* New York, 1915.

———. *Neutral Nations and the War.* New York, 1914.

Buel, R., Jr. *Securing the Revolution: Ideology in American Politics, 1789–1815.* Ithaca, NY and London, 1972.

Bullock A. and O. Stallybrass, eds. *The Harper Dictionary of Modern Thought.* New York, 1977.

Burchell, R.A. "Did the Irish and German Voters Desert the Democrats in 1920? A Tentative Statistical Answer." *Journal of American Studies* 6 (August 1972): 153–64.

Bureau of Motion Pictures. *A List of U.S. War Information Films.* Washington, D.C., 1943.

Burgh, J. *Britain's Remembrancer: or, the Danger Not Over.* London 1746; reprinted in Philadelphia, 1747 and 1748; in Boston, 1759.

Cantril, H., and M. Strunk. *Public Opinion, 1935–1946.* Princeton, NJ, 1951.

Cappon, L.J., ed. *The Adams-Jefferson Letters.* 2 vols. Chapel Hill, NC, 1959.

Cartwright, D. and Z. Zander. *Group Dynamics: Research and Theory.* Evanston, IL, 1953.

Chadwin, M.L. *The War Hawks of World War II.* Chapel Hill, 1968.

Chambers, C. "The Greeks in the United States." *Modern Greek Studies Yearbook* 1 (1985): 193–97.

Chebithes, V.I. *AHEPA, and the Progress of Hellenism in America.* New York, 1935.

Child, C.J. *The German-Americans in Politics, 1914–1917.* Madison, 1939.

Choukas, M. "Greek Americans." In *Our Racial and National Minorities,* ed. F.J. Brown and J.S. Roucek. New York, 1937: 339–57.

Christol, H., and S. Ricard, eds. *Hyphenated Diplomacy: European Immigration and U.S. Foreign Policy, 1914–1984.* University de Provence, 1985.

Clay, L.D. *Decision in Germany.* Garden City, NY, 1950.

Coburn, C.K. *Life at Four Corners: Religion, Gender and Education in a German-Lutheran Community, 1868–1945.* Lawrence, KA, 1992.

Cohen, N.W. *Not Free to Desist: The American Jewish Committee, 1906–1966.* Philadelphia, 1972.

Cole, W.S. *Roosevelt and the Isolationists, 1932–45.* Lincoln, 1983.

Commons, J.R. *Races and Immigrants in America.* 2nd ed. 1907, New York, 1920.

Cooley, C.H. *Human Nature and the Social Order.* 1st ed. 1902, 4th ed. New York, 1964.

Cooling, B.F., ed. *War, Business, and American Society: Historical Perspectives on the Military-Industrial Complex.* Port Washington, NY, 1977.

Correspondence of the Military Intelligence Division Relating to "Negro-Subversion", 1917–1941. Washington, DC, 1986.

Coser, L. *The Functions of Social Conflict.* New York, 1956.

Cottam, M.L. *Foreign Policy Decision Making: The Influence of Cognition.* Boulder, London, 1986.

Couloumbis, T.A., J.A. Petropulos and H.J. Psomiades. *Foreign Interference in Greek Politics: An Historical Perspective.* New York, 1976.

Crapol, E.P. "From Anglophobia to Fragile Rapprochement: Anglo-American Relations in the Early Twentieth Century." In *Confrontation and Cooperation. Germany and the United States in the Era of World War I, 1900–1924,* ed. H.-J. Schröder. Providence, RI., Oxford, 1993: 13–31.

———. *America for Americans: Economic Nationalism and Anglophobia in the Late Nineteenth Century.* Westport, CT, 1973.

Culbert, D.S. "'Why We Fight:' Social Engineering for a Democratic Society at War." In *Film and Radio Propaganda in World War II,* ed. K.R.M. Short. Knoxville, 1983.

———, ed. *Film and Propaganda in America: A Documentary History.* New York, 1990.

Cummings, H.S., and C. McFarland. *Federal Justice: Chapters in the History of Justice and the Federal Executive.* New York, 1937.

Curti, M. *The Growth of American Thought.* 2nd ed. New York, 1951.

Dallek, R. *Franklin D. Roosevelt and American Foreign Policy, 1932–45.* Oxford, 1979.

Daniels, R. *Asian America: Chinese and Japanese in the United States since 1850.* Seattle, 1988.

———. *Coming to America: A History of Immigration and Ethnicity in American Life.* New York, 1992.

Dann, O. *Nation und Nationalismus in Deutschland, 1770–1990.* 3rd ed. Munich, 1996.

Daugherty, W.E., ed. *A Psychological Warfare Casebook.* Baltimore, MD, 1968, orig. 1958.

Davis, D.B. *The Fear of Conspiracy: Images of Un-American Subversion from the Revolution to the Present.* Ithaca, NY, 1971.

Dawkins, R. *Das egoistische Gen.* Berlin, Heidelberg, New York, 1978.

Denisoff, S.R. *Great Day Coming: Folk Music and the American Left.* Chicago, 1971.

Detjen, D.W. *The Germans in Missouri, 1900–1918: Prohibition, Neutrality, and Assimilation.* Columbia, MO, 1985.

Devine, D.J. *The Political Culture of the United States.* Boston, 1972.

Diamond, S.A. *The Nazi Movement in the United States, 1924–1941.* Ithaca, NY, 1974.

Dimbleby, D. and D. Reynolds. *An Ocean Apart: The Relationship Between Britain and America in the Twentieth Century.* London, Sydney, Auckland, Toronto, 1988.

Dinnerstein, L. *Anti-Semitism in America.* New York, 1994.

———. *Uneasy at Home: Antisemitism and the American Jewish Experience.* New York, 1987.

Dippel, H. "Die Wirkung der amerikanischen Revolution auf Deutschland und Frankreich." In *200 Jahre amerikanische Revolution und moderne Revolutionsforschung,* ed. H.-U. Wehler. Geschichte und Gesellschaft. Sonderheft 2. Göttingen, 1976, 101–21.

———. "'Eripuit coelo fulmen sceptrumque tyrannis': Benjamin Franklin als die Personifizierung der amerikanischen Revolution." *Amerika-Studien* 23 (1978): 19–29.

———. *Germany and the American Revolution 1770–1800: A Sociohistorical Investigation of Late Eighteenth-Century Political Thinking.* Chapel Hill, NC, 1977.

Dobbert, G.A. "German-Americans between New and Old Fatherland, 1870–1914." *American Quarterly* 19 (1967): 663–80.

Dobkowski, M.N. *The Tarnished Dream: The Basis of American Anti-Semitism.* Westport, CT, 1979.

Doerries, R.R. *Imperial Challenge: Ambassador Count Bernstorff and German-American Relations, 1908–1917.* Chapel Hill, NC, 1989.

Doll, E.E. "American History as Interpreted by German Historians from 1770 to 1815." *Transactions of the American Philosophical Society,* N. S. 38/5 (1948): 421–534.

Donaldson, S. *Archibald MacLeish: An American Life.* Boston, 1992.

Donner, F. *The Age of Surveillance.* New York, 1980.

Dower, J.W. *War Without Mercy.* New York, 1986.

Eibl-Eibesfeldt, I. "Stammesgeschichtliche Anpassungen im aggressiven Verhalten des Menschen." In *Aggression und Frustration als psychologisches Problem,* ed. H.-J. Kornadt. vol. 1. Darmstadt, 1981.

Eichhoff, J. "The German Language in America." *America and the Germans: An Assessment of a Three-Hundred-Year History,* vol. 1: *Immigration, Language, Ethnicity,* ed. F. Trommler and J. McVeigh. Philadelphia, 1985, 223–40.

Ellis, M. and P. Panayi. "German Minorities in World War I: A Comparative Study of Britain and the USA." *Ethnic and Racial Studies* 17 (April 1994): 238–59.

Engelsing, R. "Deutschland und die Vereinigten Staaten im 19. Jahrhundert: Eine Periodisierung." *Die Welt als Geschichte* 18 (Stuttgart, 1958): 138–156

Epstein, B.R., and A. Foster. *The Radical Right:. Report on the John Birch Society and Its Allies.* New York, 1967.

Epstein, D.J. *Sinful Tunes and Spirituals: Black Folk Music to the Civil War.* Urbana, Chicago, 1977.

Erenberg, L. *Steppin' Out: New York Nightlife and the Transformation of American Culture, 1890–1930.* Westport, CT, 1981.

Erikson, E.H. *Childhood and the Society.* New York, 1950.

Etzold, T.H., and J.L. Gaddis, eds. *Containment: Documents on American Policy and Strategy 1945–1950.* New York, 1978.

Falkowski, L.S., ed. *Psychological Models in International Politics.* Boulder, CO, 1979.

Fein, H. "Dimensions of Antisemitism: Attitudes, Collective Accusations, and Actions." In *The Persisting Question,* ed. H. Fein. Berlin, 1987.

Feingold, H.L. *A Time For Searching: Entering the Mainstream, 1920–1945.* Baltimore, MD, 1992.

Felden, T. "Frauen Reisen: Zur literarischen Repräsentation weiblicher Geschlechterrollenerfahrung im 19. Jahrhundert." Ph.D. diss., University of Alabama, 1991.

Ferguson, E.J. *The Power of the Purse: A History of American Public Finance, 1776–1790.* Chapel Hill, NC, 1961.

Ferrell, R.H. *Woodrow Wilson and World War I.* New York, 1985.

———. *Off the Record: The Private Papers of Harry S. Truman.* New York, 1980.

Fiebig-von Hase, R. "Lateinamerika als Konfliktherd der deutsch-amerikanischen Beziehungen, 1890–1903." *Schriften der Historischen Kommission bei
der Bayrischen Akademie der Wissenschaften*. vol. 27 (Göttingen, 1986).

———. "The United States and Germany in the World Arena." In *Confrontation and Cooperation, Germany and the United States in the Era of World War I,
1900–1924*, ed. Hans-Jürgen Schröder. Providence, RI, Oxford, 1993: 33–68.

———. *Lateinamerika als Konfliktherd der deutsch-amerikanischen Beziehungen
1890–1903*. Göttingen 1986.

Fink, G.-L. "Die amerikanische Revolution und die französische Revolution:
Analogien und Unterschiede im Spiegel der deutschen Publizistik
(1789–1798)." *Modern Language Notes* 103 (1988): 540–68.

Finlay, D.J., O.R. Holsti and R.R. Fagen. *Enemies in Politics*. Chicago, 1967.

Fisch, J. *Reparationen nach dem Zweiten Weltkrieg*. Munich, 1992.

Fiske, S.T., and S.E. Taylor. *Social Cognition*. 2nd ed. New York, 1991.

Foner, Ph.S., ed. *Alexander von Humboldt on Slavery in the United States*.
Berlin, 1981.

Foong Khong, Y. *Analogies at War: Korea, Munich, Dien bien Phu, and the Vietnam Decision of 1965*. Princeton, NJ, 1992.

Foster, A.J. "The Politicians, Public Opinion and the Press: The Storm over
British Military Intervention in Greece in December 1944." *Journal of Contemporary History* 19 (1984): 453–94.

Fox, R.W. *Reinhold Niebuhr: A Biography*. New York, 1985, 43–61.

Fraenkel, E., ed. *Amerika im Spiegel des deutschen politischen Denkens: Äußerungen deutscher Staatsmänner und Staatsdenker über Staat und Gesellschaft in
den Vereinigten Staaten von Amerika*. Cologne, Opladen, 1959.

Franz, E.G. *Das Amerikabild der deutschen Revolution von 1848/49: Zum Problem
der Übertragung gewachsener Verfassungsformen*. Heidelberg, 1958.

Frederickson, G. *The Black Image in the White Mind*. New York, 1971.

Free, L.A. and H. Cantril. *The Political Beliefs of Americans*. New Brunswick,
NJ, 1967.

Freeland, R.M. *The Truman Doctrine and the Origins of McCarthyism: Foreign
Policy, Domestic Policy, and Internal Security 1946–1948*. New York, 1972.

Frei, D. *Feindbilder und Abrüstung. Die gegenseitige Einschätzung der UdSSR
und der USA*. Munich, 1985.

Freud, S. *Civilization and its Discontent*. New York, 1961.

———. *The Standard Edition of the Complete Psychological Works of Sigmund
Freud*. Translated from German under the General Editorship of James
Strachey. London, 1963.

Fromm, E. *The Anatomy of Human Destructiveness*. New York, Chicago, San
Francisco, 1973; German edition: *Anatomie der menschlichen Destruktivität*.
Hamburg, 1977.

Funke, P., ed. *Understanding the USA: A Cross-Cultural Perspective*.
Tübingen, 1989.

Gaddis, J.L. "The Insecurities of Victory: The United States and the Perception of the Soviet Threat After World War II." In *The Truman Presidency*,
ed. M.J. Lacey. Washington, D.C., 1989, 235–72.

Garden, J. *A Cold Peace: The Fight for Supremacy*. New York, 1992.

Garrow, D.J. *The FBI and Martin Luther King, Jr.* New York, 1981.

Gay, P. *The Cultivation of Hatred.* New York, 1993.

Gellner, E. *Nations and Nationalism.* Ithaca, NY, 1983.

George, A.L. *Deterrence in American Foreign Policy: Theory and Practice.* New York, 1974.

————. *Presidential Decision Making in Foreign Policy: The Effective Use of Information and Advice.* Boulder, CO, 1980.

Gerbi, A. *The Dispute of the New World: The History of a Polemic 1750–1900.* Trans. J. Moyle. Pittsburgh, 1973.

Gerndt, H., ed. *Stereotypvorstellungen im Alltagsleben: Beiträge zum Themenkreis Fremdbilder—Selbstbilder—Identität: Festschrift für Georg R. Schroubek.* Munich, 1988.

————. "Zur kulturwissenschaftlichen Stereotypenforschung." In *Stereotypvorstellungen im Alltagsleben: Beiträge zum Themenkreis Fremdbilder—Selbstbilder—Identität: Festschrift für Georg R. Schroubek,* ed. H. Gerndt. Munich, 1988, 9–12.

Gerson, L.L. *The Hyphenate in Recent American Politics and Diplomacy.* University of Kansas, 1964.

Gestle, G. *Working-Class Americanism: The Politics of Labor in a Textile City, 1914–1960.* New York, 1989.

Giddens, A. *The Nation State and Violence.* vol. 2. *A Contemporary Critique of Historical Materialism.* Cambridge, 1985.

Gienow, J.C.E. "Cultural Transmission and the U.S. Occupation in Germany: The *Neue Zeitung,* 1945–55." Ph.D. diss., Charlottesville, VA, 1995.

Gietz, A. *Die Neue Alte Welt: Roosevelt, Churchill und die Europäische Nachkriegsordnung.* Munich, 1986.

Gillis, J., ed. *The Militarization of the Western World.* New Brunswick, NJ, 1989.

Ginsberg, B. *The Fatal Embrace: Jews and the State.* Chicago, IL, 1993.

Glazer, N., and D.P. Moynihan. *Beyond the Melting Pot: The Negroes, Puerto Ricans, Jews, Italians, and Irish of New York.* Cambridge, MA, 1963.

Gleason, P. "Americans All: World War II and the Shaping of American Identity." *Review of Politics* 43 (1981): 483–518.

Gleason, P. *Speaking of Diversity: Language and Ethnicity in Twentieth-Century America.* Baltimore, 1992.

————. *The Conservative Reformers: German-American Catholics and the Social Order.* Notre Dame, IN, 1968.

Goldman, A. "Germans and Nazis." *Journal of Contemporary History* 14 (1979): 155–91.

Greeley, A.M. *Ethnicity in the United States: A Preliminary Reconnaissance.* New York, London etc. 1974.

Greene, J.P. *The Intellectual Heritage of the Constitutional Era: The Delegates' Library.* Philadelphia, 1986.

Greiner, B. *Die Morgenthau-Legende: Zur Geschichte eines umstrittenen Plans.* Hamburg, 1995.

Griffith, R. *The Politics of Fear: Joseph R. McCarthy and the Senate.* Lexington, KY, 1970.

Grothusen, K.-D. "Außenpolitik." In *Greece: Handbook on South Eastern Europe*, vol. 3, ed. K.-D. Grothusen. Göttingen, 1980, 147–90.

Grothusen, K.-D., W. Steffani and P. Zervakis, eds. *Cyprus: Handbook on Southeastern Europe, vol. 9*. Göttingen, forthcoming.

Gruber, C.S. *Mars and Minerva: World War I and the Uses of Higher Learning in America*. Baton Rouge, LA, 1975.

Gurr, T.R. "The Revolution—Social Change Nexus. Some Old Theories and New Hypotheses." *Comparative Politics* 5 (1972/73): 359–92.

———. *Why Men Rebel*. Princeton, NJ, 1970.

Habe, H. *Im Jahre Null: Ein Beitrag zur Geschichte der deutschen Presse*. Munich, 1966.

Hamilton, D.L., and T.K. Trolier. "Stereotypes and Stereotyping. An Overview of the Cognitive Approach." In *Prejudice, Discrimination, and Racism*, ed. J.F. Dovidio and S.L. Gaertner. New York, 1986: 127–63.

Hamilton, W.D. "The Genetical Evolution of Social Behavior." *Journal of Theoretical Biology* (1964): 1–52.

Hamm, Ch. *Music in the New World*. New York, 1983.

Hampton, W. *Guerrilla Minstrels. John Lennon, Joe Hill, Woody Guthrie, and Bob Dylan*. Knoxville, KY, 1986.

Harbutt, F. *The Iron Curtain, Churchill, America, and the Origins of the Cold War*. Oxford, 1986.

Harper, John Lamberton. *American Visions of Europe: Franklin D. Roosevelt, George F. Kennan, and Dean G. Acheson*. Cambridge, 1996.

Hartmann, S.M. *Truman and the 80th Congress*. Columbia, 1971.

Hatch, N.O. "The Origins of Civil Millennialism in America: New England Clergymen, War with France, and the Revolution." *William and Mary Quarterly* 31 (1974): 407–30.

———. *The Sacred Cause of Liberty: Republican Thought and the Millennium in Revolutionary New England*. New Haven, CT, 1977.

Hawgood, J.A. *The Tragedy of German-America: the Germans in the United States of America During the Nineteenth Century—and After*. New York, 1940.

Heale, M.J. *American Anticommunism: Combating the Enemy Within, 1830–1970*. Baltimore, MD, 1990.

Heartman, C.F. *The Liberty Loan: Why Americans of German and Austrian Origin Should Buy Bonds*. New York, 1918.

Heideking, J. "Amerikanische Einflüsse und Reaktionen auf die Französische Revolution." In *Die Französische Revolution und Europa, 1789–1799*, ed. H. Timmermann. Saarbrücken, 1989, 117–31.

———. "Das Englandbild in der nordamerikanischen Publizistik zur Zeit der Revolution." In *Feindbilder: Die Darstellung des Gegners in der politischen Publizistik des Mittelalters und der Neuzeit*, ed. F. Bosbach. Cologne, 1992, 179–99.

———. "The Federal Processions of 1788 and the Origins of American Civil Religion." *Soundings* 77 (3–4, 1994): 367–87.

———. *Die Verfassung vor dem Richterstuhl: Vorgeschichte und Ratifizierung der amerikanischen Verfassung, 1787–1791*. Berlin, New York, 1988.

Heine, Heinrich, *Werke und Briefe*, vol. 4, ed. H. Kaufmann. Berlin, 1961.

————. "Ludwig Börne. Eine Denkschrift." In *Heinrich Heine: Historisch-kritische Gesamtausgabe der Werke*, ed. M. Windfuhr. vol. 11. Hamburg, 1978.

Helbich, W.J. *"Alle Menschen sind dort gleich": Die deutsche Amerika-Auswanderung im 19. und 20. Jahrhundert*. Düsseldorf, 1988.

Herberg, W. *Protestant-Catholic-Jew: An Essay in American Religious Sociology*. Chicago, 1955, 1960.

Hermann, R. "The Empirical Challenge of the Cognitive Revolution: A Strategy for Drawing Inferences about Perceptions." *International Studies Quarterly* 32 (1988): 175–203.

Herrmann, D. "The Americanization Movement, 1915–1921: Chance and Challenge for American Democracy." in *Problems of Democracy in the United States*, ed. W.P. Adams et al. Berlin, 1993, 124–32.

Hersey, J. *Into the Valley: A Skirmish of the Marines*. New York, 1943.

Herzstein, R.E. *Roosevelt and Hitler: Prelude to War*. New York, 1989.

Hettling, M., and P. Nolte. *Nation und Gesellschaft in Deutschland: Historische Essays*. Munich, 1996.

Higham, J. *Send These To Me: Jews and Other Immigrants in Urban America*. New York, 1975.

————. *Strangers in the Land. Patterns of American Nativism, 1860–1925*. New Brunswick, NJ, 1955, 2nd ed. New York 1966.

Hill, T. "The Enemy Within: Censorship in Rock Music in the 1950." In *Present Tense. Rock & Roll and Culture*, ed. A. DeCurtis. Durham, NC, London, 1992, 39–72.

Hinds, L., and T.O. Windt. *The Cold War as Rhetoric: The Beginnings 1945–1950*. New York, 1991.

Hobsbawm, E.J. "Inventing Traditions." in *The Invention of Tradition*, ed. Eric J. Hobsbawm and Terrence Ranger. Cambridge, 1983, 1–14.

————. *Nations and Nationalism since 1780: Programme, Myth, Reality*. Cambridge, New York etc., 1990.

Hobson, J.A. *The Psychology of Jingoism*. London, 1901.

Hoerder, D. *"People on the Move. Migration, Acculturation, and Ethnic Interaction in Europe and North America."* German Historical Institute: Annual Lecture Series No. 6. Providence, RI, Oxford, 1993.

Hoffer, C.P. *Revolution and Regeneration: Life Cycle and Historical Vision of the Generation of 1776*. Athens, GA, 1983.

Hofstadter, R. *Social Darwinism in American Thought*. Boston, 1955.

————. *The Paranoid Style in American Politics and Other Essays*. New York, 1965.

Holenstein, E. "Koevolutionäre Erkenntnislehre." In *Evolution und Selbstbezug des Erkennens*, ed. A. Fenk. Vienna and Cologne, 1903.

Holsti, O.R. "Foreign Policy Decision Makers Viewed Psychologically: Cognitive Processes Approaches." In *Thought and Action in Foreign Policy: Proceedings of the London Conference on Cognitive Process Models for Foreign Policy, March 1973*, ed. M. Shapiro and G.M. Bonham. Basel, Stuttgart, 1977, 10–74.

————. "The Belief System and National Images: A Case Study." *Journal of Conflict Resolution* 4 (1967): 244–52.

Homan, G.D. "Post-Armistice Courts-Martial of Conscientious Objectors." *Mennonite Life* 44 (1989): 4–9.

———. "The Burning of the Mennonite Church, Fairview, Michigan, in 1918." *Mennonite Quarterly Review* 64 (1990): 99–112.

Homans, G. *The Human Group.* 5th ed. New York, 1956.

Hondrich, K.-O. "Grenzen gegen die Gewalt." *DIE ZEIT*, no. 5, 28.1.1994: 4.

Horsman, R. *The Diplomacy of the New Republic, 1776–1815.* Arlington Heights, IL, 1985.

Horton, J.O., and H. Keil. "African Americans and Germans in Mid-Nineteenth Century Buffalo." In *Free People of Color: Inside the African American Community,* ed. J.O. Horton. Washington, D.C. and London, 1993.

Hough, E. *The Web.* Chicago, 1919.

Howe, J.R., Jr. *The Changing Political Thought of John Adams.* Princeton, NJ, 1966.

Huffines, M.L. "Language-Maintenance Efforts Among German Immigrants." In *America and the Germans: An Assessment of a Three-Hundred-Year History,* vol. 1: *Immigration, Language, Ethnicity,* ed. F. Trommler and J. McVeigh. Philadelphia, 1985, 241–50.

Hull, C. *The Memoirs of Cordell Hull.* New York, 1948.

Humboldt, A. von. *Kosmos.* vol. 1. Stuttgart, Tübingen, 1845.

Huntington, S.P. "The Clash of Civilizations?" *Foreign Affairs* 72 (1993): 22–49.

———. *American Politics, the Promise of Disharmony.* Cambridge, MA, 1981.

———. *The Clash of Civilizations.* New York, 1996.

Hurstfield, J.G. *America and the French Nation, 1939–45.* Chapel Hill, NC, 1986.

Hurwitz, H. *Die Eintracht der Siegermächte und die Orientierungsnot der Deutschen 1945–1946.* Cologne, 1984.

———. *Die Stunde Null der deutschen Presse: Die amerikanische Pressepolitik in Deutschland 1945–1949.* Cologne, 1972.

Iatrides, J.O., ed. *Ambassador Mac Veagh Reports: Greece, 1933–1947.* Princeton, NJ, 1980.

———, ed. *Greece in the 1940s: A Nation in Crisis.* London, 1981.

Immelmann, K., K.R. Scherer, Ch. Vogel and P. Schmoock, ed. *Psychobiologie: Grundlagen des Verhaltens.* Stuttgart and New York, 1988.

Jaher, F.C. *A Scapegoat in the New Wilderness: The Origins of Anti-Semitism in America.* Cambridge, MA., 1994

Janis, I.L. *Crucial Decisions: Leadership in Policymaking and Crisis Management.* New York and London, 1989.

Jeffrey-Jones, R. *American Espionage: From Secret Service to C.I.A.* New York, 1977.

Jeismann, M. *Das Vaterland der Feinde: Studien zum nationalen Feindbegriff und Selbstverständnis in Deutschland und Frankreich 1792–1918.* Stuttgart, 1992.

Jensen, J.M. *The Price of Vigilance.* Chicago, 1968.

Jervis, R. "Deterrence Theory Revisited." *World Politics* 31 (1978/1979): 289–324.

————. *Perception and Misperception in International Politics.* Princeton, NJ, 1976.

————. *The Illogic of American Nuclear Strategy.* Ithaca, NY, 1984.

Johnson, D. *Challenge to American Freedoms: World War I and the Rise of the American Civil Liberties Bureau.* Lexington, KY, 1963.

Jones, H., and R.B. Woods. "Origins of the Cold War in Europe and the Near East: Recent Historiography and the National Security Imperative." *Diplomatic History* 17 (1993): 251–76

Jones, J.S. *The Fifteen Weeks.* New York, 1955.

Jordan, W. *White Over Black: American Attitudes Toward the Negro 1550–1812.* Chapel Hill, NC, 1968.

Kahn, O.H. "The Duty and Opportunity of German-Americans." *Economic World* 15 (1918): 76–78.

Kammen, M. *A Season of Youth: The American Revolution and the Historical Imagination.* New York, 1978.

Kanter, K.A. *The Jews on Tin Pan Alley: The Jewish Contribution to American Popular Music, 1830–1940.* New York, 1982.

Karalekas, A. *Britain, the United States and Greece, 1942–1945.* New York, 1988.

Katz, B. *Foreign Intelligence: Research and Analysis in the Office of Strategic Services, 1942–45.* Cambridge, 1989.

Kazal, R.A. "Revisiting Assimilation: The Rise, Fall, and Reappraisal of a Concept." *American Historical Review* 100 (1995): 437–71.

Keeley, E. *The Salonica Bay Murder, Cold War Politics and the Polk Affair.* Princeton, Second Edition, 1990.

Keil, H., and J.B. Jentz, eds. *German Workers in Chicago: A Documentary History of Working-Class Culture from 1850 to World War I.* Urbana and Chicago, 1988.

Keil, H. "Die Auswirkungen der amerikanischen Revolution auf Europa." In *Die französische Revolution. Wurzeln und Wirkungen,* ed. V. Schubert. Wissenschaft und Philosophie. Interdisziplinäre Studien. vol. 7. St. Ottilien, 1989.

Keller, P. *States of Belonging: German-American Intellectuals and the First World War.* Cambridge, MA, 1979.

Kennan, G.F. "The Sources of Soviet Conduct." *Foreign Affairs* (July, 1947): 566–82.

————. *American Diplomacy.* expanded ed. Chicago, 1984.

Kennedy, D.M. *Over Here: The First World War and American Society.* New York, 1980.

Kennedy, R.G. *Orders from France: The Americans and the French in a Revolutionary World, 1780–1820.* New York, 1989.

Kepley, D.R. *The Collapse of the Middle Way: Senate Republicans and the Bipartisan Foreign Policy, 1948–1952.* New York, 1988.

Kimball, W.F. *Swords or Ploughshares? The Morgenthau Plan for Defeated Nazi Germany, 1943–46.* Philadelphia, 1976.

Kinsella, W.E., Jr. *Leadership in Isolation: FDR and the Origins of the Second World War.* Cambridge, MA, 1978.

Kirchwey, F. "Unity for What?" *The Nation* (16 November 1940): 465–66.

Kirschbaum, E. *The Eradication of German Culture in the United States, 1917–1918.* Stuttgart, 1986.

Kitroeff, A. "The Transformation of Homeland-Diaspora Relations: The Greek Case in the 19th-20th Centuries." In *Proceedings of the First International Congress on the Hellenic Diaspora,* ed. J.M. Fossey. 2 vols. Amsterdam, 1991, vol. 2, 233–50.

Klineberg, O. *The Human Dimension in International Relations.* New York, 1964, German ed. *Die menschliche Dimension in den internationalen Beziehungen.* Bern, Stuttgart, 1966.

Kluge, F. *Etymologisches Wörterbuch der deutschen Sprache.* 22nd ed. Berlin, 1989.

Koch, A., ed. *The American Enlightenment: The Shaping of the American Experiment and a Free Society.* New York, 1956.

Koebner, Th., ed. *Deutschland nach Hitler: Zukunftspläne im Exil und aus der Besatzungszeit, 1939–49.* Opladen, 1987.

Kohn, H. *The Idea of Nationalism.* New York, 1944.

Koistinen, P.A.C. *The Military-Industrial Complex: A Historical Perspective.* New York, 1980.

Kontis, B. *I Angloamerikaniki Politiki kai to Elliniko Provlima: 1945–1949* [Anglo-American Politics and the Greek Problem]. 2nd ed. Thessaloniki, 1984.

Kontje, T.C. *The German Bildungsroman: A History of a National Genre.* Columbia, SC, 1993.

Kopan, A. "Greek Survival in Chicago: The Role of Ethnic Education, 1890–1980." In *Ethnic Chicago,* ed. M.G. Holli and P. Jones. 2nd ed. Grand Rapids, MI, 1984, 109–68.

Kornweibel, Th., Jr. *Federal Surveillance of Afro-Americans (1917–1925): The First World War, the Red Scare, and the Garvey Movement.* Frederick, MD, 1986.

Krakau, Knud, ed. *The American Nation—National Identity—Nationalism.* Münster, 1997.

Kraut, A.M., and R.D. Breitman. "Anti-Semitism in the State Department, 1933–44: Four Case Studies." In *Anti-Semitism in American History,* ed. D.A. Gerber. Urbana, IL, 1986, 167–97.

Kraut, B. "Towards the Establishment of the National Conference of Christians and Jews: The Tenuous Road to Religious Goodwill in the 1920s." *American Jewish History* 77 (1988): 388–412.

Krieger, W. *General Lucius D. Clay und die amerikanische Deutschlandpolitik 1945–1949.* Stuttgart, 1987.

Krippendorff, E. *Staat und Krieg. Die historische Logik politischer Unvernunft.* Frankfurt a.M., 1985.

Krohn, C.-D., E. Rotermund, L. Winckler and W. Koepke, eds. *Exil und Remigration.* Munich, 1991.

Kropotkin, P. *Mutual Aid: A Factor in Evolution.* New York, London, 1902.

Kurth, J. "The Real Clash." *The National Interest* 37 (1994): 3–15.

Kurth, P. *American Cassandra: The Life of Dorothy Thompson.* Boston, 1990.

Kusmer, K.L. *A Ghetto Takes Shape: Black Cleveland, 1870–1930.* Urbana, Chicago, IL, 1976.

Kyrou, A.K. "Greek Nationalism and Diaspora Politics in America, 1940–1945: Background and Analysis of Ethnic Responses to Wartime Crisis." Ph.D. diss., Indiana University, 1993.

Lach, D.F. "What They Would Do About Germany." *Journal of Modern History* 17 (September 1945): 227–43.

Laiou-Thomadakis, A. "The Politics of Hunger: Economic Aid to Greece, 1943–1945." *Journal of the Hellenic Diaspora* 7 (1980): 27–42.

Langewiesche, D. "Nation, Nationalismus, Nationalstaat: Forschungsstand und Forschungsperspektiven." *Neue Politische Literatur* 40 (1995): 190–236.

Langkau-Alex, Ursula and Thomas M. Ruprecht, eds. *Was soll aus Deutschland werden? The Council for a Democratic Germany in New York 1944–45.* Frankfurt, 1995.

Lansing, R. *War Memoirs.* Indianapolis, IN, 1935

Larson, D.W. "The Role of the Belief System and Schemas in Foreign Policy Decision Making." *Political Psychology* 15 (1994): 20–21.

———. *Origins of Containment: A Psychological Explanation.* Princeton, NJ, 1989.

Leber, G.E. *The History of the Order of AHEPA.* Washington, D.C., 1972.

Lees, L. "National Security and Ethnicity: Contrasting Views during World War II." *Diplomatic History* 11 (1987): 113–25.

Leffler, M.P. *A Preponderance of Power. National Security, the Truman Administration, and the Cold War.* Stanford, CA, 1992.

———. *The Specter of Communism.* New York, 1994.

Leonard, N. "Reactions to Ragtime." In *Ragtime: Its History, Composers, and Music,* ed. J.E. Hasse. New York, 1985.

———. *Jazz and the White Americans.* Chicago, 1962.

Lerner, D. *Propaganda in War and Crisis.* New York, 1951.

———. *Psychological Warfare Against Nazi-Germany: The Sykewar Campaign, D-Day to VE-Day.* Cambridge, MA, 1971, orig. 1949.

Levin, G.N. *Woodrow Wilson and World Politics: America's Response to War and Revolution.* London, 1968.

Levinson, D. "Authoritarian Personality and Foreign Policy." In *War,* ed. A. Lepawsky and G. Goethals. 2nd ed. New York, 1968.

Lewin, K. *Resolving Social Conflict.* New York, 1948.

Lieberman, R. *"My Song is My Weapon": People's Songs, American Communism, and the Politics of Culture, 1930–1950.* Urbana and Chicago, 1989.

Liebman, R.C., and R. Wuthnow, eds. *The New Christian Right.* New York, 1983.

Lind, M. "Reverend Robertson's Grand International Conspiracy Theory." *The New York Review of Books* (2 February 1995): 21–15.

Link, A.S. *Wilson,* vol. 5: *Campaigns for Progressivism and Peace, 1916–1917.* Princeton, NJ, 1965.

———. *Woodrow Wilson and the Progressive Era, 1910–1917.* New York, 1963.

———, ed. *Papers of Woodrow Wilson,* 69 vols. Princeton, 1966ff.

Lippmann, W. *The Cold War: A Study in US Foreign Policy.* London, 1947.

Lipset, S.M., and E. Raab. *The Politics of Unreason: Right-Wing Extremism in America, 1790–1970.* London, 1971.

Lipset, S.M. *The First New Nation: The United States in Historical and Comparative Perspective.* London, 1964.

Lipstadt, D.E. *Beyond Belief: The American Press and the Coming of the Holocaust, 1933–45.* New York, 1986.

Loomis, L.R., and T.B. Lowett, eds. *Five Great Dialogues.* Princeton, NJ, 1942.

Lotchin, R.W. *Fortress California, 1910–1961: From Warfare to Welfare.* New York, 1992.

Louis, W.R., and H. Bull, eds. *The 'Special Relationship': Anglo-American Relations Since 1945.* Oxford, 1986.

Luebke, F.C. "Images of German Immigrants in the United States and Brazil, 1890–1918: Some Comparisons." In *America and the Germans: An Assessment of a Three-Hundred-Year History,* vol. 1. *Immigration, Language, Ethnicity,* ed. F. Trommler and J. McVeigh. Philadelphia, 1985, 207–21.

———. *Bonds of Loyalty: German-Americans and World War I.* De Kalb, IL, 1974.

———. *Germans in the New World: Essays on the History of Immigration.* Urbana, IL, 1990.

———, ed. *Ethnic Voters and the Election of Lincoln.* Lincoln, NE, 1971.

Lundestad, G. *The American Non-Policy Toward Eastern Europe 1943–1947: Universalism in an Area not of Essential Interest to the United States.* Tromsö, Bergen, Oslo, 1978.

Maier, P. "John Wilkes and American Disillusionment with Britain" *William and Mary Quarterly* 20 (1963): 373–95.

Malone, M.P., and R.W. Etulain. *The West: A Twentieth Century History.* Lincoln, NE, 1989.

Mandel, R. "Psychological Approaches to International Relations." In *Political Psychology,* ed. M.G. Hermann. San Francisco, London, 1986, 251–58.

Markusen, A., S. Campbell, P. Hall and S. Deitrick, eds. *The Rise of the Gunbelt: The Military Remapping of Industrial America.* New York, 1991.

Marquardt-Bigman, P. *Amerikanische Geheimdienstanalysen über Deutschland 1942–1949.* Munich, 1995.

Marshall, Th.H. *Citizenship and Social Class.* New York, 1950.

Martin, L., and K. Segrave. *Anti-Rock: The Opposition to Rock 'n' Roll.* Hamdon, CT, 1988.

Marudas, P. "Greek-American Involvement in Contemporary Politics." In *The Greek American Community in Transition, with a Bibliographic Guide by J.C. Zenelis,* ed. H.J. Psomiades and A. Scourby. New York, 1982, 93–109.

Mason, D.G. *Tune In America* 1930. repr. Westport, CT, 1970.

Mathews, D.G. "'Spiritual Warfare': Cultural Fundamentalism and the Equal Rights Amendment." *Religion and American Culture* 3, no. 2 (1993): 129–54.

Mauch, Ch. "Pazifismus und politische Kultur: Die organisierte Friedensbewegung in den USA und Deutschland in vergleichender Perspektive, 1900–1917." In *Zwei Wege in die Moderne, Aspekte der deutsch-amerikanischen Beziehungen, 1900–1918,* ed. R. Fiebig-von Hase and J. Heideking. Trier, 1997.

Maurer, M. *Anglophilie und Aufklärung in Deutschland.* Göttingen, Zurich, 1987.

May, Ch.N. *In the Name of War: Judicial Review and the War Powers since 1918.* Cambridge, MA, 1989.

May, E.T. *Homeward Bound: American Families in the Cold War.* New York, 1988.

May, E.R. *Lessons of the Past: The Use and Misuse of History in American Foreign Policy.* New York, 1973.

McAuliffe, M.S. *Crisis on the Left: Cold War Politics and American Liberals, 1947–1954.* Amherst, MA, 1978.

McCarthy, J. "The British." In *The Immigrant's Influence on Wilson's Peace Policies,* ed. J.P. O'Grady. Lexington, KY, 1967.

McFeely, W.S. *Frederick Douglass.* New York, 1991.

Mead, G.H. *Mind, Self, and Society from the Standpoint of a Social Behaviorist,* ed. with introduction by Ch. Morris, 14th ed. Chicago, 1967.

Mehnert, U. "Deutsche Weltpolitik und amerikanisches Zweifrontendilemma. Die "japanische Gefahr" in den deutsch-amerikanischen Beziehungen 1904–1917." *Historische Zeitschrift* 257 (1993): 647–92.

———. "German *Weltpolitik* and the American Two-Front Dilemma: The 'Japanese Peril' in German-American Relations, 1904–1917." *Journal of American History* 82 (1996): 1452–1477.

———. *Deutschland, Amerika und die 'Gelbe Gefahr': Zur Karriere eines Schlagworts in der Großen Politik, 1905–1917.* Stuttgart, 1995.

Melman, S., ed. *The War Economy of the United States. Readings on Military Industry and Economy.* New York, 1971.

———. *'Pentagon Bourgeoisie.' Beyond Conflict and Containment: Critical Studies of Military and Foreign Policy.* New Brunswick, NJ, 1972.

———. *'Pentagon Capitalism.'* New York, 1970.

Mencken, H.L. *Prejudices: Second Series.* New York, 1920.

———. *Prejudices: Third Series.* New York, 1922.

Mendelsohn, E., M.R. Smith and P. Weingart, eds. *Science, Technology, and the Military.* 2 vols. Boston, 1988.

Merkley, P. *Reinhold Niebuhr: A Political Account.* Montreal, 1975.

Merritt, R.L. "The Colonists Discover America: Attention Patterns in the Colonial Press, 1735–1775." *William and Mary Quarterly* 21 (1964): 270–87.

———. "The Emergence of American Nationalism: A Quantitative Approach." *American Quarterly* 17 (1965): 319–34.

———. *Symbols of American Community, 1735–1775.* New Haven, CT, 1966.

Meyer, H. *Nordamerika im Urteil des deutschen Schrifttums bis zur Mitte des 19. Jahrhunderts: Eine Untersuchung über Kürnbergers "Amerika-Müden". Mit einer Bibliographie.* Hamburg, 1929.

Meyer, J.C. "Reflections of a Conscientious Objector in World War." *Mennonite Quarterly Review* 41 (1967): 79–96.

Middlekauff, R. *The Glorious Cause: The American Revolution, 1763–1789.* The Oxford History of the United States. vol. 2. New York, Oxford, 1982.

Miller, R. "Preface." In *States of Progress: Germans and Blacks in America over 300 Years,* ed. Randall Miller. Philadelphia, 1989.

Mock, J.R. *Censorship, 1917.* Princeton, NJ, 1941.

Mock, J.R., and Cedric Larson. *Words That Won the War: The Story of the Committee on Public Information, 1917–1919.* Princeton, NJ, 1939.

Moltmann, G. *Atlantische Blockpolitik im 19. Jahrhundert: Die Vereinigten Staaten und der deutsche Liberalismus während der Revolution von 1848–49.* Düsseldorf, 1973.

———. *Amerikas Deutschlandpolitik im Zweiten Weltkrieg: Kriegs- und Friedensziele 1941–45.* Heidelberg, 1958.

Mommsen, H., ed. *Arbeiterbewegung und Nationale Frage. Ausgewählte Aufsätze.* Göttingen, 1979.

———. "Der Nationalismus als weltgeschichtlicher Faktor: Probleme einer Theorie des Nationalismus." In *Arbeiterbewegung und Nationale Frage. Ausgewählte Aufsätze,* ed. H. Mommsen. Göttingen, 1979, 15–60.

Montalto, N.V. *A History of The Intercultural Education Movement, 1924–1941.* New York, 1982.

Moore, M.S. *Yankee Blues: Musical Culture and American Identity.* Bloomington, IN, 1985.

Morgenthau, H.J. *Politics among Nations,* 6th rev, ed. New York, 1985.

Moskos, Ch.C. *Greek Americans: Struggle and Success.* 2nd ed. New Brunswick and London, 1989.

Mosse, G.L. *German Jews Beyond Judaism.* Bloomington, IN, 1985.

Mowrer, E.A. *Germany Puts the Clock Back.* London, 1937.

Mullen, B., and G.B. Goethals, eds. *Theories of Group Behavior.* New York, 1986.

Mullen, B. *The Phenomenology of Being in a Group: Meta-Analytic Integrations of Social Cognition and Group Processes.* New York, 1991.

Nachmani, A. *International Intervention in the Greek Civil War: The United Nations Special Committee on the Balkans, 1947–1952.* New York, 1990.

Nagler, J. "Enemy Aliens in the USA, 1914–1918." In *Minorities in Wartime: National and Racial Groups in Europe, North America and Australia During the Two World Wars* ed. Panikos Panayi. Providence, RI, 1993, 191–215.

———. *Fremont contra Lincoln: Die deutsch-amerikanische Opposition in der Republikanischen Partei während des amerikanischen Bürgerkrieges.* Frankfurt a.M., 1984.

Nicholas, H.G., ed. *Washington Despatches, 1941–1945: Weekly Political Reports from the British Embassy.* Chicago, 1981.

Nicholls, A.J. "American Views of Germany's Future During World War II." In *Das 'Andere Deutschland' im Zweiten Weltkrieg: Emigration und Widerstand in internationaler Perspektive,* ed. L. Kettenacker. Stuttgart, 1977.

Niebuhr, R. "The Failure of German-Americanism." *Atlantic Monthly* 118 (1916): 13–18.

Noebel, D.A. *Rhythm, Riots and Revolution: An analysis of the Communist Use of Music—The Communist Master Music Plan.* Tulsa, OK, 1966.

Norman, A. *Our Germany Policy: Propaganda and Culture.* New York, 1951.

Norton, M.B. "The Loyalist Critique of the Revolution." In *Library of Congress Symposia on the American Revolution: The Development of a Revolutionary Mentality,* ed. Library of Congress. Washington, D.C., 1972, 127–44.

Novack, M. *The Rise of the Unmeltable Ethnics: Politics and Culture in the Seventies*. New York, 1975.

Novick, P. *That Noble Dream: The "Objectivity Question" and the American Historical Profession*. Cambridge, New York, Melbourne, 1988, reprint 1995.

O'Connor, R. *Diplomacy for Victory: FDR and Unconditional Surrender*. New York, 1971.

Office of War Information, Domestic Branch. *Information Guide: The Enemy*. Washington, D.C., April 1943.

———, Domestic Radio Bureau. *When Radio Writes for War*. Washington, D.C., 1943.

Ohlinger, G. *The German Conspiracy in Education*. New York, 1919.

Olds, F.P. "Disloyalty of the German-American Press." *Atlantic Monthly* 120 (1917): 136–40.

———. "'Kultur' in American Politics." *Atlantic Monthly* 118 (1916): 382–91.

Olson, A.G. "The London Mercantile Lobby and the Coming of the American Revolution." *Journal of American History* 69 (1982): 21–41.

Oshinsky, D.M. *A Conspiracy So Immense: The World of Joe McCarthy*. New York, 1983.

Ostendorf, B. "'America is a Mistake, a Gigantic Mistake': Patterns of Ethnocentrism in German Attitudes Towards America." *In Their Own Words*, vol. 3, no. 2 (1986): 19–47.

———. "Anthropology, Modernism, and Jazz." In: *Ralph Ellison*, ed. H. Bloom. New York, 1986, 145–72.

———. "Chicago and the Music of the Jazz Age 1920–30." *Englische und Amerikanische Studien* 2 (1980): 432–44.

———. "Ethnicity and Popular Music." Working Paper No. 2. IASPM, International Association for the Study of Popular Music. Exeter, Engl., 1983.

———. "Minstrelsy and Early Jazz." *The Massachusetts Review* 20, no. 3 (1979): 574–602.

———. "The Diluted Second Generation: German-Americans in Music 1870–1920." In *German Worker's Culture in the US: 1850–1920*, ed. H. Keil. Washington, D.C., 1988, 261–87.

———."Probleme mit der Differenz: Historische Ursachen und gesellschaftliche Konsequenzen der Selbstethnisierung in den USA." In *Die bedrängte Toleranz*, ed. W. Heitmeyer and R. Dollase. Frankfurt a.M., 1996, 155–78.

Palmer, R.R. *The Age of the Democratic Revolution: A Political History of Europe and America, 1760–1800*, vol. 1: *The Challenge*. Princeton, NJ, 1959.

Pankratz, H. "The Suppression of Alleged Disloyalty in Kansas During World War I." *Kansas Historical Quarterly* 42 (1976): 277–307.

Parsons, T. "Full Citizenship for the Negro American?" In *Sociological Theory and Modern Society*, ed. T. Parsons. New York, 1957.

———. *Essays in the Sociological Theory*, rev. ed. New York, 1947, 1964.

Paterson, Th.G. "Presidential Foreign Policy, Public Opinion, and Congress: The Truman Years." *Diplomatic History* (1979): 1–18.

———. "The Dissent of Senator Claude Pepper." In *Cold War Critics*, ed. Th.G. Paterson. New York, 1971, 114–39.

Pautsch, I.D. *Die territoriale Deutschlandplanung des amerikanischen Außenministeriums, 1941–43*. Frankfurt a.M., 1990.

Peck, A.J., ed. *The German-Jewish Legacy in America, 1938–1988: From Bildung to the Bill of Rights*. Detroit, MI, 1989.

Peterson, E.N. *The American Occupation of Germany: Retreat to Victory*. Detroit, MI, 1977.

Peterson, H.C. *Propaganda for War: The Campaign Against American Neutrality, 1914–1917*. Norman, OK, 1939.

Peterson, H.C., and Gilbert C. Fite. *Opponents of War 1917–1918*. Seattle, WA, 1963.

Phocas, A. *Biologische Aspekte politischen Verhaltens*. Munich, 1986.

Pickett, T.H. "Perspectives on a National Crisis: A German Correspondent Reports on America, 1853–1865." *Tamkang Journal of American Studies*, 4 (Spring 1988): 6–15.

———. "The Friendship of Frederick Douglass with the German, Ottilie Assing." *The Georgia Historical Quarterly*, 73 (1989): 87–105.

Pogo (as told to Walt Kelly). *The Jack Acid Society Black Book*. New York, 1962.

Powell, A.K. "Our Cradles Were in Germany: Utah's German American Community and World War I." *Utah Historical Quarterly* 58 (Fall 1990): 371–387.

Prentice-Dunn, S., and R.W. Rodgers. "Deindividuation and the Self Regulation of Behavior." In *Psychology of Group Influence*, ed. P.B. Paulus. Hillsdale, NJ, 1989), 87–109.

Preston, W., Jr. *Aliens and Dissenters: Federal Suppression of Radicals, 1903–1933*. Cambridge, MA, 1963.

Public Papers of the Presidents of the United States: Harry S. Truman, January 1 to December 31, 1947. Washington, 1963.

Radkau, J. *Die deutsche Emigration in den USA: Ihr Einfluß auf die amerikanische Europapolitik, 1933–45*. Düsseldorf, 1971.

Rainbolt, J.C. "American's Initial View of their Revolution's Significance for Other Peoples, 1776–1787." *Historian* 35 (1973): 418–33.

Rauhut, F. "Die Herkunft der Worte und Begriffe 'Kultur', 'Civilisation' und 'Bildung'." *Germanisch-Romanische Monatsschrift* 3 (April 1953): 81–91.

Raulet, G. "Die Modernität der Gemeinschaft." In *Gemeinschaft und Gerechtigkeit*, ed. M. Brumlik and H. Brunkhorst. Frankfurt a.M., 1993, 72–93.

Redekop, J.H. *The American Far Right: A Case Study of Billy James Hargis and Christian Crusade*. Grand Rapids, MI, 1968.

Reed, I. *Mumbo Jumbo*. New York, 1972.

Reed, M.E. *Seedtime for the Modern Civil Rights Movement: The President's Committee on Fair Employment Practice, 1941–1946*. Baton Rouge, LA, 1991.

Regan, P.M. *Organizing Societies for War: The Process and Consequences of Societal Militarization*. Westport, CT, 1994.

Reitzel, W., M.A. Kaplan and C.G. Coblenz. *U.S. Foreign Policy, 1945–55*. Washington, 1956.

Reynolds, D. "A 'Special Relationship'? America, Britain and the International Order Since the Second World War." *International Affairs* 62 (1985/86): 1–20.

Ribuffo, L.P. *The Old Christian Right: The Protestant Far Right from the Great Depression to the Cold War.* Philadelphia, 1983.

Richter, D. "Der Mythos der "guten" Nation." *Soziale Welt* 3 (1994): 304–21.

Rippley, La Vern J. *The German-Americans.* Boston, 1976.

Roloff, G. *Exil und Exilliteratur in der deutschen Presse 1945–1949: Ein Beitrag zur Rezeptionsgeschichte.* Worms, 1976.

Roosevelt, F.D. *F.D.R. His Personal Letters.* vol. 2. *1928–1945,* ed. Eliot Roosevelt. New York, 1950.

———. *The Complete Presidential Press Conferences of Franklin D. Roosevelt.* New York, 1972.

———. *The Public Papers and Addresses of Franklin D. Roosevelt,* ed. S.I. Rosenman. New York, 1950.

Roosevelt, Th. *The Foes of Our Own Household.* New York, 1917.

Rosati, J.A. "A Cognitive Approach to the Study of Foreign Policy." In *Foreign Policy Analysis: Continuity and Change in Its Second Generation,* ed. L. Neack et al. Englewood Cliffs, NJ, 1995, 49–70.

Rosen, St., ed. *Testing the Theory of the Military-Industrial Complex.* Lexington, MA, 1973.

Ruof, F. "Johann Wilhelm von Archenholtz (1741–1812)." In *Deutsche Publizisten des 15. bis 20. Jahrhunderts,* ed. H.-D. Fischer. Munich, Pullach, Berlin, 1971, 129–39.

———. *Johann Wilhelm von Archenholtz: Ein deutscher Schriftsteller zur Zeit der Französischen Revolution und Napoleons (1741–1812).* Berlin, 1915, reprint Vaduz, 1965.

Said, E. *Cultural Imperialism.* New York, 1993.

Salet, R. *Russian-German Settlement in the United States.* Fargo, ND, 1974.

Saloutos, Th. "Causes and Patterns of Greek Emigration to the United States." *Perspectives of American History* 7 (1973): 381–437.

———. "The Greek Orthodox Church in the United States and Assimilation." *International Migration Review* 7 (1973): 395–407.

———. *The Greeks in the United States.* Cambridge, 1964.

———. *They Remember America.* Berkeley, 1956.

Samatas, M. "Greek McCarthyism: A Comparative Assessment of Greek Post-Civil War Repressive Anticommunism and the U.S. Truman-McCarthy Era." *Journal of the Hellenic Diaspora* 13 (1986): 5–75.

Sandeen, E.J. "'Confessions of a Nazi Spy' and the German-American Bund." *American Studies* 20 (Fall 1979): 69–78.

Sarna, J.D. "Anti-Semitism and American History." *Commentary* 71 (March 1981): 42–47.

Sayer, J. "Art and Politics, Dissent and Repression: The *Masses* Magazine Versus the Government, 1917–1918." *American Journal of Legal History* 32 (Jan. 1988): 42–78.

Schaff, A. *Stereotypen und das menschliche Handeln.* Vienna, Zurich, Munich, 1980.

Scheiber, H.N. *The Wilson Administration and Civil Liberties, 1917–1921.* Ithaca, NY, 1960.

Schissler, J., and Ch. Tuschhoff. "Kognitive Schemata: Zur Bedeutung neuerer soziapsychologischer Forschung für die Politikwissenschaft." *Aus Politik und Zeitgeschichte* B 52–53/88 (23.12.1988): 3–13.

Schlabach, T., ed. *"An Account,* by Jacob Waldner: Diary of a Conscientious Objector in World War I." *Mennonite Quarterly Review* 48 (1974): 73–111.

Schlesinger, A.M. *Prelude to Independence: The Newspaper War on Britain 1764–1776.* New York, 1957.

Schlesinger, A.M., Jr. *The Disuniting of America: Reflections on a Multicultural Society.* New York, London, 1991.

Schmid-Hempel, P. "Lebenslaufstrategien, Fortpflanzungsunterschiede und biologische Optimierung." In *Fortpflanzung, Natur und Kultur im Wechselspiel, Versuch eines Dialogs zwischen Biologen und Sozialwissenschaftlern,* ed. E. Voland. Frankfurt a.M., 1992.

Scholnick, M.T. *The New Deal and Anti-Semitism in America.* New York, 1990.

Schreiner-Seip, C. *Film- und Informationspolitik als Mittel der Nationalen Verteidigung in den USA, 1939–41: Eine Studie über die Umsetzung außenpolitischer Programme in Filminhalte.* Frankfurt a.M., 1985.

Schubert, V., ed. *Die französische Revolution. Wurzeln und Wirkungen.* Wissenschaft und Philosophie. Interdisziplinäre Studien. vol. 7. St. Ottilien, 1989.

Schulze, H. *Staat und Nation in der europäischen Geschichte.* Munich, 1994.

Schulzinger, R.D. *The Wise Men of Foreign Affairs: The History of the Council on Foreign Relations.* New York, 1984.

Senghaas, D. *Rüstung und Militarismus.* Frankfurt a.M., 1972.

Shapiro, E.S. *A Time For Healing: American Jewry since World War II.* Baltimore, MD, 1992.

Shapiro, M., and G.M. Bonham. "Introduction." In *Thought and Action in Foreign Policy: Proceedings of the London Conference on Cognitive Process Models for Foreign Policy, March 1973,* ed. M. Shapiro and G.M. Bonham. Basel, Stuttgart, 1977, 1–9.

———. *Thought and Action in Foreign Policy: Proceedings of the London Conference on Cognitive Process Models for Foreign Policy, March 1973.* Basel, Stuttgart, 1977.

Shaw, M. *The Dialectics of War.* London, 1988.

Shaw, P. *American Patriots and the Rituals of Revolution.* Cambridge, MA, 1981.

Sherry, M.S. *In the Shadow of War: The United States since the 1930's.* New Haven, London, 1995.

Shirer, W.L. *Berlin Diary: The Journal of a Foreign Correspondent, 1934–41.* New York, 1941.

Sidgwick, H. *The Methods of Ethics.* London, 1884.

Silverman, K. *A Cultural History of the American Revolution, 1763–1789.* New York, 1987.

Simmel, G., *Der Streit* (1908), repr. in *Soziologie,* 3rd ed. Berlin, 1958. English ed. *Conflict,* transl. by K.H. Wolff. New York, 1955.

Sinclair, A. *Prohibition: The Era of Excess.* Boston, 1962.

Six, U. "The Functions of Stereotypes and Prejudices in the Process of Cross-Cultural Understanding: A Social Psychological Approach." In *Understanding the USA: A Cross-Cultural Perspective*, ed. P. Funke. Tübingen, 1989, 42–62.

Skaggs, W.H. *German Conspiracies in America*. London, 1915.

Smith, A.D. *The Ethnic Origins of Nations*. Oxford, 1986, repr. 1993.

———. *Theories of Nationalism*. 2nd ed. New York, 1983.

Smith, G.S. *To Save A Nation: American Countersubversives, the New Deal, and the Coming of World War II*. New York, 1973.

Smith, H.K. *Last Train from Berlin*. New York, 1943.

Sniderman, P.M., and Ph. Tetlock. "Interrelationship of Political Ideology and Public Opinion." In *Political Psychology*, ed. M.G. Hermann. San Francisco, London, 1986, 62–96.

Sniderman, P.M., Ph.E. Tetlock and E.G. Camines, eds. *Prejudice, Politics, and the American Dilemma*. Stanford, 1993.

Snyder, G.H. *Conflict among Nations: Bargaining Decision Making and System Structure in International Crises*. Princeton, NJ, 1977.

———. *From Deterrence and Defense toward a Theory of National Security*. Princeton, NJ, 1961.

Snyder, L.C. *Encyclopedia of Nationalism*. Chicago, London, 1990.

Snyder, R.C., H.W. Bruck and B. Sapin. *Decision Making as an Approach to the Study of International Politics*. Princeton, NJ, 1954.

Sollors, W. "Introduction." In *The Invention of Ethnicity*, ed. W. Sollors. New York, Oxford, 1989, ix–xx.

———. *Beyond Ethnicity: Consent and Descent in American Culture*. New York, Oxford, 1986.

Sommer, V. "Soziobiologie: Wissenschaftliche Innovation oder ideologischer Anachronismus?." In *Fortpflanzung, Natur und Kultur im Wechselspiel: Versuch eines Dialogs zwischen Biologen und Sozialwissenschaftlern*, ed. E. Voland. Frankfurt a.M., 1992.

Sorkin, D. *The Transformation of German Jewry, 1780–1840*. New York, 1987.

Sperry, E.E., and W.M. West. *German Plots and Intrigues in the United States During the Period of Our Neutrality*. Washington, D.C., 1918.

Spillmann, K.R., and K. Spillmann. "Feindbilder: Entstehung, Funktion und Möglichkeit ihres Abbaus." *Internationale Schulbuchforschung, Zeitschrift des Georg-Eckert-Instituts* 12/3 (1990): 253–83.

Spurlin, P. *Montesquieu in America, 1760–1801*. Baton Rouge, LA, 1940.

Stagg, J.C.A. *Mr. Madison's War: Politics, Diplomacy, and Warfare in the Early Republic, 1783–1830*. Princeton, NJ, 1983.

Starr, S.F. *Red & Hot: The Fate of Jazz in the Soviet Union*. New York, 1983.

Stauber, R. "Nationalismus vor dem Nationalismus? Eine Bestandsaufnahme der Forschung zu 'Nation' und 'Nationalismus' in der Frühen Neuzeit." *Geschichte in Wissenschaft und Unterricht* 47 (1996): 139–65.

Steele, R.W. "American Popular Opinion and the War Against Germany: The Issue of a Negotiated Peace, 1942." *Journal of American History* 55 (December 1978): 704–23.

———. "Franklin D. Roosevelt and His Foreign Policy Critics." *Political Science Quarterly* 94 (1979): 15–35.

———. "Preparing the Public for War: Efforts to Establish a National Propaganda Agency, 1940–41." *American Historical Review* 75 (1970): 1640–53.

———. "The Great Debate: Roosevelt, the Media, and the Coming of the War, 1940–41." *Journal of American History* 71 (1984): 69–92.

———. "'The Greatest Gangster Movie Ever Filmed:' *Prelude to War*." *Prologue* 11 (1979): 220–35.

———. "The War on Intolerance: The Reformulation of American Nationalism, 1939–1941." *Journal of American Ethnic History* (1989): 9–35.

———. *Propaganda in an Open Society: The Roosevelt Administration and the Media, 1933–1941*. Westport, CT, 1985.

Steenbergen, B. van, ed. *The Condition of Citizenship*. London, 1994.

Stephan, W.G. "Intergroup Relations." In *Handbook of Social Psychology*, ed. G. Linsey and E. Aronson. 5 vols. New York, 1985, vol. 2, 251–89.

Stoddard, R.H. *The Life Travels and Books of Alexander von Humboldt*, with an introduction by B. Taylor. New York, 1854.

Stoler, M.A. *George C. Marshall: Soldier-Statesman of the American Century*. Boston, 1989.

Stouffer, S.A., et al., eds. *The American Soldier*. Princeton, 1949.

Strauss, H.A., and W. Röder. *International Biographical Dictionary of Central European Emigrés 1933–1945*. Munich, 1980–1983.

Strother, F. *Fighting Germany's Spies: A Revelation of German Intrigue in America*. New York, 1918.

Sussman, L.J. "'Toward Better Understanding': The Rise of the Interfaith Movement in America and the Role of Rabbi Isaac Landman." *American Jewish Archives* 34 (1982): 35–51.

Tajfel, H., ed. *Social Identity and Intergroup Relations*. Cambridge, 1982.

———. *Differentiation between Social Groups*. London, 1978.

———. *Human Groups and Social Categories: Studies in Social Psychology*. Cambridge, 1981.

Talbert, R., Jr. *Negative Intelligence: The Army and the American Left, 1917–1941*. Jackson, MS, 1991.

Teichrowe, A. "Military Surveillance of Mennonites in World War I." *Mennonite Quarterly Review*, 53 (April 1979): 95–127.

———. "World War I and the Mennonite Migration to Canada to Avoid the Draft." *Mennonite Quarterly Review* 45 (1971): 219–49.

Terra, H. de. "Alexander von Humboldt's Correspondence with Jefferson, Madison, and Gallatin." *Proceedings of the American Philosophical Society* 103 (1959): 783–806.

———. "Studies of the Documentation of Alexander von Humboldt." *Proceedings of the American Philosophical Society* 102 (1958): 136–141.

———. *Humboldt: The Life and Times of Alexander von Humboldt, 1769–1859*. New York, 1955.

The Gallup Poll: Public Opinion, 1935–71. vol. 1. *1935–1948*. New York, 1972.

The Soldier's Pocket Guide to Germany. Washington, 1944.

Thernstrom, St., ed. *Harvard Encyclopedia of American Ethnic Groups.* Cambridge, MA, 1980.

Thomas, A. *Grundriß der Sozialpsychologie.* 2 vols. Göttingen et al., 1992.

Thompson, K. "The Ethics of Major American Foreign Policies." *British Journal of International Studies* 6 (1980): 111–124.

Thurow, L. *Head to Head: The Coming Economic Battle among Japan, Europe & America.* New York, 1992.

Timberlake, J.H. *Prohibition and the Progressive Movement, 1900–1920.* Cambridge, MA, 1966.

Tocqueville, A. de. *Democracy in America,* ed. Richard D. Heffner. New York, 1956.

Toynbee, A.J. *The German Terror in Belgium: An Historical Record.* New York, 1917.

———. *The German Terror in France: An Historical Record.* New York, 1917.

Trivers, R. *Social Evolution.* Menlo Park, CA, 1985.

Trommler, F., and J. McVeigh, eds. *America and the Germans: An Assessment of a Three-Hundred-Year History,* vol. 1: *Immigration, Language, Ethnicity.* Philadelphia, 1985.

Truman, H.S. *Memoirs: Years of Trial and Hope.* 2 vols. New York, 1956.

Tsoucalas, C. "The Ideological Impact of the Civil War." In *Greece in the 1940s: A Nation in Crisis,* ed. J.O. Iatrides. Hanover, N.H., 1981, 319–41.

Tuchman, B.W. *The First Salute.* New York, 1988.

Tuttle, W.M., Jr. "Aid-to-the-Allies-Short-of-War versus American Intervention, 1940: A Reappraisal of William Allen White's Leadership." *Journal of American History* 56 (1970): 840–58.

———. *"Daddy's Gone to War": The Second World War in the Lives of America's Children.* New York, 1993.

Tuveson, E.L. *Redeemer Nation: The Idea of America's Millennial Role.* Chicago, 1968.

US Office of Strategic Services (OSS). *Foreign Nationalities Branch (FNB), Files, 1942–1945.* 2 vols. Washington, D.C., 1988.

Van den Berghe, P.L. *Race and Racism: A Comparative Perspective.* New York, 1967.

Van der Meulen, J. *The Politics of Aircraft: Building an American Military Industry.* Lawrence, KA, 1991.

Van Evera, St. "The Cult of the Offensive and the Origins of the First World War." In *Military Strategy and the Origins of the First World War. An International Security Reader,* ed. St.E. Miller. Princeton, NJ, 1985, 58–107.

Van Everen, B. "Franklin D. Roosevelt and the German Problem: 1914–45" Ph.D. diss., University of Colorado, 1970.

Vaughn, St. *Holding Fast the Inner Lines: Democracy, Nationalism, and the Committee on Public Information.* Chapel Hill, NC, 1980.

Villa, B.L. "The U.S. Army, Unconditional Surrender, and the Potsdam Proclamation." *Journal of American History* 63 (June 1976): 66–92.

Vlanton, E., ed. "The O.S.S. and Greek Americans." *Journal of the Hellenic Diaspora* 9 (1982) 53–82.

Vogel, Ch. *Vom Töten zum Mord: Das wirkliche Böse in der Evolutionsgeschichte.* Munich, Vienna, 1987.

Voland, E. *Grundriss der Soziobiologie*. Stuttgart, Jena, 1993.

Vossler, O. *Die amerikanischen Revolutionsideale in ihrem Verhältnis zu den europäischen untersucht an Thomas Jefferson*. Munich, Berlin, 1929.

Wagner, M., ed. and transl. *Reports from America in German Newspapers, 1828 to 1865*. Stuttgart, 1985.

Wala, M. *Winning the Peace: Amerikanische Außenpolitik und der Council on Foreign Relations, 1945–50*. Stuttgart, 1990 [Engl. version: *The Council on Foreign Relations and American Foreign Policy in the Early Cold War*. Providence, RI, 1994.]

Wallace, H.A. *Democracy Reborn*. New York, 1973.

Wang, P.H. "The Immigration Act of 1924 and the Problem of Assimilation." *Journal of Ethnic Studies* 2 (1974): 73–75.

Ward, P.D. *The Threat of Peace: James F. Byrnes and the Council of Foreign Ministers 1945–1946*. Kent, OH, 1979.

Weber, M. *Wirtschaft und Gesellschaft*. Tübingen, 1968.

Weber, P.C. *America in Imaginative German Literature in the First Half of the Nineteenth Century*. New York, 1929.

Wehler, H.-U., ed. *200 Jahre amerikanische Revolution und moderne Revolutionsforschung*. Geschichte und Gesellschaft. Sonderheft 2. Göttingen, 1976.

———. "Nationalismus und Nation in der deutschen Geschichte." In *Nationales Bewußtsein und kollektive Identität: Studien zur Entwicklung des kollektiven Bewußtseins in der Neuzeit*, ed. H. Berding. Frankfurt a.M., 1994, vol. 2, 163–75.

Wehner, J. *Kulturpolitik und Volksfront: Ein Beitrag zur Geschichte der Sojwetischen Besatzungszone Deutschlands 1945–1949*. Frankfurt a.M., 1992.

Weinberg, D.E. "The Ethnic Technician and the Foreign-Born: Another Look at Americanization Ideology and Goals." *Societas* 7 (1977): 209–27.

Weinberg, G.L. *A World At Arms: A Global History of World War II*. New York, 1994.

Weinberg, S. "What to Tell America: The Writers' Quarrel in the Office of War Information." *Journal of American History* 55 (1968): 73–89.

Welch, R. *The Blue Book of the John Birch Society*. Boston, Los Angeles, 1959.

———. *The Politician*. Belmont, MA, 1963.

Wellenreuther, H., and C. Schnurmann, eds. *Die amerikanische Verfassung und deutsch-amerikanisches Verfassungsdenken: Ein Rückblick über 200 Jahre*. New York, Oxford, 1990.

Wersich, R. *Zeitgenössischer Rechtsextremismus in den Vereinigten Staaten*. Munich, 1978.

White, R. *Nobody Wanted War: Misperception in Vietnam and Other Wars*. Garden City, NJ, 1966.

Whitfield, St.J. *The Culture of the Cold War*. 2nd ed. Baltimore, MD, 1996.

Wile, F.W. *The German-American Plot*. London, 1915.

Williamson, J. *The Crucible of Race: Black-White Relations in the American South Since Emancipation*. New York, 1984.

Wills, G. *Inventing America: Jefferson's Declaration of Independence*. Garden City, NY, 1978.

Wilson, E.O. *Sociobiology: The New Synthesis*. Cambridge, MA, 1975.

Winkler, A.M. *Politics of Propaganda: The Office of War Information, 1942–45.* New Haven, CT, 1978.

Winkler, H.A., and H. Kaelble, eds. *Nationalismus, Nationalitäten, Supranationalität. Europa nach 1945.* Stuttgart, 1993.

Winkler, H.A. "Einleitung: Der Nationalismus und seine Funktionen." In *Nationalismus,* ed. H.A. Winkler. 2d ed. Königstein, Ts., 1985, 5–46.

Wistrich, R.S. *Antisemitism: The Longest Hatred.* New York, 1991.

Wittke, C. *The German-Language Press in America.* Lexington, KY, 1957.

Wittner, L. *American Intervention in Greece 1943–49.* New York, 1982.

Wolfe, R., ed. *Americans As Proconsuls: United States Military Government in Germany and Japan, 1944–1952.* Carbondale, 1984.

Wood, G.S. "Conspiracy and the Paranoid Style: Causality and Deceit in the Eighteenth Century." *William and Mary Quarterly* 39 (1982): 401–41.

Wright, G. *The Ordeal of Total War, 1939–45.* New York, 1968.

Wust, K. "German-Americans: Eight Million Individual Transplants." In *Germans in America: Retrospect and Prospect,* ed. R.M. Miller. Philadelphia, 1984.

———. *The Virginia Germans.* Charlottesville, VA, 1975.

Wyman, D.S. *Abandonment of the Jews: America and the Holocaust, 1941–1945.* New York, 1985.

Xydis, St. "America, Britain, and the USSR in the Greek Arena, 1944–1947." *Political Science Quarterly* 478 (1963): 581–96.

Yavis, C. *Propaganda in the Greek American Community. Foreign Agents Registration. War Division. Department of Justice.* Washington, D.C., 21. April 1944.

Zalampas, M. *Adolf Hitler and the Third Reich in American Magazines, 1923–1939.* Bowling Green, 1989.

Zervakis, P.A. *Justice for Greece: Der Einfluß einer gräkoamerikanischen Interessengruppe auf die Außenpolitik der USA gegenüber Griechenland, 1945–1947.* Stuttgart, 1994.

INDEX

Jackson, Andrew, 105, 347
James, William, 344
Jameson, Egon, 293
Jefferson, Thomas, 94, 98–99, 101–2, 144, 271
Jeffreys-Jones, Rhodri, 189
Jervis, Robert, 10
Jordan, Winthrop, 174
Joyce, James, 169

Kantorowicz, Alfred, 293–4
Kenilworth, Walter Winston, 176
Kennan, George F., 244, 302, 339–40
Kepley, David R., 324
Khrushchev, Nikita S., 167
King, William H., 324
King Jr., Martin Luther, 172, 228
King Constantine I, 305
King George II, 244, 309
King George III, 92, 94
Kirchwey, Freda, 214
Kirschbaum, Erik, 183
Kirstein, Lincoln, 171
Kissinger, Heinz, 300
Krassner, Paul, 159
Kropotkin, Peter, 52
Kühl, Gustav, 177

Labat, Jean Baptiste, 178
La Follette, Robert, 206
LaGuardia, Fiorello, 251
Landsman, David, 169
Latrobe, Benjamin, 178
Laud, William, 43
Lauder, Harry, 191
Ledbetter, Huddie, 171
Leffler, Melvyn P., 302
Le Jau, Reverend, 175
Lenin, Vladimir, 163
Lennon, John, 169
Levin, Rahel, 148
Leyhausen, Paul, 53
Lieberman, Robbie, 171
Liljas, Eric, 226
Lincoln, Abraham, 106, 138, 153, 271
Locke, Alain, 171
Locke, John, 179

Lodge, Henry Cabot 322
Lorenz, Konrad, 46
Lowenfels, Walter, 171
Löwenstein, Karl, 284
Ludwig, Emil, 260
Luebke, Frederick, 192

MacVeagh, Lincoln, 332
Madison, James, 144
Manatos, Michael, 323
Marshall, Gen. George C., 268, 270
Marshall, Thomas H., 74
Martigopolus, Gus, 226
Mason, Daniel Gregory, 176
Matthews, H. Freeman, 286
Maurois, André, 211
Maxwell, Bob, 225
Mayer, Hans, 294
McCarthy, Joseph, 295
McClellan, John, 151
McClure, Robert, 286
McCormack, John, 319, 332
McElroy, Robert McNutt, 198, 200, 207
McGhee, Brownie, 171
McMahon, Bernard, 288
Mead, James, 314, 324
Mencken, H. L., 205
Merriam, Charles, 328
Merrow, Chester E., 324
Metaxas, Ioannis, 307–9, 311
Metternich, Prince Klemens von, 124, 129
Mineth, Joe, 226
Mitscherlich, Alexander, 75
Molotov, Vyacheslav M., 328
Monroe, James, 105
Monsarrat, Alice English, 170
Montesquieu, Baron de, 100
Morros, Boris, 166
Mowrer, Edgar A., 260
Moynihan, Daniel Patrick, 21
Muck, Hans, 176
Mühlenberg, Friedrich August, 121, 125–6
Mühlenberg, Heinrich, 125–6
Murphy, Robert, 286, 292
Myrdal, Gunnar, 178